Missions, Missionaries, and Native Americans

UNIVERSITY PRESS OF FLORIDA

Florida A&M University, Tallahassee
Florida Atlantic University, Boca Raton
Florida Gulf Coast University, Ft. Myers
Florida International University, Miami
Florida State University, Tallahassee
New College of Florida, Sarasota
University of Central Florida, Orlando
University of Florida, Gainesville
University of North Florida, Jacksonville
University of South Florida, Tampa
University of West Florida, Pensacola

Missions, Missionaries, and Native Americans

Long-Term Processes and Daily Practices

Maria F. Wade

University Press of Florida
Gainesville/Tallahassee/Tampa/Boca Raton
Pensacola/Orlando/Miami/Jacksonville/Ft. Myers/Sarasota

First cloth printing, 2008
First paperback printing, 2011

Wade, Maria de Fátima, 1948–
Missions, missionaries, and Native Americans: long-term processes and daily
practices / Maria F. Wade.
p. cm.
Includes bibliographical references and index.
ISBN 978-0-8130-3280-1 (alk. paper)
ISBN 978-0-8130-3801-8 (pbk.)
1. Indians of North America—Missions—History. 2. Indians of North
America—Social life and customs. 3. Indians of North America—Religion.
4. Franciscans—Missions—North America—History. 5. Jesuits—Missions—
North America—History. 6. Missions, Spanish—North America—History.
7. Culture conflict—North America—History. 8. Christianity and culture—
North America—History. 9. North America—Religious life and customs.
10. Spain—Colonies—America—History. I. Title.
E98.M6W23 2008
970.004'979–dc22   2008030317

The University Press of Florida is the scholarly publishing agency for the State
University System of Florida, comprising Florida A&M University, Florida At-
lantic University, Florida Gulf Coast University, Florida International University,
Florida State University, New College of Florida, University of Central Florida,
University of Florida, University of North Florida, University of South Florida,
and University of West Florida.

University Press of Florida
15 Northwest 15th Street
Gainesville, FL 32611-2079
http://www.upf.com

To Tom Campbell, as promised

Contents

List of Illustrations

Acknowledgments

Every book is an overt dialogue with many authors and their ideas and a covert, ongoing questioning and debating with oneself. I hope I have found the right tone for the dialogue and have posed the right questions. For me this book is also a conversation with friends, especially with a particular friend, Dr. Thomas Nolan Campbell. In fact, this book is a posthumous birthday present for him. I discussed many of the issues in this book with him, but he has been gone quite awhile and I often find myself trying to read mental tea leaves to decipher how he would react to this or that idea and anticipate his sharp and relentless criticism. To make up for his absence, his daughter, T. J. Campbell, read drafts of this book, commented on it, edited it, and supplied a genuine Campbell criticism. There are no words to thank them both: just my effort.

Other people have been so helpful that my debt of gratitude may take a while to repay. One of those most influential and helpful to my work has been Robert Jackson, whose generosity with ideas, materials, and criticism is unparalleled. Liz and Karl Butzer, Tom Hester, Jim Neely, Joel Sherzer, Carole Smith, and Katie Stewart read portions of the book, endured discussions, made suggestions, and provided support. A special thanks to Sam Wilson, who in his quiet manner was a source of unfailing encouragement, and to the University of Texas College of Liberal Arts for a very helpful Deans' Fellowship. Graduate students who took my Spanish Missions Seminar helped generate ideas; theirs is an ongoing, invaluable contribution and I hope that my research and this book will spur questions and further research.

Archival researchers rely on flair, serendipity, and most of all librarians. My sincere thanks to the staff of the Center for American History in Austin, to Nancy Sparrow at the University of Texas Alexander Architectural Archive, and to Susan Snyder at the Bancroft Library, Berkeley. I am equally grateful to Adán Benavides, Michael Hieronymus, Christian Kelleher, and Jorge Salinas at the Nettie Lee Benson Latin American Library in Austin, who in various ways remove obstacles to research.

That said, a scholar needs a willing and supporting press and a trusting and caring editor to bring ideas to fruition. John Byram and the University Press of Florida have been there for me from the start with their support. Eli

Bortz has provided his unfailing trust and care as have many other members of the staff: to Eli, especially, my gratitude.

My heartfelt thanks to the anonymous and not-so-anonymous readers; they undoubtedly made this book better with their criticisms and suggestions. Their help was invaluable and their work and intellectual engagement amply validate the notion that every book is, or should be, a collaborative dialogue.

Finally, my gratitude to Claire Huie, who digitized the maps included in this book. To Don, for preparing the maps and for everything else, my thanks and my love.

Introduction

One Stone Throw and Many Ripples

Colonial Spanish missions from Florida to California have long fascinated visitors and have been the loci of controversy for scholars and particularly for Native Americans. This book addresses the conceptual world of the missionaries who came to New Spain, compares the long-term strategies and the daily practices of the Franciscans and Jesuits in their missionary work, and contextualizes all of the above in terms of the object of the mission: Native American populations. Within that framework, the objective of the book is to show the processes and strategies missionaries used to socialize and convert Native Americans, particularly hunting and gathering populations who were missionized. I also aim to demonstrate the plight of missionaries who felt trapped by the system they created.

This work started with a simple question: What did Native Americans do in a mission? It seemed easy to collect the information about the daily and yearly activities within a mission, though mission histories followed different trajectories, practices changed over time, and there was a great diversity among Native groups and among missionaries. It was far more difficult to make sense of the reasons some practices were put in place and the effect of those practices on Native populations. Thus, one innocuous question led to many ripples.

To understand the impact of Spanish missionary work among Native American groups in New Spain it became necessary to question differences in background and motivation of the European missionaries and understand how such differences affected the processes and practices they used to convert Native populations. New Spain was a vast territory that was culturally and socially diverse, the time span of the colonial encounters was too long, and the historical tracings of conversion ideologies and practices are too varied and often too tenuous to be garnered. My question also arose from my previous work with Native American populations in Texas and northeastern Mexico. With few exceptions, all those groups made a living by gathering and hunting. In addition, I wanted to compare the methodology and the conversion strategies of the Franciscans and the Jesuits, but the Franciscans operated missions in Texas and the Jesuits' work in northeastern Mexico was restricted in time and space, providing a poor basis for comparison. Because I sought to examine and compare missionary practices specifically among hunter-gatherers, this book deals mostly with Franciscan and Jesuit missionary work from the sixteenth through the late eighteenth centuries in the territories of New Spain that were known as the Californias, Coahuila, Nuevo León, and Texas.

I have included in the analysis the missionaries' experiences with the Calusa from the Florida peninsula for three reasons. First, work with the Calusa is one of the earliest and best documented examples of missionary activity. Second, Jesuits and Franciscans alternated working among the Calusa. Third, as settled hunter-gatherers, the Calusa provide a useful contrast to the Texas Hasinai groups, who were settled horticulturists but relied substantially on hunting and gathering, and to the nomadic hunter-gatherer populations housed in the San Antonio missions.

Hunter-gatherer populations posed specific problems to the establishment of missions and particularly to their sustainability because they were nomadic, they did not grow crops, and their lifestyle and work habits did not fit western concepts of what constituted labor. The founding of missions among settled agriculturalist Native groups, such as those of the Southwest Pueblo country, was inherently different because subsistence requirements and access to potential converts were facilitated by preexisting agricultural settlement patterns. Different settlement patterns raised specific logistic problems that thwarted missionary expectations. Still, the missionaries could count on a readily available food supply, benefit from a variety of local skills essential for building dwellings and missions, monitor neophytes, and use scheduled routines and civic-ceremonial centers of Natives to proselytize. Hunter-gatherers provided none of those benefits and the indeterminacy of their lifestyle taxed the colonial psyche. In addition, hunter-gatherers' fluid decision-making processes challenged the organizational principles and rigid hierarchical training of the missionaries. Interestingly, while hunter-gatherer populations posed specific problems for the work of conversion, their lifestyle tapped into the deepest conversion fervor of the early missionaries, particularly the Mendicant Orders.

To understand the work of conversion—its methodologies and pedagogic strategies and practices—one has to start with the missionaries. Franciscans and Jesuits vowed to follow the rules and precepts of their institutions, and the early history of both orders shaped their approaches to conversion and their views of the people they wished to convert. The historical events that marked the consolidation of Catholic dogma and religious practices in Europe and the conflicts within the religious orders were essential formative elements of the missionary ethos. Part One, which includes the first four chapters of this book, briefly addresses some of these events and conflicts as it looks at the historical development of Franciscans and Jesuits and discusses how European religious practices and coeval Native practices were perceived and judged differently. The double standard used to determine the thresholds between good and evil in Europe and in the colonial worlds deeply affected the conversion process. The missionaries' purposeful excising of Native shamanic practices left a numinous hole filled with shreds of memories of the old and pieces of the new from which, out of necessity, modern Native Americans made whole cloth. It would be unwise to consider the resultant cultural fabric a product of the dominant western culture. The long-term process of adaptation fostered recombination and reinvention and in so doing often encouraged ethnogenesis.

The missionaries' background shaped their perception of the role of Native labor in the missions. In turn, the need for Native labor affected the development of the missions. Whether or not those labor needs could be fulfilled ultimately determined the success or failure of a mission. Western cultural notions of what constituted labor privileged farming as Christian and civilized and stigmatized hunting and gathering as barbaric. Despite this conceptual framework, missionaries often recognized and admired the intense effort Natives expended in subsisting by hunting and gathering. This ambivalence produced a bifurcated discourse that affected missionary practices and may have caused missionaries to give mixed messages to Native groups. Native labor was essential to the secular colonizing process, and it was the foundation and basis of sustainability of missions as well as the nexus of never-ending contention between the settlers, the military, and the church.

Other parameters influenced and constrained the missionaries' process of adaptation and the conversion practices that process produced. Religious principles, missionary rules, and royal decrees shaped missionary practices as much as they created legal loopholes and fostered transgression by attentive actors. Legal documents from the period of the transition from the Hapsburg to the Bourbon colonizing paradigm demonstrate the accuracy of the crown's knowledge about the pedestrian conditions in specific areas of New Spain. These textual mementoes demonstrate either a naiveté about what laws could do or a tacit acknowledgment that the more things changed the more they stayed the same. Colonial rules and legislation operated in tandem with cultural mores that viewed the Natives, particularly the nomadic "barbaric hordes" of the inhospitable frontier, as inveterate children, irrecoverable sinners, or simply as a labor resource.

As missionaries felt their way through a harsh frontier, earning a foothold here and a martyrdom there, they tried out conversion strategies and tactics that evolved into broad models. Regardless of which model a mission adopted, missionary practices were frontal attacks on Native American beliefs and practices. As such, they provoked a range of reactions from vehement rejection to silent refusal and flight.

To understand the process of development of missionary models, it is necessary to take a long-term perspective. To understand how those models were translated into daily practices, it is necessary to focus on discrete events. A perspective of the *longue durée* (Braudel 1972) helps us analyze multiple factors that affected the development of models of conversion. Discrete events, on the other hand, are ethnographic moments that exemplify the viewpoints of some of the participants. In order to trace the effects of religious practices on Native Americans, I added a short-term perspective to the other two methodological approaches. This perspective is based on the concept of life course,[1] which I qualify by calling it a sacramental life course, whereby the neophyte's life was marked by the reception of sacraments that replaced Native traditional rites of passage. These were translated into specific statuses and roles that marked a neophyte's advancement in the conversion process.

Although this perspective was very helpful, how to locate and interpret the Native perspectives that were so seldom provided in the archival sources remained a conundrum. The choice of issues had to be pertinent to the daily lives of Native Americans because it was at that daily level that conversion practices meant the most and had the most impact. Furthermore, it was the repetitive and relentless character of daily practices that mollified resistance and refashioned the Native habitus. To weave my arguments, I chose to concentrate on the missionaries' drive to convert and on the minutiae of social, religious, and economic practices that sought to socialize Native Americans into good Christians. To be sure, the missionary discourse that determined what was good and what was evil marked traditional Native practices accordingly. But missionization was even more insidious because it tightly interwove daily economic and subsistence practices with religious activities: economic sanctions were religious sanctions and vice versa. The missionaries took the Lord's Prayer literally; for them, daily bread was intertwined with moral trespasses.

Using similar doctrinal paths, Franciscans and Jesuits adopted different models of conversion. The wilderness model and the rotational model discussed in Part Two had short-term consequences that benefited Native populations and, as I suggest, facilitated the work of conversion. Yet when missionaries reassessed their mission programs, either because of revolts, as the Jesuits did in Baja California, or because they entered a new area, as the Franciscans did in Alta California, they discarded or rationalized away the root causes of their problems and imposed tighter controls instead of capitalizing on Native initiative and autochthonous social mechanisms. Faced with the impossibility of uprooting traditions and modifying Native behavior to their Christian standards, missionaries chose the pragmatic solution: they blamed Native neophytes and chose to intensify their segregation and repression of Native converts. As I hope to show, except for the early period of colonization, missionaries expected Native populations to adapt to the mission models, not the other way around. Had the missionaries questioned their approaches to conversion, would the results have been different? It is possible, but the missionaries were only some of the key players in a colonial historical conjuncture rooted on Native land and in Native labor, and every colonial player wanted a piece of both. And yes, I mean to include the missionaries, because without land there was no settlement, without a settlement there was no mission, and without Natives there was no one to convert—ergo no mission.

A Plan of Thought and a Textual Path

This book is divided into three parts organized around three principal and interconnected objectives. Part One provides context for the discussions that follow and establishes a thematic and discursive link with Part Three. The first and second chapters endeavor to set a conceptual frame for the larger underlying issues that shaped the practice of conversion that became the mission. It is short-sighted to consider the evolution of the mission in any specific region of New Spain without even a shorthand notation of the issues that permeated and gave shape to the experiences of the missionaries before they embarked for the New World. As missionaries came in different waves, their imaginations and attitudes were shaped by the great European contests of the time between good and evil, such as the religious reform movements, the Inquisition and witchcraft, and day-to-day tussles with village folk traditions that coupled what was becoming heretical behavior with Christian teachings. In that light, chapter 2 surveys, albeit briefly, the religious practices of European folk from king to peon. This exercise unveils, I hope, how cultures define and enact different thresholds between good and evil and how practices that were deemed pious and were highly encouraged in Europe had counterparts in the New World that were demonized and excised. This long-term process abridged and shaped modern Native American practices.

Chapters 3 and 4 briefly introduce Francis of Assisi and Ignatius of Loyola because aspects of their lives and the core tenets of their respective religious orders were as important to their perspectives on conversion as they were to the disciples they attracted and how they were trained. The long-term controversies between Franciscan Spirituals and Conventuals, particularly those over the definition of abnegation and poverty, were vital to the Franciscan paradigm of conversion. These controversies, though they changed over time, cropped up in the frontier in debates over how to manage the missions. For the Jesuits, their approach to learning, their practice of the Spiritual Exercises, and their innovative management skills affected who they attracted, how they acted, and how they were perceived by secular entities. These issues acquire relevance and take practical shape in the events discussed in the subsequent chapters.

The chapters in Part Two compare the results of the differing approaches of the Jesuits and the Franciscans in their efforts to convert Native American hunter-gatherer populations in specific areas of Florida, Texas, California, and northeastern Mexico. The material in each chapter is arranged chronologically and whenever possible discusses the sequential presence of Jesuits and Franciscans in particular geographical areas. Florida and Baja California provide that sequential contrast while Texas and Alta California do not. Northeastern Mexico is anomalous in many respects. Jesuits and Franciscans both worked in the region but in different areas and mostly at different times. Also, northeastern Mexico was plagued with the *encomienda* system that raised specific issues between settlers, soldiers, missionaries, and Natives. Those issues resulted in royal legislation and approaches to conversion that reflected the complexity of the problems in the region.

The arrangement of the chapters in Part Two is essential to the premise of this work, as I aim to show the similarities and differences between Native preoccupations and reactions to conversion and changes in missionary practice. Throughout the six chapters in this section, I look at the unfolding of the practice of the mission as it congealed into a concept and an institution shaped by the conditions present in the regions discussed and by the timing of the establishment of the missions in each region. I suggest that there are three broad periods that characterize the missionary trajectory within New Spain and in the regions mentioned above. These periods are exemplified first by the early missionary work among the Calusa in western Florida and the work in Coahuila and Baja California. The second and third phases can be delineated by the work in Texas and in Alta California. These periods are characterized broadly by missionary practices of entrenchment and increased control over the Natives. Another aspect of this periodicity is the impact of conversion efforts on the contact generation as well as the influence of that generation on missionary conversion practices. The study of generation gaps among Native Americans in response to contact is beyond the scope of this work, but the differences between the contact generation and Natives born and raised within the mission system are important and perceptible. No doubt other regions of the colonial missionary world followed different trajectories, particularly those that include urban and settled agricultural populations, but these populations are outside the purview of my analysis.

The Calusa of Florida (chapter 5) provide a unique view of Native American reaction to the missionaries because the attempts to convert them occurred at an early date and were short lived and because the Franciscans followed the Jesuits. Including the Calusa in this study also permits a comparison between settled hunter-gatherers (the Calusa) and settled horticulturalists that relied heavily on hunting and gathering (the Texas Hasinai). Both groups were targeted for conversion early on and both rejected conversion and dismissed the missionaries. The Calusas' and the Hasinais' peremptory rejection of Catholic religious practices raises the issue of the importance for Native Americans of a complex and well-structured ritual system and social organization, likely enshrined in their respective settlement patterns.

Franciscans and Jesuits worked in different areas in northeastern Mexico, and chapter 6 introduces events that provide snapshots of the complexity of frontier life in those areas. This mission frontier had unique characteristics that challenged missionaries and highlighted the best and the worst conversion practices. The result was specific conversion models characterized mostly by the location of the Native populations and the use of their labor. Extensive landholdings and the *encomienda* system and its institutional subterfuges created a high demand for a cheap, controllable labor force that could only be obtained by mobilizing Native laborers. The concentration of power in the hands of wealthy miners and landowners, who also occupied the top leadership positions in civil society and in the military, guaranteed that this small elite controlled the very institutions that were supposed to defend the rights of the Natives. Collusion, real or perceived, between missionaries and the *encomenderos* bred distrust and resentment.

In this setting of high tension that included nomadic groups, Tlaxcalans, *encomenderos*, soldiers, settlers, secular clerics, and missionaries, the example of Fr. Larios and his companions demonstrates conversion at its best.

Like St. Francis, and taking the cue from the Spirituals, Fr. Larios practiced conversion by following hunter-gatherer groups as they moved in search of sustenance. Like the work of Fr. Larios, the work of a handful of Jesuits in the Parras-Laguna areas illustrates the brief adoption of a wilderness model of conversion that was soon replaced by the more common urban-rural model, a version of the pueblo-mission model of conversion.

The last part of chapter 6 includes a royal edict issued in 1715. This is a long document paraphrased almost in total. Although it was issued for the kingdom of Nuevo León, the edict exposes problems in the whole of northeastern Mexico. The legislative measures show the detailed knowledge the crown and the viceroyalty had of the plight of Native Americans and the complexity of conflicting interests. I follow this document with a set of documents that demonstrate the ineffectiveness of the king's laws.

I examine the work of the Franciscans in Texas in chapter 7. The Franciscans were in Texas for a long time and built many missions there, although some of them were very short lived. My discussion concentrates mainly on the early missions Franciscans established for the Hasinai in east Texas, the Rio Grande missions, and the mission complex in San Antonio, Texas. The Hasinai were settled horticulturalists that were organized in complex polities, or chiefdoms, while the groups in the San Antonio missions were hunter-gatherers organized as extended family groups, or bands. The case of the Hasinai permits us to compare the reactions of horticulturalist groups to conversion to those of the hunter-gatherer groups housed in the San Antonio missions. The strategies the friars adopted in their efforts to convert both sets of groups call attention to the methodological and pedagogical problems with their strategies of conversion.

Colonial Texas did not suffer the injury of the *encomienda* system nor did it profit from the *encomienda's* economic benefits. Still, the provincial territory had its share of problems. The presence of the bellicose Apache and other groups led the Spanish army and the citizenry to conduct mercenary raids on them and helped justify the creation of walled mission compounds. I suggest that walled missions were built as much to keep Natives in as they were to keep others out and that this change in the built environment marked both a shift in attitude toward conversion and the second period of mission-building and characterized what Fr. Font called "the Texas method" (chapter 7). The main catalyst for this change was, I believe, the 1758 attack on Mission San Sabá in Texas perpetrated by Native groups located north of the modern Texas territory. This event served as a marker for the later part of the mission period in Texas and affected the Franciscans who moved into Alta California. I also suggest that these walled precincts were the result of a mutation of the urban-rural model of conversion used earlier in Coahuila and that the San Antonio missions coupled features and objectives of the hacienda and the presidio. Like the hacienda, the mission was meant to be a profitable enterprise with a reliable labor force; like the presidio, a mission needed fortified walls for its defense and to prevent Native flight.

At the end of the Texas mission period, unresolved issues between Spirituals and Conventuals flared up again when friars such as Fr. Oliva questioned the appropriateness of Franciscan involvement with things material. I find the Franciscans' debates about the management of the affairs of the missions crucial to an understanding of the essentials of conversion and the way the mission system webbed missionaries.

The conversion of the Native groups of Baja California is the subject of chapter 8. As in Florida, the Jesuits preceded the Franciscans in efforts to convert the hunter-gatherers of the peninsula. Unlike in Florida, however, in Baja California the Jesuits established long-term missions and were forced to leave by the Spanish crown. Their departure led to a reshuffling of Franciscan resources and manpower that shaped mission programs in the Californias and changed the contours of mission administration in Texas.

In Baja California, the Jesuits implemented a rotational system whereby selected Native groups came to the mission each week to learn Christian doctrine and then returned to their respective campgrounds or *rancherías*. Regardless of why they used this model, it provided a measure of freedom for Native groups that was far from negligible. In contrast, the Native populations that resided at the mission headquarters were subject to strict age and gender segregation. The discussion of Jesuit conversion practices focuses primarily on the administration of sacraments and the forked discourse that contrasts Native incapacities and incomprehension with Native expertise and cunning. A crucial aspect of the Jesuit missions in Baja California was the source of their finances, which permitted a good measure of Jesuit control over the management of the missions and the military force. These two elements were, in my opinion, essential to the way the Jesuit missions were run, and they were a direct result of the Society of Jesus' independence and worldview.

After the Jesuits were expelled in 1767–1768, Franciscan methods of mission work did not help the Baja California missions that were already experiencing problems. Consciously or not, and even though the missions continued to be funded primarily by the Jesuit Pious Fund, the Franciscans perceived the Jesuit missions as "old" and problematic hand-me-downs. But the Franciscans had to contend with army officials bent on interfering, a harsh environment, and intractable Natives, and it was difficult to show progress and measure conversion because many Natives had perished and most of those who were alive had been baptized long ago. As it is often the case, the fervor of conversion stalled in the daily grind of religious life.

But the Franciscans yearned for Alta California, the subject of chapter 9. The Franciscan conversion of Native groups in Alta California constitutes the end product of a religious-economic system that had become more economic and less religious. Franciscans' reports emphasized the physical appearance of the churches, the edification of the Natives through ceremonial sacra, and the overall economic condition of the missions. In comparison, the attention reports devote to the living conditions of the mission population is small to nonexistent. Also, the age and gender segregation measures previously adopted in Texas were intensified in Alta California with the creation of female and male dormitories and attempts to control Native sexual practices.

Conversion work was fundamentally about daily practices, and Part Two ends with a detailed compilation of the daily routines and weekly schedules of mission life. In chapter 10, I compare Franciscan and Jesuit strategies of socialization and conversion and evaluate the effects of those practices on the lives of Native neophytes. The litany of daily and weekly practices provides a vision of Native life from sunrise to sunset as well as the missionaries' viewpoints on their use of punishment and their opinions of Native performance. I should note that the doctrinal and management manuals analyzed in this chapter were prepared by the Franciscans while the information about Jesuit daily and weekly routines and sacramental procedures was retrieved from a variety of published primary sources.

Fr. Diego Martín García stated that "the most important task of the apostolic worker is to provide his flock with spiritual sustenance and the second is to make sure they labor in order that, united and congregated in pueblos, [the friars] can provide them with spiritual nourishment" (1745, 33). The work of conversion was a web of religious and economic practices so efficiently interwoven that it is hard to tease them apart. In chapters 11 and 12, I examine, respectively, the mission's religious and economic practices.

In chapter 11, I discuss the Catholic sacraments administered to Native neophytes and the possible social and material repercussions that neophytes experienced when they chose to accept these sacraments. Central to my discussion are the methods the missionaries used to measure conversion and how modern researchers assess conversion. In chapter 12, I explore in detail the calendar of monthly and yearly scheduled activities that were the economic lifeblood of the missions. Religious practices were inseparable from economic practices because the missionaries intended them to be inseparable. Weaving economic practices with religious practices placed a premium on Native American compliance, resulting in either rewards or punishments, issues that crop up throughout the book.

Apart from showing what Native Americans did in a mission, the list of tasks that filled a day or a year of a Native's life shows the grinding power of such activities on populations of hunter-gatherers and how these activities worked to produce cultural change. Fr. Oliva's arguments against the economic management of the missions discussed in chapter 7 tell us as much about the missionaries' spiritual dilemmas as they do about the Natives who were at the receiving end of such management.

Finally, this work makes no attempt to be a comprehensive history of Catholic missions in the areas studied, nor does it endeavor to cover all aspects of missionizing. That was never the objective. This work is just one more attempt to get the story straight.

Part 1

Good and Evil

A Battleground

One of the most important cultural changes brought to the New World was the conceptual framework that defined, or redefined, the boundaries between good and evil (Burkhart 1989; Cervantes 1994; Taussig 1987). This subliminal change was translated into a cultural program that affected colonizers and colonized, albeit at different levels and degrees. The confrontation between Europeans and Amerindians was not so much one of religions as one of spirituality. This confrontation took shape through missionary work and took place in the context of several key religious debates, principally the nature of heresy, the classification of heretical practices as defined by Inquisition practices, and the defining of Native practices as heretical and devilish.[1] From this confrontation resulted the most momentous change for the Native populations of the Americas: a severing of the natural from the spiritual. What today some call syncretism, the imbrication of the spiritual with the religious, is simply the puncturing of the natural realm into the spiritual realm manifested in the practices of Native Americans and other ethnic groups, or the imperfect accomplishment of the western spiritual conquest sometimes called imperfect Christianization (Mello e Souza 2003, 47). To contextualize the central debates that shaped missionary practices in the New World, it is necessary to outline the relevance of missionary work to the conquest of the Americas. I will use two early treatises, one written by a Franciscan, Fr. Andrés Olmos, and one by a Jesuit, Father Pérez de Ribas, as vehicles to explore the influence of the Inquisition and to gauge missionary perceptions of Native spiritual practices.

A Mission Statement

In 1494, the Treaty of Tordesillas cleaved the sixteenth-century world into two geographical areas cum religious domains. With the blessing of the church, the treaty and later negotiations formalized the "discoveries" made by the crowns of Portugal and Spain, imbued them with a religious mandate, and left the door open for an expanding universe of lands to be discovered and Christianized. The pope's protection and incentives guaranteed the Iberian crowns a divine right to dominate all peoples they encountered regardless of whether they were "civilized" or not (Baudot 1990, 18; Sneed 1992, 189, 196, 202–3). Prophetic and eschatological writings led Columbus to see himself as God's "messenger of the New Heaven and the New Earth of which He spoke in the Apocalypse by St. John" (Columbus as quoted in West 1989, 302–3), and to urge the Catholic kings to heed God's command to spread the gospel to the pagan world. Indeed, the Spanish code of laws—the *Recopilación de las leyes de los Reynos de Indias*—and its various revisions firmly wedded church to crown in its ends if not in its means. The rights and privileges accorded by the Patronato Real "placed the king and the king's representatives in almost complete control of the Church in America" (Curley 1940, 10–11, quote on 13).[2] Together with secular priests and other religious orders, Franciscans and Jesuits were sent at different times and often to different areas of the new lands to serve church and crown. For the church, the religious orders were the advance laborers plowing the fields of the Lord in the expectation of fruit. For the crown, missionaries were willing participants in the enterprise of conquest who metamorphosed into discoverers, ambassadors, peacemakers and policy makers, inquisitors, judges, hospitalers, ethnographers, linguists, geographers, architects, healers, spies, guides, and (sometimes) soldiers.

Unlike the missionaries of the Society of Jesus, the resilience of Franciscan missionaries had been well tried in Europe and elsewhere by the time they were called to missions in the New World (Moorman 1988, 226–39). Such experiences left the Franciscans with hagiographies, relics, and a trail of martyrs. The Franciscans of the thirteenth and fourteenth centuries were deeply divided over what the doctrine of poverty meant and how friars should conduct themselves to comply with its principles. The debates between Franciscan theologians and the papacy weakened the tenets of the doctrine and resulted in multiple and enduring fissures among those who followed the religious ideals of St. Francis (Lambert 1961). The internal dysfunction of Spirituals (who followed the Rule of St. Francis strictly) and Conventuals (who wanted a lifestyle that accommodated the physical needs of scholars and preachers) was eventually muted by papal intervention that punished or reined in recalcitrant and radical Spirituals.[3]

During the fifteenth and sixteenth centuries, a reform movement took shape in the Extremadura region of southern Portugal and Spain under the leadership of Fr. Juan de Guadalupe, who called for stricter observance of St. Francis's Rule and obtained papal permission to establish several monasteries in the region (Baudot 1990, 18–21). Among the reformers was Fr. Martín de Valencia, one of the most "fervent adepts of Fr. Guadalupe's reforms and ideas" (Baudot 1990, 23), and the leader of the first Franciscan group to reach Mexico.[4] Fr. Guadalupe's visionary and millenarian inclinations were not isolated, nor was his movement unique. Eventually a compromise was reached that produced an ideological and pragmatic position whose adherents, by the sixteenth century, were called Franciscans of the Regular Observance, or Observants (Chauvet 1981, 15; Moorman 1988, 582–85).

The sixteenth century was a time of self-reflection for Christians in general and the Catholic church in particular. Protestant calls for reforms forced the Catholic hierarchy to review its practices, explain them in theological terms, and revise the structure of religious orders. By convening the Council of Trent (1545–1563), which worked for over two decades, Pope Paul III signaled the papacy's determination to codify practices, curtail abuses, and exercise control over the religious orders; in short, to put the house of God in order. From excesses and corruption the church moved to dogmatism and repression, a program of renewal that began more as a reaction to the Protestant Reformation than to the future of the Catholic church.

Coincidental or not, the Council of Trent's reforms overlapped with the progressive unveiling and domination of new lands and the desire to expand Christian and European empires. Likewise, the Society of Jesus came of age amid the euphoria and conflicts of the worlds being unveiled. The order was not immune to the trends established by the Protestant Reformation and the Catholic Counter-Reformation, and it influenced and benefited from the directions established by the Council of Trent (O'Malley 2000, 23–25). In 1550, Pope Julius III, the same pope who convened the Council of Trent for the second time (1551–1552), finally confirmed the Society of Jesus.

The exponential growth of the Jesuits was not without woes. Like the Franciscans, the Jesuits experienced dissension, particularly in Spain and Portugal during the late sixteenth century and especially under the leadership of the Jesuit general Claudio Aquaviva (Bangert 1972, 110–19; Lewy 1960, 141–60). Struggles for control over the society's constitutions and the overarching authority of the society's general pitted the Iberian crown, the Inquisition, Dominicans, the dissenters, and sometimes the papacy against the society's leadership and those who saw the reforms as unnecessary or detrimental. Unlike Franciscan leaders, Jesuit leaders managed to ward off major changes in the order's constitutions and maintain rules of obedience that restricted outside influence on the affairs and policies of the order.

An argument can be made that the Franciscan catharsis that led to splinter movements and the formation of other orders, such as the Capuchins, helped the Franciscans manage conflict and adapt to the growth of the order and to political, social, and religious changes. Conversely, the Jesuits' intense desire to maintain unity and avoid change to the constitutional spirit of the order contributed, according to Pope Clement XIV, to the suppression of the Society of Jesus in 1773 (Lewy 1960, 158). In any event, the deep-seated divisions between Franciscan Spirituals and Conventuals and the Jesuits' expulsion from New Spain influenced the missionary work of the two orders, albeit in different ways.

The mission started as a practice of missionaries. "A field of knowledge [was] born out of practice" (de Certeau 2000, 44), and became the institution of the mission (Bolton 1917). In time, the practice became a concept, possibly as a result of the project of telling its story (Taussig 1987, 107). Charles Polzer emphasized that the key element of mission as an activity was that missionaries were *sent* (1976, 4). Other authors point to the historical changes in the concept and practice of missionary work, although the physical separation of the person going on a mission from his or her physical and social environment seems to be the enduring characteristic of such work regardless of time period (Medgyessy 2004, 99–101; Wood 2001, 3–5, 247). The alienation from one's zone of comfort and the necessary immersion of the missionary in the world of the other resulted, in my opinion, in revulsion toward the other and a longing for that which was known and reassuring— the world left behind. Being sent was the desire, but being there was the challenge.

In his work *The Spiritual Conquest of Mexico*, Ricard grouped different mission arrangements according to their location on the land and their intended function (1933/1982). Ricard's scheme included geopolitical considerations as well as stages in the process of conversion. "Missions of penetration" were brief trips meant to assess the possibilities of converting residents on the land, extend missionary coverage, or deal with specific geographic or political conditions. Conversely, "missions of occupation" and "missions of liaison" connoted an established presence either through a "relatively dense network [of missions] within a reasonable distance of one another" that were possibly grouped around a center or through a network of spaced missions of the same religious order that could serve as way stations and provide support (77–78). Ricard's scheme related to sixteenth-century Mexico, but its categories are viable for later missions as well. The nexus of Franciscan missions in San Antonio can be described as missions of occupation, while the Rio Grande missions and their mission connections to the south can be described as missions of liaison, although both the San Antonio and Rio Grande missions were established in the late seventeenth and eighteenth centuries. In Texas and northeastern Mexico, as in Baja California, the great distances between missions and between those missions and the respective central convents in Zacatecas, Querétaro, or Mexico City created critical problems in the transmission of information that were made worse by logistical difficulties.

From the onset of colonization, the importance of the epistemological and heuristic background of the Old World religious practitioners was apparent. The missionaries who arrived in the New World from Europe were still in the midst of confrontations with heretic and diabolical manifestations. In *The Possession at Loudon*, Michel de Certeau recounts a series of events of possession and fraud that took place in France in the seventeenth century and observes, "All stability rests on unstable balances that are disturbed by every intervention intended to reinforce them" (2000, 2). In Europe, missionaries were engaged in a concerted battle against folk practices that anchored the practical and religious life of urban and suburban populations. The life of European agricultural societies was largely shaped by vows, relics, fairs, and cycles of saints' feasts as farmers attempted to account for epidemics, temperamental weather, and ravenous pests. What made the folk religious also made them heretics. The task of separating the religious wheat (doxa) from the heretic chaff (heterodoxy) continuously preoccupied the Catholic church (Ricard 1933/1982, 286).[5] In the New World the missionaries pursued their labors against heresy, shifting their vision and defining new boundaries of doctrine.

Local Native American societies also were engaged in maintaining the equilibrium of unstable balances that had long sustained their relationship to the natural-cum-spiritual world. The manifestations of that equilibrium could be as elaborate and visible as those of the Aztec, Maya, or Mississippian groups or as elaborate and mirage-like as those of the innumerable populations of hunter-gatherers in what is now California, Florida, Texas, and northern Mexico. In the process of protecting the fundamental fulcra of their world, Native societies confronted and redefined the boundaries of the divine.

The battleground was never the same, the battles were never equal, and the outcomes depended on context and were sometimes reluctant agreements to disagree punctuated by bloodshed. There are perceivable differences between the early period of conquest and later contacts (Ricard 1933/1982, 223–90). In Central Mexico and in Yucatán, European contacts with Native groups were often marked by astonishment and efforts to comprehend, which were rewarded with tolerance and compliance. In other places, such as in southern Florida among the Calusa, even gestures to accommodate Native paradigms were fruitless. In the effort to know and comprehend what to expunge, missionaries peered into the conceptual world of the other. To destroy codices, Bernardino de Sahagún and Diego de Landa (Franciscan missionaries in the New World) had to view, acknowledge, and reject the cultural and religious information contained in the codices. To write about heretical practices of Natives, Father Andrés Pérez de Ribas had to procure information, learn, witness, "handle crude idols," and destroy what he considered to be evidence of heretical practices. In order to argue with the Calusa, Father Rogel had to face and conceptualize the logic of the faithless, and that elicited imaginings and left memories. Knowledge is implacable and it penetrates; it produces power but it burdens the producer with memories that in the long run also affect the producer.[6] Later, as the wonderment of conquest dissipated and the process of conquest ground northward, the missionaries' effort to comprehend waned. The realization that the other was not overtaken by the God the missionaries hailed, that rejection cut both ways, and that refusal could be mute and wrapped in a package that looked like acquiescence led the missionaries to classify the Natives as perennial adolescents, always in the process of becoming and never reaching the comprehension of maturity. To conceive of the Natives as children maintained the possibility of maturity while arresting development and justifying what might otherwise be perceived as failure. The danger zone was reached when the missionaries assumed they understood the Natives and took them for granted. At that point, comprehension ceased and with it tolerance.

Neither group remained untouched or unscathed by contact; in the end both exhibited scars that marked the religious itineraries of their future and of our shared present. These scars took many forms, from the ritual use of peyote to the cult of the Virgin of Guadalupe or from Juan Sabeata's cross (Wade 2003, 78, 239) to ritualized steam baths (Wallis 2003, 200–226). What remains are spiritual grafts: appropriations of bodies, signs, and practices to mediate a spiritual conquest and redefine the boundaries of religiosity for both worlds.

Heresy and *Inquisitio*

The concept of heresy grew spasmodically and not always under the same exegesis, although it always "dreamed of a different society . . . based on another conception of truth, another conception of the relations between the flesh and the spirit, the visible and the invisible" (Duby 1980, 131). At its root, the problem of heresy is one of choosing and defining domains. Some scholars have pointed out that the process of defining heresy is dialogic because the shifting definition of heresy stands in counterposition to its modes of repression (Ginzburgh 1991; Martin 2002; Mitchell 2001). Heretics could be freethinkers and seekers of learning. They could also be raving lunatics, visionaries, healers, or saints and often were considered all of the above, depending on the time and the context. They could also simply refuse to obey the pope, as was the case of the Franciscan Spirituals (Verbeke 1976, 180). Their refusal to stop preaching a "distorted" truth and faith made them vulnerable to excommunication and the Inquisition (de Nicolas 1986, 15). For the Medieval church, the posture of the Spirituals was "a species of unbelief (*infidelitas*) worthy of death" (McGrade 1999, 111, 114).

Atheists fared no better. In 1645, Pérez de Ribas, a Jesuit missionary in the New World, stated, "Because they cannot defend their errors, they go from heresy to atheism, slamming the door on any understanding of sound truth. They fear neither a God who punishes nor a law that forbids, becoming brute animals who recognize only the visible, the corporeal, and the worldly, paying no heed to the blessed and eternal purpose for which God created man" (1645/1999, 96).

Confrontation with the novel practice, the unforeseen or unimagined, led to on-the-job training, expedient solutions, and the building of a corpus of repressive tactics that defined heretical practices. This pragmatic background became the conceptual, theological, and juridical basis for repression and the work of conversion. The texts of the *Malleus Maleficarum* (The Hammer of the Witches) by Kramer and Sprenger (1928/1971) or the *Directorium Inquisitorum* (1595) by Nicholas Eymeric, all churchmen, exemplify these processes quite clearly. The testimonies of witches about their practices were used to demonstrate the existence of such practices deemed heretical, and their testimony provided the backbone for the repressive measures that were imposed on them (see Few 2004, 30–31; Mello e Souza 2003, 179–217; and especially Ginzburg 1992).

Confession was the central issue in the Inquisition trials. The confessional manuals permitted discovery of cultural "sins" and extended the definition of what would be deemed illicit. Unwillingly, Native informers shaped the repression they suffered by their responses during confession. As Foucault noted, "Confession is a ritual of disclosure in which the speaking subject is also the subject of the statement" (1990, 61). Raymond Williams theorized that tradition is "an actively shaping force" whereby "certain meanings and practices are selected for emphasis and certain other meanings and practices are neglected or excluded" (1977, 115). As in the lost-wax method, selective Native traditions and their repression provided the mold that held and shaped Catholic practices in the New World.

Those interrogated in this process of *inquisitio* deployed various strategies and often compromised their "innocence" by attempting to evade the accusations. The efforts of the accused to explain their actions in order to meet the expectations of inquisitors or confessors filled in the blanks that provided coherence to the Catholic picture of devil worship, witchcraft, sorcery, blasphemy, Jewish practices, homosexual and lesbian practices, and any form of "deviance" inquisitors could imagine. More important, as the Inquisition prosecuted the deviant, it legitimized the imaginary and made it "real." The blur that enveloped the accused when they entered the universe of fear and torture brought about a phantasmagoric theme that fed on itself (Taussig 1987, 5, 8). When this happened, heresy entered the theme of the fantastic.

The missionaries who came to the New World had been raised in the context of the multitude of heretical movements that enveloped Europe in the sixteenth and seventeenth centuries (de Nicolas 1986, 9; Ricard 1933/1982, 35). For them, conversion included the hunt for and eradication of heresy. Martin points out that "religion, conceived as a 'cultural system,' is not only a reflection of society but also a model for society, a way of ordering the mundane as well as the religious life" (2002, 18). Neither missionaries nor their prospective converts seemed to distinguish between religious and secular practices. For westerners, the dreams that invaded sleep or what one did in the bedroom and how one prepared food were events as potentially heretical as crushing the Holy Host on the church floor. For Native societies in the New World, life was spiritual from the concept of being to the concept of becoming. Yet the compartmentalization of the numinous and the mundane and the momentous severing of the two did not occur until the nineteenth century in the Old World. Until then religion dominated life, although as Febvre notes about Europe, we know little about how the religious permeated the daily practices of generations (1982, 335–36).

A Treatise and a History of Religious Triumph

Except for the first decades of the conquest, Native Americans were not under the jurisdiction of the Inquisition, but the works of the devil were, and what you did not know about the devil could hurt you. In 1553, Fr. Andrés de Olmos wrote a treatise on witchcraft and sortilege in Nahuatl (Baudot 1553/1979). Before coming to the New World, Fr. Olmos had been deeply involved in the persecution of witchcraft in Biscay, where he had been the protégé of Bishop Juan de Zumárraga, who was later the first inquisitor of New Spain, and their partnership continued in the New World (Pilling 1895,

43–60). Fr. Olmos constructed his treatise around the dialogic relationship between good and evil, God and Satan, and the treatise is a textual tour de force that tailors Catholic religious concepts to Nahuatl comprehension. Using Bakhtin (1968, 95) to explain how texts are made to live in other people's minds, Burkhart notes that "the authors of these texts, whether Nahua or European, had to re-imagine Old World discourse in relation to the developing Christianity of indigenous Mesoamericans and the colonial power relations in which their religious life was entangled" (2001, 5). Fr. Olmos had to imagine, or should I say reinvent, an indigenous spiritual context within which Christian concepts of good and evil could be read.

In the exhortation to the Native (Indian) reader, Olmos stated, "I implore you my child, to pay very close attention in order that you do not misunderstand what I say. But if something appears obscure, difficult to understand, ask questions to the father who has spoken to you. That is all" (Baudot 1553/1979, 38). After positioning the priest as carnal and spiritual father, Fr. Olmos solicited a father-son dialogue through which the reader could pose questions and assuage doubts. As in a multiple-choice test, Fr. Olmos would then know how to modulate his text and teachings to Nahua cultural understanding. Parent, priest, and teacher, he would use the questions to shape the answers.

The content and language of the treatise clearly indicate that it was written for young men. The work documents a detailed preoccupation with the ontological nature of Satan, how Satan wants to be honored, and how he entraps those who wish to know the secret of life and how to do secret things. The treatise is not so much about the knowledge one should have (the nature of God and good) as it is about the secretive knowledge one should not have (the nature of Satan and evil). It admonished the Native reader that contact with shamans or seers to seek healing or foresee the future would anger God. Time and health are in God's hands, and evil tinkers with both. Unlike other texts that comment on Native shamanic beliefs, this one contrasted the good sacraments of the Catholic church with the anti-sacraments of the devil (Baudot 1553/1979, 70). In a series of rhetorical questions about why God permits the works of the devil, Fr. Olmos cited Saint Paul, "And as Saint Paul stated: It is necessary that heretics exist in order that the avowed Christians be well recognized" (82).[7] Recognition of God and Christianity required a heterodox heretic discourse, and the treatise targeted specific ethnic groups, such as Jews and Moors, along with an indiscriminate mass of unbelievers. The treatise pointed to cultural and everyday practices and asserted that foods such as water, bread, wine, and olive oil were associated with the Christian sacraments and were good to eat. Conversely, the anti-sacraments included foods that were not good to eat, such as birds and wild animals (72). In another work entitled *Tratado de los Pecados Mortales*, Fr. Olmos advocated fasting as the means to combat lust and sins of the flesh (Baudot 1990, 157–58). Such proscriptions called to mind and reinforced the distinction between "civilized" agricultural practices and "uncivilized" hunting and gathering practices, both in terms of the choice of foods and self-restraint.

In Chapter IV of the treatise, Olmos identified the ministers of the devil as sorceresses, necromancers, and magicians and declared that they would pay for their sins by fire because God wanted them to be burned (Baudot 1553/1979, 86). Time and again, the treatise emphasized the nefarious role of women in witchcraft and divination and spoke of how women caused men to fall from grace (74, 90, 96, 98; compare Burkhart 2001 for texts that mitigate this perspective). Olmos said that women were vulnerable to the devil's trickery for several reasons that marked them from birth as soiled, undeserving, and intrinsically unredeemable. First, because Eve, not Adam, was the first to be seduced by the words of the devil, women, as progeny of Eve, served the master of darkness. Second, because women avidly pursued knowledge of all things secret and because their lives were not centered on learning to succeed, they resorted to the teachings of the devil. Third, the devil knew that unlike men, women talked too much, did not ponder what they say, and gossiped about secrets and evil things, and the devil used these characteristics to keep his hold on women. Also, women could easily be overcome by ire; they were jealous and envious and often wanted to kill someone. Women entered into pacts with the devil to achieve the evil desires they harbored in their hearts. Olmos added that many of the sorcerers were women, particularly old women who were no longer desired by anyone and for that reason were taken by the devil as his tools (Baudot 1553/1979, 96, 98; see Few 2004 for women as targets of the Inquisition). Regardless of the pre-Columbian position of women in the many societies that were colonized, the effects of these views had to have been significant.

But the treatise went further. Fr. Olmos discussed those who made pacts with the devil and were thus capable of traveling through the air. He affirmed that although some decried belief in such practices, demons had the power to fly and said that some people had witnessed women doing the same. He cited the scriptures and explained that there are two types of sorcerers who served the devil: those who made a pact with him, belonged to him, and were transported by him to the forest, the fields, the air, and maybe even the sea and those who lost consciousness as if they were in a deep sleep and who received revelations about occult facts while in that state. These revelations were false, although those who experienced them with their bodies and their senses believed them (Baudot 1553/1979, 102–6). To illustrate his teachings, Fr. Olmos told stories of women who made pacts with the devil or people who were transmuted into animals, such as deer or cougars (see Few 2004, 61, 63, 67). Olmos said that although the devil could permit the sorcerer to take the form of a bird, a cougar, or a tiger, the sorcerer (*nahuali*) could not actually enter or leave the body of the animal: it was all an illusion created by the devil (Baudot 1553/1979, 112). Olmos explained that the devil had the power to perform these corporeal changes but that such power emanated from Satan, not from the sorcerers' skill. Unambiguously, the treatise delegitimized Native spiritual practitioners and portrayed them not as powerful mediators but as emasculated puppets and mouthpieces of evil.

Fr. Olmos associated places of devil worship with darkness, dishonor, shame, and laziness as well as with filth, cloacae, excrement, and latrines (Baudot 1553/1979, 116–20 and 1990, 155; see Delumeau 1977, 166 for European examples of excrement associated with witchcraft). To discuss the sacrificial offerings made to the devil by his followers, to exemplify the potential results of a "bad vow," and to demonstrate how easy it was to misunderstand signs and be tricked by the forces of evil, Fr. Olmos used the biblical episode when God ordered Abraham to sacrifice his son, Isaac (for the use of the same passage with different objectives see Burkhart 2001, 92–93). The Franciscan stated that in ancient times many people were killed by the acts of the devil. Such was the case in Mexico when people killed other humans and consumed human flesh communally until the Spaniards arrived and put an end to such devilish practices. In fact, Olmos constituted the devil as a *precolonial* barbaric historic presence in the New World with specific periods of activity (Baudot 1990, 124, 140). Fr. Olmos admonished his Nahuatl readers that the devil continued his works through the work of old women sorcerers who drained the blood of small children. For that purpose the devil taught midwives horrendous practices so they could eat the flesh and drink the blood of infants (Baudot 1553/1979, 124–26). Whether or not there was any evidence for such or similar practices in the New World, these demonic admonitions oozed into the Native psyche. These and other archetypal characteristics of the witchcraft discourse, such as flying through the air, bodily transmutation and pacts with the devil, which made the corpus of the *Malleus Maleficarum*, appeared in other parts of the American colonial world (Mello e Souza 2003, 155–75), and in various ways applied the European discourse of sorcery and witchcraft to Native shamanic practices.

For European Christians, the wilds of the New World contained a substratum of evil. Just a few decades before the publication of Fr. Olmos's work,

Cabeza de Vaca (1528–36), while in the land that would be known as Texas, reported that the Natives told him about a being they called the "Bad Thing" (*Mala Cosa*), whom they feared and who could transform himself into an animal or a woman (Cabeza de Vaca 1993, 81). This being would appear suddenly in the night and attack and injure them. Those who reported these apparitions to Cabeza de Vaca authenticated the shamanic encounters with the wounds the Bad Thing inflicted on their bodies. Likewise, the first Jesuits in the Laguna-Parras area noted the Natives' belief in a bloody black man whose appearance terrified them (Peláez, Barraza, Serrato, and Sakanassi 1991, 45–46).

A century after Fr. Olmos, Jesuit Pérez de Ribas (1645/1999) commented extensively on the shamanic practices of Native groups. Pérez de Ribas devoted Book XI of his *History of the Triumphs of Our Holy Faith* mostly to the conversion of the Laguna-Parras areas. There are many similarities between what he witnessed or reported from other areas and what he observed in the Laguna-Parras area. Pérez de Ribas's complaints mirror those of other missionaries: the sorcerers did the bidding of the devil, persuaded the people to rebel, burned the churches, and returned to the wild to continue their barbaric lifestyle (97, 673–74, 668).

Like the Franciscan Fr. Olmos, the Jesuit Pérez de Ribas commented on the bodily transformations of shamans whereby they appeared as deer, tigers, serpents, and other animals and sometimes as black men (1645/1999, 657, 673–74). Referring to the Parras area, the Jesuit stated, "It is well known from the Indians' oral traditions that the devil, for whom they had their own native term, appeared to them on innumerable occasions" (657). Pérez de Ribas described the shaman's sacra as representative of the pact made between the sorcerers and the devil. Pérez de Ribas stated that this pact was "kept bound up in small pieces of rawhide made from the pelts of animals similar to the ferret. They make small pouches out of this material, in which they keep colored pebbles or nearly transparent marbles. They guard this little pouch as though it held relics, so when they hand it over at the time of their Baptism, it is a good indication that they are truly receiving Christ's Faith and divorcing themselves from their intimacy with the devil" (97).

Throughout the Americas during the colonial period the sacra of shamans in the form of bundles or pouches were exposed and considered evil. Similarly, shaman bundles (*mandinga* pouches) produced by African slaves and others that were used for a variety of *maleficio* were objects of intense scrutiny by the Brazilian inquisitors and used as proofs of pacts with the devil (Mello e Souza 2003, 130–41). Indeed, although Inquisition activities were generally not visible in northernmost New Spain, official representatives of the Holy Office were present throughout and were assigned to missions and discovery expeditions. In the frontier, the presence of the Inquisition was felt in the discourse of *malleficio*, which grounded and indicted Native shamanic practices.

Pérez de Ribas continued to explain the relationship and form of contact between the Natives and the devil as well as its signifiers, though its representational forms were not considered idolatrous.

> The devil frequently spoke to the Indians when they were gentiles, appearing to them in the form of animals, fish or serpents; he has not forgotten how successful he was in assuming this same shape to cause the downfall of our first mother. The Indians greatly respected and feared him whenever he appeared, and as a title of respect they called him "Grandfather." They did so without distinguishing whether he was creature or creator. Even though they recognized the shape of the animal or serpent in which the devil appeared to them, painting it in their own fashion or sometimes erecting a stone or pole as an idol, they clearly did not seem to recognize a deity or supreme power of the universe. Most of the idolatry found among these people turned out to be of this kind. However, among other peoples . . . greater evidence of formal idolatry did exist. (Pérez de Ribas 1645/1999, 97)

Missionaries feared and continuously challenged shamans, yet despite the intense confrontation between missionary and shaman, which the former framed as the combat between good and evil and the latter probably viewed as one of spiritual survival, the friars co-opted some of the shaman's responsibilities and practices. Similarly, Native shamans adopted Catholic names and rituals (Hann 1991, 158–60, 167, 422–25; Metcalf 2005, 101, 203). Once a shaman received baptism, the missionaries used him as a mouthpiece; the sophisticated oratorical practices of shamans were better vehicles for exhorting the Native populace. Pérez de Ribas often referred to these speakers as preachers and noted the repetitive nature of the speech as well as the speaker's appeal to kinship connections (1645/1999, 97). As Cervantes notes, "In Mesoamerican thought rhetoric and ritual were unified in an effort to sustain a social order sufficiently in harmony with natural order" (1994, 43). In many cases, however, missionaries apparently did not relate the repetitive aspect of Native oratory to the pedagogic methods the missionaries utilized to teach the Christian doctrine. Missionaries' complaints that Natives worshiped the devil, did not remember what they were taught, and could not repeat the teachings appropriately should have alerted them to the resistance of Native populations to learn what they pointedly rejected or were simply not interested in.

Because missionaries relied on the oratory excellence of shamans in persuading Native groups to adopt Christian practices, shamans gained increasing control of the message they delivered, and often they used this ability to incite Natives to covert resistance and open revolt. But this genre of exhorting speech did not occur without absorbing Christian teachings, possibly not within a Christian conceptual framework but instead structured in the uniquely and imaginative manner in which people under control revive themselves and their culture.

Raymond Williams has posited that "the dominant culture . . . at once produces and limits its own forms of counter-culture" (1977, 114). I suggest that the vulnerability of dominant cultures to newly encountered and unknown cultural formations led the dominated cultures to subvert Christian doctrine and practices. Thus, in the long term, dominated cultures produced and limited the influence of the dominant Christian culture while at the same time subjecting it to scrutiny and forcing its practitioners into accommodating postures. Williams foresaw such situations when he stated that "it would be wrong to overlook the importance of works and ideas which, while clearly affected by hegemonic limits and pressures, are at least in part significant breaks beyond them, which may again in part be neutralized, reduced, or incorporated, but which in their most active elements nevertheless come through as independent and original" (1977, 114). In the New World such elements, which were visible in multiple cultural practices were, and are, indeed independent and original.

When the missionaries adopted the practice of breaking up families by separating males from females and children from the family unit, they succeeded in diminishing the influence of local leaders and communal practices. In the short term, these changes in social practices facilitated the work of the missionaries by undermining the importance of local elders and shamans and by curtailing the performance and importance of spiritual Native practices. In the long run, they also diminished the ability of Native leaders to influence and attract Native populations to Christianity.

Pérez de Ribas affirmed that the greatest achievements of the missionaries were "snatching from the devil's clutches the souls of bedeviled sorcerers" and "the great reform that one can see with respect to the vice of sorcery," leaving no doubt that despite the absence of "formal idolatry," the battle was between the Christian good and the shamanic evil (1645/1999, 245, 97).

Interestingly, the devil "testified" to the progress of the Jesuits, because as Pérez de Ribas stated, "the devil has confessed (as is told in several stories) that it is Saint Ignatius who wages the greatest war against him in the world" (1645/1999, 245, parenthesis in the original). The presence of the devil was needed to measure the difficulty of the task. The missionaries co-opted the devil to certify to the efficacy of conversion and authenticate the battle between good and evil. As Fr. Olmos believed, the devil not only validated but also vitalized the work of conversion.

Pérez de Ribas provides an important example of this devilish validation. A shaman who had converted declared that the devil appeared to his people in a thousand different forms, donned different names according to the reason for his appearance, and provided them with different gifts, which were related to the reason he was summoned. In war, the devil was "the fortress" and his gifts were the weapons for war; in pleasure, the devil was "delight" and he provided people with soft items such as feathers; he was "the lord of the rains" when he was called to provide rain for a copious harvest, and he was called "the lord of life and death" when he appeared as a bolt of lightning and could kill whomever he wished. He could spread pestilence and disease. Sometimes he was called "the Angel of Light" or the "Light of Midday," and he revealed the location of things lost or future events. Pérez de Ribas added that not everyone could see the devil, nor could all sorcerers communicate with the different personae of the devil. The devil answered specific needs and his manifestation was associated with explicit items or acts: arrows with war; feathers with pleasure; harvest with rain; lightning with life and death; light with vision and premonition (1645/1999, 245–46).

As will be discussed off and on throughout this work, the information provided by shamans, whether they had converted or not, modeled the Native "devil," sometimes making it Christian-like and familiar, other times portraying it as wild and ungraspable. The devil's appellations reveal the mutability and multiplicity of his personae as well as the functions he performed in Native spiritual-cum-social realms. The devil saw past the present; he had the power to see the past and the future. He also had the power to teach sorcerers spells to kill others and even to snuff out the lives of newborn children, a recurrent malefic theme. Pérez de Ribas affirmed that the episode retold above culminated when the missionary exorcized the devil by destroying and burying his simulacra (stone or gnarled poles) and by placing a cross over the buried idols, signaling victory. In spite of differences in culture, the tactics of power were generally the same whether the target was a stone temple or a single stone figurine: raze and superimpose (1645/1999).

In hunting-gathering societies, shamans had unique and essential roles as healers and spiritual mediators, and attacks on them were attacks on the group. It appears that shamans were convinced that once baptized "their familiar spirits left" them and they were "no longer any good at healing," a prospect that would leave them dispossessed of power as well as vulnerable and bare of spiritual protection (Pérez de Ribas 1645/1999, 250). If that were correct, transiting to such a liminal state would require enormous courage and place shamans in grave danger. Shamans engaged in these battles of conversion were unable to assist their people, were generally punished by the friars and the soldiers, and sometimes perished (249–250, 668, 673–74).

To understand how similarly "devilish" and "absurd" practices were acceptable and reasonable among the folk in Catholic Europe and barbaric and unacceptable in the New World, it is necessary to suspend disbelief. Just as Catholics did in Europe, Natives sought the help of spiritual protectors against natural phenomena or against the outcome of events beyond their control. These shamans often used a secretive and unintelligible language to access the numinous realm. The Natives had "idols" from which they requested healthy offspring, victories in war, protection for crops, rain, profitable hunts, or good fishing (Pérez de Ribas 1645/1999, 250). These "idols" had diverse shapes, and often the shamans' sacra amounted simply to unusual stones or rocks, little sticks, thorns, and human bones (494). Likewise, missionaries prayed in an esoteric language and performed ceremonies to ward off natural dangers and ensure the success of Christian endeavors using sacred objects such as the rosary, the cross, and other sacra or even natural elements such as water and bread. Missionaries read signs to ascertain God's will, performed exorcisms, said invocations, and used human relics and the images of the Virgin Mary and saints to liberate those who were bewitched and to expel demons (Delumeau 1977, 163–65, 168; Pérez de Ribas 1645/1999, 246–47, 668; Ricard 1933/1982, 92, 103). Such practices resonated with American Native populations, while the demotion of shamans and proscription of their practices had to be perceived as confrontations between the power of different gods and different spiritual paradigms (Alberro 1999, 40–47, 54). The premise that Natives worshipped "false idols" in contrast to a Christian true God and His sanctioned mediators did violence to the Native American cultural essence. To deal with the massive attack of such spiritual contagion, Native populations split conceptual threads and made new cultural fabric. Without diminishing the trials and efforts of the missionaries, it is to Native ingenuity and conceptual wizardry that we should pay homage.

Commenting on the cultural changes that resulted from missionary work, Pérez de Ribas stated, "These include dealings and familiarity with demons, idolatry and diabolical superstitions" (1645/1999, 448). Once converted, shamans presumably discarded their items of sorcery, but Pérez de Ribas understood the equivalence of spiritual affect and value these sacra held for the shaman. He stated, "The Indian sorcerers loved these items in the same way that Catholic Christians love their holy and sacred relics" (449). The Jesuit understood the equivalence but placed it at marked polar opposites—relics were holy, but a shaman's pouch was devilish. There lay the battleground.

Conclusion

At the root of the religious conversion of the New World was a battle about good and evil, the outcome of which forever changed colonized and colonizer. In the still-smoldering cauldron of this brew the missionaries, and others, stirred the essentials of the crucial debates that confronted modern Europe and came to afflict the worlds of discovery. Central to the definition of the boundaries of what was good and what was evil were the definition of heresy and principally the institution of the Inquisition, not so much for its presence in New Spain as for the questions it raised, the solutions it reached, and the dogmatic foundation it gave to the Catholic Church. The problem was that in *recognizing* good and evil, the missionaries established a double standard and all that was ineffable became evil. The next chapter fleshes out some ways this double standard was implemented.

The Religious and the Spiritual

Europe and the Americas

The missionaries who came to the New World left home with conceptual knapsacks loaded with Christian zeal, preconceived notions about those they came to convert, and unrealistic expectations. Most important, they brought along European models of conversion that were steeped in combat with Jews, Muslims, and Protestants but most of all with witchcraft, sorcery, and heretical and deviant practices. Catholic missionaries honed their arguments and conversion skills among the European urban and country folk who, from crib to coffin, engaged in an emotional dialectic of promises and devotion to a pantheon of saints.

In New Spain, particularly in the Basin of Mexico and Yucatán, the Spanish encountered sophisticated civilizations with sacrificial and ritual cannibalistic practices that the conquistadors found threatening, monstrous, and abhorrent. In California, Texas, northeastern Mexico, and even in Florida, the hunter-gatherer societies the Europeans encountered posed a physical threat and were perceived as barbaric but generally did not provoke the religious repugnance missionaries experienced in other places. Although Europeans saw hunter-gatherers as devil-worshippers, the absence of visible structured religious practices, temples, and idols among hunter-gatherer groups caused the Europeans to sway between destructive rage, contempt, and pity. European missionaries were knowledgeable about many superstitious folk practices, and missionaries born in New Spain would certainly have been wise to local "heretical" practices. Yet many of the folk practices of Europe were not that different from the practices of Native Americans. What was perceived as acceptable and even sanctioned in Europe was excised and punished in New Spain. At issue is how analogous spiritual or cultural practices were treated differently in the Old World and in New Spain. Similarly, it is instructive to briefly compare the roles performed by shamans and missionaries as actors engaged in the transaction of knowledge among Native American mission populations.

Folk Practices

The work of William Christian (1989a, 1989b) is essential for understanding the folk religious practices of Iberia and for making sense of the experiences of many of the missionaries who came to the New World. Christian based some of his conclusions on the questionnaires issued by Philip II that were sent to New Castile, in Central Spain, from 1575 to 1580. These elicited responses from the residents of local Spanish communities on a variety of subjects, some of which related to religious practices. Christian's study concentrates on two issues on the questionnaires: first, "the notable relics that the churches and towns possessed; and the well-known chapels and oratories in the territory and the miracles that have taken place there"; and second, "the holy days on which work could not be done, and the fast days and the days on which meat could not be eaten that are observed in the town by a special vow, in addition to those of the Church, and the reasons for them and their origin" (1989a, 6).

Apart from Philip II's lifelong obsession with relics, the questionnaire demonstrates the inseparability of religious and economic practices. Vows, miracles, shrines, and saints held the key to a healthy economy, but the number of days people were not working had to be kept in check lest the crops rot in the fields. Christian's analysis of the questionnaires (1989a), as well as his study of apparitions (1989b), demonstrates that the region was dotted with monasteries, convents, churches, and shrines run or sponsored by the Mendicant Orders and the Jesuits.

In the sixteenth and seventeenth centuries, European religious life centered more on vows, festivals, processions, pilgrimages, and the miraculous than on the sacramental (Christian 1989b, 13). The miraculous saturated the economic and religious life of Europeans and made the two spheres concentric. The records show that villagers confessed and received communion only once a year and that most did so under duress. In fact, "a manual of 1530 instructed the parish visitors [clerics] to '[teach the priests] how they should treat more gently the *letrados* and nobles and virtuous people who bring with them great shame . . . than the rustics and the ignorant who if they are not rebuked neither have shame nor realize the gravity of their sin'" (Christian 1989a, 142). Moreover, the Council of Trent, which codified most Catholic practices, established that nuns were to confess and receive communion at least once a month, which implies that even nuns seldom received those sacraments (Delumeau 1977, 196). Most Catholics in Europe did not know much more than the Our Father and the Hail Mary in terms of prayer and doctrine. Few could identify any of the Ten Commandments, which are essential for a proper confession, until the eighteenth century. On the other hand, theft, murder, adultery, inebriation, and deviant sexual practices had long been acknowledged as antisocial behaviors punishable by law and the church, as is clearly evident from the medieval books of penance (McNeill and Gamer 1938). Overall, Europeans displayed poor knowledge of doctrine and even poorer compliance with the sacramental requirements of the Catholic church (Delumeau 1977, 175, 196).

In the New World, missionaries complained constantly about the incapacity of Natives to confess properly and to know and recall their sins. In Tlaxcala, "only twenty percent of the faithful confessed annually" and in Mexico the figure was less than ten percent, while in other parishes the number "varied between six and forty percent" (Gurzinski 1989, 104), even though some Native populations in Mexico traditionally practiced a "kind of confession" (Ricard 1933/1982, 32). Parishioners seldom fulfilled the confession precept whether they were Spanish or Native Americans (Taylor 1996, 241–42). Within the missions discussed in this work, however, it is likely that the numbers were higher since the annual confession was part of the set of structured religious and economic practices. Besides, failure to confess during Lent could result in forty-four lashes.

As for the sacrament of matrimony, Europe struggled with solutions to the sociocultural, economic, and religious problems the union of man and woman presented (Reid 2004, 25–68). Marriage's tortuous history did not coalesce into a body of laws until the Council of Trent, while the application of the laws regulating coupling and procreation took about another two centuries to be accepted. In the New World things were not very different, and sometimes those who refused to contract matrimony were whipped, while others were not allowed to marry (Taylor 1996, 244). Missionaries were particularly concerned with the sexual behavior of Native populations, as the confessionary manuals demonstrate, but it was the church's insistence on a single partner (wife) that probably caused more overt conflicts between missionaries and mission Natives and led to the recognition of unions Natives had begun before they entered the missions (Harrington 1934, 25). The harsh control missionaries exercised over coupling and sexual practices were hardly better accepted in the New World than they were in Europe. But the methods available to missionaries in the New World were much harsher than the methods priests typically used in the Old World. While in Iberia the church could peer into the household through confession, gossip, and peer pressure, in the missions it could control Native behavior through structuring their living arrangements and, in the late period, by locking up people.

The sacraments of baptism and last rites are poor indicators of sacramental knowledge because they bracket the beginning and end of a life course, are individual legal markers, and could be administered without the consent of the person. Baptism also marked entry into a kin group and society and placed people within a genealogy that had legal and social implications, including inheritance rights. Likewise, the sacrament of last rites was intrinsically tied to wills and testaments and the division of property. In Europe, as in the New World, Catholic death rituals concentrated on the sacrament of last rites. In the New World, mission Natives seldom asked for last rites, particularly early in the contact period, and in most cases the elaborate ritual was reduced to the use of holy water or anointment with holy oils. In terms of doctrinal and sacramental knowledge, urban and rural folk in Europe, who had been exposed to the tenets of the Catholic faith for several centuries, did not perform much better than Native Americans. Aside from the special cases of baptism and last rites, the insistence of the missionaries that Natives in the New World had a poor grasp on the mysteries of the faith, failed to understand the significance of confession and communion, and were therefore unfit to receive either sacrament becomes problematic.

Similar to Native American populations, the religiosity of European urban and rural dwellers responded to a variety of concerns, from fertility to epidemics to drought, floods, and agricultural pests (Harrington 1934, 13; Taylor 1996, 49). During the sixteenth century, entire villages disappeared due to epidemics and to economic problems that resulted from natural phenomena (Christian 1989a, 23–28). Spain's populace and friars were used to the wrath of God, which often translated into very high mortality. God gave it and God took it away was a living paradigm. The hope that the Virgin Mary and a host of saints would intervene was often the only alternative to utter despair. After Europeans arrived in the New World, devastating epidemics created similar distress situations. Some Christianized Native populations in urban areas appealed to the Catholic pantheon and negotiated tradeoffs with traditional Native deities, much like Europeans did to engage the best saint for the task at hand. But most reacted to physical stress and social dislocation from within their own moral and spiritual universes. Hunter-gatherer and horticulturalist populations attributed disease to contact with Europeans (Cabeza de Vaca 1993, 59; Pérez de Ribas 1645/1999, 501, 673, 677, 680); threatened, expelled, and killed missionaries (Casañas 1691; Pérez de Ribas 1645/1999, 124–25); fled rancherías and missions (Pérez de Ribas 1645/1999, 675, 681; Wade 2003, 6); and relied on Native spiritual practitioners for help (Geiger and Meighan 1976, 49, 74–75; Pérez de Ribas 1645/1999, 668, 673–74, 681; Swanton 1942, 220–21, 224), some to the point of recanting Christianity and refusing last rites (Harrington 1934, 14, 49–50, 55).

It would be unwise to equate Native American urbanized agriculturists or frontier hunter-gatherers with Iberian populations living at the same time, yet human reactions to widespread pestilence and death are predictable. Christian points out that in 1575, New Castile was not the backwater we might imagine but "the heartland of the most powerful nation in Europe" with a well-informed and mobile citizenry (1989a, 22). But when the epidemic of 1506–1507 struck New Castile, "villagers fled infected towns hastening the spread of the disease" (Christian 1989, 25), just as Native American populations did under similar circumstances. Other epidemics struck New Castile in 1545–1546, 1556–1557, 1557–1570, and 1580. Grasshoppers devastated crops in 1545–1549, and vines and trees suffered pest infestations (25–28). In the grip of collective panic, the affected groups appealed to the saints through vows, pilgrimages, processions, prayers, and exorcisms. They hired itinerant necromancers, enpsalmers and conjurers to chase the clouds to prevent hail and lightning and summon rainclouds during drought. Town leaders even held trials to condemn locusts, rats, or swallows and excommunicate them (29). One such trial took place near Segovia in 1650 at the Hieronymite monastery, "and the judge who pronounced the excommunication on the grasshoppers was Our Lady Saint Mary, 'constant advocate of men, particularly those in anguish and need,' speaking through her lieutenant, the prior of the monastery" (30). The sentence the Virgin Mary delivered, "after consultation with her advisors Saint Jerome, Saint Francis, Saint Lawrence and Saint Michael the Archangel, was that the insects would automatically fall under excommunication if they did not leave the territory" (30). The Virgin Mary spoke through the prior of the monastery, just as Native American deities spoke through shaman and other spiritual practitioners, and excommunication of insects and animals is no more preposterous than the shaman's intercession with prey animals among hunter-gatherer groups (Fletcher and La Flesche 1972, 441, 518; Geiger and Meighan 1976, 47, 50–51; Harrington 1934, 46; Swanton 1942, 136, 219). Similarly, in New Spain and in the areas discussed in this book, epidemics ravaged mission populations, and floods and plagues destroyed crops (Casañas 1691; Engelhardt 1929, 479, 481, 483–84; Lopez 1786, 16, 19; Pérez de Ribas 1645/1999, 686–87; Santa Ana 1748). These trials were sent by God and by the devil to harvest Native souls and test the resolve of the missionaries. The devil took the shape of animals and insects, and locusts frequently devastated mission crops in California, but I could not find evidence that animals were ever put on trial in the New World.

In Europe, necromancers, fortunetellers, and sorcerers competed with friars and priests, who performed the same ceremonies but did so according to Catholic practices. Signs such as a fire, hail, or a freak storm that occurred on a given saint's day were understood as an expression of that saint's anger. To placate the saint, a vow would be made, followed by appropriate processions and prayers, and the effectiveness and power of that saint were assessed according to the resolution of the problem. A complex language of signs was interpreted according to a liturgical calendar and a saint's proven relationship to specific phenomena. In some cases lotteries were held "to find helper saints in times of need" (Christian 1989a, 47). Sometimes the community would determine which saint they should approach by selecting twelve candles of equal size and height. Each candle was assigned to a different saint. When the candles were lit, the last candle left burning determined which saint should be chosen. According to Christian, this procedure was used throughout Europe (47). All these instances issued from faith in the outcome and imply "the possibility of interaction between a visible and an invisible domain" (Turner and Turner 1978, 205) in which a liminal boundary has to be pierced to allow for transformation and intervention. This porous membrane between visible and invisible realms permits the flow of transformations, an important aspect of a process often called syncretism.

Images were used for curing and local shrines dedicated to a multitude of saints were the site of prayers and nocturnal vigils (Christian 1989a, 101). "Miracles were critical, dramatic evidence of the power of the shrine image," enhanced its value in economic and religious terms, and guaranteed the continuous outpouring of offerings (102). Vows, shrines, and processions were instruments of mediation between the divine and the anguished folk while also establishing a self-perpetuating votive economy.

Likewise, Native American spiritual practitioners accessed spiritual domains to preempt the negative consequences of hunting and gathering or to placate the forces of nature. They read natural phenomena such as wind, dust devils, earthquakes, and cosmic events as portents with spiritual significance. Similar to European populations that "located sacred images in places of universal significance . . . near water, near important trees, on cliffs or peaks," the Native American landscape was (and is) a spiritual register dotted with places imbued with significance and power (Christian 1989a, 91; cf. Geiger and Meighan 1976, 51, 58; Harrington 1934, 57–59; Schneider 2007). The importance of sacred places enshrined in the land to Native lifeways and to the acquisition of resources is amply confirmed by the large gatherings of Native groups at certain times and places, practices the friars continuously decried.

The intense devotion to the Virgin Mary exhibited by the Catholic rulers and some of the most ruthless conquistadors of the New World leaves no doubt as to the importance of visions, signs, and propitiatory rites that accompanied the work of conquest and conversion (Burkhart 2001, 2–3; Hall 2004, 45–79). In Mexico, the Virgin Mary was deeply venerated, as were Catholic saints, and they were also used to appropriate the landscape and to reinforce the links between ancient Native traditions and the Catholic rites and feasts (García 2006, 37–61; Ricard 1933/1982, 36; Taylor 1996, 279–80). For instance, in the case of Our Lady of Ocotlán, Fr. Martín Sarmiento de Hojacastro was not concerned about whether the Natives saw the apparition of the Virgin Mary as the Aztec goddess Xochiquetzalli, or any other deity for that matter, providing they came "eventually to venerate the mother of God" (Cervantes 1994, 54). At issue is not whether the Natives "confused" or conflated the deities but simply that the Franciscan would suggest that they do so or expect them to do so. The important point is the equivalence of perceptions and practices, not the identity of the entities or objects venerated. Equally, the missionaries' insistence on finding parallels between Native practices and Christian teachings blurred (and blurs) the boundaries between pre- and postcolonial traditions (Harrington 1934, 48, 52).

Like the economic dimension of vows and indulgences, the Christian relic business was extremely lucrative, and its development foregrounds a fascination with death, body parts, bones, fluids, and saintly odors (Christian 1989a, 151–52, 155–57; Turner and Turner 1978, 196). Franciscans, Jesuits, the papacy, and the crowns of Europe participated in this religious commerce and some kings, such as Philip II, developed a world-renowned collection of relics. This cultic practice extended early to New Spain (García 2006, 48–49). The devotional example of the heads of the Eleven Thousand Virgins is particularly relevant for its number and gruesome reality. These heads were venerated by the crown, the church, and the populace (Christian 1989a, 134–38, 152). In Mexico City there were two heads of these virgins and a tooth said to belong to one of them. There were also slivers of Christ's cross, many bones from saints, hair from Saint Theresa, and even a sliver from the table of the Last Supper (Vetancurt 1971, 47). While the heads of the virgins were displayed and touched as saintly relics, heads of enemies displayed by Native Americans on poles were considered barbaric and devilish. More to the point, throughout Europe, criminals were punished and their body parts and heads displayed as a deterrent to an audience of potential delinquents and as edifying spectacles to redress the offense made to the body of the king. In the "liturgy of public execution" (Foucault 1979, 65), heads rolled to assert the power of kings in search of a state, but when Native

Americans displayed the heads of vanquished enemies, they were labeled as savages.

Even a brief perusal of the religious practices of Europeans and Iberians demonstrates that neither their motivations nor their practices were very different from the ones missionaries encountered in the New World. Native American shamans as well as shamans all over the world strove to access entities of the spiritual world to obtain good crops, rain, and health; to avoid pestilence and disease; to guarantee fertility and healthy offspring; and to affect the future. Images and cultic objects were used in both spiritual contexts as mediators and signifiers. Communication with the dead, "the good dead, but not the damned" (Turner and Turner 1978, 204), was the basis for miracles and was expressed in out-of-body experiences, dreams, apparitions, and visions. In some cases, death and the dismembered body served propitiatory purposes in the New World, while in Europe they were objects of fervor, reverence, or kingly revenge and power. Body parts as relics held the feverish imagination of kings and commoners alike and were, and are, responsible for the renown of many sanctuaries, pilgrimages, and local healthy economies (Turner and Turner 1978). In Europe, as in the New World, people used herbal preparations for cures and mediation, and relics were sometimes ingested as medicine in Europe (Christian 1989a, 129; Conklin 2001, 9–12; Harrington 1934, 49). While Christians ingest the body and blood of Christ to reenact Christ's redemptive sacrifice and strengthen the receiver against attacks from evil, Native groups ingested the ashes or body parts of relatives to embody and honor them. As well, Native groups ingested remains of enemies and animals to extract and be empowered by their skill and strength (Cabeza de Vaca 1993, 60; Pérez de Ribas 1645/1999, 667; Ricard 1933/1982, 31). Despite modern reluctance to or even repugnance about associating Christian practices with Native practices, the parallels are obvious.

Healing practices of shamans and missionaries were extremely similar, and although they may have appeared so to Native populations, generally missionaries did not see the parallels. Missionaries attributed the shamans' healing practices to maleficent forces (see Harrington 1934, 54–55). Similarly, once shamans viewed the missionaries as competitors or were forced to do so, the shamans either acquiesced and were co-opted by the missionaries' teachings or fought back. Either way, shamans and missionaries were involved in continuous spiritual dueling, sometimes with tragic consequences, but the similarity of their practices is clear.

Shamans and missionaries accessed the spiritual world through prayer using an esoteric language—Latin, in the case of the missionaries. In heal-

Figure 2.1. San José Mission, San Antonio, Texas. Robert Runyon Photograph Collection, image number 04188. Courtesy of the Center for American History, University of Texas at Austin.

ing performances both used ritualized gestures, both called on the power of special objects, and both used herbs, potions, and phlebotomy. The practices and interpretations resulting from the outcome of a healing could be very different, however. Generally, gifts, either prayers or objects, were offered as thanks for cures. Unsuccessful healing sessions might cost the shaman his or her reputation or even his or her life (Swanton 1942, 222), but the missionary won either way, because the outcome reflected God's will (Pérez de Ribas 1645/1999, 673). That was an enormous advantage for the missionary, whose mediating powers were not put to an exacting test with a required outcome. Likely the Natives saw matters otherwise, and they often shopped for the best provider (Harrington 1934, 54–56).

In a few cases, we hear dissonant missionary voices that speak through the normal Christian discourse with a questioning curiosity, if not a tinge of respect. In California, Fr. Boscana reported that Luiseño males and females had

> the power of enchantment, to such a degree, that no one can withstand their powers. . . . The incantation is performed thus: Beneath the left arm, in a small leather bag, they carry a black ball, called by them 'aguet,' composed of a plaster of mescal, and wild honey, or, as they term it, 'quijotes,' or 'sejat.' When they wish to make use of same, to exercise its virtues upon any one, the right hand is placed upon

the leather bag, and without any other ceremony, the sorcery is effected. . . . The said 'aguet,' is a composition unknown to all but the sorcerers, and of course, only used by them. How it possesses so much virtue, I have never been enabled to discover. Nevertheless, they give up whatever is asked of them. (Robinson 1969, 296–97)

Though convinced that the powers of the shaman derived from the devil, Boscana nevertheless was perturbed by their efficacy, and he related the case of a young woman at Mission La Purísima who suffered dysentery and fevers for over one year and "was to all appearances dying; having received the holy sacrament preparatory to her supposed departure" (Robinson 1969, 312–13). Soon after, Fr. Boscana saw her working in the garden and looking well. When asked how she felt, her mother, who was working next to her, explained that a shaman had "taken from her some bear's hairs, which were the cause of her illness, and immediately, she was restored" (Robinson 1969, 313). The hairs had been deposited in her stomach before she reached womanhood and were responsible for the illness. Though Boscana found the explanation a fraud, he had to admit that "still it happened from that day, that the girl improved in health, and, in a short time, was robust and hearty as any one" (Robinson 1969, 313). Likely the problem was related to the onset of menses, but if the mysterious 'cure' had been the result of the friar's intervention and prayers, he might well have called it a miracle and required no further explanation.

The belief in *malleficio* due to the insertion into the body of strange substances or objects such as hairs, worms, and sticks was widespread in the Americas (Behar 1987, 37–38, 45; Blaine 2000, 618; Cabeza de Vaca 1993, 62, 79–80; DuBois 1908, 81; Geiger and Meighan 1976, 49, 72, 74–75; Harrington 1934, 49–50; Radding 2005, 206; Sparkman 1908, 216), and these objects were extracted through the laying on of hands, ritual movements over the body, blowing, and suction. In response to a questionnaire sent to the Franciscans in Alta California in 1813–1815, most friars acknowledged that Native shamans used a great assortment of herbs and minerals for physical and spiritual healing as well as bleeding, scarification, bathing, and sweat baths (Geiger and Meighan 1976, 71–80; Sparkman 1908, 218).[1] Fr. Boscana also noted that the Luiseño used herbs such as "sage, rosemary and the nettle-plant" (Robinson 1969, 310). Like Fr. Boscana (Robinson 1969, 310), Fr. Antonio Peyri (Geiger and Meighan 1976, 72), who missionized the Chumash at San Luis Obispo, recognized that healing ceremonies were secretive and enveloped in great mystery, a fundamental difference of Native rituals from Christian ones.

Out of context, European popular religious practices or Native spiritual practices may appear abhorrent or ridiculous to the uninitiated. The issue of context is relevant because, aberrant or not, discussions of European religious practices or of Native practices associated with Christian conversion are often contextualized while Native American spiritual practices are not, thus neutralizing or ridiculing their relevance. It is hard to understand why excommunicating locusts or swallows would appear more logical or less devilish to the missionaries than seeking protection against the forces of nature through ritualized drinking and dancing. Similarly, why would missionaries perceive that Christian Agnus Dei scapulars worn next to the body were effective and sanction them while judging shamans' pouches, sacred bundles, and talismans as devilish frauds and banning them (see Behar 1987, 37–38; and Mello e Souza 2003, 131)?[2] The perceived and actualized chasm between Christian and non-Christian practices resulted from the absolute expectation that the Native other was a being who did not know God, a God commensurate with the Catholic conception of God; therefore missionaries believed that all practices that contravened religious teachings were intrinsically barbaric or the work of the devil.

Recent research on the concept of "wickedness" has focused on the Basin of Mexico and other nonfrontier areas and is based on the evidence from a variety of texts from different regions (see Alberro 1999; Burkhart 1989; Cervantes 1994; Florescano 1997; Sousa 2002). The pictorial and textual evidence from these regions shows how the Church demonized Native practices and deities while it saw the devil as the agent provocateur who was responsible for deviant behavior. But the evidence from the hunter-gatherer populations discussed in this work is challenging because the devil as evil comes through the discourse of the missionaries. Even in the rare occasions when we presumably hear a Native voice, it is unclear if the Natives were simply using Christian terminology in order to be understood, whether they were mocking Christian concepts, or if they had stitched the Christian devil or the saints to their spiritual protectors and multifunctional deities. Such is the problem with the Calusa, the Hasinai, and the many events recorded by Father Ribas (1645/1999), where shamans were understood as proxy actors for the devil.

The process by which Native spiritual practices, mainly those of hunter-gatherer populations, became the domain of a Christian devil is yet to be fully dissected. Obsession with evil forces and a multivocal and ever-present devil were widespread in Europe since the Middle Ages. Ginzburg's (1992) research on the *benandanti* and their forced metamorphosis from witch-fighters to witches exemplifies the slippery process of transmuting amorphous folk traditions beliefs into the devil's work. Similarly, witchcraft manuals defined the devil's role in witchcraft by a process based on cumulative testimony provided by the victims of the Inquisition, often under torture. If nothing else, the process of retelling and shaping a narrative to accommodate potential dreamlike experiences and inconsistencies framed a discourse of the devil that was destined to shape the future as it stereotyped women and racialized the devil (Peláez, Barraza, Serrato, and Sakanassi 1991, 45–46).

This research on evilness has addressed the ambivalence of concepts of good and evil in the New World as well as the preoccupation of colonial institutions with understanding, curbing, or eliminating Native practices (Burkhart 1989; Cervantes 1994; MacCormack 1991; Mello e Souza 2003; Taylor 1996). As a result of its geographic and textual emphasis, most of the research, however, has focused on urban or settled agricultural societies with elaborate social structures anchored by strong spiritual components whereby sacred communal practices, either overt or covert, permeated and validated those very structures.

For settled folk, the conflation of the domain of the devil and the wild and savage frontier occupied the colonial imaginary as a "chicamec" cancer. In fact, as late as the early 1800s Fr. Boscana compared the California groups to the "chichimecs" (Harrington 1934, 8). In Veracruz, the discalced Carmelite nuns were afflicted by ants that they perceived as one of the many embodiments of the devil. They noted that some ants called "chichimecas cause a great burning and stinging sensation" (López 2002, 190; cf. also Blaine 2000, 618 and Ingham 1986, 103). Lewis notes that "Spaniards and others attributed the most powerful forms of witchcraft to Chichimecs" (2003, 108), and Cervantes briefly touches on the subject when he looks at Native nomadic groups (*chichimecs*) as sources of a diabolism that spread from the "wild" to the "civilized" world (1994, 90–97). The notion that wilderness folk harbored contagion that could infect civilized urban folk etched the boundary between "savage" hunter-gatherer and "civilized" agriculturists (see Radding 1998b, 198). A significant point is the tradition among the Luiseño in California of the use of ants in rites of passage and the connotation that the sting of ants had health benefits (DuBois 1908, 91). We are far from understanding what evil lurked in hunting and gathering societies and how conversion mimetically appropriated a European devil to make sense of and to muzzle the practices of Native American nomadic societies.

Mitchell describes the fixation of southern Spaniards with the devil and points out that "the ecclesiastical mind was hardly less prone to superstition than the popular" (1990, 25–26). In fact, according to Jean Weir (Flores 1976, 47), a staunch witch hunter, there were no less than 7,405,926 devils that composed 1,111 legions. These computations led the inquisitors to determine that Weir could have obtained that information only from satanic sources, a typical Inquisition move. In Spain, people believed that demons took all possible disguises and found them in "amulets, furniture, animals, voices and even heads of lettuce" (Mitchell 1990, 26), but in Mexico the Virgin Mary could appear inside a kernel of corn (Taylor 2003). Natural phenomena like hurricanes and high winds and cosmological phenomena were associated with the devil's work in parts of the Old and New Worlds (Ingham 1986, 106, 116; Mitchell 1990, 26; Pérez de Ribas 1645/1999, 657; Radding 2005, 205). In Parras, the local Natives feared dust devils and when they saw one they dropped to the ground in fright and awe. It is little wonder that the Jesuits considered the Natives' reaction to dust devils as an invocation of the devil (Pérez de Ribas 1645/1999, 657). But signs live double lives. In the exercise of reading signs, a high wind during an Inquisition auto-de-fé in Lima was understood as God's intervention on behalf of the condemned (Silverblatt 2004, 95). In 1696, in southern Spain, town healers and curanderos were skilled in exorcizing devils and chasing plagues. After passing tests, such as walking barefoot on a red-hot iron bar, they could be officially employed by a town as healers (Mitchell 1990, 32–33). Native Americans who performed identical services and feats of endurance, on the other hand, were flogged, imprisoned, and exiled. Perception is nine-tenths of reality.

Shamans and Missionaries

There are many roads to shamanism and many ways to heed the shamanic call (Bean and Vane 1991, 713–23; Taussig 1987, 171–87). Whether a shaman inherited his or her position or actively sought his or her job, most had unusual skills and talents and underwent long periods of apprenticeship as well as rites of passage. Shamans sought and were guided by signs and needed a community of believers to confirm their power (Bean and Vane 1991, 717; Sparkman 1908, 216). The community also checked the shaman's skill by assessing the results obtained when his or her services were requested. Equally, there are many roads to God and many ways to answer a vocational call. Missionaries often had unusual talents, they certainly went through extensive learning and training, and they underwent various types of rites of passage designated as vows. Signs from God were sought and many missionary careers were decided on a web of signs and symbols studiously read and reworked. Finally, the missionary could not perform without a community of believers; without it his mission was void. What was often denied to the missionary was the faithful, at least later when enough mission Natives were poached by disease.

For the Native who sought help from the missionary, poor performance in curing or the death of the patient would be assessed negatively, as it would be with a Native shaman (Bean 1991, 730). But negative appraisal of a Christian life and its spiritual value took other forms. In 1817, Fr. Boscana tried to help a baptized young man from Mission San Juan Capistrano who was dying. He was well instructed in religion and was a good Spanish speaker, but he violently rejected the friar. According to Fr. Boscana, the dying man stated that he would not confess "because I do not want to: having lived deceived, I do not want to die deceived" (Harrington 1934, 55–56). Epidemics and conflicts over labor and social organization eroded the curiosity and the goodwill of mission Natives, though these events may have done much to enhance the role of Native shamans. The truth is that while the Franciscan and Jesuit programs of conversion were under way, the manna of the missionaries never proved powerful enough to displace Native beliefs wholesale, as revolts and continuous spiritual wrestling of missionaries with shamans prove. Unlike the shaman, a strict specialist, the missionary performed many tasks and assumed many roles out of necessity. Frequently, the missionary also had to rely on the expertise and help of others. In a certain sense, the many roles the missionary assumed and his dependence on others devalued and undermined his capabilities as a spiritual specialist.

Conclusion

The missionaries who came to New Spain encountered Native spiritual traditions that they struggled to comprehend and catalogue according to their notions of heresy and idolatry. Culturally, missionaries could not associate Catholic paraliturgical traditions that engaged kings and priests in devotional ecstasy, such as the veneration of relics, with similar Native American spiritual traditions, nor did they admit the parallels between European folk traditions and Native American practices. Folk superstitions that priests regarded as merely misguided in Europe became barbaric rites when they were practiced by Natives. As arbiters of the definition of what was good and what was evil, missionaries demonized Native practices and produced cultural change. Today many Native American groups who descend from mission communities claim Catholicism as their religion. One might say that God works in mysterious ways.

The historical development of the Order of Friars Minor and the Society of Jesus imparted their missionaries with distinct characteristics that facilitated their conversion work. The next two chapters identify these characteristics and focus on gauging their relevance.

The Franciscans

Men of the Cloth

To understand the lives and acts of the missionaries who came to the Americas it is necessary to consider the conceptual world and experiences that shaped their perceptions. Without knowledge of their cultural background and the core tenets of the religious orders they joined, we might read their acts as if their lives in the New World were remade out of new cloth. That would be misleading; they were shaped by the order they served and their lives were patched with other missions, other trials, and other truths. Coming from many areas of the western world, missionaries brought to the Americas their quilted cultural knowledge plus all their misconceptions about the New World and its peoples.

The original thematic and historical development of the Order of Friars Minor was central to the spread of Christianity among indigenous populations in the Americas. The Franciscan apocalyptic vision and the dialogic undertow of the Spirituals and Conventuals, which eventually led to the emergence of the Observants, left an indelible wash on the religious practices of the Americas. This chapter discusses some of the early characteristics of the Franciscan Brotherhood and the development of the Franciscan Order and relates them to the Franciscans who came to the New World and the practices they used in their attempts to convert the Native people there.

A Beginning

St. Francis of Assisi was born Giovanni di Bernardone. His father was a prosperous cloth merchant. Giovanni was renamed Francesco by his father, and he later adopted that name. Francis followed a tortuous route to salvation, flirting with debauchery, corruption, and the Crusades, finally falling in love with God.

Most of the narratives of St. Francis's life, whether they are well researched or romanticized, try to identify the point when his life changed and his search for God found a response. This modern quest for the moment of epiphany reflects our need for a plot with a denouement and discounts the process of becoming. In a certain sense, this quest parallels the attitudes we have when analyzing the actions of the missionaries. Epiphanic signposts that point the way from sinner to saint characterize the way the histories of the early Franciscans and Jesuits have been told. Interestingly, researchers have often read the signs in the same way as the medieval saints and missionaries read them (de Nicolas 1986). Julien Green has pointed out that "if we edited all the dreams out of the history of the Middle Ages, the whole thing would grind to a halt" (1987, 119). I would include in that statement all the signs that people received in various forms. A language of dreams, visions, and revelations constituted a corpus of signs that scripted many a life change and the contours of sainthood (de Nicolas 1986; Frugoni 1996, 161–90).

Francis was not unique in his behavior or quest. There were others, such as Joachin of Fiori from Calabria or Robert d'Arbrissel, who chose to dispossess themselves of all worldly goods in order to live like Christ and preach the gospel. Some were viewed as mystics, others as revolutionaries; some died at the stake as heretics, while others were co-opted by the very principles and people they vowed to change. The end of the twelfth century was a time of great debate about the nature of good and evil and of intensely lived movements such as those of the Bogomils, the Cathars, and the Albigensis, whose members questioned the sanctioned path to salvation and rejected the structures and practices of the Catholic church as well as its teachings.

What we know of St. Francis's episodic process of conversion appears to reveal a series of attempts to discern a path almost by trial and error, each attempt followed by a revelatory event that redirected or confirmed the path he chose. These affective mystic moments, which were heuristic moments, occurred in specific places such as caves, continuing a medieval trope that was used in the New World until at least the eighteenth century and that harmonized well with several Native shamanic traditions. Francis's starts and stops and their affirmation by appropriate revelations created the basic tenets of what would become the Rule of the Franciscan Order. These tenets and the controversies that surrounded them during St. Francis's lifetime and long after created deep rifts within the Franciscan Order and among its practitioners. As we shall see, these conceptual and practical rifts were very much alive in the religious frontiers of New Spain.

From the beginning, Francis's stories highlighted certain themes that differentiated the order from a multitude of others that were created during the twelfth to the sixteenth centuries, the period of explosion of religious organizations. These themes marked the appeal of the order to those who joined it and eventually resulted in both internal divisions and a program of conversion (Roest 2000).

At the Church of the Lady of the Angels (La Porciúncula) in Assisi, Francis had a revelation that commanded that he and his followers "take no gold, silver or copper in your belts, no pack for the road, not two tunics, nor sandals, nor a staff . . . and Preach as you go, saying, 'The Kingdom of heaven is at hand'" (Le Goff 2000, 148). Discounting the millennial aspects of the commandment, the instructions were clear. First, Francis and his followers were to journey and teach the gospel; they were to be itinerant preachers. They would take to the road and have no permanent abode. They were to possess or carry nothing except one tunic: just enough to cover their nakedness. They were to have no shoes, no staff, no money. Theirs would be an order of absolutes with no compromise; that would remain the challenge and the danger of the order. Its members would rebuild churches. They would beg for food and lodging. They would have no books. All teachings would emanate from the Lord; no other teachings would be needed. They would owe complete obedience to their superiors, would strictly abstain from any sexual intercourse, and would perform harsh penance for their sins. Throughout his life St. Francis battled against the institutionalization of the brotherhood; he struggled to maintain its nomadic tradition and the absence of a place of abode to retain, as Michel de Certeau would say, a "proper" (1988, 36).[1]

The close association of the Franciscans with the dispossessed, the forsaken, and the diseased as well as the order's complete prohibition of possession of material goods created a close relationship and empathy with the native groups of the New World, particularly the hunting and gathering populations. Unlike other orders, the Franciscans sought an itinerant lifestyle that fitted well with the mode of living of nonsettled populations that moved frequently to obtain their sustenance. Francis's prescriptions to perform manual work for one's sustenance and never accept money for one's labor, to beg for food and the necessities of life, and to be joyful in poverty and austerity created a mindset and social framework that made the Franciscans (at least the early ones) perfect for working with hunter-gatherers all over the world.

Francis did not allow his followers to use or own books. He believed that knowledge nourished pride and "he regarded knowledge as a form of possession and property and the educated (*doutos*) as an especially formidable section of the powerful" (Le Goff 2004, 84). In his view, knowledge damned more souls than it saved. Throughout his life Francis sharpened the contrast between poverty, indigence, and ignorance and wealth, power, and knowledge (85). For him the greatest social evil was power based on birthright, wealth, and knowledge (91). It is no accident that the first order was called Friars Minor (where "minor" is synonymous with "subject" and "pauper" [*subditi et paupers*] [89–91, 94]) and that it recognized a hierarchical structure of masters and subjects. Francis felt, and intrinsically understood, the symbiosis of power/knowledge, and his actions and words indicated that he believed that books and philosophical debates distanced people from faith; he knew that questioning unravels faith. His gospel was one of orality positioned in the present that emphasized the role of memory and refused any ties to a textual religious past, with the exception of the gospels (152).

Rome and the papacy of the thirteenth century could not withstand the contrast between their wealth and Faustian behavior and the raw, minimalist approach of the Franciscans to Christianity. God's command to Francis, or Francis's interpretation of it, may not have questioned directly the behavior of the pope and the Curia, but the order's proscriptions and the practices of those who joined the brotherhood were an overt indictment of the church. Also, the questions raised by the tenets of Francis's rule bordered too closely on issues raised by other visionaries and by the cults Rome was intent on destroying, such as the Cathars and the Albigensis. Besieged by dissent, Rome called to arms its faithful to destroy the heretical cults in crusades and instituted inquisitory procedures to burn heretics in public demonstrations of purification and power. Tongues of fire swabbed ideas and burned dissent.

The affective charm and public appeal of Francis's work and rule (*Regula non bullata*) were not lost on the papacy. Sanitized of its nonorthodox elements, such as the refusal to obey immoral orders and the prohibition against using money or books, and provided with a permanent residence (convent), the brotherhood or fraternity of Francis's followers metamorphosed into a legitimate religious order by the official rule (*Regula bullata*) issued by Pope Honorius III on November 29, 1223.

The institutionalization of the Franciscan Order aggravated the growing rift among its members and marginalized those who had joined because of the ascetic and rigorous aspects of the rules, particularly the emphasis on poverty and lack of a domicile. Many of the Observants,[2] who advocated stricter adherence to the rule of poverty (Spirituals, *Zelanti*, or *Fraticelli*) did not abide by the *Regula bullata* and were excommunicated and persecuted by the church and by the Inquisition (Burr 2001, 312). The Conventuals, who wanted to amend the rule of poverty and allow members of the order a place of residence, saw their requests sanctioned by the official rule. Unhappy with a sanitized order, Francis, tired, sick, and disheartened, retired to his Golgotha to await stigmata and deliverance. St. Francis died in 1226. His order, which would envelop the world in rapture and rupture, reached "the people, tribes, languages, nations and all men, present and future, throughout the earth," as he had commanded (Le Goff 2000, 108).

For centuries after St. Francis's death, internal dissension among the Franciscans convulsed the order, leading to the disillusionment, banishment, and Inquisition trials of many of its members as well as to spin-offs of other religious orders, such as the Capuchins and the discalced Franciscans. The need for a string of papal bulls to bring about a consensus among the various factions while increasing papal control over the Franciscans is indicative of the extent and difficulty of the problem. The reform movement centered in Spain during the fourteenth and fifteenth centuries was essential to the final resolution. It was supported by such iconic Franciscan figures as Cardinal Cisneros and Fr. San Buenaventura (Saranyana 1991, 33–34).[3] By the sixteenth century a solution had been reached that gave the Observants the upper hand but also reflected an agreement to disagree. The point of disagreement was how rigorously the rule of poverty should be applied to the daily practices of Franciscans (Moorman 1988, 484, 487, 508–9). That debate, which cannot be divorced from the issue of power and how the missions were administered, resurfaced in the Americas (see chapter 6).

Across the Sea and over the Hill

Does this land belong to the kings of Spain or not? The second alternative no one dares to suggest, because it means being thrown out of the land and exiled from the kingdom.

Fr. Francisco Ribera (Chapa 1997, 78)

Three centuries after St. Francis's death, the first Franciscans arrived at Veracruz, followed by the Dominicans in 1526, the Augustinians in 1533, and the Jesuits in 1572. Fr. Martín de Valencia led the first twelve Franciscans, called the Twelve Apostles, whose mission was to create the kingdom of heaven on earth—a city of God and men. The New World and its Native populations would enable them to re-create the ultimate kingdom of God. The choice of twelve Franciscans was as clear a message of their messianic mission as it was possible to convey in a single act (Phelan 1956, 44). The Amerindians, as Gerónimo de Mendieta perceived them, were meek, gentle, simple of heart, humble, obedient, patient, and content with poverty (56). Mendieta saw them as tabulae rasae imbued with natural reason but lacking the emotions and desires conducive to sin. Native Americans were the perfect utopian vessels for grace. Primed for goodness, in reality like angels, they were closer to God presumably because they were still trapped in pre-limbo. Yet Mendieta was clear about how the Scriptures outlined the role of friars: "He meant that the Gentiles should be compelled in the sense of being guided by the power and authority of fathers who have the faculty to discipline their children for committing evil and harmful actions and to reward them for good and beneficial deeds, especially in all those matters relating to the obligations necessary for eternal salvation" (9). In order to accomplish the apocalyptic renewal of the church, it would be necessary to use force, although some, like Fr. Bartolomé de las Casas, a Dominican, vehemently disagreed with the procedure but not with the process. From 1524 to the 1600s, revolts, epidemics, conflicts, Inquisition trials, and the realization that Natives were neither meek nor obedient nor patient led to disenchantment. Angelic children had turned into rebellious adolescents.

In New Spain, the Franciscans operated mostly in California, central and northeastern Mexico, New Mexico, Texas, and the Southeast. The members of the Society of Jesus, the Jesuits, operated in California, northwestern and central Mexico, and in the Southeast. The two orders often missionized the same areas at different times, especially in Florida during the early period (from the 1500s through the mid–1700s) and in California after the expulsion of the Jesuits in 1767–1768.

In the early period, the Franciscans who came to New Spain adhered to the ideals of the Spirituals, who clung to St. Francis's vow and practice of poverty (Weber 1992, 93–94). The influence of Cardinal Ximénez de Cisneros with the crown, the Inquisition, and the wide distribution of Franciscan centers of religious and political power were all central to Franciscan theological supremacy (Ricard 1933/1982, 68). Amid empires of gold and human sacrifice, the encounter between the missionary, who was poor by choice, and the Native laborer, who was poor by condition, seemed to validate at last the long struggle of the Spirituals; they had found the appropriate place and folk for their mission of renewal. Later, on the inhospitable and untamed frontier, their encounter with hunters and gatherers reaffirmed this connection while it challenged the friars' capacity to imitate St. Francis and to re-create the city of God on earth.

In central Mexico, the honeymoon between Franciscans and civil authorities was short lived. The clashes between the Audiencia de Mexico and the Franciscans over civil and criminal jurisdiction culminated in 1530 with Bishop Juan de Zumárraga's excommunication issued for the people of Mexico City (Baudot 1990, 38–40). Regardless of the bitter arguments and subplots that marked these clashes, the core issues were control of the Natives and their labor. The movement northward of Franciscans from the Central

Basin of Mexico was erratic. Conversion accompanied military and commercial ventures, particularly mining and ranching, the two most prevalent industries of northeast New Spain. Hunting and gathering Native populations, who the colonizers feared and described as warlike, occupied this vast area. Most of the early campaigns of the northward conquest involved violent and protracted military actions that resulted in massive displacement of local Native populations, often after successive waves of Native revolts. From the settlers' point of view, these populations had nothing of value to contribute except their labor. For the Franciscans, a limitless horizon of possible converts kept alive a messianic dream. Ahead lay pristine fields of souls—a trope to behold.

Conclusion

About 300 years separated the founding of the Franciscan Order by a homeless and joyful Francis and the arrival of Franciscan missionaries in the New World. St. Francis envisioned that his brotherhood would convert all tribes and all nations, present and future. And they did, and they do. The tenets of the order as established by St. Francis were particularly suited for work among nomadic Native populations. The foundational debates between Spirituals and Conventuals brought to New Spain, particularly to the frontier, a controversy that became embedded in mission policy. Those debates, which were ontological in their essence but pragmatic in their effects, were translated into mission models and conversion practices.

4

The Jesuits

Diversity of Spirits

I shall not speak of the hundred other prophecies concerning the conversion of heathens. . . . But may I ask, what of the particular prophecy of Christ in Matthew xxiv that, before the end of the world arrives, the Gospel shall be preached everywhere and to all nations? (Baegert 1979, 159)

Just a few decades after the Society of Jesus was formed, it began its work in New Spain in the late 1500s. The establishment and development of the society were deeply enmeshed in the rough tide of momentous changes occurring in the world of ideas and in the very idea of what constituted the world. The life and experiences of St. Ignatius of Loyola shaped the concept and practices of Jesuit missionizing. In particular, Loyola's *Spiritual Exercises* provided a mechanism of religious renewal for the fathers and equipped them with ways to structure change in the habits of Native Americans.

A Society of Jesus

Iñigo López de Loyola was born about 1491 in Basque country. When he was born, Erasmus was twenty-five years old, Machiavelli twenty-two, Copernicus eighteen, Michelangelo sixteen, Thomas Moore eleven, and Martin Luther had just reached the age of reason. It would be one year before the kingdoms of Navarre and Castile were unified; Antonio de Nebrija published the *Arte de la lengua castellana*, the first Spanish grammar; and Christopher Columbus discovered the New World (Lacouture 1993, 1:13). By the time of Iñigo's conversion in 1521, Francis of Assisi had been dead for 300 years, waves of heretical movements and religious crusades had swept Europe, Luther had been excommunicated, Henry VIII was head of the Anglican church, the Catholic church was deeply engaged in organizing a comprehensive doctrinal corpus, and Cortés had just began the conquest of Mexico (Ganss 1991, 10). During Iñigo's lifetime, portentous events radically changed how people conceived of the world and their place in it: the Earth was no longer the center of the universe, Europe was not alone in the ocean blue, God had created beings who might be beyond eternal salvation, and seeing was believing as the printed word supplanted oral learning (de Nicolas 1986, 7–9). One might as well be living on Mars.

Like St. Francis, Iñigo was born into a well-to-do family and he also flirted with chivalry and moral laxity. Unlike Francis, Iñigo was brought up near the court, learned to read and write, and developed a taste for calligraphy, books, and learning. A brush with the military shattered one of his legs and injured the other. This event, which led to several makeshift operations and a long-term convalescence, had repercussions for his faith and conversion. To pass the time, Iñigo read the life of Christ and the lives of saints and methodically put down his thoughts in elaborate, colored calligraphy. This synthesizing process resulted in a 300-page folio of personal thoughts that became the basis for *Spiritual Exercises* (Ganss 1991, 72), the work matrix for the practices of the Society of Jesus. During this same period, Iñigo also read novels of chivalry and indulged in daydreaming, switching from damsels in distress to the knights of God who "performed resplendent deeds" in the service of the Lord (16). According to Iñigo's *Autobiography*, the fleeting quality of his delight with things mundane and the enduring feeling of happiness that resulted from his engagement with saintly thoughts led him to ponder the meaning of the difference between the two states (71). This introspective and mystical approach led to what he later called "discernment of the spirits." Like those of other mystics, Iñigo's quest for the appropriate spiritual path for serving God was guided by a hermeneutics of signs that directed his decision-making processes (de Nicolas 1986, 28, 48–49). Unlike some of the earlier mystics, Ignatius, as he become known, filtered those signs through meticulous study of how he felt and thought.

During the years that followed, Ignatius sensed visions that seemed always to be beyond his grasp and comprehension, like one who awakes from a dream and knows what the dream was about but cannot describe the images that invaded sleep. Ignatius "saw *clearly with his understanding*," and "*with interior eyes*" he comprehended the humanity of Christ (Leturia quoted in Ganss 1991, 29, italics in the original; Delumeau 1977, 52). Ignatius lived at a time when visions and signs could be misread, and he feared that he could not tell whether these insights were divine or the work of the devil. This dilemma, which confronted Christ with Satan, the supreme Good and the supreme Evil, mimicked Ignatius's self-reflective vacillations and the weeding of his doubts. These cleansing processes (*askesis*) were executed through the sequence of practices set in *Spiritual Exercises*, a pragmatic and performative text. This text "articulates a language of images, organizes memory and re-sensitizes the body of the exercitants to the will of God" (de Nicolas

1986, 28). In short, *Spiritual Exercises* remade, or attempted to remake, the habitus of the Jesuit novitiate, closely bonding spirit and body so the unity of mind-body would become the instrument of change for God's work (35–36, 39, 48).[1]

The cumulative result of Ignatius's "discernment"[2] episodes was a life path that included intense learning, the creation of *Spiritual Exercises* as a regime for maintaining the soul, and the formation of the Society of Jesus. During the ten years Ignatius studied in universities in Spain and Paris (1524–1535), his activities and proselytizing aroused the interest of the Inquisition and the censure of his teachers (Ganss 1991, 92–95). From 1526 to 1527, Ignatius was investigated and sentenced by the Spanish Inquisition. Despite scholastic and ideological frictions, Ignatius obtained his Licentiate in Arts in 1533. By then he had met several of the founding members of what would be the Society of Jesus, including Francisco Xavier. The members of the initial group were largely Mediterranean—French, Italian, Portuguese, and Spanish—and their goal was to dedicate their lives to the greater glory of God.

Three hundred years after St. Francis, the mystical lure of Jerusalem prevailed, but just as with St. Francis, Jerusalem did not produce the results Loyola desired because he was unable to remain in Jerusalem. Instead, Rome and the pope held the key to the future of the society. And unlike Francis, that key fit well with Ignatius's vision and plans. While awaiting the pope's decision to approve the formation of the Society of Jesus, Ignatius and his followers taught and guided people through *Spiritual Exercises* (Delumeau 1977, 55; Olin 1974, 98). Pope Paul III approved the constitution of the Society of Jesus on September 3, 1539 (de Nicolas 1986, xxv).[3] The first paragraphs of the constitution emphasized learning. They stated:

> Whoever desires to serve as a soldier of God beneath the banner of the cross in our society, which we desire to be designated by the name of Jesus, and in it to serve the Lord alone and his vicar on earth, should, after a solemn vow of chastity, keep what follows in mind.
>
> He is a member of a community founded chiefly to strive for the progress of souls in Christian life and doctrine and for the propagation of the faith by means of the ministry of the word, the Spiritual Exercises, and works of charity, and specifically by the instruction of children and unlettered persons in Christianity. (Ganss 1991, 45)

By the time Ignatius died in 1556, a scant fourteen years after official papal approval, the Society of Jesus had extended to Portugal, Spain, Italy, Sicily, France, Germany, India, Japan, and the Americas (Delumeau 1977, 34). The world of the Society of Jesus and Ignatius's vision were almost coterminous with the frontiers of the geographically known world. The Jesuits (as they became known) were deeply involved in the Counter-Reformation, the Council of Trent, and the establishment of numerous prestigious colleges and universities that became the premier places of learning (Ganss 1991, 48).

For the Jesuits of Loyola, religion, morality, discipline, and academic pursuits were a totality to be integrated into the process of conversion and education. This pedagogic program sought to synthesize theory and practice, thinking and doing, knowing and experiencing, reasoning and believing in order to couple learning with the practice of the knowledge acquired (Gil, Labrador, Escanciano, and de la Escalera 1992, 47).

Signs and Seers

Ignatius's practice of reading signs, ascertaining their godly origin and value, and foreseeing a future sanctioned by God's will may have differed from Native American shamanic practices in its procedures but not in its goals or results (see de Nicolas 1986, 10, 20, 49–50). In fact, Ignatius's readings were generally informed by his *sensed* technology, repeated experiences, and attribution of the correct meaning to the event. His interpretation of the meaning of signs resulted from agonizing introspection or from isolating a singular event from a multitude of similar but nondramatic occurrences. As an example, St. Ignatius often kept the other fathers in the refectory after dinner so he could read them his notes on obedience, despite the fathers' wish to retire to the garden. One day while St. Ignatius was reading his notes, the roof over the garden arbor where the fathers would have been sitting collapsed. St. Ignatius read this event as a signal of God's pleasure with the rule of obedience and the readings (de Nicolas 1986, 49–50). He plucked the unusual event out of a frequent practice and gave it singular and divine meaning. Every day, all over the world and in every culture, people interpret events as fateful occurrences often laden with spiritual meanings, yet few manage their lives and the lives of thousands of others by such signposts. Native American cultures (and others), however, did just that through a personal search for signs, like the vision quest,[4] or through the guidance of shamans who directed camp movements, procurement of resources, buffalo hunts, rites of passage, and group engagement in socialization or conflict.

To achieve proficiency and accuracy in the reading of signs and to acquire knowledge through the capabilities and exercise of the imagination, St. Ignatius developed the regimen of *Spiritual Exercises* whereby the retreatant vacated prior world experiences to make room for spiritual renewal under the guidance of a spiritual mentor (de Nicolas 1986, 22, 43). Both the mentor and the confessor helped the Jesuit initiate to navigate the psychological ebb and flow of *Spiritual Exercises* and to read and interpret the signs that shaped his path (de Nicolas 1986, 43–45, 58). Similarly, Native American shamans advised and guided the vision seeker, helped interpret the signs, and mediated between the world of the spirits and the person seeking their guardianship. When the Jesuits recognized these similarities, they reduced the labors of the shaman to the devil's bidding and work and could not, or would not, see the similarities in language, practices, and objectives. This was not always the case, however. For example, in the early years of missionary work in Brazil, the Jesuits used persuasion to co-opt local shamans and used Native children and women as catechists (Metcalf 2005, 97–98, 101). Although priests did not change their obdurate point of view, they did profit from Native knowledge and expertise. In the long term, the hybridism of good-evil practices in the New World produced a fabric of unique spiritual and cultural discourses woven out of practices milled through Native heuristic systems.

Men from the North

The Society of Jesus had a complex relationship with the Spanish crown from the onset of its work in the New World. But the Jesuits' work in Florida and in north central Mexico and Sonora taught them important lessons about running a mission, and by the time Father Juan María Salvatierra reached Baja California, the Jesuits had devised a plan to provide for the missions without much help from the crown. From 1697 to 1768, the Jesuits established eighteen missions in Baja California, but consolidations and closings had reduced that number to fifteen by 1768. Although for most of their time in the New World the Jesuits received some funds from the crown, wealthy donors provided the initial capital for the establishment of the missions. Gifts in land, mines, and other property allowed the Jesuits to amass a considerable trust fund. In reality, they established the model nonprofit organization. The income from these properties, proceeds from loans, shrewd investments, and wise financial management provided the Jesuits with income on which they drew to maintain the missions. The fathers supplemented this income with the sale of agricultural products and livestock (see Palou 1994, 117–20). Each mission and missionary had a yearly allowance, and every year in March the missionaries ordered the things required for each mission from an administrator who lived in Mexico City.

Jesuit missionary efforts in southern Florida were unsuccessful, but their work in Baja California was a very successful missionary program, particularly when the local environment and degree of isolation are taken into account. As Dunne noted, it is indeed ironic that the Jesuit mission to Alta California expanded while Charles III was planning the expulsion of the order from the New World in 1767–1768 (1968, 399). Indeed, Mission Santa María de los Ángeles, located in northern Baja California, was established during the period of the expulsion.

In the eighteenth century, Jesuit Jacob Baegert summed up the value of European ingress in the New World: "The only purpose of Divine Providence in the discovery of the route to the East Indies around the Cape of Good Hope and the finding of the fourth continent seems beyond a doubt to have been the expansion of the Christian Faith and the eternal salvation of the many heathen who live in the East and the West. Aside from this, as Saint Theresa has said, these discoveries have brought to Europe and Europeans more harm than good" (1979, 107). Such was indeed the case for the missionaries of the Society of Jesus.

Conclusion

The founding of the Society of Jesus soon after the conquest of Mexico and amid the tumult of the Protestant Reformation brought missionaries to New Spain with innovative ideas and different approaches to conversion. Loyola's indomitable personality and his insistence on practices that combined learning with applied knowledge shaped the Jesuit conversion paradigm. The phenomenal expansion of Jesuit missions in Asia, Africa, and the Americas testifies to the zeal of the fathers and the appeal of the order to those who joined it.

St. Ignatius and many of his followers decoded events to find God's guidance, a practice that paralleled the spiritual behavior of Native shamans. In spite of the Jesuits' antagonism toward the Native shamans, both groups of practitioners confirmed their mission by reading the natural and the unsolvable (Reff 1998, 27–28). But the most important aspect of the formation of the Jesuit fathers for their work with hunter-gatherer populations was the practice of *Spiritual Exercises*. The introspective deconstruction of even the most insignificant acts and thoughts trained the Jesuits to observe, record, and recognize the importance of changing a neophyte's habitus. The practice of *Spiritual Exercises* was meant to change behavior, and the Jesuits excelled at performing them.

Part 2

Southern Florida

Jesuits and Franciscans

Spanish contact with the Native people of Florida's coastlands preceded the conquest of Mexico by Hernán Cortes (1519–1521). Despite periodic attempts of missionaries to convert Native groups and the prolonged contact of shipwrecked Spanish survivors with Floridians, contact of Europeans with Florida's Native groups did not materialize into colonial settlements or missionary activities until the 1560s (Hann 2003, 12–13; Milanich 1998, 128, 136). The missionary efforts of Jesuit fathers Juan Rogel and Pedro Martínez and of Francisco Villarreal, a lay brother, began in 1567 with groups located on Florida's western coast. Father Pedro Martínez was killed before he could begin his work, but Brother Villarreal worked with the Tequesta and Father Rogel with the Calusa (Hann 1991, 220).

From 1697 to 1698 the Franciscans undertook a second period of missionary work among the Calusa, but the results were abysmal. The Jesuits returned in 1743 for a last attempt to convert the Calusa; that, too, was unsuccessful. Sequential efforts of Jesuits and Franciscans to convert the Calusa for short, well-defined periods of time provide useful contrasts to coeval missionary efforts and underline the variety of Native responses to the process of conversion. Although other missionary efforts with Florida's Native groups took place earlier (Bushnell 1994), this chapter focuses primarily on the well-documented dialogue between the Calusa and the first Jesuit missionary and spotlights the intellectual, theological, and pragmatic fencing strategies the Calusa used as they negotiated conversion.

The Jesuits: 1567–1568 and 1743

The Calusa were sedentary hunter-gatherers who developed a sophisticated socioeconomic system based on coastal fishing and tribute exacted from surrounding Native communities (Goggin and Sturtevant 1964, 183–85; 187–88; MacMahon and Marquardt 2004, 2–4; Widmer 1988, 224–76). The location of the Calusa settlements along major maritime routes and the

Calusas' knowledge of coastal waters and proximity to Cuba resulted in early contacts with French, Spanish, Dutch, and English colonizers and seafarers. These interactions primed the Calusa to have measured reactions toward the Europeans and sharpened their negotiating and cosmopolitan skills. Neither the army nor the Jesuits were matches for them; they exploited the relationships between both to their advantage. Even such a valiant fight was, in the long run, futile: disease, internal fighting, and colonial attrition eventually brought the Calusa to the brink of extinction.

The early period of conversion work the Jesuits undertook is atypical with regard to the type of interactions they had with Native groups and the setting. Father Rogel, who ministered to the Calusa, lived at the Spanish fort and so did the cacique (chief) of the Calusa. The Natives congregated daily with the permission of the Calusa cacique and, if they so wished, at a designated place marked by a cross. The missionary's activities were, however, largely dependent on the goodwill of the cacique and his vassals.

From the start, Father Rogel's contacts with the Calusa were based on a regime change. The Spanish murdered the principal Calusa chief, Carlos, in 1567, which eventually led to the chieftainship of Felipe, nephew of the slain Carlos. While Carlos had played a game of cat and mouse with the Spanish and the missionaries, Felipe masked his reluctance in philosophical arguments and postponements (Hann 1991, 266–67). Until Carlos was assassinated, Father Rogel lived at the Spanish fort and was greatly limited in his movements and ability to proselytize (Hann 1991, 248). Carlos, and later Felipe, treated apprenticeship in the Christian religion as an economic resource; the Calusa did not submit to doctrinal teachings unless they received adequate goods in exchange. The Calusas' attachment to the cosmological precepts and spiritual traditions of their forefathers notwithstanding, the price of political and religious allegiance to the Spanish had to be commensurate with their traditions: they would not sell themselves short.

The Spanish saw their enterprise as colonization: the Calusa were to accept, learn, and abide by Catholic teachings; labor for them; provide them with food; fight the French and other enemies of Spain; and be content with the gifts the Spanish thought appropriate to provide. The Calusa saw it differently; even though the alliance with the Spanish was unequal and difficult, it was still one to be negotiated. The Calusa insisted on their own sense of hegemony whereby their whole lived social process was articulated with "specific distributions of power and influence," which they experienced as traditions and practices (Williams 1977, 108–11). Several distinctive aspects of Calusa demands and expectations emerge from the historical record as

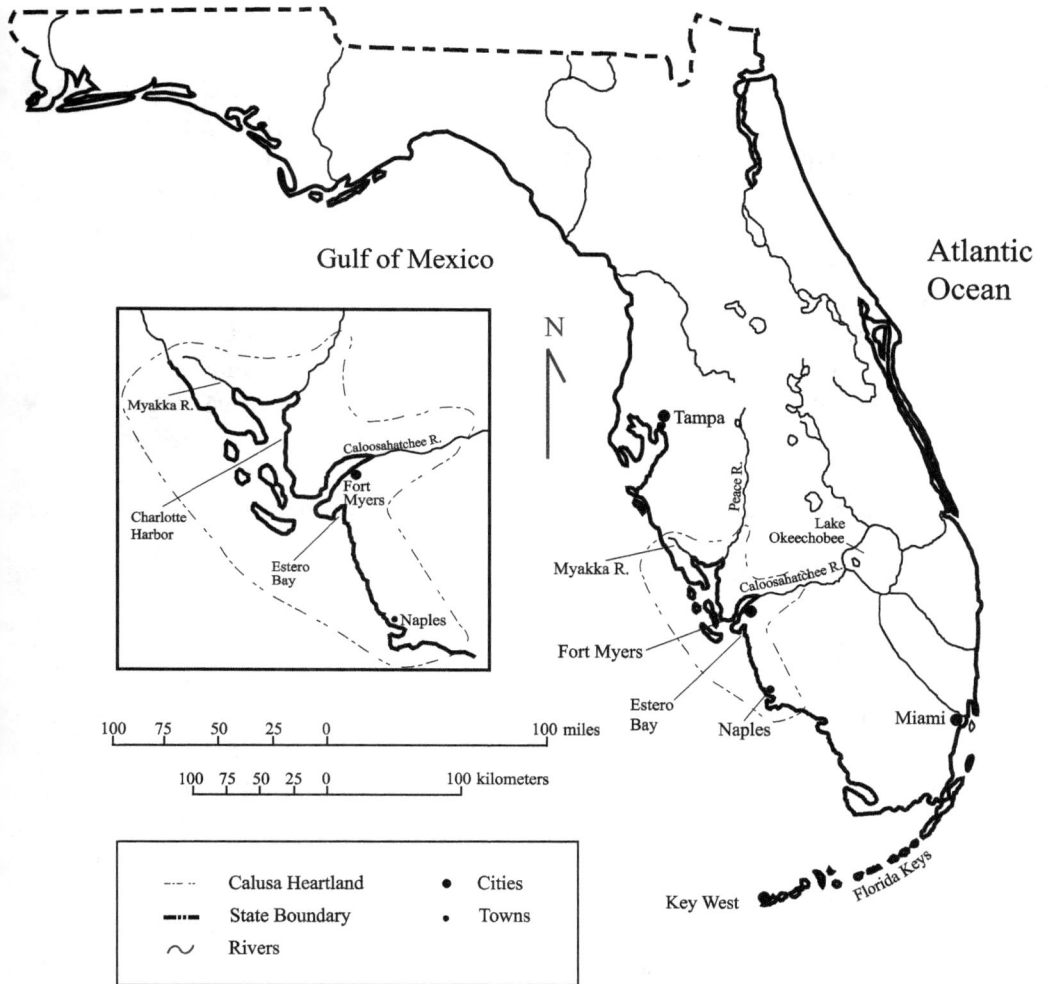

Map 5.1. The Calusa heartland of southern Florida. Map prepared by Claire Huie and Don Wade.

well as concerns and patterns of behavior that can be connected to other Native groups.

Firstly, the Calusa did not appear to mind other spiritual practices in addition to (but not to the exclusion of) their own (Hann 1991, 236). In fact, by the time Father Rogel began working with them in 1567, the Calusa children "knew the Christian doctrine in Spanish, that is to say, the four prayers" (235). The youngsters had learned the essential prayers through contact with Spanish soldiers. It also appears that the Calusa wisely appraised concepts and practices independently and debated the former while sometimes rejecting the latter. They pondered concepts such as the immortal nature of the soul, transubstantiation, the resurrection, and the Trinity and examined them in light of their own cosmological beliefs and the intrinsic logic of the Christian arguments, while they rejected outright the missionaries' bans on polygamy and incestuous marriages (237). Obviously, from the Catholic point of view, practices were the direct result of accepted concepts, but the Calusa took a "best-fit" approach to what could, or could not, be meshed with their beliefs. This means that the core of their cosmological and spiritual beliefs remained about the same; acceptance of Christian precepts was not based on a change of heart and faith but on reasoning and expediency.

Second, the contact generation[1] understood that changes in cosmological beliefs were bound to occur and might well be accepted by their children and grandchildren. But the contact generation was deeply invested in the accepted belief system that sanctioned and authorized a structure of responsibilities and duties with correspondent statuses and roles. The importance of this evidence is twofold. First, it indicates that the Calusa had encountered such situations before European contact, were prepared to deal with them, and could foresee the outcomes. Their cosmological beliefs were not static and may have undergone significant changes, albeit within commensurate spiritual and cosmological schemes. Second, they assessed, measured, and integrated some aspects of cultural change and retained some core beliefs. For instance, when the Spanish *adelantado*,[2] Menéndez de Avilés, arrived, cacique Carlos gave him his sister as a bride to establish a classic alliance between nations according to Calusa diplomatic rules (Goggin and Sturtevant 1964, 189). But when the Spanish demanded that Carlos and the Calusa make core changes in their spiritual and kinship structures by destroying their "idols" and changing marriage rules, Carlos was prepared to burn along with his "idols" (Hann 1991, 236). What seems to have been lost in translation was the type of alliance and settlement Carlos was bargaining for versus that which the Spanish wanted to impose. Faced with the external threat of the Spanish and with internal conflicts represented by his nephew's claims to the caciqueship, Carlos steered a neutral political course that banked on a conservative policy and minimized change while profiting from the elements of the Spanish-Calusa alliance that enhanced his prestige and reinforced his authority. Yet there was a blind spot in Carlos's political reasoning: Felipe, his nephew and the pretender to the Calusa caciqueship, was part of the younger generation. Because of Felipe's complicity with the Spanish, the Spanish assassinated Carlos and installed Felipe as cacique. Felipe's alliances and behind-the-scenes political moves with malice aforethought led to a change in leadership but not necessarily in governance. Machiavelli would have been proud.

Felipe's bargain with the Spanish military did not ease his cultural conscience, nor did it pave the way to a compromise with his ancestral beliefs: his role and acceptance as cacique was still predicated on custom. Felipe found himself debating his cultural hybridity and struggling with the differences between learned principles and novel ideas. Enamored of the clothing, the goods, the weapons, and the status that connections with the Europeans provided, the Calusa feared a loss of prestige if their Native competitors superseded them with the Spanish. The hegemony and trading advantages of the Calusa were intertwined with polygamy and incestuous coupling, and with practices the Calusa cosmology undoubtedly sanctioned. Sociocultural change is never compartmentalized and its repercussions are generally exponential. To accept Europeans without Christianity was logical and feasible; to accept both was cultural suicide. "A lived hegemony is always a process," and the poignancy of the Calusas' dilemma and its modernity and relevance to the subject of conversion bears discussing (Williams 1977, 112).

Conversations about Conversion

Father Rogel began teaching the basic tenets of the Catholic faith to cacique Felipe through an interpreter. They agreed on a space defined by the erection of a cross, and for a while, Felipe and his entourage came to the appointed place to hear Rogel. After teaching them the basic prayers in Castilian, Father Rogel explained that those prayers were a way to talk to God and request favors. The missionary explained the essence of God: creator and almighty. The Calusa had no problem with the concept of a creator God or with his overarching power. As for the Trinity, they conceived of it as three people who governed the world, each with specific jobs (Goggin and Sturtevant 1964, 197). The first and most important person controlled the heavens and the seasons, the second ruled kingdoms, and the third controlled the world of warfare. The Calusa solved the mystery of the Trinity by superimposing on it the grid of roles and statuses of their own officials: the numinous mediator, the secular ruler, and the war captain. Yet the Calusa appeared to place the king (cacique) above the head shaman (Goggin and Sturtevant 1964, 190, 192; Hann 1991, 246), and cacique Felipe stated that esoteric knowledge of God was unique to the caciques (Hann 1991, 241). Be that as it may, concepts of supreme power and assignment and division of ruling responsibilities were readily made commensurate with the Calusas' cosmology. The Calusa did not fail to challenge what they saw as the incongruity of the concept of one Creator God and a powerful Trinity (247). Rogel noted that they may not have believed in Christian ideas, but they were paying close attention to make sense of the teachings, to challenge them, and to determine whether to accept or reject them.

When Father Rogel explained the nature of the soul, Felipe discarded the notion of a single soul and explained that the Calusa believed that each person had three souls. The first was located in the pupil of the eye, the second was constituted by a person's shadow, and the third was the self-image in a reflective surface such as a mirror or a pool of water.[3] Upon a person's death the last two souls left the person; only the soul residing in the pupil remained forever. It is noteworthy that all the souls were connected with the sense of vision, but only the one that resided in the body remained with it. When a Calusa died, one of the two souls external to the person entered an animal or a fish. If and when that animal was killed, the soul re-entered another lesser animal and so on, until the soul was reduced to nothing. People who were sick had lost one of their souls, which could be retrieved by shamans and made to stay in the body by placing fires at all house openings to bar the soul from fleeing. It appears that in Calusa cosmology, the soul was vulnerable to disease and could be lost. This loss of soul magnified the importance of epidemics well beyond the possibility of death. The Calusa mocked the Jesuits' concepts of the uniqueness of the soul and its immortality, and despite Rogel's multiple attempts to explain the concept, the Calusa could not, and did not, find a place for the concept within their cosmological framework. Obviously, belief in only one soul would abridge the Calusas' chance of cosmological renewal.

Rogel did not relent: he rhetorically cornered Felipe by asking him if he believed that God was omnipotent and truthful, to which Felipe answered he did. The missionary continued that if Felipe believed this and if God had revealed these truths to the world, why would Felipe not accept them? In turn, Felipe asked how Rogel could know that those were the words of God. Rogel explained that the word of God had been written down long ago and preserved. For Felipe, evidence in writing superseded evidence obtained

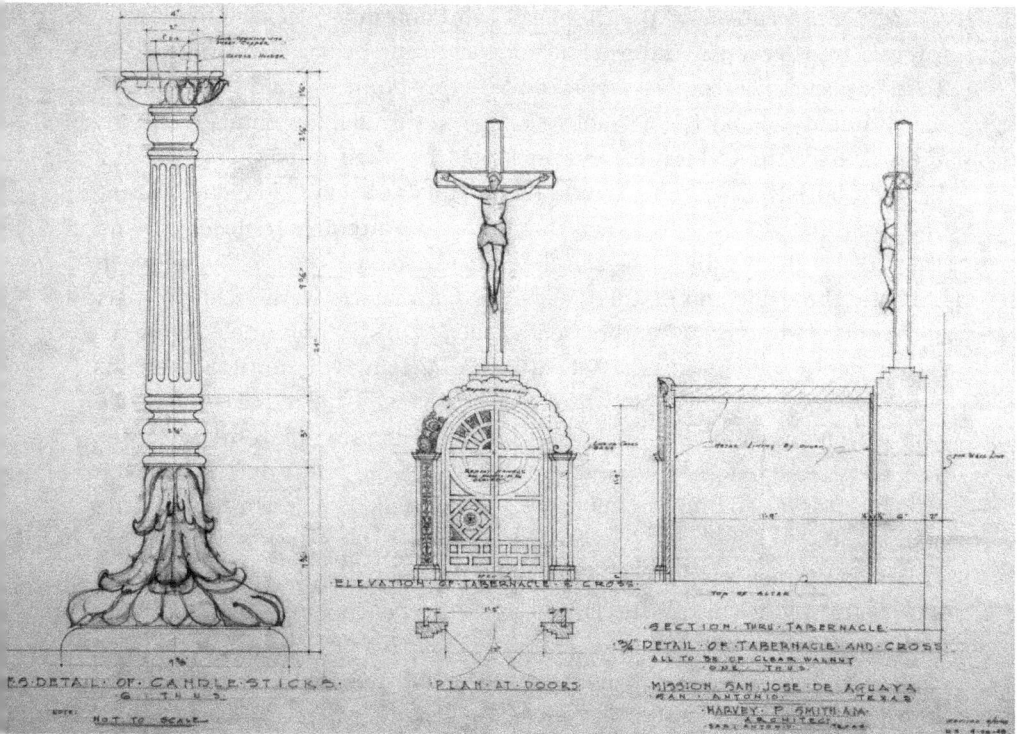

Figure 5.1. Detail of tabernacle and cross at Mission San José y San Miguel de Aguayo, San Antonio, Texas, 1948. Harvey P. Smith Drawings of San Antonio Missions. Courtesy of Alexander Architectural Archive, University of Texas Libraries, University of Texas at Austin.

by oral tradition, which, according to Rogel, Felipe considered to be liable to change as it was transmitted through generations (Hann 1991, 241). In an ironic modern twist, Felipe questioned the validity of tradition because he believed that unlike oral tradition, that which had been written was unchangeable.

Father Rogel chastised the Calusa for their adoration of wooden "idols" and was rebuked by them for his adoration of a wooden cross, whereupon the Jesuit explained the symbolic value of the cross as the symbol of Christ's death and the expiation of mankind's sins. To this the Calusa responded with the faith of tradition. As Father Rogel stated, "They said to me that their forebears had lived under this law from the beginning of time and that they also wanted to live under it, that I should let them be, that they did not want to listen to me" (Hann 1991, 239). The Calusas' continued refusal to believe denied Father Rogel a community of believers, and without that he had no mission.

The Calusa consulted the deceased, who continued to see after death, forecast future events, and provide counsel to the living (Hann 1991, 238). The deceased's privilege to see beyond earthly bounds could be related to the chthonic capabilities of shamans acquired through hereditary positions and practice. The Calusa told Father Rogel that their forefathers saw God "on their burials" (242), whereupon Rogel explained that God did not have a body and that what they saw was the devil in his attempts to deceive them. The Calusa rejected this understanding of the nature of the conflict between God and the devil, and neither Felipe nor his subjects were willing to part with their traditions. When pressed by the Jesuit's admonitions, Felipe retorted that he "had permission to live according to his rites until the Adelantado" returned (243). Felipe, who lived at the Spanish presidio, must have been struggling with changes because Rogel noted that he sometimes was found kneeling before the cross. Apparently Felipe told Rogel that in the evenings he offered the Christian God a sacrifice like the one he customarily offered his gods.

If Felipe maneuvered through turbulent waters, so did Rogel. While Felipe was trying to mesh his spiritual traditions with the teachings of the Catholic faith, the Jesuit was shaping the tenets of the faith to make them acceptable to the Calusa (245–46). In this struggle, neither remained untouched. Father Rogel admitted that Felipe "in his own fashion" offered himself to God, but the Jesuit was perturbed by Felipe's version of conversion (243). Rogel wanted visible proofs of conversion. He repeatedly asked Felipe to burn the idols, cut his hair, and dress like a Spaniard or, as Father Rogel saw it, to don "the clothing of a Christian" (261). To Rogel, practices were signs of belief, as if the former signified comprehension and acceptance. His presumption was that actions spoke louder than words, but the entire confrontation was based on words.

The stakes were even higher. According to custom and in order to fulfill the requirements of his caciqueship, Felipe married his blood sister and kept many wives given to him by allied nations. When confronted with the Catholic prohibition against such behaviors, Felipe reiterated that he had asked for permission to live according to his cultural customs until the return of the *adelantado*. More important, Felipe stated that his subjects demanded that he follow custom and in his position as cacique he was required to satisfy them (Hann 1991, 244–45). This was a delicate issue, as the Spaniards' position among the Calusa depended on Felipe's goodwill and protection as much as it did on the attitude of Felipe's vassals and neighbors. In turn, Felipe's subjects, when pressed to comply with the precepts of the Catholic faith, stated that they could not abide by them unless and until their cacique did so (246–47). While these statements reflect a structural social reality and a colonial conundrum, they nonetheless served to deflect decision making and bought precious time.

Felipe and his vassals frequently seemed eager to decry the falsity of their beliefs while contending that the legitimacy of the caciqueship depended on the performance of appropriate practices (Hann 1991, 247). In spite of Felipe's assurances that conversion would be forthcoming and that he and his subjects would give visible proofs of change, when Felipe's daughter became seriously ill, Felipe refused to have her baptized and instead cured her using traditional medicines and shamanic practices (246–47). This rejection of Christian solace at life's liminal moments, such as birth and death, appears sometimes in the historical record, raising doubts about the commitment of Native neophytes to their professed conversions.

On one occasion, unable to evade Father Rogel, Felipe discouraged the priest from trying to change the behaviors of the contact generation and encouraged him to concentrate on the young people, as they knew little of the customs of their elders and were likely to be more amenable to the new doctrine. As for the older adults, however, the missionary "could not strip them of everything" and leave them culture-bare (Hann 1991, 245). Felipe bluntly stated that Rogel should be satisfied that he was willing to forsake his "idols" and shamanic practices, remove sodomites, abolish the custom of sacrificing children at burials, stop decorating his body with black paint, cut his hair, and do other things Rogel had requested. However, he adamantly refused to have only one wife. The Jesuit capitulated: "And thus I see no impediment to the implantation of the faith of our Lord Jesus Christ in this entire heathendom" (246). A hegemonic face-off came to a draw.

The example of the Calusa is important for our understanding of the permutations and ambiguities of the process of conversion. This case demonstrates the effort of the Calusa to learn, evaluate, and carefully consider which Christian concepts could be grafted onto their beliefs without destroying fundamental spiritual-social structures. This process provides a window into the interweaving of Calusa cultural concepts and discourses with those of the colonizer, pinpoints some of the Calusas' essential tenets that did not allow compromise, and demonstrates just how far the Calusa were willing to go to appropriate and use the benefits provided by the colonizers.

The Calusa anticipated and outlined patterns of behavior that were later visible among other Native groups. The conflicts between Carlos and Felipe and the options each chose exemplify the gap between the contact generation and later generations and demonstrate how the different generations as well as the missionaries explored that cleavage. Generational power shifts such as the shift from Carlos's leadership to that of Felipe resulted in reversals and alterations of statuses and roles. In other words, cultural change occurred along generational lines and likely along gender lines. Add to that the incalculable effects of disease, and one can surmise that generations were skipped and that sociocultural patterns of organization and transmission of knowledge were greatly disrupted or became maladaptive.

By 1568, the tiny Jesuit contingent had realized the futility of its conversion efforts. The Franciscans had tried their conversion methods among the Calusa in 1697–1698, only to be forcefully expelled. Forgetful or undaunted, the Jesuits tried again in 1743, 175 years later. By then the Calusa had been whipped by waves of wars, epidemics, migrations to Cuba, social disruption, and an unhealthy appetite for rum. Two centuries after contact with the Europeans, the Calusa were still living by hunting, gathering, fishing, and trading. Despite the fact that the Calusa once more requested the presence of missionaries, Father Joseph de Alaña discovered that they continued to stipulate conditions for conversion. Calusa who agreed to be baptized were not to perform any work and the crown was to supply them with food, clothing, and rum. They were to continue their traditional spiritual practices, and the missionaries were not to punish their children (Hann 1991, 421). If the missionaries wished them to build a church, they were to pay them wages to do so, and if the Spanish decided to settle within Calusa territory they were to pay tribute to the cacique, as the lands belonged to him and not to the king of Spain. Indeed, as Father Alaña fully realized, the Calusa were convinced that "in admitting our religion in any manner, they are doing us a great favor" (421). When the priests refused to supply them with rum, the Calusa berated the missionaries about using wine for Mass, appropriated a Catholic status by calling their shaman bishop, and refused Catholic burial practices while maintaining their own (422–25). The Calusa neither mellowed nor melted.

The Franciscans: 1697–1698

> But did not you or your caciques ask the señor bishop to send ministers so that they might baptize them? They replied that the old chief had made this request, but that he was no longer in charge, and that just as the Christians could not cease to be Christians and live without the rosary, neither could they abandon their law and become Christians.
>
> Fray Miguel Carrillo, quoted in Hann 1991, 174–75

After the Jesuits departed in 1568, the Calusa had frequent contact with the Spanish through trade, shipwrecks, and voyages to Cuba. In 1688, the son of the Calusa cacique declared that they were ready to accept the Catholic faith, and in 1689 the cacique visited Cuba to ask that missions be established on his lands (Hann 1991, 36–38). The Calusa experience with the Jesuits in 1568 had taught them useful lessons about Spanish behavior and how far they could push the missionaries and the army, yet their desire for trade goods and favors from the Spanish was matched by the resiliency of their spiritual beliefs and traditions.

In September 1697, the Franciscans finally reached the Calusa. The friars were lodged in a section of the cacique's dwelling for thirteen days while the Calusa constructed a structure of palm thatch to house them (Hann 1991, 165). Eager to start missionizing, the six Franciscans erected a cross and some poles with bells to demarcate the sacred place for prayer. The Calusa were curious but noncommittal. In October the friars moved into their own dwelling, which they divided into a place for worship and living quarters (174). The friars set up an oratory but apparently minimized the display of sacra such as the baptismal font and the ciborium,[4] fearing depredations by the Calusa. The Calusa submitted some children for baptism, but when they did not receive what they deemed adequate gifts in exchange for those baptisms, they complained (166). In doing so, the Calusa inverted the terms of salvation; the price of admission was to be borne by the Christians.

Unlike Father Rogel, who attempted to explain the mysteries of the Catholic faith and engaged in vibrant discourse with the Calusa, the Franciscans adopted a policy of intervention and attempted to disrupt and destroy the Calusas' "idols." When the friars said that the "superstitious" practices of the Calusa offended the Christian God, the Calusa replied in kind: *su santo* (their saint) was offended by the presence of the friars and angry with the Calusa for allowing the friars' presence (Hann 1991, 167; for similar statements in Brazil see Metcalf 2005, 101, 203). The Calusa requested and accepted the missionaries while presumably inviting the wrath of their own gods, a dangerous spiritual game. It could be that their spiritual precepts permitted other spiritual mediators if they did not displace traditional spiritual entities or that bargaining with the spiritual realm was permissible. On the other hand, the Calusa might have been playing their customary game of tit for tat.

When the Franciscans led a procession to the Calusas' "synagogue" on the hill to disrupt their spiritual practices, the Calusa manhandled and insulted them and removed them forcefully from the area. These confrontations continued, and according to the testimony of the friars, the Calusa urinated on the friars and rubbed feces on their faces, either a demonstration of the Calusas' view of waste and humiliation or their perfect understanding of the western abhorrence of bodily excretions (Hann 1991, 166–68). By December 1697, the Franciscans had been evicted from Calusa lands and left naked and starving on the shore, presumably to perish. A Spanish ship passing by the Florida Keys rescued the desperate friars.

Throughout the short period of missionization, the Calusa displayed keen knowledge of Catholic concepts, specific language, and pointed argumentation. They demonstrated that it was not lack of knowledge or incomprehension that dissuaded them from becoming Christians but rather a clear and determined preference for the structure of their spiritual beliefs and traditions. The Calusa called their temple the "house of Mahoma"; they told Fr. Feliciano Lopéz, the Franciscan head of the missionary group, that the Calusa god was as powerful as the Christian God; and they addressed their god as *santo* (Hann 1991, 158–60). In doing so, they positioned themselves outside the Catholic faith, as de facto heretics, while at the same time equating the validity of their beliefs with those of the Christians. Likewise, it is significant that friars and civilians referred to the Calusa temple as a "synagogue" (170, 196). The Spanish use of such terms and particularly the adoption by the Calusa of the heretical terminology shows that the Calusa were aware of the links between and implications of the terms "synagogue," "Mohammed," and "heretics" and located themselves within that discourse. Indeed, their use of such terms underscores the extent to which stereotypes of the Inquisition had permeated colonial discourse. The Calusa mistreated and degraded the friars through physical and mental means but did not kill them, always refraining from the ultimate act of disrespect.

The Calusa coveted Spanish goods and clothing but did not change their hunting and gathering way of life. They never congregated around the mission church, few received baptism, and what prayers they learned appear to have been learned more out of curiosity than an intent to adopt Catholic practices. Nevertheless, they may have learned more about the tenets of the Christian faith than many other Native groups. The Calusa understood well the coupling of knowledge and power: to overpower the Christians, they had to know Christian culture.

Conclusion

During the early Jesuit conversion period, the Calusa, quite genuinely, I think, engaged in discussion, assessed the value of adopting Christianity, and chose to refuse the price to be paid for it. Once the Calusa realized the importance of the conversion program to the Spanish, they requested that the Spanish pay a price in exchange for the mere possibility that the

Calusa might consider accepting Christianity. The request for missionaries that resulted in the presence of the Franciscans was an overt attempt by the Calusa to obtain goods and food in exchange for flirting with Christianity. It is possible, however, that the Calusa had envisioned another period of debate about religious practices like the one they had enjoyed with the Jesuits and were not prepared for the interventionist proselytizing of the Franciscans. It is also possible that the Calusa were actually engaged in attempting to convert the friars to their spiritual beliefs. Father Rogel realized that the Calusa tried to convince the Jesuits of the validity and true nature of their gods (Hann 1991, 285, 287–88).

The Calusa provide a useful comparison to other hunter-gatherer populations made sedentary by entering a mission. Their behaviors also draw attention to the similarities and differences between them and settled horticulturists, such as the Hasinai. The processes and models of conversion used in northeastern Mexico and Texas and discussed in the next two chapters highlight how missionaries adapted to the local social and environmental circumstances and how their models of conversion work shaped the lives of Native Americans.

Northeastern Mexico

Franciscans and Jesuits

In northeastern Mexico, as in almost everywhere else in New Spain, attempts to convert local groups followed the discovery of regions previously unknown to Europeans. Missionaries accompanied the army and settlers as they pushed the frontier northward, and missionary activities often served as an incentive or pretext for new forays. During the early period, many minor players cemented the mosaic of colonization and a few major players, by simply pursuing their interests, sculpted the frontier.

In northeastern Mexico, contact between missionaries and Native populations was sporadic during the sixteenth and early seventeenth centuries. After the middle of the sixteenth century and partly as a result of the Royal Orders for New Discoveries of 1573 (Weber 1992, 95), the Spanish penetrated the territory that today encompasses the Mexican states of Coahuila, Nuevo León, and Tamaulipas. Most of the early conversion work in northeastern Mexico was undertaken by one or two missionaries, who, guided by Natives, searched out non-Christian groups or were contacted by groups that were said to wish conversion. Such is the case of a Franciscan who visited the Saltillo area in 1562 and was killed by the Guachichile (Arlégui as quoted in Alessio Robles 1978, 76). Although Saltillo was probably established around 1578 (Alessio Robles 1978, 77), prior to that date the area was inhabited by a small group of settlers attracted by the region's mining and agricultural potential (71). The same is true for the area that encompassed what would become known as the Mexican states of Nuevo León and Coahuila. Early settlement towns such as Saltillo, Monterrey, Monclova, and Parras concentrated economic and religious activities and served to seed other settlements on the frontier.

In northeastern Mexico, the work of conversion followed very specific pathways that reflected systemic problems present in many areas of the Spanish colonial world. In order to emphasize the multifaceted nature of these problems, this discussion is divided into two sections. The first section wades through the complex, and often obscure, process of early settlement

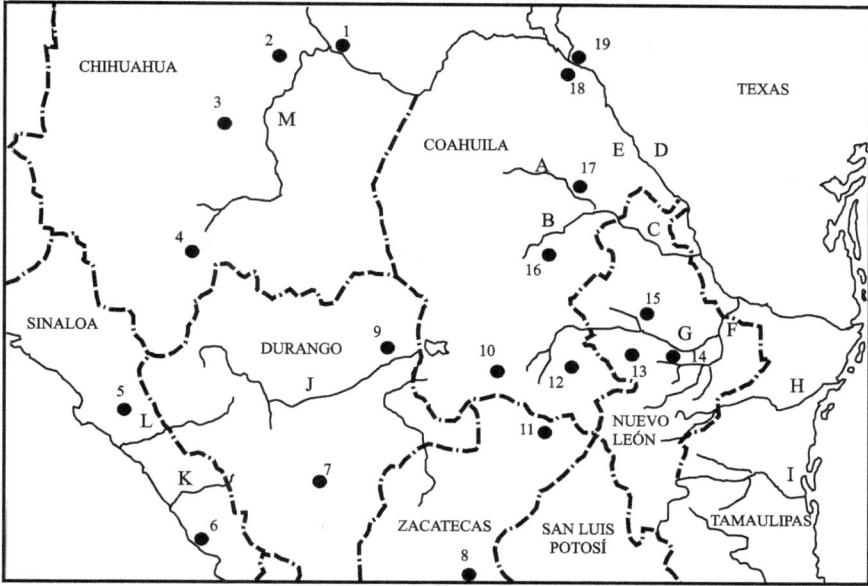

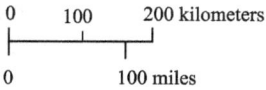

Map 6.1. Northern Mexico, showing states, selected cities, towns, and rivers. Map prepared by Claire Huie and Don Wade.

Cities and Towns

1 Presidio	11 Mazapil
2 La Junta de los Ríos	12 Saltillo
3 Chihuahua	13 Monterrey
4 Hidalgo del Parral	14 Cadereyta
5 Culiacán	15 Cerralvo
6 Mazatlán	16 Monclova
7 Durango	17 Sabinas
8 Zacatecas	18 Ciudad Acuña
9 Mapimi	19 Del Río
10 Parras	

Rivers

A Río Sabinas	G Río Pesqueira
B Río Nadadores	H Río Conchos
C Río Salado	I Río Purificación
D Río Grande	J Río Ramos
E Río Bravo	K Río Piaxta
F Río San Juan	L Río San Lorenzo
	M Río Conchos

in northeastern Mexico as it outlines two models of conversion. These were based on where Native populations were located and how they were going to be used as a labor force. The first model, the urban-rural model, is broadly defined by two practices: the friars missionized Natives working in urban households and businesses or in rural haciendas, and these Natives constituted an unfree labor force. This model fit well in regions like northeastern Mexico where the *encomienda*[1] and *repartimiento* systems existed. In the second model, the wilderness model, missionaries worked to convert Native groups by following along as the Natives pursued their social and subsistence schedules. In this model the Natives were free to move about and did not constitute a kept labor force.

While these two basic models characterized the early work of conversion, the urban-rural model was a poor fit for some regions and the wilderness model proved unsustainable because it could not result in settlement. The middle ground was the mission-pueblo model, which emerged partly as a compromise between the other two models and was often coeval with them. The evidence in this chapter concerns mostly the work of Franciscans in northeastern Mexico. The Jesuits experimented briefly with the wilderness model in Coahuila, but soon reverted to a mission model, though with slightly different parameters than the models the Franciscans used.

The second section of the chapter uses a royal edict from 1715 to demonstrate how accurate the crown's knowledge was of the problems in the frontier and what measures it proposed to protect the living conditions of the Native populations. This document enables us to contextualize and provide legal background for the multiplicity of interests and complex nature of the interactions among the different players in the frontier.

Early Settlement: Major Players, Minor Players

In 1579, Luis de Carvajal y de la Cueva from the villa of Mougadouro in the northeast mountains of Portugal obtained a large land grant that encompassed most of Coahuila and modern Texas west of San Antonio (Alessio Robles 1978, 90). Carvajal had lived in the northeast of New Spain since 1567 and knew the area well. After obtaining his land grant, he established Villa de Cerralvo (Ciudad de Nuevo León), Villa de San Luís (Monterrey), and Villa de Almadén (Monclova). But by 1590, Carvajal, a Portuguese Jewish converso, had been arrested by the Inquisition, most likely on trumped-up charges. He died in prison without ever being formally charged by the inquisitors (Rodríguez-Sala, Cué, and Ignacio Gómezgil 1995, 110–14).

Francisco de Urdiñola, a Basque from near Guipúzcoa, started his career in New Spain in association with the Ibarra[2] family and with mining and agriculture. He sharpened his skills as an Indian fighter early in his life (Alessio Robles 1978, 110). Sometime at the end of the 1570s he moved to Mazapil, where he became known as an expert military commander. His arrival in the area just about coincided with the heyday of Carvajal in Nuevo León. In the 1580s, Urdiñola was engaged in a series of campaigns around Saltillo against various Native groups, including the Guachichile and the Pacho, groups that lived in the Saltillo area before the arrival of the Europeans (Rodríguez-Sala, Cué, and Ignacio Gómezgil 1995, 116). In spite of a discourse of bloodless victories or slave raids, it is quite clear that relentless pressure by frontiersmen was applied on both sides of the contested frontier and that the former hunter-gatherer Native residents were losing the battle. As Europeans tried to move the frontier northward, Native Americans reacted to push it back. This resulted in a situation that, from the perspective of the Spaniards, meant continuous attacks by Natives. The correct way to describe the series of events is that the Native groups were being attacked by Spaniards who were trying to move into Native lands. That is how history would be written had Native populations recorded it.

The Urban-Rural Model

In 1582, Fr. Lorenzo de Gavira established a Franciscan convent in Saltillo, but the site was soon abandoned because of Native attacks (Alessio Robles 1978, 114). The Native Americans' refusal to let the convent stand was as much about their displeasure with Christian religion as it was an indictment of the settlers' invasion of their territory. By the 1590s, after Viceroy Álvaro Manrique de Zúñiga was replaced with Viceroy Luís de Velasco, the Spanish strategy of armed conquest had shifted to a strategy of armed "encouragement." The change in leadership and tactics brought about negotiations with Gregorio Nanciaceno, head of the republic of Tlaxcala, who, in 1591, selected 400 Tlaxcalan couples to colonize the north and establish pueblos where local Native American nations would congregate. This program of colonization by "insiders" granted the Tlaxcalan families the status of *hijos de algo* (gentlemen), which allowed them to ride horses, possess weapons, and have separate pueblos from those of the other Native groups (Butzer 2001, 11–14). They were to be given water rights and title to lands and were to be exempt from taxes for specific periods. Several mission pueblos in northern Mexico were settled and established by these Tlaxcalans and their descendants. One of these, San Esteban de Nueva Tlaxcala, was established in Saltillo in 1591 for the Tlaxcalans and the Guachichile under the guidance of Urdiñola (Butzer 2001, 14–18). By then, the Guachichile and other groups that occupied the area where the town of Saltillo was established had been subdued and their populations had been diminished.

Viceroy Velasco's policy really aimed at *reducción*[3] by proxy, whereby the Tlaxcalans were the mediators between the "barbaric tribes" and the Spanish and provided the settlement environment for nomadic groups. This was a clever idea that placed the success of a settlement on the Tlaxcalans rather than the Spanish. On the other hand, the Spanish campaigns against the Natives and the establishment of San Esteban gave Urdiñola prestige and provided him with extensive properties, particularly La Hacienda de Parras, Las Palomas, La Hacienda de los Patos, and a host of other properties, in addition to several mines (Rodríguez-Sala, Cué, and Ignacio Gómezgil 1995, 185–86). The labor force for these agricultural haciendas and mines came from the Native people Urdiñola fought and *reduced*. Despite the good works of the friars, their connection with the church and with the Spanish conquest of lands and displacement of Native populations was not lost on the Natives. As an aside but also as a clue to his continued success, Francisco de Urdiñola was a familiar (informant) for the Inquisition (Alessio Robles 1978, 143).

The Jesuits: Sixteenth–Seventeenth Centuries

Despite the establishment of a mission in the Valley of Parras in 1578, the conversion work of the Society of Jesus did not begin in earnest in the Parras-Laguna area until the period 1591 to 1594. The Jesuits maintained their missions there until the middle of the seventeenth century (Peláez, Barraza, Serrato, and Sakanassi 1991, 15, 21, 200; Pérez de Ribas 1645/1999, 659n7). Six Jesuits worked in this vast area, serving mainly two kinds of groups: medium-sized populations of settled horticulturists and nomadic hunter-gatherers dispersed throughout the Laguna Grande and in the hills and mountains around Parras (Alegre 1956, 420–22; 1958, 106–9; Pérez de Ribas 1645/1999, 690). In August 1594, Father Gerónimo Ramírez stated that he took the Natives "holy water and whatever food he could provide" and that he went "from bed to bed preaching the gospels" (Alegre 1956, 422–23) during an epidemic of smallpox, a scourge that would recur often. The Jesuit priests tried to convince some Natives to resettle closer together and in some cases were successful. Bishop Mota Escobar is explicit about the problems and some of the strategies the Jesuits adopted. He states:

The distance between the first pueblo and the last is over 30 leagues [78 miles] and although we have tried to congregate them we had limited success and they are still far apart. [This is] because we have always tried to shape our resource needs to those of the Indians which consist mainly in fishing and exploiting the maguey fields. Nowhere are these resources concentrated in abundance to feed them . . . and [if we were to congregate them] we would remove them from their natural and social environment. To press them to move and congregate in one place would be to agitate them. Besides, there is no location around with enough resources to sustain them all. (Alessio Robles 1978, 160)

Thus, even though the Jesuits began by using a wilderness-centered model, they soon discarded it. The Jesuits' recognition of their inability to provide for the Native populations together with their understanding of the importance of Native resource needs were recurring characteristics of Jesuit conversion strategies. Fathers Juan Agustín de Espinoza, Gerónimo Ramírez, Martín Peláez, and Francisco Arista were some of the first Jesuits to work in the area during the last decades of the sixteenth century. From Durango, the fathers traveled eastward and established missions and pueblos in the Nazas River and Laguna areas among nomadic groups that subsisted by fishing, hunting, and gathering plant foods, particularly maguey, lechuguilla, mesquite, and the tuna of the prickly pear (Peláez, Barraza, Serrato, and Sakanassi 1991, 22, 28, 41). As the fathers began their work of conversion, children attended teachings of Christian doctrine every day, but the adults came only on Sundays or feast days. For a while, the Jesuits conducted Mass and other religious ceremonies in a borrowed chapel (*capilla de prestado*), possibly belonging to one of the local haciendas (58). By 1599, however, the fathers had set up their missions with houses, churches, and gardens (59).

During the early phase of their work, the Jesuits used some interesting strategies to convert local populations. Sometimes they invited caciques to dine and even to hold dances and festivities at the Jesuit house. They held processions and targeted the usual reticent old men (Pérez de Ribas 1645/1999, 662–64). As they succeeded in congregating the children in the school, they appointed a bright male child, who they called "the little fiscal," to monitor the activities of others and to round everyone up for Christian doctrine and religious ceremonies. These strategies might have been successful had it not been for the severe distress brought about by epidemics, which prompted people to revolt and abandon the area (Pérez de Ribas

1645/1999, 666, 690). Using children to teach and monitor the elders constituted a complete reversal of traditional roles and was likely perceived by the elders as a social infraction.

Even so, before the tide turned against the Jesuits, there were positive interactions. The first Christmas in Parras was celebrated with the presence of several Native groups, a great bonfire, and the adoration of baby Jesus. The Natives sang and danced adorned with feathers and arrows, and cattle were butchered for the festivities. Apparently wealthy folk from the haciendas of Isabel de Urdiñola and Lorenzo García attended the celebrations (Peláez, Barraza, Serrato, and Sakanassi 1991, 49–50). On January 1, as commanded by law, the Natives elected pueblo officials, and on January 6, a day of celebration of the Epiphany and Three Kings Day, baptisms and marriages took place and the priests heard the confessions of some Natives (50). According to Father Nicolás de Arnaya, who visited the area in 1599, there soon would be about 5,000 people congregated in the area and the Jesuits were planning to establish four or five new pueblos (55–56). Once the town of Parras and the mission of Santa María de Parras were organized, the adults came to the Christian doctrine twice a day. The catechism was taught in two languages at the Jesuit house, and neophytes learned songs in Nahuatl. Curiously, the neophytes attended Mass until the reading of the Gospels and then left the church to join the gentiles, who remained in the atrium outside the church.[4] Those who had been baptized remained in church till the end of Mass. The Jesuits established a school for children, later called Colegio de San Ignacio de Loyola, and all Natives received instruction before being baptized (115).

Those who came to settle in Parras received land for a house and garden, seed for planting, and the so-called king's ration: corn, salt, chiles, and some clothing (Pérez de Ribas 1645/1999, 665). Sometimes they were provided with meat, possibly from local wealthy *hacendados* (Peláez, Barraza, Serrato, and Sakanassi 1991, 48, 58). Once several groups congregated in the area, the Jesuits noted that they had different dancing traditions and that during these celebrations men were segregated from women. The fathers commented that the Natives no longer sang their pagan songs or practiced "idolatrous" acts and that they had abandoned polygamy, yet they noted that the elders continued those practices in secret (Alegre 1956, 423; Peláez, Barraza, Serrato, and Sakanassi 1991, 58). The behavioral differences between the contact generation and those raised or born within mission life would continue to affect Jesuit conversion strategies.

From 1594 to 1645, a series of epidemics devastated the region, resulting in great loss of life. The epidemics killed old and young alike, and most people were baptized in *artículo mortis* (Pérez de Ribas 1645/1999, 680,

COAHUILA   • Del Río   TEXAS

† 1

San Rodrigo
† 2

• Eagle Pass

† 3

Río Sabinas

Sabinas

Río Salado

Río Grande

† 5   † 4

Cuatro Ciénegas •

† 7

† 6   Monclova

8
†

Los Cabazos

TAMAULIPAS

N

Mapimi
•

Nazas

Parras
•
† 10

Saltillo

† 9

• Monterrey

Conchos

DURANGO

NUEVO LEÓN

| 0 | 100 | 200 kilometers |
| 0 | | 100 miles |

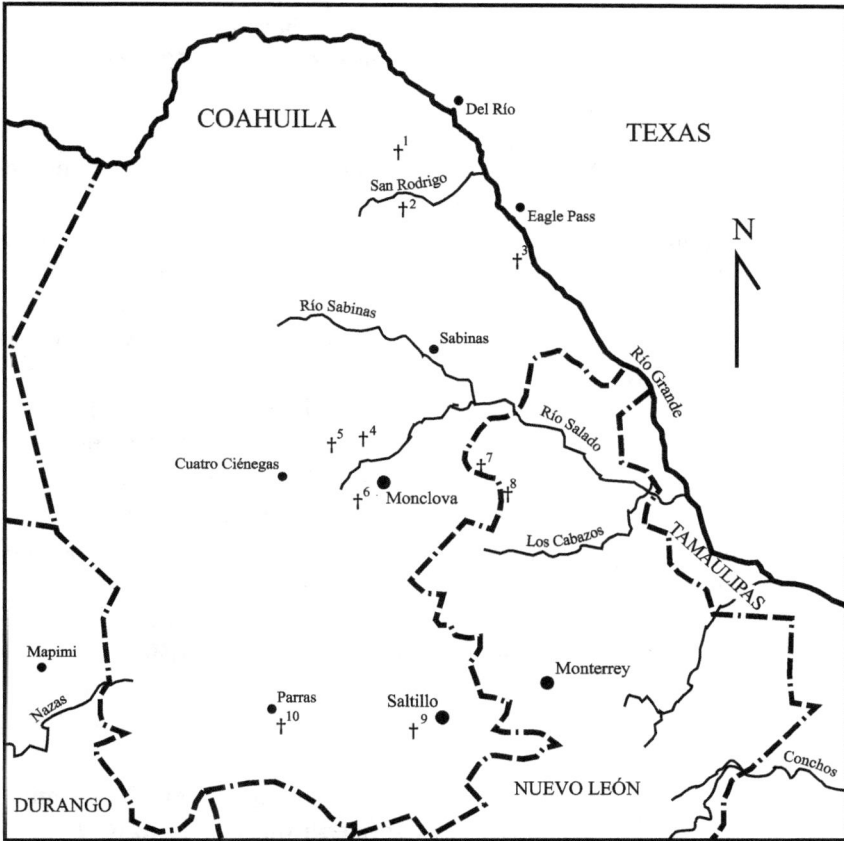

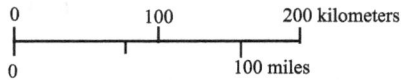

† 1	San Ildefonso	† 7	San Phelipe de Santiago	Cities	•
† 2	SSMO Nombre de Jesus		de Valladares	Towns	•
† 3	San Juan Bautista	† 8	San Bernardino de la		
† 4	Santa Rosa		Candela	Rivers	∼
† 5	Cuatro Ciénegas	† 9	San Esteban (Saltillo)	State Lines	▬·▬
† 6	San Francisco de Coahuila	† 10	S. María de Parras	Missions	†

Map 6.2. Selected Coahuila Spanish missions of northern Mexico. Map prepared by Claire Huie and Don Wade.

682). The Jesuits saw some of those epidemics as a battle between God and the devil over the souls of the sick. The fathers believed that "God was seeking the fruits that He harvests through these illnesses" (673) and that the devil fought God through the local shamans and used them to stir up trouble by attributing the pestilence to the administration of baptism (673). The devil appeared to the Natives as fire, serpents, and deer and sometimes as a woman, once all dressed in white and another time robed as a Jesuit. In these apparitions the devil admonished against baptism and threatened to kill everyone if they became Christians (668, 673–74, 685). In the fierce battle against evil, the Jesuits burned Native sacra and interpreted the surge in disease as God's way of snatching souls from the devil through baptism at the hour of death (668).

Notwithstanding the promising reports of the Jesuits, and without respite from the epidemics the Native populations revolted in 1599, the same year the mission was established. Headed by older men, the revolt involved over 1,000 people; only five or six Natives remained at the mission. The rebellious Natives attacked and sacked the haciendas, killed several people, and took refuge in the mountains. One week later they were suffering with measles and smallpox; many died. Accompanied by soldiers and other Natives, Father Agustín contacted the rebels, only to find a scene of desolation. Many returned with the father; others came back later. The army punished the leaders of the revolt and hanged at least one (Peláez et al. 1991, 67, 71–72).

This was not the only upheaval. One shaman from Nuevo León sent a "preacher" to Parras. This "preacher" traveled from pueblo to pueblo admonishing the Natives that high winds would cause never-before-seen chaos; men would turn into women and women into men.[5] Another shaman, described as being over 100 years old with long hair, long nails, and extraordinary agility and strength, threatened to kill a priest when he refused to permit a ceremonial dance (Peláez et al. 1991, 73). These prophecies and events are indicative of the stress felt by the communities. They terrified the people and placed them between the shamans and the friars, desperately appealing to both for deliverance from the pestilence. As smallpox raged, the shaman lost face and may have been killed; the Jesuits considered the epidemics a mercy of God.

The Jesuits found the Natives in Parras to be smart, hard working, neat, well-dressed folks who got along very well with the Spaniards. Commenting on the enormous population loss due to epidemics, Father Pérez de Ribas said that those who survived had these desirable qualities and were concerned with their salvation. He stated, "And this is worth much more than the great number of gentiles who once existed" (Pérez de Ribas 1645/1999, 691). For the Jesuit, as for most missionaries, population loss had its rewards. In 1645, there was a widespread revolt followed by famine and epidemics, and despite some missionary success, in 1652 the missions were turned over to parish priests (secularized), except for the Jesuit residence in Parras (Alegre 1956, 3:38–39, 266, 278).

The Franciscans: Sixteenth and Seventeenth Centuries

Information about conversion practices during this early period is scant and controversial (Alessio Robles 1978, 63; Hoyo 1985, 14–17) and comes primarily from Juan Bautista Chapa's *Historia del Nuevo Reino de León* (1997), a chronicle that recounts the accomplishments and trials of the Spanish settlers, who were mostly engaged in military campaigns or *encomiendas*.

The last two decades of the sixteenth century were marked by four major Native revolts in the northeastern frontier as the local native population fought displacement and the *encomenderos* (Rodríguez-Sala, Cué, and Ignacio Gómezgil 1995, 179). The most reliable historical information indicates that the first missionary in the area was Fr. Lorenzo de Gavira, who established the Convent of San Esteban in Saltillo in 1582 and that the friar came in with Luís de Carvajal (Cavazos Garza 1994, 31; Hoyo 1990, 105). There were a few secular priests in the area, some of whom were also miners and *encomenderos* and had very unsavory reputations (Hoyo 1990, 106). After the pueblo of San Esteban de la Nueva Tlaxcala was established in 1591, two friars worked in the area: Fr. Cristóbal de Espinosa and Fr. Antonio Zalduendo. Eugenio Hoyo points out that there is no evidence that these friars missionized the Natives (107). In 1596, several settlers from Saltillo established what later became known as the town of Monterrey, and by 1603 Fr. Lorenzo Gonzáles and Fr. Martín de Altamira had begun working to convert the local residents (109). Fr. Altamira was killed in 1607 while proselytizing among the Quamoquane in eastern Coahuila, apparently inside a small chapel (11). This event brought Francisco de Urdiñola to the area of the Rio Grande to avenge the death of the friar.

In 1622, Fr. Damián de Acevedo, the Franciscan *guardián* of the Convent of San Andrés in Monterrey, made a request for information about the Native groups that inhabited the area, an indication that the friars had little information about the Native population (Hoyo 1985, 55–56). Two years later there was a general Native uprising in the Monterrey area headed by a Guachichile captain named Cuaujuco and another Native named Colmillo who rode horses. Cuaujuco, a ladino, commanded a great deal of respect and supplied the Spaniards with Native laborers from other areas (de León, Chapa, and de Zamora 1961, 65–67, 73).[6] The revolts continued despite the punishments the Spanish inflicted on Native groups, partly because, as Alonso de León stated, no Spanish male would consider himself a man unless he took Native children from their mothers whether the group was friendly or not (63). These *piezas*, as Natives who were apprehended in war and were considered slaves were called, were promptly sold for labor.

As governor of Nuevo León, Martín de Zavala reestablished the towns of Cerralvo in 1626 and Cadeyreta in 1637 and attempted to reestablish Nuevo Almadén (Monclova) in 1643. In 1626, Fr. Lorenzo Cantú worked with Natives and local African populations near the modern town of General Zaragoza, but it was another twenty years (1648) before the Río Blanco missions were established near modern Aramberri, Nuevo León (Cavazos Garza 1994, 32).

By 1632, the settlers were complaining about repeated attacks by many groups of Natives. The targets of these attacks, as reported by the settlers, were the Spanish, other Native Americans, haciendas, mines, crops, merchandise convoys, and horses and cattle. The Spanish declared a "war of fire and blood" on the Native populations and stipulated a series of harsh punishments to curb the hostilities. Faced with the problem of whether or not to sanction the activities and punishments the settlers proposed, Governor Zavala sent the settlers' petition to Fr. Francisco de Ribera for his opinion. The friar approved it.

Fr. Ribera's document includes interesting comments that indicate specific attitudes of Natives and friars at this early period. According to Ribera, Guapale, a baptized ladino, led the Natives in rebellion. The friar stated that "[the Natives] tell each other, that there is no reason to fear the Spanish; that if they kill us we will also kill them and eat [consume the products of] their haciendas, [and that] no one should falter because, at most they will place us in Zacatecas for a few years" (Hoyo 1985, 69). Ribera justified his agreement with the punishments with the following reasons: "First, if anyone has a different opinion from mine . . . he should come and live here for a while; he will see that he changes his opinion, as I changed mine after I experienced these matters. Second, if we do not change things, we will give the natives all authority over the lives and possessions of the Spanish, tie the hands of the Spanish and impede their defense" (71, 77, 79). Fr. Ribera declared that a legitimate and just war pursued with a clear conscience required four conditions: "legitimate authority, sufficient cause, good intentions and convenient means" (Chapa 1997, 81). Ribera found that all the conditions were present for a legitimate war to be waged without scruples.

Fr. Ribera had a disparaging but pragmatic view of the Natives. In his view, "all of them follow no law, because once baptized they discard the evangelical teachings they received as can be seen by the way they despised the cross . . . and they do not have any rites or ceremonies with idols or false gods; they live like animals or deer without civility, permanent abode or possessions, and they go about outfitted only with bows and arrows" (Hoyo 1985, 75). As the missionaries repeated frequently, if the Natives had idols they were heretics; if not, they were animals. Ribera's unusual document is particularly important because it was signed by eleven friars and reflects the feelings of a significant group of the local Franciscan community.

The events connected with Fr. Rivera's report emphasize several recurrent themes in the relationships among Natives, friars, soldiers, and settlers. First, Native revolts were often led by Christianized and ladino Natives, a pattern that underlines the complex and problematic nature of sustained colonial contact. As Natives learned the language and became socialized to Spanish customs, they also became proficient in detecting and exploiting the colonizers' weaknesses. In colonial contexts, acculturation means to become accustomed to the culture of the colonizer, and it provided, as it still does, the means to subvert that same culture. The symbiotic relationship between the processes of conversion and socialization made it impossible for the Natives or the friars to dissociate the two; they were part of the same civilizing project and acts of revolt targeted both. This is not to say that Native peoples confused the work of the missionaries with the actions of the *encomenderos*. It is well demonstrated that missions and missionaries were often the only refuge available to Native populations, but the missionaries' dependence on the settlers and the military and their complicity in the violence against Native groups implicated the church in a program of control that cannot be described as benevolent (compare Bolton 1917, 44; and see Sweet 1995, 1–48 for a pertinent discussion).

In 1640, Fr. Andrés Ocampo of Zacatecas proposed Fr. Francisco Lavado as minister to the citizens of the Villa de Cadereyta and to "the Indians who might be there" (Hoyo 1985, 87–90). Fr. Lavado asked to be given land for a church, garden, and convent. Nine years later, Alonso de León the elder commented that since the friars had begun the work of conversion in the area, "there was not a [single] Indian who could be reduced, or was Christian in name and deeds" (94). Like Fr. Ribera, Alonso de León, an *encomendero*, advocated the use of force to convert the Native groups, but Alonso de León did so with less vehemence and with considerably more empathy toward the Natives.

By 1657, Fr. Juan Salas was the *guardián* of the Convent of San Francisco in Monterrey; his ecclesiastic jurisdiction included Cadereyta and Valle de las Salinas (Monterrey). Fr. Salas visited the haciendas of the *encomenderos* to say Mass and teach Christian doctrine to the Native groups as required by law, but he complained that he could not even set up a brush arbor (*ramada*) where he could say Mass and preach. The *encomenderos* had not built chapels as they were legally required to do, and Fr. Salas protested that he should not be expected to travel to their *rancherías* to administer the sacraments to the Natives. Salas's statement, which implies that he had traveled to the *rancherías*, was less about his discomfort than about the noncompliance of the *encomenderos* with the law and their disregard for the Natives' welfare. In his letter to Governor Martín de Zavala, Fr. Salas requested that "when the priest calls on the Indians to minister to them, all the citizens of this town who have Indians working for them should not neglect to send the natives [to the doctrine] with the excuse that they are busy with other chores" (Hoyo 1985, 101–2). This shows that the friars ministered to Natives living in urban areas and to those working in haciendas, whether they resided on the hacienda or in *rancherías* near or within the hacienda's lands. Zavala's response clarifies that Fr. Salas had made personal requests to the *encomenderos* to correct problems and build chapels but to no avail. Martín de Zavala ordered a visual inspection of the state of construction of the chapels and noted that of twelve haciendas within the area covered by Fr. Salas, only two had chapels. The report concluded that some of the *hacendados* had begun construction on the chapels but had not finished and alleged that the Native workers had suddenly abandoned the area (104). In his Spanish transcription of these original documents, Hoyo notes that a century and a half later the situation and excuses were precisely the same (111).

Though there were exceptions, these documents and others clearly indicate that the friars rarely traveled around the countryside to locate Native groups to convert, did not bring groups to the mission pueblos (except for those conscripted or enslaved through warfare), and did not actively engage in conversion by following the Natives as they pursued their social and subsistence schedules. Instead, the friars used an urban-rural model of conversion, whereby the friars ministered to the Natives who were domestic servants or were under *encomienda* and the *encomenderos* invested as little as possible on the Natives' socialization and conversion. The documents also show that the *encomenderos* circumvented the laws and exercised control over Native workers in terms of schedules, working conditions, and missionary practices, but this does not mean that there were no exceptions to this pattern of urban missionizing.

A Wilderness Model

In 1658, some Jumano and Babane representatives who resided in *encomiendas* near Saltillo asked to set up a pueblo. Witnesses who testified during the proceedings were not reticent about the treatment of the Natives. The *encomenderos* had rounded up Natives in Coahuila and had "imprisoned the children of Native workers to force their parents to remain in the haciendas, and did not pay the Natives for their work" (Wade 2003, 2). Despite the legal proceedings sent to the viceroy, the Duque de Albuquérque, for review, the request was eventually denied: the *encomenderos'* need for a labor force outweighed de facto enslavement practices. Though they were outmaneuvered this time, the Natives did not give up, and in 1673 they tried again to obtain permission to set up an autonomous pueblo, this time supported by Fr. Juan Larios and several influential businessmen.

Fr. Larios may not have been unique, but he was certainly unusual in the empathy and commitment he felt for the Natives, particularly in the way he approached conversion. In a real sense, Larios was an activist friar who followed St. Francis's rule of poverty, worked and begged for his food, had no permanent abode, and shared the life of those he wished to convert. Some of the Franciscans who became involved in his project to establish mission pueblos for Native groups shared Larios's Spiritual ideals, and the documents show that these friars had little help from their superiors. The latent conflict between Spirituals and Conventuals sometimes surfaced in dialectical debates and in practices of conversion.

The encounter between persistent Babane and Jumano Natives and Fr. Larios was fortuitous but critical. As interpreter for the legal proceedings of this new Native request for a pueblo, Fr. Larios was able to devise a legal strategy that forced the hand of the law and resulted in permission to establish missions. Yet it must not be forgotten that the Native groups had set the process in motion and that Fr. Larios was the instrument of change, not the initiator (Wade 2003, 4–6).

Fr. Larios's intervention on behalf of the Natives later led to the establishment of several mission-pueblos where large coalitions of Native groups from north and south of the Rio Grande congregated. Unlike other friars who traveled in and out of urbanized areas to missionize, seeking Natives in haciendas and mines but returning to urban convents, Fr. Larios and his companions followed the Natives as they pursued their social and subsistence rounds. However, Larios strove to keep the groups together and tried to induce them to settle, farm the land, and raise cattle. This model of contact

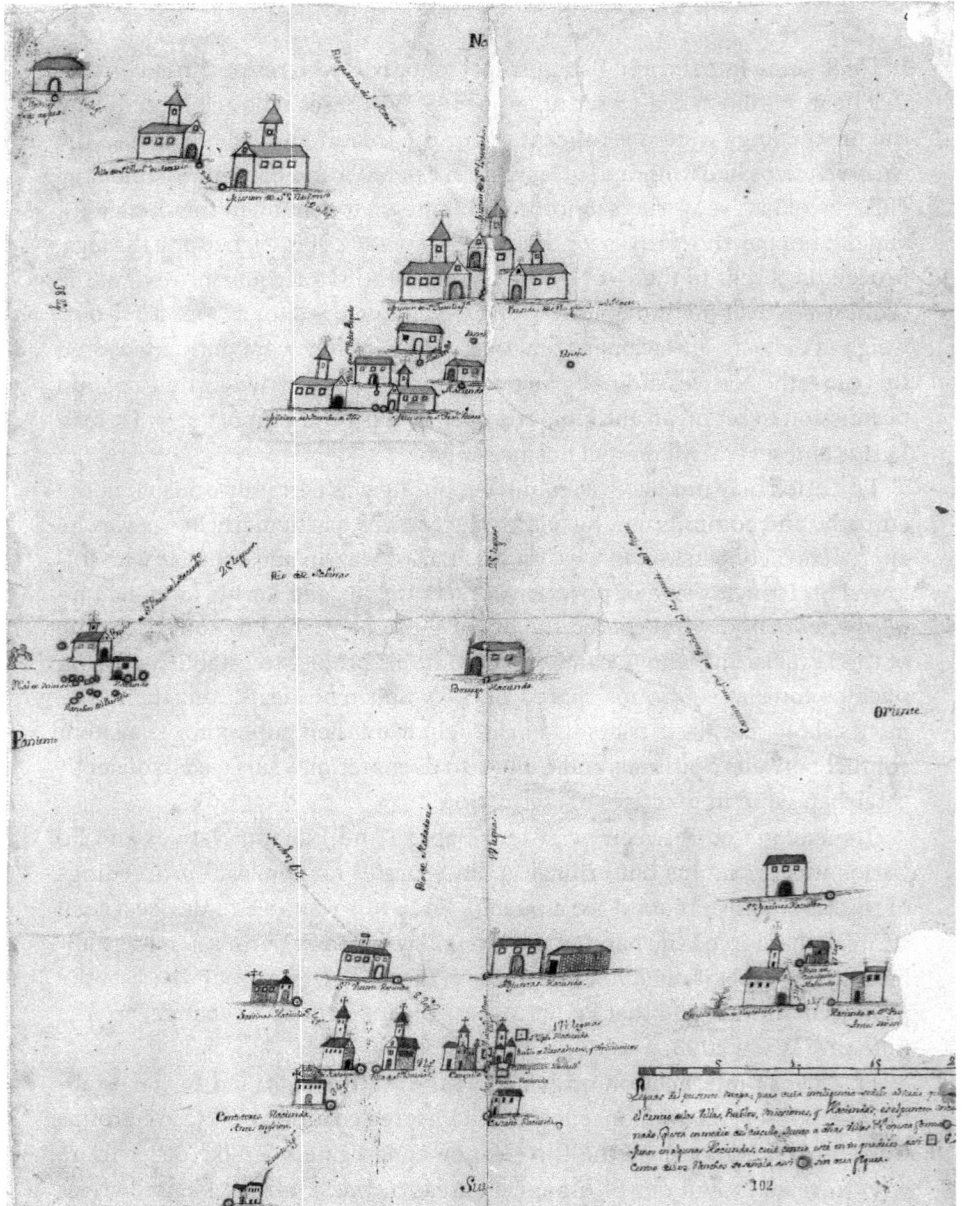

Map 6.3. Tlascaltecos and Chichimecos haciendas in northern Mexico south of the Rio Grande, 1750. Courtesy of the Benson Latin American Library, University of Texas at Austin.

with intent to convert was well adapted to the lifestyle of hunter-gatherers. But it could not be sustained because the ultimate aim of the wilderness model was settlement.

Hunter-gatherer populations who lived just south and north of the Rio Grande subsisted on a variety of floral and faunal resources. Some of these resources, such as deer, bison, and the fruit of the prickly pear, were available only in certain areas and at certain times of the year (Wade 2003, 55–57). Native groups carefully scheduled their seasonal rounds to make full use of these resources. Social gatherings to perform ceremonies, choose mates, trade, establish coalitions, and plan future raids were scheduled to coincide with the abundance of certain resources. Bison and ripe prickly-pear fruit supplied enough food for these large gatherings and made it possible to schedule raids by providing food for both the raiders and those left behind.

Despite the scarcity of information about the social organization of these groups, there is sufficient evidence to affirm that groups were guided by charismatic spokespersons and that some of these may have held positions of leadership regarding warfare and camp movements (Wade 2003, 20–23). Likewise, the presence of shamans or curing practitioners can be inferred from Cabeza de Vaca's narrative and the services he rendered. It is easy to comprehend that neither friars nor Natives understood the implications of the changes they contemplated. Native groups that lived by hunting and gathering may have liked the idea of a settled life but failed to realize that such radical change in their social and subsistence structures could not be accomplished in a short period of time. Native groups' fission-fusion patterns suited the hunting-and-gathering style of diluted leadership and the timely access to certain resources. Social intercourse and specific events related to the gathering of resources took place at the same time. The role of the spiritual practitioner was likely central to the welfare of the group, and the demotion of such practitioners by the missionaries was probably socially emasculating.

Despite temporary success, Fr. Larios, who had shunned the presence of the military in 1673 because of its ties to the *encomenderos*, ended up requesting a presidio. It is well to remember that military officials and *encomenderos* were also state officials in Saltillo, a minority holding power and frightened of a Native majority. Fr. Larios and his colleagues had been able to wrestle only meager resources from reluctant church and secular authorities and feared, correctly, that a few attacks by some Natives would destroy established mission-pueblos.

The sequence of events that began in 1658 resulted in the entrada[7] of Fr. Manuel de la Cruz into what would become Texas territory and culminated with the 1675 expedition of Lieutenant Fernando del Bosque and Fr. Juan Larios to Texas. Although Spaniards crossed the Rio Grande several times before 1675, it was almost two decades before the crown expressed interest in converting Native peoples north of the Rio Grande.

In 1679, Fr. Manuel de la Cruz, one of Fr. Larios's companions, reported on the missions Larios and his group had established in Coahuila. Fr. Manuel understood that although some Natives had made the mission their home, others used the produce and cattle of the mission only as a food cache on their scheduled food rounds (Wade 2003, 63). Some groups, however, left the women and children at the mission, which indicates that they treated the mission as their *ranchería* and as a refuge. It is not clear if those who left their families at the mission were the same as those who raided the mission larder. If they were the same people, they were merely gathering their own resources, though the friars would not have seen it that way. These and other clues leave little doubt that there was a clear distinction between how Native groups perceived the mission-pueblos and how they saw life in the *encomiendas*. These clues cannot be found when mission-pueblos were first established; they are present in the historical record only after the Natives tired of the novelty of the mission-pueblos and incorporated them into their routines.

On the other hand, it would be wrong to assume that what went on in Coahuila, Saltillo, or Monterrey also took place in other areas such as modern Chihuahua. Griffen's work on the Conchería and La Junta de los Ríos areas shows that the Natives preferred paid work at the *encomiendas* and sojourned at the missions only temporarily (1979/1991). Furthermore, the existence of Native governors who were empowered by the Spanish and who procured Native workers for mines and haciendas over wide areas differs from the pattern recorded for Coahuila (103–4), although the example of Cuaujuco mentioned above and Susan Deeds' (2003, 57, 71) work for Nueva Vizcaya indicate the pattern was not unique to Chihuahua. Griffen could not trace the presence of "general governors" beyond the 1650s, but there is no doubt that the *encomienda* system persisted well into the mid-eighteenth century in the area (1979/1991, 104). Natives and Native leadership were certainly co-opted by the *encomendero* labor market, and it is undeniable that many Natives willingly worked for the Spanish commercial ventures and that many of the ladinos did not come from the mission fold. Nonetheless, several revolts exploded throughout the northern Mexico region during the seventeenth century, and many were led by the unpredictable and resourceful ladinos, who did not come from the mission fold (Deeds 2003, 34–35, 64–65, 69–70). No doubt there were laws to prevent the abuse of

Native laborers conscripted through the *encomienda* or *repartimiento* systems (Griffen 1979/1991, 104–5), but the correspondence between the spirit of the law and the implementation of the law was rather poor (Deeds 2003, 62–63, 66).

The picture that emerges from the records on labor practices and the activities of missionaries and *encomenderos* is far from clear. In 1684, Fr. Francisco de Ayeta, former custodian and procurator general of all the provinces of the Indias, wrote to the king about the missions in the northern frontier. Fr. Ayeta responded and refuted the complaints, including those of Alonso de León,[8] but the letter is an indictment of the state of the missions in the kingdom of Nuevo León:

> because of the poor attention paid to them by the friars and because, although they attend to the missions the only result is that the Indians complain that the friars make them work and keep their daily wages. Others complain they cannot obtain permission [to work?], that they do not get assistance from the parish priests, and [complain] about the lack of language skills of the friars. These [issues] lead to the seizure [of Natives] from other doctrinas,[9] which means they have no appointed priest, and do not advance in religious knowledge. Finally, [it is also] because in some missions, serious crimes have been permitted with the complicity of some of the friars. (Hoyo 1985, 127–28)

If a friar's religious zeal was questionable, so was his authority. In 1676, long after Martín de Zavala's death, Fr. José de Arcocha visited Nuevo León to request the release of Natives who had been Zavala's servants. Zavala's will and testament released them from bondage and specified that they were to return either to the farm from whence they had come or to the Native pueblo he had founded. Many of Zavala's servants, however, had been appropriated by other *encomenderos*, who had kept them and their families without pay for some nine or ten years, mostly as workers in the mines. When Fr. Arcocha arrived, several of the Natives who were to be freed were said to be gathering prickly-pear fruit. Others, who were working for Captain Antonio de Palacios, were laboring in the coal furnaces of silver and lead mines. After the inquiries and testimony and despite the efforts of the friar, several Natives freed by law remained at work in the mines (Hoyo 1985, 117–24).

This case and the Babane and Jumano request of 1658 provide information about the social and legal situation of the Natives and their labor conditions and, by inference, about the missionizing activities of the friars. First, the friars' attempts to intervene on behalf of the Natives in matters that involved *encomenderos* and Natives were generally ineffective. Second, colonizers disregarded legal instruments that protected or released Native people from bondage because they valued Native labor more than they valued the law. Third, Natives were quite often not paid for their labor, which means that their labor produced an income for colonizers that was decreased only by the cost of their food. Fourth, Natives either fled or were allowed to procure prickly-pear fruit and other foods so they could subsist, which also decreased the cost of sustaining them. Further, the Natives' presumed absence made them unavailable for release from bondage. Finally, these cases show how little the friars were able to affect the lives of Natives outside of missions and how the interests of the *encomenderos* shaped the work and models of conversion, since all haciendas were supposed to have friars to minister to the Natives, protect their interests, and see to their welfare. Colonial Spain had systems of checks and balances, but on the frontier such systems often went unchecked and remained unbalanced.

In response to all these problems, the king issued a royal edict in 1689 that acknowledged the problems the Native populations were experiencing. This edict and other legislation issued before and after (Deeds 2003, 66, 74) make clear that the king knew that the owners of haciendas stole the wives and children from "'los miserables Indios,' abuse[d] them against the laws of God, and [sold] them in Mexico, Puebla and Querétaro as slaves" (Alessio Robles 1978, 193).

In 1682, Bishop Juan de Santiago de León Garavito informed the viceroy that he was going to visit Coahuila because he had been contacted by three Natives from Coahuila and two Tlaxcalans who were deeply upset with the missionaries and with their Indian protector, Pascual Vallejo. They complained about the humiliating treatment they had suffered at the hands of both. Bishop Garavito noted that the letters he had received made it apparent that the Natives were unwilling to share food with or serve the friars or the captain protector. Garavito informed the viceroy that he had instructed the friars and Vallejo to treat the Natives with pretense and guile [*con disimulo y mana*] to keep them quiet (Alessio Robles 1978, 282). He also stated that to mollify the friars, he had ordered a priest from Nuevo León to provide a servant who, at Garavito's expense, would prepare food for the friars. No doubt frontier conditions were difficult, but Native complaints of mistreatment were reduced to the friars contravening complaints of lack of servant help and Native refusal to share food with the friars. The scant archival references to the sharing of food with the missionaries by Natives are especially important because they indicate that despite their rhetoric, friars often depended on Natives for their sustenance and that Natives, whom friars decried as inept farmers, were often the food producers (Wade 2003, 7).

Garavito was appalled at the deplorable conditions under which the friars were ministering to the Natives. At San Buenaventura de las Cuatro Ciénegas, the sacred altar stones were broken and the friars were using oils that had been consecrated two years earlier. Moreover, the missionaries were apparently working without diocesan approval and could not pass their exams in theology or in Nahuatl (Castañeda 1984, 78–79). No doubt the service of the Lord deserved the best and native language skills were essential, but surely preaching in the wilderness was more important than freshly consecrated oils. Aside from recurring conflicts between the missionary orders and the secular church, these two groups of religious officials held very different perceptions of the essential nature of missionary work, and these differences were intrinsic to the wilderness and mission models of conversion. What Bishop Garavito considered "indecent" was likely the decency of poverty (Castañeda 1984, 79).

Bishop Garavito's intervention was ineffective, and in 1687 he reported that the situation of the Native missions had deteriorated. According to the bishop, mismanagement and suppression of the royal storehouses that supplied food to the Natives were chief reasons for the problems because it forced them to procure their own food. Delays in establishing towns, the greed and inexperience of local officials, and the friars' abandonment of the missions contributed to the state of disarray of the missions. The bishop felt that reopening the royal storehouses to supply the Natives with food for eight to ten years would help. He believed that further development of the frontier was needed to attract settlers and minimize the problems with the Native population and that changes in local leadership were essential.

These proposed remedies draw attention to some persistent issues. Neither the missions nor the *encomiendas* were able or willing to feed the Native population, while at the same time the Natives with hunter-gatherer economic traditions had not become productive farmers after a century of consistent contact and interaction. This discourse, however, contradicts statements of reluctance to share food and declarations that the Natives who worked for the *encomiendas* generally procured their own sustenance. Surely all those comments could be pertinent, but there is no historical discourse to mediate them. The panacea of further urban development would only have increased the requirements for labor, although it would have shored up Spanish defenses. As for changes in leadership, the incestuous relationship between landed gentry, crown officials, and the military added up to concentrations of power, as the case of Echeverz y Subiza discussed below exemplifies. The discontent of the friars likely was more problematic than it appears, since the relationship between missionaries and the secular clergy was generally less than amiable, and the relationship between Bishop Garavito and the missionaries in Coahuila was no exception.

In 1684, the (in)famous Agustín de Echeverz y Subiza, the principal obstacle to the mission pueblo plan for Natives Fr. Larios sponsored, was appointed governor of Nuevo León. In 1699, he married the granddaughter of Francisco de Urdiñola, Francisca de Valdés Alcega y Urdiñola. At the time, Echeverz y Subiza was protector of the Indians at the Mazapil mines, a position once held by his grandfather-in-law. Prior to that, Echeverz y Subiza had been the protector of Indians at San Esteban de Nueva Tlaxcala in Saltillo. On the basis of his services to the king and the immense property he acquired through marriage, he obtained the title of Marqués de San Miguel de Aguayo (Alessio Robles 1978, 293–95). Echeverz y Subiza's case is one of the most egregious examples of how the continuous commingling of judicial, political, and military powers into the hands of the elite left the Natives vulnerable to abuse and placed some friars, like Fr. Larios, in intolerable positions (Wade 2003, 60).

Turn of the Century

From the end of the seventeenth century through the eighteenth century, the jurisdictional conflicts between Nueva Vizcaya, Coahuila, Texas, and the Audiencia de Guadalajara; the grinding frictions between the Franciscan Colleges and the bishoprics; and the constant acrimony between *encomenderos* and priests created a state of unrest. Central to all these disagreements was not the issue of conversion, on which everyone agreed in principle providing it did not interfere with each group's interests, but the use of Native labor.

Native groups assaulted convoys and haciendas mostly to raid for cattle, horses, and supplies, although they did kill some people (Chapa 1997, 63, 66, 70–71, 90, 92; Deeds 1998, 27). For example, when the mission of Contotores in Coahuila was attacked in 1673, the people who remained in the area took refuge in San Francisco de Coahuila. The younger Alonso de León's inquiries and the testimony of several Native leaders accused of the attacks underscore the relationships between mission Natives and rebels, showing the connections between and common interests of both communities as well as the pressures those on the outside imposed on those inside. Ultimately, the inquiries pointed to the porous nature of the worlds of inside and outside, how they were intertwined, and how the flux of Natives in and out of missions reinforced the links between both worlds, particularly through the Native ladinos, whose roles and statuses often collapsed cultural brokering with leadership of revolts.

In 1697, the archbishop of Guadalajara, Fr. Felipe Galindo Chávez y Pineda, wrote the king regarding the problems with the missions and *encomenderos*. He stated,

> The governor allows [the *encomenderos*] to go to the lands of non-Christian Indians, who they call Borrados,[10] and bring all those they can to labor. They gather them by force and these trips cause many deaths of innocent people who live in their lands and bother no one. . . . Those Spaniards who bring [the Natives] say that they will feed and clothe them and keep them as slaves, but they certainly do not cloth them and the food [they provide] is so meager you can see [the result] in their bodies. They say they teach [the Natives] the Christian doctrine but if you ask [the Natives], there are no pueblos or congregations [of Natives] and the Bishop does not visit the haciendas or mines to inspect the situation, which in all conscience he should. As such, my Lord, 80 years after the foundation [of this area] [Natives] live like people without reason, as beasts in the hills and mountains. (Hoyo 1985, 139–40)

The repetitious blame game and dueling among missionaries, secular priests, and *encomenderos* seemed never to improve or cease. In 1712, Diego Camacho y Ávila, bishop of Guadalajara, visited Nuevo León and reported that the Franciscans had not presented reports on the Natives under their care. The bishop noted that no information was provided on whether the Natives had fulfilled the annual precept of confession (Hoyo 1985, 154–56). In response to the bishop's order for information, Fr. Juan de Carvajal confirmed that he could not supply a list of the people who had received sacraments because the registers had burned along with the church and convent. Besides, he could not provide such an account because if one year five or six hundred Natives might confess and receive communion, in another there would only be some three hundred. According to Fr. Carvajal (156–58), the *encomenderos* explained the discrepancy by stating that the Natives had returned to their wild ways (*gentilidad*). The friar could not get the *encomenderos* to send the Natives to Mass on Sunday, though the governor threatened the *encomenderos* with pecuniary fines. Equally, he could not get the *encomenderos* to bring the dead for a Christian burial; instead, they buried the Natives in the fields. When Fr. Carvajal asked Sergeant Major Francisco de la Garza to have the *encomenderos* deliver the bodies for burial, he refused, declaring that he had permission from a bishop to bury them in the fields. The friar testified that he was never called to confess and administer last rites to those who perished in the fields and that only those who managed to flee their masters got married because the *encomenderos* rarely allowed them to contract matrimony. The friar added that the only Natives who could be accounted for were those who worked within the city in the ranchos and kitchens of their masters (156–58). Only urban Natives had reached the stage of Christian learning that would enable them to receive the sacraments, and even with those he could seldom do more than confess and administer last rites at the moment of death. Fr. Carvajal insisted that the majority of the Natives would not be *reduced* unless forced by their owners and that he could not fulfill his obligation to convert them because the Natives moved around.

Bishop Camacho y Ávila also interviewed Francisco de la Calancha, a priest, commissary of the Holy Office and ecclesiastic judge who had lived in Nuevo León for over thirty years. He testified that the Franciscan *doctrinas* in Nuevo León, Cadereyta, and Cerralvo did not have Natives under doctrine (*sujetos a son de campana*) because the latter lived at great distances and were owned by the *hacendados*, who they called *encomenderos* (*en poder de los dueños de haciendas, que llaman encomenderos*) (Hoyo 1985, 160–61). The bishop concluded that no Natives came to church because they were all under the power of the *encomenderos* who, under the guise of congregating them, kept them in their farms and houses, forced them to work without remuneration, and provided them with little food (158–60). The *encomenderos* removed the Natives from their lands by force and did not congregate them in pueblos as the law required, and few *encomenderos* saw to it that the Natives received Christian instruction. Conversely, the friars used the *encomenderos* as the excuse for their failure to fulfill their religious duties, although the friars received the crown stipend (*sínodo*) for ministering to the Natives.

Other witnesses confirmed all of this information and reemphasized the inadequacies of the urban-rural model of conversion. Some testimonies explained part of the migratory pattern of presence/absence of Native populations. According to various witnesses, the Natives left the area to harvest the tuna of the prickly pear and other natural resources not only because these were their traditional foods but also because they needed the nourishment. At harvest time the *encomenderos* hunted the Natives down, tied them up, and brought them to the haciendas and mines. Soldiers, paid by the *encomenderos*, raided Native *rancherías* and were paid with the offspring of the Natives who were raided. Children who were not sold were kept by the *encomenderos* to ensure that the parents remained in the haciendas. The adult males worked in the fields and mines, while the females gathered roots and plants to sustain their menfolk. After a day's work, they were given three ears of corn and no salary. As for the missions, all the witnesses confirmed that they had few Native residents.

These reports stress a crucial point in labor practices whereby patterns of gathering wild foods were grafted onto unfree labor. This strategy guaranteed a male labor force that relied on female food-gathering for sustenance, decreasing the cost of maintaining a labor force and increasing potential profits. In other cases, as detailed below, males were made to labor and provide for their own sustenance by hunting and gathering while the *encomenderos* kept females and children as hostages to assure the return of the men. Either way, such practices ensured higher potential profits.

Lieutenant Manuel de Mendoza, a 46-year-old Spaniard, made some important observations. He confirmed most of what the other witnesses had stated, but he added that the friars did not visit the haciendas because of the distances to be covered. He also stated that even though the Natives received baptism they did not have the religious education to know the meaning of the sacrament and so returned to a barbaric way of life. He said that because of the cruel way soldiers conducted the raids for labor, many Natives were killed. This had occurred in the past and was continuing in the present (1712). He reported that many Natives were buried in the corrals where animals were kept. The *encomenderos* did not allow the Native women to marry; instead, women were kept inside their masters' houses. The houses were too small for privacy, and males and females were kept together, creating serious problems. The cruel treatment of the *encomenderos* corrupted those who did not own *encomiendas* but were hired as soldiers to get Native laborers, sometimes in raids as far away as 100 leagues (260 miles) or more. The soldiers were paid with young boys, girls, or adult women, whom they sold away from Nuevo León, removing them from their land (*desnaturalizandolos de su tierra*) (Hoyo 1985, 165–71). He testified that many times, realizing the fate that awaited their menfolk and their children, the women would follow them to the *encomenderos'* haciendas and would kill their children (*las indias, sabiendo con el conocimiento racional, que, aunque gentiles, no les falta, van aperseguirlos así, por el trabajo de sus maridos, como por sus hijos, los cogen y los matan [a sus hijos]*) (167–68, parenthesis in the original). Statements such as these reinforce the notion that almost two centuries after the initial colonization of the northern frontier, the need for labor continued to poison the relationship between Natives, friars, and settlers. The *encomenderos* held the majority of the Natives by force or blackmail and strove to produce wealth while investing the minimum amount of resources in a labor force. The law implicated the *encomenderos* in the process of conversion and instead they contravened it.

On the other hand, most friars, whether in charge of *doctrinas* or missions, did not engage in conversion outside the mission compounds except for in the safer and easier urbanized areas. The chasm between urban and rural Natives appears to have become institutionalized and emphasized by specific practices of action or neglect. Regardless of the greed and sins of the *encomenderos*, the friars were often complacent about and compliant with a corrupt system that at various decision nodes involved the church, the army, and the citizenry. Captain Juan Esteban Ballesteros, for instance, stated that when the governor visited a mission, the friars recruited the most proficient ladino Natives to recite the four prayers after Mass under the direction of the Native fiscal (Hoyo 1985, 164–65). Likewise, when the governor visited the *encomenderos* to evaluate the state and learning of the Natives, the *encomenderos* called on the Natives who served in the house and were reared among the Spanish. No one checked to see if other Natives who were working for the *encomenderos* and were under their protection had learned Christian doctrine, if they were paid for their labor, or how many they were. Perhaps the most disturbing facet of Lieutenant Manuel de Mendoza's deposition was his statement that the cruelty of the *encomenderos* had created a gang mentality whereby even those who had less to gain became corrupt (168).

As always, however, there were voices of wisdom, honesty, and sadness. Around 1714, Fr. Vicente Santa María acknowledged that these *congregas* (*pueblos*) were created simply as pretexts to attract the Natives or bring them by force to the pueblos that the Spaniards were supposed to establish (Alessio Robles 1978, 190–91). Once there, the Natives were grouped and delivered to the Spanish settlers, who pledged to be their protectors and were charged with providing for their sustenance and well-being. These settlers were to socialize the Natives to Spanish ways and make sure they learned religious doctrine, but things did not turn out as planned. The Natives in *congregas* were compelled to work continuously without any benefit, and the males were encouraged to go to the mountains to gather roots and wild plants, saving the *encomendero* the trouble and expense of sharing the crops the Natives labored to harvest with them. The *encomenderos* kept the women and children as hostages to guarantee the return of the males. These Native groups, decimated by disease, malnutrition, internal strife, and labor conditions, were replaced by new groups of Natives as needed. Hired soldiers and others took trips to uncolonized areas to gather new members for these *congregas*, which were, in reality, human labor pools. As the Franciscan friar stated, "In fact they returned from the expeditions with a considerable number of savages, whom they gathered like deer or animals, without wanting from them anything but their labor and without considering that in some manner the Indians needed to acquire notions of christianity and civility. Then the masters sold them as slaves, fathers separated from sons, wives from husbands for whom they clamored in their fashion, and the sale value of the *congregas* was estimated according to the number of Indians in them," a statement that implies that the sale value of the land was contingent on the available Native labor force and that the *congregas* were akin to *encomiendas* (Alessio Robles 1978, 191–92). There is little that can be added to these testimonies; they are eloquent enough. The only question remaining is: What did the crown do about it?

The Law: What the King Knew and When He Knew It

In 1715, King Phillip V issued legislation to address the problems of the Indian Pueblos in Nuevo León.[11] This legislation covers issues that existed in one form or another in all of northern New Spain and serves as a good synopsis of the problems discussed above. The rules the crown established also demonstrate the king's knowledge of the problems in his colonial domains. This document was chosen because it was promulgated at the beginning of the eighteenth century and covers broad legislative issues such as establishing the office of *protector de indios* (Indian protector) as well as mundane details such as what the salary should be for a Native woman who worked for a master for a long period of time or how many bulls could be killed on feast days.

The document is long and self-explanatory, but it often seems to cover one issue only to add legislative details later in the text. Due to the length and breath of the document, I have decided to paraphrase it but seldom did I change the original order of the text. Because of this and because I do not want to interrupt the flow of the source document, I will include my comments at the end and only one reference will appear at the end of the document.

The Document

Following a tortuous legal path and a long tradition of protectorship and tutelage of people deemed in need of legal representation, the crown established (or reestablished) and defined the position of an independent Indian protector who was responsible for Natives of any nation and who was to administer justice in all civil, juridical, and criminal matters (Cutter 1986,

7–20). The document outlines the job description of the *protector de Indios*, adapting it to local needs and conditions. The protector had the authority to pursue Natives who fled, but Spanish authorities were not to force Natives to go to war unless they volunteered, and even then they needed the permission of the protector. The king stated that when the Natives departed to harvest the tuna of the prickly pear and remained in their lands for four or five months or failed to return, such was not to be understood as a rebellious act or as an act of war because when the harvest was over, if they had not been molested, the Natives would return to their pueblos without much effort on the part of the Spanish. The king emphasized that if such policies were adopted, many Natives would not die without sacraments, be buried in the fields, or return to their "barbaric" rites.

The king stipulated that if Natives wanted to harvest salt, even if they were armed, they were to be allowed to do so providing they had the protector's permission. Natives were permitted to appropriate stray cattle and horses as long as the animals were not branded. If they were branded, the owner would pay four reales (half a peso) for a horse and one peso for mules or donkeys. If Natives were attacked or their animals were stolen, they could immediately pursue their attackers if they had permission from the Native governor of the pueblo. The king ordered that no Native be given the title of captain and that no Native be used for escort duty.

Each pueblo was to have a Tlaxcalan governor regardless of what other Native nations were present in the pueblo. He was to be elected for one year by all the other Native officials of the pueblo in consultation with the resident friar. After the governor was elected, the officials would elect the *alcaldes*, *regidores* (elected pueblo officials), and *alguaciles* (constables). Natives appointed to posts of justice were to display their insignia even when outside their area of jurisdiction (the pueblo). Tlaxcalans were not to be drafted for war, were to be allowed to have horses and weapons, and were to have their guns (*escopetas*) ready. A Tlaxcalan scribe was to be appointed in perpetuity for each pueblo; he was to keep the records of the pueblo, including sales records and wills. Also, he was to teach the children to read and write and was to compel the friar to buy books for that purpose. After leaving school, in the morning and in the afternoon, the pupils were to sing the Alabado[12] hymn and recite doctrine. Pueblo officials were not to be whipped except for grave crimes.

The church was to be furnished with two benches; one was to be placed on the side of the pulpit used for the reading of the Gospels and was destined for the Tlaxcalan officials, while on the opposite side a bench would be provided for the officials of the other Native nations who lived in the pueblo. The Tlaxcalans were not allowed to leave Nuevo León, even if they had permission from their pueblo governor. The crown ordered that a book be kept with a list of all the belongings of the pueblo, from farming implements to cattle. This inventory book was to be maintained in good order by the Tlaxcalan governor, who was responsible for the items listed, while the resident friar was to make sure the pueblo possessions were not misused. The Tlaxcalan governor was to pass this registry on to his replacement.

If a lawsuit regarding land and water rights was to be brought against the Natives, individually or in common, the matter was to be decided by the viceroy and the Natives could plead the lawsuit before local authorities depending on the opinion of the protector. Under no circumstances were the lands or water rights of the Native pueblos to be sold, alienated, or rented, and if such a transaction occurred the buyers would lose the property they had purchased, taken, or leased. Those who rented Native pueblo property would pay a fine of 100 pesos; this amount was to be divided between the pueblo church and the person who disclosed the transaction.

The king ordered that the pueblos plant as much corn as possible to make sure that the Natives had plenty to eat. The friar was to manage the harvest, and food rations were to be given throughout the year, daily or weekly, according to the needs of each family. No Native was to be excused from farming chores; the survival of the pueblo depended on the labor of all. Missions and pueblos should aim to produce a surplus to be sold and used for the other needs of the pueblo. If the friar sold the grain to a third party, he was required to explain the transaction to the Natives to avoid the perception that he had stolen the Natives' harvest.

Some of the revenue accumulated was to be used for church ornaments, which were to be decent but not extravagant. If the harvest allowed, some of the profits were to be used to clothe Natives who had greater need. Those who did not get garments one year were to get them the following year. The king also stipulated that some revenue was to be reserved to establish a hospital (infirmary) in every pueblo and to purchase blankets and other necessary items to outfit the hospital.

From 1716 onward, the Tlaxcalans were to be given lands and water rights so they could cultivate their lands apart from the other Native nations. Their expenses and harvests were not to be mixed with those of the other Natives. The Tlaxcalans were to be allowed to cultivate the land individually or as a group, as they wished. They were to be given farm implements and cattle according to the number of people who farmed the land, and if problems arose the protector was to decide the issues. Any Tlaxcalan who wished to cultivate the land individually was also compelled to farm for the community to compensate for those who were unable to work, were ill, or were orphans. The harvest surplus was to be used as they saw fit. During the first years, the Tlaxcalan governor was to make sure that the Natives of other nations (always called *chichimecos*) worked the lands, and he was to help them. If the pueblo governor saw that the land assigned to the other nations was not being farmed, he was to ensure that the Tlaxcalans worked the land communally so the pueblo would not fail. To guarantee that the work was performed and to teach by example, the friar was to entreat the Natives with apostolic zeal and with his participation in the harvest. The eight or ten Tlaxcalans who contributed to the harvest of other Native nations were to be supported by other eight or ten Tlaxcalans who did not and who had worked solely on the Tlaxcalan lands. If necessary this work could be done in turns. The king thought that it would be very good if each member of the other Native nations (*chichimecos*) owned his plot of land and farmed it, but he considered that this would be unlikely because the Natives consumed all their harvest in a fortnight or gambled it away. He entreated the friar, however, to encourage them, little by little, to cultivate their own plots.

The king ordered that no pueblo Native was to work for the haciendas more than twelve to fifteen days, otherwise they would not attend to their own harvest, from which they derived their yearly sustenance. The king wanted all the Natives to be engaged in the harvest, and if some were found working for *encomenderos* without the friar's permission they were to be brought to the pueblo, tied up, and punished with twelve lashes. Any Spaniard who used a Native's labor without permission of the pueblo governor or the friar was to pay six pesos for each person hired and the proceeds of the fine would revert to the pueblo church. The crown ordered that great care be given to this provision, otherwise there would be no one to work the lands of the pueblo. This provision did not apply to the Natives who had been serving under agreement (*concierto*) for many years, but the pueblo was not to support them with food. The king ordered that Natives who came from their lands with the intention of settling in a pueblo be given land, a garden, a dwelling (*jacal*), and rations like those provided for the pueblo residents. If some Natives abandoned the pueblo, those who remained were to continue to farm their land because if those who left decided to return they would not be able to survive without food. If those who abandoned the pueblo failed to return, the corn was to be sold and the proceeds used to purchase farming implements. In the latter case, the protector and the viceroy were to be informed of the situation.

The king stated that it was to be expected that the Spanish would take advantage of the Natives and lead them to believe they would be hired for a full year when they contracted them in April. Instead they would keep them only through August, the harvest period when the settlers needed laborers the most. The king ordered that such labor contracts were to cover the period from September through January to avoid that problem. Natives who accepted contracts outside of that period were to be brought to the pueblo and whipped twelve times. The king was aware that the Spaniards would oppose this ruling and stated that the Indian protector should be vigilant about that fact. The Natives were to work for the friar in exchange for burials, baptisms, and marriages or any other service or practice that pertained to the administration of the pueblo.

The king emphasized the need to have the Natives build their dwellings and work their gardens. As well, the Natives were to be encouraged to plant fruit trees, new corn (*elotes*), and other crops at the appropriate times. Each pueblo was to have a square, a residence for the governor (*casas reales*) if he so wished, and a room for town meetings (*cabildo*). There should also be a house to serve as hospital for the Tlaxcalans and other Natives. Older women who had no one to care for were to be in charge of the sick and cleaning the hospital. The Tlaxcalans were allowed thirty square varas[13] (about 227 square feet) each for the house and garden, while the other Natives were allowed twenty square varas each (about 151 square feet), which is not much different from the housing stipulated for the Texas missions (where each house varied between twenty square varas, or about 146 square feet, and twenty-four square varas, or about 175.2 square feet). The irrigation ditch (*acequía*) was to run through the middle of the pueblo and was to serve both sides of the pueblo—the Tlaxcalan side as well as the side of the other Native nations. The layout of the pueblo was to be as stated, and the pueblo of Nuestra Señora de Guadalupe (Monclova) was to serve as the model.

The Natives (other than Tlaxcalans) were not to carry arms inside the pueblo, except for those who kept watch at night. The Natives who belonged to one pueblo were not allowed to move to another unless they had a good reason that was determined by the friar and the governor. Spaniards, mestizos, and mulattos were forbidden from living in the Native pueblo and they were not to be given land except when an unmarried Native woman bore a child from a member of those groups.

In view of the high price of goods, the king ordered that the daily labor of the males be compensated at two reales a day with food and three without food. Females were to receive two reales daily without food and one with food.[14] The Natives were to be forced to participate in the communal labor of the pueblo, and they should use whatever wages they made to clothe themselves and their families and for other things that benefited them. Pueblo officials could leave the pueblo to work, but they had to find a replacement acceptable to the governor. The pueblo governor was not allowed to work outside the pueblo under any circumstances, and legal officials (*justicias*) could not be absent for more than fifteen days or they would forfeit their positions. The pueblo friars and the governor were to decide who would be allowed to work outside the pueblo when they received requests for laborers. Those allowed to work were to do it in turns and for short periods. The king recognized that it was an old custom in the kingdom not to pay Natives for their labor; therefore he stressed that crown rulings were to be followed strictly. Any payment made to the Natives for personal labor without the permission and intervention of the friars and the governor was void, and even if the Native, male or female, had received payment, he or she could still complain and request payment again. The penalty to the employer who did not execute payment in the presence of the friar and the governor would be the amount of the first salary due. This measure was intended to prevent employers from paying for labor with one or two handfuls of tobacco or using similar scams.

The king was aware that, against his expressed will, some people were trying to do away with the congregation of Native populations in pueblos (*congregas*). Those who acted to accomplish this purpose were liable to lose all their possessions and be condemned to ten years in prison. If the culprit was of low class, he would be subject to 200 lashes and ten years of hard labor, and the king insisted that special attention be paid to make sure that these penalties were applied.

The king knew that Spaniards circumvented the law by procuring nomadic Natives who lived in the wilderness and secured these laborers personally or through the efforts of others. The king was aware that to humor the Natives, the Spanish let them live as they wished and without proper marriages until they no longer needed their labor. The king forbade this conduct and insisted that those who engaged in it would suffer the pecuniary penalties established. The king also admonished that it would not be a defense to allege that the Natives had willingly entered the house of Spaniards accused of this practice as Spaniards were not allowed to harbor the Natives. No Spaniard could hire any Native not registered in the pueblo. The penalty for such an infraction was four pesos for each person hired, with the proceeds reverting to the nearest pueblo.

Beginning on March 6, 1715, when the law was to be posted in Monterrey, all the Native women over the age of fourteen who had remained voluntarily in the domiciles of Spaniards would be paid one real as daily wages. In accordance with these stipulations, Native women were to be promptly paid all of their wages when they left the house of their master to work elsewhere, when they left to settle in a pueblo, or when they left to marry. The women were to be given their children, boys or girls, whenever and wherever they chose to go. If the Native woman confessed that she began to serve her master without expecting a salary but then requested one, she was to be paid. The same disposition applied to all (male) Natives who worked voluntarily, who were to receive two reales daily as wages. In all these cases, the masters could not allege that their Native employees had stolen from them or use any other excuse to avoid payment. All such allegations would be considered only after payment of wages was made. As well, any Native who had served the Spanish for a long period was to be paid and payment was to be made in the presence of the friar and the pueblo governor. These persons, however, could continue to serve their masters if they so wished. If the master did not pay them as stipulated, he was obligated to pay the Native when he or she claimed the wages, which were to be two reales a day for every day spent in the master's house. The master could not claim what he (or she) had paid beforehand if such payment had not been done in the manner prescribed by the edict.

The law was to be applied with all vigor to punish those who bought or sold Natives, as was customary; those who gave Native children as gifts, either males or females; and those who impeded or forbade free marriage. The law did not admit interpretation or exclusion. The crown forbade the use of ropes tied around the neck of Natives. If Natives were to be restrained, they were to have only their hands and arms tied. No one was allowed to have a prison cell in the house or to use domiciles to imprison Natives. Anyone who violated this law was subject to the laws covering private prisons. The king stipulated that no Tlaxcalan or any other Native (*chichimeco*) was permitted to sell any real estate without permission from their protector and without known benefit. Natives could not, under any circumstance or for any motive, obligate their community and take or move from it anything without the permission of their protector.

On feast days pueblo officials could kill two bulls or oxen belonging to the pueblo and distribute the meat among the members of the community. For this to take place the permission of the friar or the governor of the pueblo sufficed; however, this was to be done only when there were surplus animals, otherwise no bull should be killed for any motive or on any day.

The king acknowledged that it had been the practice in Nuevo León to sell Natives a few items of clothing. He also knew that the price of any merchandise was exorbitant, even for the Spanish, and that the Natives had little understanding of this. As a result, Natives could never fully repay what they owed and spent their lives serving the master or ran away without paying their debts. To curtail these problems, the king ordered that no more than five pesos be loaned to any Native of any nation. If the total exceeded the stipulated amount, the lender forfeited the remainder because he had violated the king's law. The protector was to pay special attention to this point. These provisions applied only to Natives who lived in Nuevo León, because those who worked as shepherds came from outside the province and were not under the jurisdiction of the protector.

The king declared that care should be exercised to prevent the Natives of the pueblos, males or females, from marking (tattooing) their faces. The king expressed the wish that, with gentleness, the Natives be dissuaded from holding *mitotes* (ceremonial dances), because those practices were connected with their wild lifeways and led to problems due to the large gatherings associated with the *mitote* celebrations. The king wished that the non-Tlaxcalan nations be gently dissuaded from riding horses because they became very reluctant to enter the rugged hills on foot, a mode of traveling at which they were very adept if horses were not provided. Also, non-Tlaxcalan Natives were not to be allowed to leave the kingdom (Nuevo León) without permission from the pueblo governor.

The king stipulated the responsibilities of the Indian protector. The protector was to see that the laws were observed. If, in the performance of his duties, the protector faced difficulties from the local authorities, he was to immediately inform the viceroy so the latter could punish those who attempted to obstruct the law. The protector was to live most of the year near the pueblos, and he was to visit all the pueblos each year to address the necessary issues. The protector was to be informed of the progress of the harvest, and if there was a pueblo where the work was delayed, he was to render his personal assistance, even if temporarily. In the case of distant pueblos, the protector could appoint a person who would make sure his instructions were followed, and that person would have the same powers as the royal justice officials.

On his personal authority, the protector could take Natives from any house where they might be so they could perform work in the pueblos. The protector and the friar were to maintain good relations. The protector was to deliver these royal provisions to all the pueblos and make sure that all concerned understood what they should do. Also, the protector was to inform the viceroy of all other things required that might not be addressed in the royal provisions. The king ordered that the governor of the kingdom (of Nuevo León) and all his officials provide the protector with all help he might require, orally or in writing. If they were remiss, the protector was to inform the viceroy. The Spanish governor was ordered to make sure that all subjects were informed of these laws, be they Spaniards, mulattoes, chinos,[15] and so forth to ensure that everyone knew how to act regarding Natives and so that one month after the publication of these laws, no one could allege that he or she was unaware of the punishment ordered (Hoyo 1985, 171–95).

Analysis

The king's laws emphatically made the protector the central authority on the welfare of Natives, while they charged the Tlaxcalans with the job of socializing and acculturating all non-Tlaxcalan Natives. Obviously, these provisions applied to areas where Tlaxcalans were, by proxy, the Native colonizing agents, as was the case in several parts of northeastern Mexico. Even in Texas, and as late as 1758, a group of Tlaxcalans was sent to the failed mission of San Sabá to help with the settlement of the Apache.

The authority of the missionaries is clearly deemphasized and the military is excluded from Native issues except to enforce the crown's rulings. Nevertheless, friars and the native pueblo governor were responsible for decisions about Native labor and for authorization to work outside the pueblo. Furthermore, the king decriminalized several issues that the Spanish frequently presented as reasons to pursue Native groups, such as the Natives' failure to return to the pueblos or when they took horses and other property. Also, the king uncoupled just payment for work performed from Spanish allegations that Natives had committed robberies or other infractions.

In various ways the king marked and rewarded the roles of the Tlaxcalans with status symbols and practical benefits, and he made sure that clear divisions were instituted between Tlaxcalans and non-Tlaxcalans in terms of the pueblo layout, property, surplus goods, revenue, and even their place in church. Such laws recognized preexisting perceptions of difference between civilized agriculturists and hunter-gatherers. As a result, the law confirmed a hierarchy among Native Americans. Similarly, the king's penalty system extended to all subjects and distinguished between high- and low-class settlers. Also, the king was clear in the intended exclusion from Native lands of all but recognized Natives. This provision, like many others, was not unique to this region (Deeds 2003, 111). Further, the granting of the king's ration and the proscription on selling or alienating Native lands and water rights leaves no doubt that the king intended those lands to be the property of the Natives (*pueblos de Yndios*).

The crown's emphasis at this early date on the economic self-sufficiency of the pueblos and the creation of a surplus to hedge against the vagaries of the harvest and to provide other essential items for the Natives confirms the king's intention that missions or mission-pueblos were to be self-sustaining. To accomplish that, the king stipulated first that the Tlaxcalans pay for their privileges by being responsible for their Native brethren. Second, corporal punishment was to be meted to those who did not labor in and for the pueblo. Third, Natives were not allowed to leave, but if they left, they were welcome to return and could do so without penalty, a directive no one followed. Those who remained were to guarantee the success of the pueblo so that if those who left happened to return, there would be food to sustain them. As such, the burden of performance was always on those who remained, the implication being that those who stayed would pressure those who desired to leave into staying. The king's plan created internal pressures among the pueblo-mission inhabitants to force compliance and productivity. These measures placed the onus for the success of the missions and pueblos on the Natives; the role of the friars was to guide and instruct by example. Interestingly, the king assigned responsibility for school instruction to the Tlaxcalans and not to the friars, as would be expected. Also, little is said about religious instruction or the civilizing role of the church. Thus, the law's intention was to employ innovative notions of sustained development, though the reality was far different.

The king was wise to the stratagems the Spanish used to circumvent the law. Accordingly, the king stipulated that all Natives regardless of gender or profession were entitled to be paid for their labor. Natives were, however, to exchange their labor for Christian services and for food. The crown restricted the length of time Native laborers could spend working for *hacendados* or *encomenderos*, and it levied enough fines and restrictions on hiring, inadequate pay, and debt peonage that one would have expected the system to work. Yet the sources show that it did not. Because the law distinguished between settled and unsettled Natives (or wild ones), the Spanish continued to procure the latter Natives for their labor. This conflict continued throughout the colonial period and underscores the lack of protection afforded to those who continued to live as hunters and gatherers. Although settled life exacted a premium and was certainly a mixed blessing, the pressures to abandon a hunting-and-gathering lifestyle were real and continuous. Conversely, the *encomenderos* delivered the opposite message. *Encomenderos* expected the Natives to hunt and gather to survive when they dismissed them and when they could not, or would not, feed them.

The crown clearly envisioned what the Native pueblo should look like and how much land was to be provided to the Natives. It is interesting to realize that the king was aware that there were those who wanted to do away with the *congregas* or the Native pueblo system. Evidently the king, and his advisors, felt that gathering Natives in settlements was the most efficient and productive way to change their culture and produce Christian subjects of the crown. Still, as Fr. Vicente Santa María stated, the *congregas* were nothing but labor pools where the Natives were gathered to serve the needs of *encomenderos*.

Four years after the king issued these laws, the governor of Nuevo León, Juan Ignacio Flores Mogollón, wrote to Baltasar de Zúñiga y Guzmán Sotomayor y Mendoza, a member of the council of the king and governor general of New Spain, to complain about the Franciscan friars. According to a series of letters by Governor Mogollón, the friars complicated the work of the pueblo governors because they sent Natives to work on the haciendas simply to show their authority over that of the governor (Hoyo 1985, 195–99). As an example, Mogollón sent Baltasar de Zúñiga a letter from a citizen of Nuevo León who had in his household two young Native women, aged seven and twelve, whom he had obtained from Coahuila. The citizen argued that the young women were from another region and did not belong to the nations of Nuevo León. In accordance with the king's orders, the girls were taken to the Native pueblo of Guadalupe, but Governor Mogollón asked the Native governor of the pueblo to return them to their master. The governor complied with Mogollón's request and delivered the eldest female. The younger female remained working in the friar's kitchen, and although the pueblo governor went to fetch her, the friar responded that he would not let her go unless he received a written order from Mogollón. When the friar received the written request, he is said to have responded that he did not answer written requests and kept the Native girl. In view of this, Governor Mogollón sent the information to the Franciscan commissary general and asked him to correct the problem. In turn, the viceroy asked that civil and religious officials improve their communication and work in harmony (195–97). Citizens circumvented the law by acquiring or abducting Native servants and slaves from areas outside the jurisdiction to which the Natives belonged.

Stratagems to find loopholes in the law abounded, and while the ploys changed, the aims did not. A century earlier, ranchers had had their male servants court young Native women so the ranchers could steal them as servants. When the opportunity arose, the male servant married the girl and removed her to the house of his master. Because the church prescribed that husbands were to live with their wives, this system of abduction was legal (Valdés 1995, 171).

Spanish governors complained about obstructionist friars. Native governors played the middle ground, making every effort to please all parties while protecting their self-interest. Friars had low tolerance for interference from secular authorities and often were guided by a religious compass that admitted little compromise. The Native "peon" got shuffled around while the game was played but tried to use the fault lines of these conflicts to his or her best advantage and sometimes succeeded. The bottom line of many of these confrontations was the use and abuse of Native labor, but the pivotal issue was power. As always, knowledge of the law buttressed the possibility of success in subverting the word of the law. At the level of parochial daily life, the "articulation of power on knowledge and knowledge on power" had real effects on people's lives (Gordon 1980, 52). Resistance may simply be a form of living.

Regardless of the patterns of movement in precolonial times, throughout the colonial period Natives were moved, and moved, from area to area for economic and military reasons (Chipman 1967, 88, 94, 234; Deeds 2003, 63, 71; Flint and Flint 2005, 135–37; Radding 1998a, 60). These Native peoples became integrated in communities, possibly creating small ethnic enclaves or, in time, simply merging into other ethnic groups.

Coexistence between Tlaxcalans, local Spanish officials, friars, and other Native groups was also problematic. In 1722, the Tlaxcalans of the Pueblo de Candela made a formal complaint to the governor of Coahuila, the Marqués de Aguayo, against their friar alleging mistreatment. The complaint stated that for twenty-four years the Tlaxcalans had fulfilled all their obligations and assisted the officials in all aspects, including providing escorts for mail, for convoys, and for personal travel, particularly for the friars (Hoyo 1985, 199–204). Despite their compliance, the services they had rendered, and the fact that they had used their own resources to build the pueblo church and convent, they had suffered beatings and whippings by the friar. They asked that these excesses be redressed and to be excused from all services to individuals that impeded their work in the pueblo and would result in its abandonment. The petition was sent to the general commissary for the missions, which ordered the missionaries to make sure that the privileges granted to the Tlaxcalans were not violated and to correct the abuses. These instructions were transmitted also to the military officials to make sure the Tlaxcalans were not asked to provide escorts for mail or convoys (202–4). Thus, the Tlaxcalan privileges acquired by charter in 1591 and restated by the crown in 1715 did not protect Tlaxcalan communities from abuse and conflict, but they did give them the legal means to complain and ask for redress.

In 1726, the Tlaxcalan governor of the pueblo San Antonio de Los Llanos in Nuevo León asked Viceroy Marqués de Casafuerte to let his people leave the pueblo. The Tlaxcalans complained that they were being attacked and killed by other Native nations and that they had neither the weapons nor the manpower to withstand the attacks (Hoyo 1985, 204–6). They asked to be helped with people and weapons or be allowed to leave for San Cristóbal de los Gualagüises because the governor of this pueblo, Juan de Molina, was experiencing similar difficulties and needed people to protect his pueblo. This request was accepted but postponed because the crown could not support the cost of transporting the Tlaxcalan families and belongings as requested. This petition led to a similar one made by the Pueblo de la Concepción, located in the Pilón Valley.

Licenciado Francisco de Barbadillo was contacted for his legal opinion on the matter. As Barbadillo explained, the Tlaxcalans were asking for individual land plots to which they would hold deeds and which their women and children could inherit (Hoyo 1985, 206–12). At the time of the founding of the first Tlaxcalan pueblo, the king had ruled that they should be given this privilege after two years of settlement. If these stipulations were accepted, the privilege would extend to all Tlaxcalans as well as to members of all other nations except those considered *chichimecos*. Despite the king's orders issued in 1715, the corn crop harvested from the pueblos was stored in the common granary, whether it belonged to the Tlaxcalans or to *chichimecos*. From that harvest, the missionary distributed rations every eight days in proportion to the number of family members. This system was favorable to non-Tlaxcalan groups, but it did not advance the situation of the Tlaxcalans. The situation was aggravated because the Tlaxcalans did not have a parcel of land to leave their children, which was their sole desire. Barbadillo found that they were justified in their request, but he warned that if the king approved the request for the Pueblo de la Concepción, others would rebel if they did not receive equal treatment. He suggested that after providing for the Tlaxcalans, some large expanse of land be given to the other Natives, keeping in mind that if their number was small for the moment, it was likely that in time there would be many more. The land remaining would be given to other (non-*chichimeco*) Natives to farm. As the water was plentiful, he recommended that everyone share in the rights and duties regarding the *acequía* and that they share the oxen teams, which were the property of the pueblo. He thought that these were difficult provisions to put into practice and that only the governor of the kingdom of Nuevo León (in this case) had the wherewithal and authority to implement them.

The frontier was a web of interlocked interests and conflicts, with each constituency vying for the best position and consequent allocation of resources. The Tlaxcalan investment in Spanish hegemony, on which their own autonomy resided, placed them in continuously precarious negotiating positions because they lived among other Natives but were beholden to the Spanish. Eleven years after the king's edict had been promulgated, the Tlaxcalans and the other Native groups still had not been given their land allotments. Also, in spite of the autonomy the king granted the Tlaxcalans and the privileges and duties they had, the relationships between friars and Tlaxcalans and between Tlaxcalans and other Native groups were less than promising. Carving hegemonic spaces out of Spanish colonial hegemony required continued attention and retooling, and some groups were better equipped than others to sustain the effort.

In November 1726, the viceroy ordered that the inhabitants of several pueblos be given lands as prescribed. The law established that a pueblo or *reducción* would have a common area (*egido*) of a league (2.6 miles), that the cattle ranches be at least 1.5 leagues (3.9 miles) away from the area of the old *reducciones*, that stray cattle within pueblo lands could be killed by the Natives, and that no cattle ranches or haciendas be granted to anyone if conflicts with the Native pueblos were anticipated. If the latter provision was no longer feasible, the ranches were to be located as far away from Native pueblos as possible to avoid damage to the Natives' crops. To that end, the owners were to employ as many shepherds as needed to avoid problems. If, in spite of these measures, the animals trespassed into the fields, the Natives were to be compensated. The governor of Nuevo León was told to follow the instructions laid out by Francisco de Barbadillo (Hoyo 1985, 208–12).

As required, in the 1730s and in the 1740s Franciscan friars inspected the convents and missions of Nuevo León (Cortinas 1745; Losada 1730). The documents refer very briefly to the condition of the church buildings and sacred vessels and to possible complaints of the resident friars against others. In the two inspections (*visitas*) mentioned above, which covered all missions and convents in that kingdom, all that was said about the Native neophytes was that the Tlaxcalans neglected their duties and that the others (*chichimecos*) had dispersed (Cortinas 1745).

In 1763, the Natives of the pueblo and mission of La Purísima Concepción in Nuevo León learned that Antonio Ladrón Guevara, their previous Indian protector, was to resume his duties. They made repeated requests to the friars and to the interim protector to prevent Guevara from returning, and two other Native pueblos joined in the petition. The request was based on Guevara's cruelty, and the members of a local Native group, the Cometunas, were afraid that Guevara would kill them because they had refused to return to the pueblo when he had urged them to do so. According to the Natives, the pueblo was quite prosperous and its members had plenty to eat. The Natives stated they no longer needed to hunt deer, javelina, birds, or rabbits to

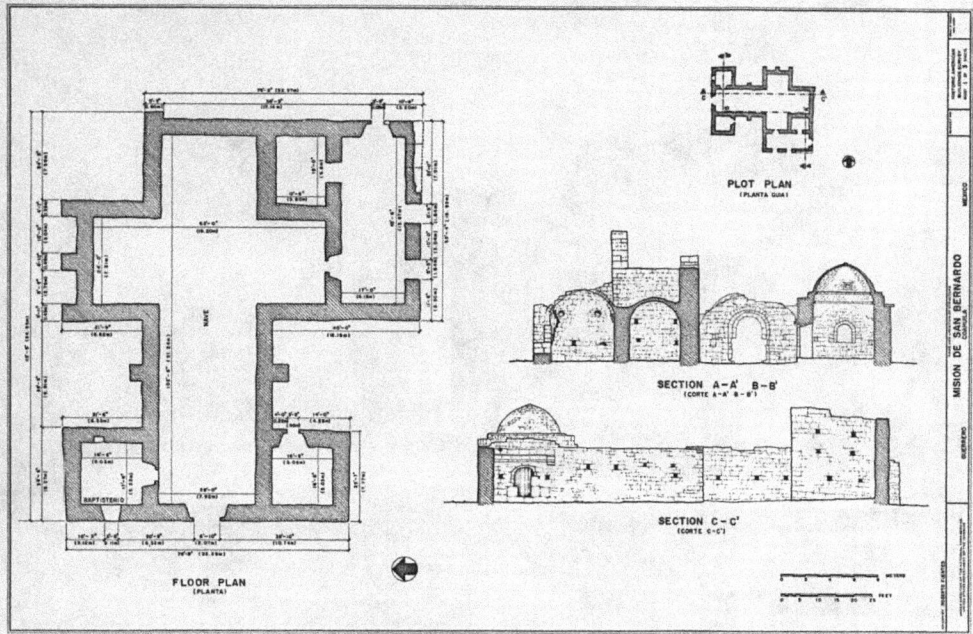

Figure 6.1. Mission de San Bernardo, Guerrero, Coahuila, Mexico. Drawing by Roberto Fuentes Cardenal. Courtesy of Alexander Architectural Archive, University of Texas Libraries, University of Texas at Austin.

sustain their families because they were growing sufficient crops to live and eat well.

In 1774, the fifty-six Native families of the Mission Punta de Lampazos, in Nuevo León, presented a complaint against their own Native *alcalde mayor* because he took fifteen days of *acequía* water and left them with only five days' worth, which was not enough for the pueblo. Further, they asked that herds of horses and cattle be removed from their lands because the animals destroyed the crops. Also, they asked to be allowed to get more land because neighbors were crowding them (Hoyo 1985, 229–37). In light of these complaints, Bachiller Pedro Joseph de Esparza argued that the Natives had not raised a single crop and that Spanish settlers should use pueblo lands to raise cattle because the Natives had not used the lands for that purpose in twenty-six years (since 1748) and because these lands compared to the best in Nuevo León.

Esparza explained that in 1769, when he took charge of the pueblo, he had realized how fertile the land was. He talked with the Natives and learned that they needed someone to help them manage the pueblo. In light of that,

Figure 6.2. Mission de San Bernardo in Coahuila, Mexico, 2006. Photograph by Robert Jackson.

in the first year Esparza paid someone to help them, and although they produced abundant harvests with this help, they made no profit because they consumed the whole crop. The following year he adopted a different tactic and rented the Spanish settlers half of the Native water. Under this arrangement the settlers were obligated to provide the pueblo with an *almude* (about 0.13 of a bushel) of corn for each day of water the Natives provided. The other half of the water was left for the Natives, but the Natives lost most of the grain because they did not farm and consumed the rest of the crop. The third year the Natives decided they did not like competing with the settlers and told Esparza they did not want any help and wanted to manage their lands freely. Despite their ingratitude, as Esparza saw it, he informed them they still had to cultivate the land on their own because that was the king's command. Esparza explained that the Natives proceeded to redistribute the lands and water rights and in less than eight days had rented it all to their Spanish neighbors: some even rented the same land to three or four different settlers. Esparza commented that the Natives continued to show a preference for idleness. They consumed and destroyed all they had, he said. Esparza stated that they should be treated like children who had just started on solid foods. He continued:

> What I mean is; we need to treat them with much commiseration to make sure they do not starve, because they are such miserable children that even when one hands them food they do not know how to masticate. The Indians who, like these ones, are proud but have been congregated in a pueblo or are under the control of a mission or encomendero (and I mean an encomendero who is a good Christian) are doing well. However, if they abandon the pueblo or hacienda they do very poorly because their natural inclination is to take off for the wilds, and with their disdain for what their labor can provide they subsist on the wild plants and resources provided by nature. They subsist on tuna [prickly-pear fruit], mesquite, javelina, deer, and mescal. With this style of living comes laziness, dances, games, and complete disaffection from the land and its cultivation. Thus, despite all the king's laws and dispositions in their favor nothing helps them because they will not get accustomed to work [*reducirse al trabajo*]. I think the only way is to force them to receive the favors given to them. I mean, they need to be fed by others [*comer por mano ajena*], or one might as well give up all the work of conquest, and all the gifts of land and water the king bestowed on them. When they were under the tutelage of the mission and someone provided for them and made sure there was food, they were many. After 26 years of living under their own government, one cannot tell which is the lesser number; theirs or their possessions. The same can be said about Candela, Coahuila, Santa Rosa and other places. It is my duty to report that although the first two still have the title of mission and the latter of encomienda, they often do not have the government and management of either, and so they might as well be lost. To conclude, I state that to achieve [the Natives'] submission and have them under government [*para su sujecion y gobierno*] one of two things is indispensable. Either to aggregate some pueblos with others, give the Natives what they need, and place them under the special authority of a protector, who needs to be a good Christian man who fears God and the king as the crown stipulated, or place the few left from each area under the special protection of an encomendero. That's how it all started and that's when the best results were achieved. (Hoyo 1985, 234–37 parenthesis in the original)

Conclusion

The practice and process of conversion followed two basic models: one that reflected deep spiritual convictions and the other that reflected an opportunistic and opportune recognition of the pragmatic conditions of the frontier. The first, a wilderness-based model, was seldom adopted and though it was friendly to hunter-gatherer Native populations, it was, in the long run, utopian and maladaptive. The second, an urban-rural–based model, was well adapted to settled Native populations and the dynamics of the frontier but yielded poor results because it was used mostly with hunter-gatherers who were congregated by force and because of the conflicts between secular and religious authorities. In this latter model, the crown and the church often engaged settled Native American populations with long traditions as food and crafts producers in order to teach and induce hunter-gatherer populations to become settled farmers.

Notwithstanding regional differences, hunter-gatherer populations shared specific ways of exploiting the landscape and tightly interwove social needs with the procurement of resources. It was not easy for Natives to relinquish the intimate relationship between spiritual and social activities and the availability of certain resources, such as prickly-pear tuna, deer, or buffalo, even if they were willing to try. Besides, had they been successful, the pressures to conform to the exigencies of Christianization and the labor demands of settlers and *encomenderos* likely would have resulted in diminished returns.

Despite the crown's attention and the laws it promulgated, the crux of the conflicts in the northeastern frontier of New Spain remained basically the same: who had power over the bodies of Natives. This exercise of power, either presumed benevolent or clearly exploitative, aimed at making deep changes in the cultures and lifestyles of Native populations. Settlers, miners, *hacendados*, and *encomenderos* wanted, and needed, to use Native labor for their own self-interest, but those people were also soldiers, civil and judicial officials, and *protectores de Indios*. The interlocking and cumulative effect of these diverse threads of power and interests produced a tight web few Natives who interacted with the colonizers could escape. The church and the crown wanted Natives to be good, productive Christians, but most often Natives could not, or would not, measure up to expectations. Amid the wants and needs of the various constituencies and interests, there was little room for a Native perspective. And so it was that by the end of the eighteenth century, not much had changed except for the disillusionment and discontent of all involved and a drastic decline in Native populations.

Texas

The Franciscans and Their Method

The Franciscans entered Texas in 1528 with Álvar Núñez Cabeza de Vaca, but they did not survive the experience. Exposure to the Catholic practices of the Spaniards who made landfall, particularly the religious practices of Cabeza de Vaca and the other three survivors, left a deep impression on the Native groups that came in contact with them (Cabeza de Vaca 1993). Cabeza de Vaca's description of his encounter with Nuño Beltrán de Guzmán's henchmen is a good example of the plight of Native populations at contact on the northern frontier of New Spain; if they were friendly to the Spanish they were frequently enslaved; if they fought back, they were enslaved or killed (109–10). For Native peoples, often the only solution was to relocate and enter into alliances with or engage in conflict with the groups occupying the lands where they wished to relocate.

Texas did not have regional and legal boundaries until the middle of the eighteenth century, and its geographical boundaries as a province of New Spain barely resemble modern Texas. For most of the period under discussion, Texas was treated as a de facto part of Coahuila.

Texas Missions

Through its colleges of Santa Cruz de Querétaro, Zacatecas, and San Fernando, the Order of Friars Minor, the Franciscans, established and ran all the Spanish missions in Texas. There are four basic periods of mission-building in Texas. The first period took place in the late seventeenth century (1689–1691) with the creation of missions south of the Rio Grande and among the Hasinai, which were east Texas Caddoan-speaking groups. The second period took place during the first three decades of the 1700s and included several missions in east Texas, the Mission of Los Adaes near modern Robeline, Louisiana, and missions in the Rio Grande area, the San Antonio River, and the Gulf Coast. The third period took place during the middle eighteenth century and was largely fruitless. It included the San Xavier River missions near modern Rockdale, Texas; a mission on the Guadalupe River; the Apache missions at San Sabá, near modern Menard, Texas; and missions on the Nueces River near Camp Wood in Texas. Two missions were built, or rebuilt, on the Texas coast in the middle eighteenth century. Several missions were originally built on a particular spot but were moved to other nearby places, often more than once. The history of the Texas missions as part of the built environment is often as complicated as their political and religious history is.

The discussion that follows focuses almost exclusively on the first and second periods of mission-building, specifically on the east Texas, Rio Grande, and San Antonio missions. The aim is to compare the two periods to locate and analyze changes in mission development through time and to understand how those changes related to the lifestyle and social organization of the Native groups for whom the missions were built. The east Texas Hasinai were horticulturists organized in polities headed by spiritual and political-military chiefs. The Hasinai supplemented their diet by hunting and gathering wild resources and lived in dispersed settlements. They provide a good contrast to the hunter-gatherers in the Rio Grande missions, particularly those in the San Antonio missions who were the object of the second period of mission-building. The Hasinai also provide a useful contrast to the Calusa, who were also led by chiefs and who were settled but were not horticulturists.

In 1689, the Spanish crown finally considered colonizing Texas in response to the French threat posed by Le Sieur de La Salle's settlement on the Gulf Coast, near modern Garcitas Creek. One year later, the explorer Alonso de León, son of Alonso de León the elder, traveled to central Texas accompanied by Franciscans Fr. Massanet, Fr. Casañas, Fr. Bordoy, Fr. Fuentcuberta, and a lay brother. Fr. Massanet returned to Mexico and Fr. Fuentcuberta died in an epidemic that ravaged the area in 1691. The missionaries established two missions among the Hasinai in response to a request from the Natives. In 1691, a military expedition commanded by Terán de los Rios traveled once again to Texas with Fr. Massanet and Fr. Hidalgo. Although the Hasinai had requested the presence of the Spanish, it was not long before they peremptorily dismissed them. The reasons for this dismissal are not clear, particularly considering later efforts the Hasinai made to entice the friars to return to east Texas. The return of the Franciscans in 1716 at the behest of the Hasinai is equally perplexing because the Hasinai refused to congregate around the missions established in their lands, and their attitude toward the friars and their teachings never changed. By 1730, virtually all the missions previously established among the Caddoan-speaking groups had closed and moved to San Antonio, except for the Mission San Miguel de Los Adaes, located in the

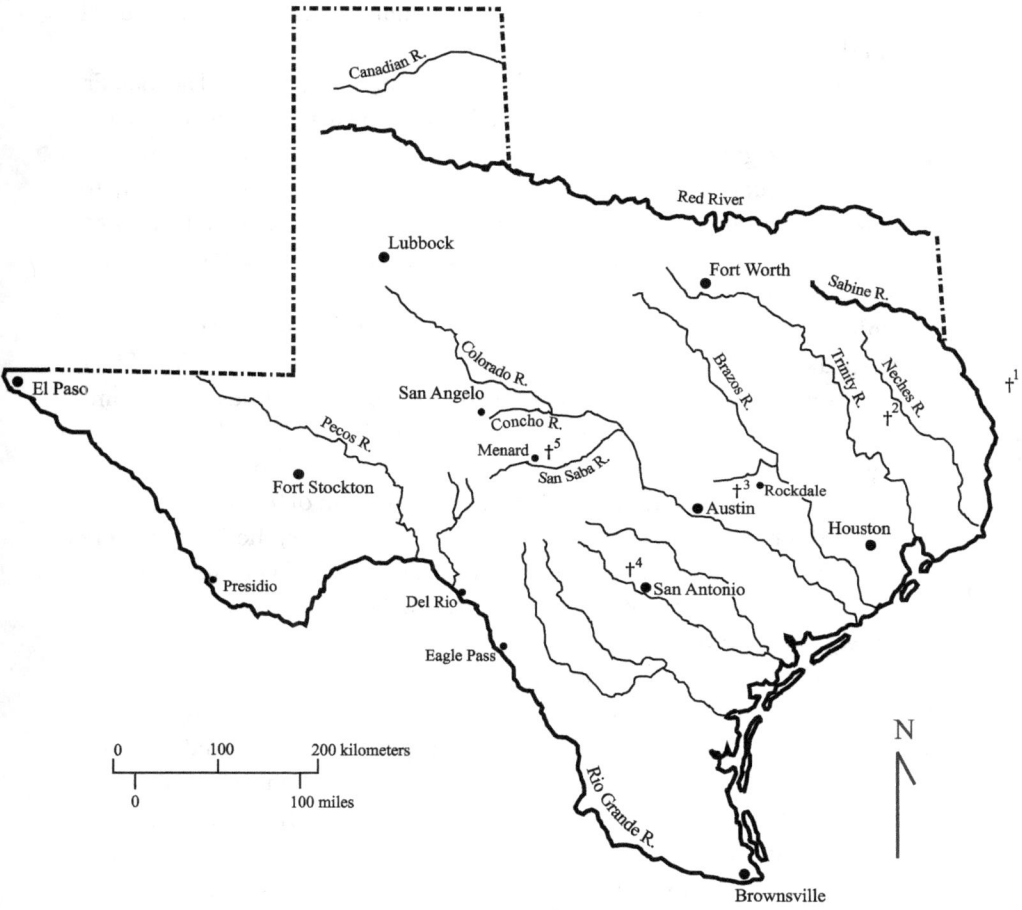

Map 7.1. Selected Spanish missions in Texas. Map prepared by Claire Huie and Don Wade.

lands of the Adai and in the area that would remain the capital of Texas until late in the eighteenth century.

In 1749, about twenty-five years after the Franciscans left the Hasinai, Fr. Ygnacio Ciprián explained why they had not been successful in converting the east Texas groups (Leutenegger 1979, 27).[1] First, the Hasinai nations were not conquered by the force of arms and it was morally impossible to change their traditions and government (*politica*). Second, the friars had little leverage with the Hasinai because these groups grew abundant crops, to the extent that the local presidio bought crops from them.

Unlike all other missionized groups in Texas (except for some of the Caddoan speakers on the Red River), the Hasinai of the Neches-Angelina River area had an observable rich ritual life, were organized in polities with a complex hierarchy of social and spiritual leaders, lived in dispersed farmsteads, and grew crops and supplemented their diet with extensive hunting and seasonal gathering. In essence, they fit the Spanish notion of "civilized Indians" and held the most promise for conversion. For the friars, the Hasinai were the puebloans of Texas, but unlike the New Mexico Pueblo groups that generally lived in agglomerated pueblos and traveled to their fields, the Hasinai, and the groups on the Red River, located their houses amid the cultivated fields. Fr. Ciprián explained that the settlements of each nation or division (*parcialidad*) were at distances from 3, 5, 10, and even 18 to 20 leagues (7.8, 13, 26, and 46.8 to 52 miles, respectively). Crop fields were located near rivers and arroyos since the Hasinai depended on them whenever rainfall was insufficient. Because Hasinai dwellings were made of thatched straw and reeds, they dispersed their households to minimize the danger that a fire would destroy the whole settlement. If they were attacked by the Apache, who normally burned dwellings, others would see the smoke and would be able to react in time. Also, as the Hasinai explained, distance between households made for fewer conflicts among neighbors. Aware of the linguistic problems involved in calling the settlements of the Hasinai "pueblos," Fr. Ciprián explained that he used the word because the Hasinai always had this type of settlement, which was the most useful for them in terms of their sociocultural and subsistence needs (Leutenegger 1979, 42–44).

The friars pressed the Hasinai to congregate around the mission, but they refused. This simple fact meant that the friars had to travel from farmstead to farmstead to proselytize and had to do it on a family-to-family basis. Thus, it was very difficult for the friars to institute their preferred teaching methods of communal recitation and memorization of doctrine and to establish a religious schedule. The friars could not round up the Natives for religious ceremonies or to teach doctrine; instead they had to wait for the Hasinai to come to them. Likewise, dispersed dwellings precluded missionary control over the daily activities of the Hasinai. This settlement pattern made the friars dependent on the generosity of the Hasinai for at least part of their food, for essential supplies, and for defense. These were important considerations because of the poor supply system that typified the early mission period before the development of San Antonio and because of the enduring threat of the French.

The Hasinai and the other Caddoan groups of the Red River could not modify their settlement pattern because it was intrinsic to their cosmology. Quite possibly the Hasinai were willing and maybe wanted to integrate others into their community, providing that these others did not disturb their "cosmological landscape" (Sabo 1998, 159–74). Evidence from Fr. Casañas as well as later evidence provided by Juan Sabeata, a Jumano and a frequent visitor to the Hasinai, also make it clear that the *xinesí*'s office restricted him to the area and likely to a specific spiritual ground (Wade 2003, 239).[2] For the Hasinai, including a Spanish community within their model of dispersed settlements was desirable and possible only if the Hasinai community's spiritual space retained its characteristics. These circumstances forced the friars to adopt a modified wilderness model of conversion that they could not sustain because the Hasinai were uncooperative and because the friars had to cover great distances to minister to them. Conversely, the friars could not use the urban-rural model as they did in Coahuila or Nuevo León because the Hasinai were free nations; they had not been conquered by force and were not subjugated as laborers. The mission had little to offer to the Hasinai. They grew abundant crops and were well organized politically, civilly, and spiritually. What the friars had to offer was a different belief and cosmology, and those the Hasinai rejected.

Other factors contributed to discontent among the Natives and the frustration of the friars. The principal archival source for this period is Fr. Casañas's 1691 *Relación*, a document of exceeding importance for understanding the early relationship between missionaries and Native groups in Texas. Casañas mentioned several events that likely contributed to conflicts between the missionaries and the Hasinai (1691, 103–23). The epidemic of 1691, poor harvests in 1691 and 1692, and a major flood that destroyed the Mission Santo Nombre de María, where Casañas resided, did not bode well for the relationship. These events could not but be interpreted as signs of foreboding, particularly for people who intently read the skies and for whom crops were so essential.

There were other issues as well. Fr. Casañas questioned and challenged the supreme spiritual authority, the *xinesí* (1691, 116). In a heated exchange,

Casañas tried to burn Hasinai sacra and scorned the *coninisi*, the two children who came from the other side of the heavens and whose role was to interface between the *xinesí* and the Hasinai Supreme Being, the Ayo Caddi Aymay. This exchange caused a confrontation between two elders, apparently women, who were present at the event. While one of the witnesses sided with Casañas, the other did not. This and other episodes during which Casañas and possibly the other friars questioned the cosmological and spiritual beliefs of the Hasinai and destroyed, or attempted to destroy, Hasinai sacra exemplify tactics of conversion that proved ineffective. Such tactics together with the natural disasters that befell the Hasinai during the three years the Spanish were present likely contributed to their final dismissal of the friars. Also, the Hasinai association of baptismal water with death ensured that the sacrament was administered only in *artículo mortis* and was even then controversial and unwelcome (117). In fact, speaking of the second period of missionization among the Hasinai, Fr. Ciprián acknowledged that all baptisms were administered to people who had died or were dying, half of whom were children (Leutenegger 1979, 50–51).

While Casañas, like most missionaries, interpreted events such as the speedy recovery of a baptized *xinesí* or the death of a hardcore shaman as God's timely and propitious intervention, he refrained from assigning meaning to the devastation caused by epidemics, floods, and crop failures. In the context of sign reading, the Hasinai had long practice and did not fail to attribute sinister meanings to the co-occurrence of the arrival of the friars and the disasters that had befallen their communities.

More pragmatic issues affected the relationship. The Hasinai had insisted on a settlement composed of Spanish families and did not want single males, showing they were aware of the Europeans' reputation for sexual misconduct. Yet during the first period, the settlement was composed of seven males—four friars and three soldiers—and the latter, according to the friars, were far from suitable. The Hasinai wanted a Spanish settlement with constituted families that would live side by side with them, afford a trade link to the Spanish in the Rio Grande and westward, confer prestige on them through exchange of goods and services, and establish the Spanish as partners in defense. In sum, the Hasinai wanted a prestigious ally, one that could help them deal with and control outside affairs, not one that aimed at controlling their domestic affairs. Their previous experience with the French in the 1680s had raised political and social expectations that the Spanish did not meet.

Despite these problems, in the first decade of the eighteenth century the

Hasinai traveled to the Rio Grande and insisted that the friars return, particularly Fr. Hidalgo, who earlier had spent about two years among them. Nothing could have pleased the Franciscans more than this request, and although they had to convince the crown of the advantages of reestablishing missions among the Hasinai, they finally succeeded. In 1716, the Spanish established several missions among the Hasinai and among other Caddoan-speaking groups located in the Red River area. Again, the presence of the French in and around the Red River was pivotal to the crown's assent.

This second conversion experiment, which included six missions among the Hasinai, did not fare any better, nor did Mission San Miguel de Los Adaes. But while the missions among the Hasinai were either closed or transplanted to San Antonio in 1731, Mission San Miguel remained a functional mission until 1773, when the Spanish closed it and the nearby presidio. San Miguel de los Adaes remained open because it was located on the border between Spanish and French territory and because it served the French, the Spanish, and the Natives. What short-term conversion did not accomplish, long-term presence may have done. Some of the descendents of the Adai community remain a Catholic enclave to this day.

It is useful to briefly compare the responses of the Hasinai and those of the Calusa to attempts to convert them. Despite the fact that the Jesuit archival materials on the Calusa are superior to those of Franciscans on the Hasinai, several points of comparison can be made. Although the settlement pattern of the Natives contributed to the difficulties of the missionaries, it may not have been the determining factor, and it seems to have mattered little for their work among the Calusa. Instead, the relentless refusal of the Calusa and the Hasinai to convert was paramount in the failure of the missionaries. Also, it seems that while the Hasinai were peremptory about their dismissal of the friars, they used less violent means.

The Jesuits' detailed documentation may reinforce the impression of more argumentative dueling between the Calusa and the missionaries than the Franciscan documentation does for the Hasinai. From Fr. Casañas's report it appears that early on the Hasinai were less prepared to challenge the missionaries, though both the Hasinai and the Calusa had intricate spiritual-cum-sociocultural structures. Both groups sought military, political, and trade connections; tried to balance their needs with the directives of the Spanish; and made some compromises. Apparently the arrival of the Europeans created severe political and leadership changes for both groups, because leaders took sides in deciding how best to deal with the conquerors.

The Rio Grande and San Antonio Missions: Eighteenth Century

From 1699 to 1703 the Franciscans established three missions in the Rio Grande area: San Juan Bautista, San Francisco Solano, and San Bernardo, all somewhat close to the modern town of Guerrero, Coahuila. The founding documents of these missions emphasized the need to introduce the Natives to agriculture to ensure that in a few years they would be self-sufficient and productive. In 1717–1718, Mission Solano was moved to San Antonio and was renamed Mission San Antonio de Valero, the first mission to be established in San Antonio by the Franciscan College of Querétaro and today is known as the Alamo. Mission Valero's founding was coeval with the establishment of the second wave of east Texas missions, but it aimed at hunter-gatherer populations that could not dismiss the friars as their Native brethren had. Instead, when the novelty of the mission and trinkets wore off or when Natives tired of the requirements imposed by a life that may have made little sense to them, some left, some perished, and others chose to stay.

Between 1717 and 1721, when the Marqués de Aguayo entered Texas in a tour de force designed to quash French hopes of controlling Texas territory, San Antonio was a small settlement and Mission Valero likely no more than an agglomeration of temporary wooden buildings (Heusinger 1936, 76–77). Natives could come and go as they pleased. There was minimal military protection, and without that, the friars could do little to force Natives to stay. The arrival of Aguayo and the establishment of the Presidio of San Antonio de Béxar and the Mission San José y San Miguel de Aguayo changed the situation. Presidial soldiers provided protection and enforcement, while San José provided support (de la Teja 1991, 31–35). It is significant that only after the arrival of Aguayo did the Apache openly and consistently express their displeasure with the Spanish presence by sticking arrow shafts in the ground marked with red rags (Wade 2003, 161). Until then, the Spanish in Texas were not a real threat to the Apache and the missions were more like temporary refuges than enclosures. It was also at this time that Aguayo established Mission Espíritu Santo de Zúñiga near the coast and the Presidio Nuestra Señora del Pilar de los Adaes and reestablished Mission Los Adaes, which had been closed due to a ruse attack by the French in 1719.

All the San Antonio missions were established and built for nomadic populations who made a living hunting and gathering, and except for San Francisco Xavier de Nájera the other five missions remained viable until they were secularized. These missions were set up as pueblos where the Natives were congregated and taught Christian doctrine and where they raised crops and cattle. Some Natives entered the missions willingly, but if they left, they were often brought back by force. The missions could survive only if there was enough food to feed the neophytes, and that meant that the Natives were required to remain and work in the missions. Many left or died. Although walled missions protected residents from exterior attack (a real concern from the late 1720s onward particularly because of the Apache), this solution also made it easier for the Spanish to control the population and harder for the Natives to leave. Later the walled missions were sometimes protected by artillery. However, the walls were built late in the mission period and the Apache threat was very serious from the 1720s to the 1740s. I suggest that the principal catalyst that led to the transformation of walled missions into fortress-like compounds was the 1758 attack of San Sabá mission, which resulted in the destruction of the mission and the killing of two Franciscan friars and several other people. A letter by Fr. Mariano de los Dolores written immediately after the attack asked for ammunition and emphasized the need for a larger defense force, expert Native warriors, and his expectation that the Province would be defended with the available resources and with the *allied* Apache (de los Dolores 1758).

Be that as it may, the urban-rural model of conversion mutated into a built environment that incorporated features of the hacienda and the presidio, which addressed the need to enclose a large labor force and provide protection from outside attacks. This physical arrangement permitted closer monitoring of the Native population, which I contend was further emphasized later in Alta California (see also Jackson 2005, 300–1). This model, which came to be known as "the Texas method" (*el método de Tejas*), was developed over time, applied in other areas, and deemed ineffective by some Franciscans (Fr. Pedro Font as quoted in Brown 2006, 114). In 1777, Fr. Font, for instance, evaluated the model as being impracticable for settling the land "which is one of the purposes of the missions, that after eighty years in which the Holy Colegio had that field in its charge, and after our Lord King spent over two million [pesos] upon those missions with their presidio garrisons, without getting any especial temporal advantage from that country, the moment they were given up and their administration was changed, they became uninhabited" (114, brackets in the original). Fr. Font was comparing the Texas model, which aimed at hunter-gatherer populations, to the models used with horticultural and agricultural Native groups in the southwest pueblo country, and he aptly noted that "the Indians of Texas, working in common and for the community and even though their bellies were well filled, did not view [the mission] as their own affair, and consequently did not contract an affection for the land" (114). In contrast, the Natives of the Pimería Alta, where Fr. Font was staying, worked for the mission but "labor[ed] also for themselves and so contract[ed] an affection for the piece of land they cultivate[d] and [held] as their own" (114). Fr. Font noted that the Texas model was being used in Monterrey, California, and that the model was only "applicable . . . when Indians who have never had any knowledge of cultivation" had to be enticed by food supplies "and even then it must not be forever but for a limited time" (115). Still, Fr. Font considered the control imposed in Texas and the submissiveness of the Native population it produced as a good and essential measure for maintaining the authority of the friars and securing the missions (115). Regarding issues of control, as he recognized, he was preaching to the choir because his addressee was Fr. Diego Jiménez (Ximénez), a veteran of Texas missions who had been deeply involved with San Sabá and the Nueces Canyon missions built for the Apache.

In Texas the problem of the *encomenderos* did not exist, although ranching became a profitable endeavor for settlers, particularly after the 1750s. From the outset, the missions, particularly those in San Antonio and on the coast, were the major owners of land, cattle, and assets. The frequent campaigns of the Spanish soldiers and citizenry to "punish" and round up Natives, particularly the Apache, resulted in the hatred of the Natives (*el odio de los Yndios*), as those campaigns aimed not only at obtaining slaves (*piezas*), particularly women and children, but also horses and hides (Habig 1978, 64). In general, though, the Franciscans in Texas did not purposely displace populations from one region to another, except in the beginning when they knew little about the province or when they moved a mission.

In the 1750s, one friar discussed the different ways Natives congregated in missions in terms of the effectiveness of conversion (Anonymous 1756). The first type occurred when most of the members of a group came or were brought to the mission on a single occasion. The second type took place when the captains of nations joined the mission with their families, and the third type took place when only one or two families entered the mission. The first seldom occurred, the second was the most successful when the friars courted the leaders of groups and therefore enticed the larger portion of the group, and the third occurred frequently but was not very successful in terms of converting the whole group. The first method required the cooperation of the army and it raises the question of how the friars knew the extent of the group. An assessment (Lopez 1786) of the Texas missions made by a Franciscan close to the end of the mission period pointed out that previously the missionaries had traveled with army escorts to proselytize and bring Natives back to the mission, where, according to Fr. Lopez, they

Figure 7.1. Old Fort of Mission San José, San Antonio, Texas. Robert Runyon Photograph Collection, image number 04149. Courtesy of the Center for American History, University of Texas at Austin.

were taught doctrine. If they decided to receive baptism, they remained in the mission. In the 1780s, the missionaries no longer had the cooperation of the army nor did they have sufficient food to feed new converts because there were so few to perform the work needed. As the friar stated, the missions were suffering in both the formal and the material (*formal y material*) sense (22).

The case of Antonio Arcón, a ladino who had been the governor of Mission Valero, exemplifies the ramifications of the problem (Alegre y Capetillo n.d.). When Arcón fled the mission with his family and others, the soldier escort at the mission was so small it was unable to bring them back. Arcón, who was well informed about the routine of the missions and presidios, joined a coalition of northern groups as a chief (*caudillo*) and helped and guided it in its forays against the Spanish. When neophytes left a mission, the mission lost Native labor power, and those who left possessed useful knowledge about the mission and had the ability to raid its assets.

When mission numbers declined so low that the friars were unable to run the mission, new "converts" were brought in. Unquestionably the objective was conversion, but it is disingenuous to pretend that two friars and a handful of Natives could perform the labor needed to grow crops, raise cattle, and maintain a prosperous mission.

A Case of Possession and Ethnicity: The Pamaque

In the early 1750s, a group of Pamaque Natives led by Juan Joseph left Mission San Juan Capistrano in Texas for Mission Vizarrón in Coahuila. Mission Vizarrón, administered by Fr. José Antonio Rodríguez, belonged to the Franciscan College of Xalisco and was part of Coahuila, while Mission Capistrano, located in San Antonio, Texas, was administered by Fr. Juan Domingos de Arricivita and belonged to the College of Querétaro. Although it was the Pamaque who relocated, at least two other groups were involved: the Painacan (Pagnacane) and the Piguique (Anonymous 1756, 1402). The controversy was about the relationships between several groups—the Pausane, the Pamaque, the Orejones, the Tenipaguai (Tinapihuaya), the Viayan (Biayan), the Pagnacane, and the Piguique (Pihuique)—as well as what these designations meant (see Campbell and Campbell 1985, 30–31, 34–35, 37–38, 57 for some of those relationships). Were these nations, that is, larger groupings of groups with very fluid leadership, or were they bands, autonomous extended families? Who was Pamaque, and were the members of extended families who had intermarried with other extended families that went by a different name to be considered Pamaque? According to the reports of the friars (Anonymous n.d.b; de Guadalupe 1754a, 1754b; Rabago y Theran 1754; Vizarraras 1754), the Pamaque had allied and intermarried with the Orejones prior to entering any mission, but several members had intermarried with people from other named groups such as the Viayan and Tenipaguai. The juridical need to resolve the problem of possession between missions Vizarrón and Capistrano brought to light the complexity of Native ethnic and territorial boundaries and had the friars scrambling for evidence that would bolster their respective legal positions.

The Pamaques' simple change of residence resulted in a complex debate over ownership of the Natives and Native ownership of mission lands and assets. There were four basic points in contention. First, which mission was founded first and which mission was established for the Pamaque? Second, what were the legal implications of the Pamaques' relocation, since the law did not permit Natives to move from mission to mission? Third, could a mission founded for a particular set of Native groups that later accepted another group claim the latter group if the baptismal books showed that no member of that group had been baptized earlier elsewhere? Fourth, possession of mission lands and some assets were given to the groups for which the missions were founded. Would these groups lose right of possession to those assets if they abandoned the mission? These were essential legal issues and both colleges pled their case using various arguments and data. The acrimonious debate raged around two fundamental questions: who "possessed" the "Indians" and what was their group ethnicity? The answers to these questions were essential because if Natives were allowed to leave missions such as Mission Capistrano, it would destroy the missions because it would leave them without a labor force. As the Querétaro friars saw it, their efforts to convert, feed, and clothe the Natives gave the college "ownership" of the Pamaque (Abassolo 1750; Guardian y Discretorio n.d., 6). The essential evidence for possession and ethnicity was the baptismal registry, and Mission Capistrano's register showed that Pamaque Natives had been baptized as early as 1733, three years before Mission Vizarrón was established (1736), legitimizing the claim of Capistrano.

A memorial, possibly prepared by Fr. Mariano de los Dolores, sheds light on the process and procedures for establishing a mission (Anonymous 1756). The writer assumed that Native possession ceremonies took place at the request of missionaries and stated that missionaries gave possession of a mission's lands to specific groups of Natives because they expected those Natives to convert. The missionaries, however, were so eager to obtain Natives (but knew so little about them) that they took any small sign as indication that the Natives were willing to convert. As the writer points out, the friars did not know who belonged to a nation, nor did they understand what "nation" meant to the Natives (1400). When a group of Natives joined or were brought to a mission without a commitment from their captains, the full nation did not join, which meant that different groups of the same nation could join different missions.[3] To stress his point, the writer stated that even though Mission San José had given possession to the Pampopa, Tacame, and Tiopane, it could not convert them (1401). The Tiopane (who were called Chayopine, according to the writer) were actually converted at San Juan Capistrano, the Tacame at Concepción, and the Pampopa at San Juan Bautista on the Rio Grande. In fact, according to the writer, only catechumen or Christian Natives should be considered mission Natives and only the sacramental registers should be used to verify their statuses and be used to establish possession rights. Possession ceremonies could not be held for Natives who entered the mission after its founding; acts of possession were to be understood simply as foundational acts that empowered the Natives present at the ceremony. The obvious implication was that acts of possession were not to exclude groups that joined a mission after its founding.

This unusual legal case illustrates how the Natives and their labor were essential to the survival of a mission. They influenced its future, but they also constituted its past (Delumeau 1977, 151). Unlike the death of a neophyte, departure, in a sense, rendered null the labor of the past, because abandonment was rejection. Likewise, departure forfeited a Native group's right to the mission's lands. On the other hand, holding founding ceremonies for specific groups did not necessarily mean that those groups were the only ones that had rights to the mission. The case also brings to the fore the importance of baptismal records; they were not just individual religious, legal, and ethnic records but were also group or tribal records that asserted property rights because they committed and entitled the group through the baptism of individual members. The preoccupation of the friars with re-searching the genealogy and ethnicity of the groups involved is rare because in this case, it mattered who had joined which mission and when.

The Pamaque wanted to change missions because they had kinfolk at Mission Vizarrón. Today several Native American groups claim to be descen-dents from San Antonio mission groups. One such group is the Pamaque Band of Mission San Juan (Thoms, Alexander, and Benavides 2001, 12), also known as the Pamaque Clan of Coahuila y Tejas. In 2003, the Pamaque Clan of Coahuila y Tejas filed a letter of intent to request federal recognition (Bureau of Indian Affairs 2003). Genealogical research conducted by Adán Benavides on a family connected to Mission San Juan but not necessarily associated with the Pamaque did not produce appreciable results (2001, 65–73). Benavides concluded, "This study failed to link descendants of San-tiago Díaz and Josefa Gutiérrez to Indian neophytes of Mission San Juan Capistrano" (73). Nevertheless the result was based primarily on censuses and sacramental records. Then, as now, the value of sacramental records as genealogical tools and legal instruments continues to be paramount in as-sessing and validating ethnic identity.

The Pamaque were not unique. A similar case occurred with the Pam-popa when Missions San Juan Bautista (on the Rio Grande) and San José y San Miguel de Aguayo (in San Antonio) disputed who "owned" the Pam-popa. Apart from arguing that the Pampopa belonged to the jurisdiction of Coahuila because their lands and dwellings were located in that area, the officials at San Juan Bautista also argued that the Pampopa had been con-gregated there by Captain Diego Ramón in 1715, six years before the found-ing of the San José mission, and that the Pampopa had planted crops and in doing so had taken possession of the mission lands (Anonymous n.d.a). In this case, de facto possession was argued on the basis of land use. In addi-tion, Mission San José was experiencing problems and could not convert the Pampopa. Yet, according to the documentation presented by Feliz Almaráz, the 1727 San Juan Bautista baptismal registry does not include the Pampopa, although they do appear in the registry for 1738 (1979, 51–53). Aside from the debates over ownership, the fact that planting seed was understood as taking possession and belonging to a mission underscores the integration of the religious with the economic.

The State of the Missions

The religious and economic state of the missions was generally evaluated through timely mission reports. These are good indicators of the material conditions of the missions and of the use and extent of Native labor, but they are poor indicators of the living conditions of the neophytes and of the work of conversion.

A mission report prepared by Fr. Benito de Santa Ana in February 1740 provides ample information about the environment and location of the five San Antonio missions but does not record information about the buildings of the various missions or about Native housing. An epidemic had ravaged the mission population[4] and between those who had perished and those who had survived or joined the mission afterward, 2,529 people had been baptized and 816 remained at the missions (Habig 1978, 52–65). A report made in December 1740 by the commander of the San Antonio presidio stated that the San Antonio missions had only thatched-roof buildings, some of which were in disrepair, and that most did not have dwellings for the 987 Natives housed in all the missions (79–82). A mission report made five years later provides important information about the state of the Texas missions from the beginning of missionization through the middle of the eighteenth century. The Autos de Visita (Xavier Ortiz 1745; see also Almaráz 1989, 15) show that at Missions San Juan Bautista, San Bernardo, San Antonio de Valero, San Juan Capistrano, San Francisco de la Espada, N. S. de la Concepción, and La Punta de Lampazos, a Coahuila mission included in the report, 5,404 Natives had been baptized, of which 681 were from La Punta de Lampazos mission. At Valero, the only mission addressed in detail, the Native dwellings were made of adobe and the mission had enough land to plant five fanegas of corn (eight bushels) and one of cotton; it also had a garden where watermelons and melons were grown. Before an uprising, the mission had 500 head of cattle, but since the uprising the herd had been reduced to 208. The same was true for the sheep and goats; only 550 sheep and 200 goats were left. The report emphasizes the incapacity of the Natives to govern and feed themselves and expresses the need for the friars to continue managing the affairs and the property of the Natives, albeit reluctantly. In 1749, Fr. Ygnacio Ciprián reported on Mission San José, the only Zacatecan mission in San Antonio (Habig 1978, 96–99). According to the friar, the mission housed 200 Natives, had 2,000 head of cattle and 1,000 sheep and

Figure 7.2. Mission Concepción, San Antonio, Texas, 1917. Image number 04142. Courtesy of the Center for American History, University of Texas at Austin.

harvested 1,500 fanegas of corn annually (2,400 bushels), though the Natives could produce more if they wished.

A mission report from 1727 (Almaráz 1979, 13–14) shows that the buildings of Mission San Juan Bautista on the Rio Grande were rather substantial and that the Natives had flat-roofed houses and adobe dwellings, perhaps because San Juan Bautista had been in existence far longer than the San Antonio missions. A 1756 report from Fr. Francisco Ortiz indicates that San Juan Bautista continued to do well and that Mission San Bernardo had been moved to a better location nearby and was being rebuilt (Almaráz 1979, 23). The convent and two granaries had been built to form a crescent-shaped compound, but construction of Native housing had been postponed to the next phase of work.

In 1759, the Texas Querétaro missions were again evaluated (Alegre y Capetillo[5] 1759). From 1700 to 1759, San Juan Bautista registered a total of 436 residents. In those six decades, 436 people had been baptized but only twenty had received baptism since the last inspection in 1756. From 1700 to 1759, 1,580 people had been buried, of which 40 had been buried since

1756. At the time of the report, the mission housed 206 people and some Pampopa from Mission San José. The mission buildings and furnishings were in good condition except for the church tower, which had six bells but was in disrepair. The complex had a weaving room with four looms, a carpenter's shop, a kitchen, a granary that stored 1,300 fanegas of corn (about 2,080 bushels), and a *ranchería* (mission ranch). The pueblo had one row of Native houses. Mission San Bernardo housed 376 people constituted in 104 families (an average of 3.6 persons per family). The dwellings are not described but they were furnished with chests, griddles (*comales*), pottery vessels (*ollas*), metates, and large metal pots (*calderas*). The complex had carpentry and masonry shops and a room where Natives wove cotton and wool fabrics.

At the time of the report, Mission Espada had 220 people. Seven hundred and sixty Natives had been baptized since the mission had been founded, 120 since the 1756 visit. Four hundred and forty one Natives had been buried, 69 since 1756, which means that over half of those baptized had either received the sacrament in *artículo mortis* or had since perished. The small church was built of stone and rubble (*cal y canto*) and the complex had fields and weaving shops. The Natives lived in rows of stone houses and another pueblo was being built.

San Juan Capistrano housed 226 people (in fifty-nine families, an average of 3.8 people per family), a number that excluded those at Vizarrón and those who had fled to the wild (*monte*). Since the founding, 812 people had been baptized, 64 after 1756. Eight "infidels" had also been baptized. In total, 557 people had been buried, 72 after 1756, a higher number than those baptized. The report described a building that was serving as the church but stated that the church had not been erected yet. The library contained eighty-one books. The Natives at Mission Concepción lived in two rows of houses, some made of wattle and daub and some of stone. The dwellings were furnished with seventy-two chests, twenty pottery vessels, fifty griddles, sixty metates, and forty large metal pots.

Mission San Antonio housed 286 people. Since its founding, 1,406 people had been baptized, 82 after 1756. Likewise 1,057 people had been buried, 80 since 1756, again a number close to the number of baptisms. The complex had a convent, cells, carpentry and masonry shops, a room with four weaving looms, storage rooms, stables, and a sugar-cane mill with all the appurtenances to make sugar cones such as ladles and molds. Natives at the mission planted maize, beans, chile, cotton, and sugar cane. The Native pueblo was formed by several rows of stone houses outlining a plaza. The dwellings were furnished with chests, griddles, large pottery jars, and metates. The *Autos de*

Visita (Alegre y Capetillo 1759) greatly emphasizes the quality and beauty of the church furnishings but accords little space to Native matters or to the work of conversion.

A report prepared in 1762 by Fr. Mariano de los Dolores y Viana[6], who was the father president of the Texas Querétaro missions and had extensive knowledge of the province (de los Dolores et al. 1762, 38–76; Leutenegger 1985, 328–54), highlights fundamental problems with the Franciscan missionary system and lays bare the conundrum of the friars. All missions had a convent, a sacristy, missionary quarters, a refectory, a kitchen, storage rooms, and specialized working rooms such as weaving rooms, although the size and number of friars' cells and working rooms varied. Most buildings were in good condition, but the church at Valero had collapsed and Espada's church was not complete. The Native housing compounds at Valero, Concepción, and Espada had either stone houses or straw dwellings; Capistrano had only straw houses. The Native dwellings at Valero were clearly superior to all others since the report emphasizes that the houses were provided with doors, windows, beds, and chests, luxuries in an austere environment. Missions Valero and Concepción had rock walls and fences enclosing the Natives' living quarters, but there is no mention of a stone wall surrounding the compound as there is in a later report of 1785. All missions had at least one ranch away from the mission where cattle and horses were kept. In total, the missions had about 1,164 horses and mares, 33 mules and donkeys, 12,000 sheep and goats, and about 2,987 head of cattle. The granaries held about 3,700 fanegas of corn (about 5,920 bushels), over 110 fanegas of beans (about 176 bushels), and unspecified amounts of cotton, wool, chiles, and salt. The inventory, which was issued in March, presumably shows the crop surplus that was still available after the winter, close to its lowest point in the season.

Since the founding of Mission Valero, 1,972 Natives had been baptized, of which 1,247 were children. At the time of the report, the mission had 275 Natives. At Mission Concepción 792 people had been baptized, 558 had died, and 207 Natives were left. At Mission Capistrano, 847 had been baptized and 203 people were living at the mission. At Mission Espada, 815 people had been baptized, 513 had died, and 207 remained at the mission. The total Native population at the missions was 892 people with an average of 223 people in each mission, excluding Mission San José. Not allowing for spoilage, the amount of corn in storage would provide about four fanegas of corn (2.13 bushels per month) per person until the next harvest, an amount insufficient for survival. Judging from the number of Natives normally present at missions, and as a rough estimate, it is possible that the San

Antonio missions could not be run with less than about 200 people per mission, of which probably one-quarter to one-third needed to be young strong males. In December 1788, though, the five San Antonio missions (San José included) housed only 290 Natives, of which 114 were at San José, leaving a scant 176 people in the other four Querétaro missions. Abandonment of the Texas Province was a reasonable option.

Like other reports, Fr. Mariano's report dwelled on extensive descriptions of the churches, particularly the church ornaments and other paraphernalia (de los Dolores et al. 1762, 38–76). His emphasis on gilded tabernacles, silver chalices, and exotic cloths cannot be overlooked, although it is completely understandable that the appearance of the church was a matter of pride, certainly for the friars and possibly for the Natives. The report also pointedly stressed the economic endeavors and situation of the missions, their wealth and manufacturing capabilities as self-sustaining enterprises. The contrast between these descriptions and the time and space devoted to the work of conversion and Native housing and furnishings is conspicuous. Native dwellings had minimal furnishings (griddles, metates and manos, kettles, and clay pots), and only the report for Mission Valero mentions beds and chests. To these should be added the clothes furnished the Natives, but these, as well as the food Natives consumed, were produced by their own labor under the management of the missionaries. Besides, the basic king's ration included clothing.

In 1785, the father president of the Texas missions reported on the missions at the request of Viceroy Conde de Galvéz (Lopez 1786). This report included an estimation of the monetary value of the various missions and their properties. Mission Valero was laid out as a quadrangle (*en quadro*) surrounded by a stone wall. This wall served as the back wall for the fifteen or sixteen Native dwellings made of wattle and daub (*madera y tierra*). The granary was built to contain 2,000 fanegas of corn (3,200 bushels) and 200 or more fanegas of beans (320 bushels). The sacristy of the old church was being used for religious services because the work on a new church had stopped due to lack of workers. Fifty-two Native people were left at the mission, and these were of mixed ethnicity because most had married blacks and other ethnic groups (*mulatos y mestizos*), but all were the offspring of Natives who had been baptized as adults. The church and its furnishings were valued at 28,000 pesos.

Mission Concepción was also built in a quadrangle surrounded by a stone and mud wall that served as the back wall for the Native houses. There were twenty-three Native dwellings with flat roofs, some of which were in poor shape but were easily reparable. In 1783, the Native dwellings had all collapsed, but they had been rebuilt. Seventy-one people were left at the mission, and most were the offspring of individuals who had been baptized as adults. The church and sacristy and their furnishings were valued at 33 to 34 thousand pesos. The granary, which was fifteen to twenty varas long and eight or nine wide, was valued at 1,000 pesos.

A wall of stone and mud encircled Mission San José, the only original Zacatecas mission. The Native dwellings ran contiguously and each was equipped with a kitchen. One hundred thirty-eight people were at the mission, thirty-two of which were Borrado Natives brought in from the coast in 1784. The Native population of this mission had suffered greatly with the spread of syphilis (*bubas*). The church and sacristy and their furnishings were valued at 30 to 40 thousand pesos.

Mission San Juan Capistrano likewise was set in a walled quadrangle against which were set the Native houses. These houses were mostly of stone and mud with flat roofs. Fifty-eight Natives were left. The church and sacristy and their furnishings were valued at 3,000 pesos, but another church and sacristy complex had begun to be constructed on which 3,000 pesos had been spent, excluding the value of the labor of the Natives. Construction had stopped because of the lack of Natives (*la causa de haverse parado esta Fabrica, es la misma que lo ha sido en San Antonio, que es la falta de Yndios*). Mission Espada was also in the shape of a quadrangle surrounded by a stone and mud wall that constituted the back wall for the Native dwellings. The Native houses were also constructed of stone and mud. Fifty-seven people were left at the mission. They had suffered a serious epidemic of measles in 1780 and were much affected by syphilis. The church and sacristy were valued at three to four thousand pesos.

Mission Espíritu Santo, then located in modern Goliad, Texas, also was built as a walled square; the Native dwellings had either flat roofs or roofs thatched with zacate. One hundred sixteen people were left at the mission. The report stated that twelve years earlier (1773), the mission had had over 15,000 cattle branded and counted at the entry to the corral and many more unbranded cattle. As of the date of the report, the number of branded cattle did not exceed 3,000, and that number together with the unbranded cattle did not surpass 15,000. The church and sacristy and their furnishings were valued at 12,000 pesos. As for Mission Rosario, the report states that it had been closed and demolished[7] because the coastal Natives had run away, incited by a rebellious and dangerous Native who was the best Castilian speaker. Apparently this ladino was so persuasive and his influence so widespread that he was responsible for the decision of many Natives fleeing other missions. The wealth of Mission Rosario was in its cattle and horses.

Of the 10,000 head of branded cattle there were none left; the Apache and the coastal Natives had taken them all.

The various reports make clear that all missions were walled compounds. In fact, the 1780 instructions for the establishment of pueblos on the Colorado River issued by the comandante general of the Províncias Internas, Caballero de Croix, stipulated that each pueblo had to have an exterior wall with a tower at each of the four corners (Matson and Fontana 1977, 102). These reports also place great stock on the appearance of the church and on religious ceremonies as well as on the economic status of the missions and the value of mission churches and sacristies and their furnishings. Little is said about the Natives' living conditions and even less about conversion practices. They indicate a clear concern with the small number of neophytes, the shortage of Native labor, and the capacity of the missions to remain self-sustaining. These preoccupations presage the content of Fr. José Rafael Oliva's report issued two years later, which addressed the thorny question of whether or not the Franciscans should abandon the Texas missions (Leutenegger 1977, 227–54).

Oliva's dissertation used the traditional form of questions and answers followed by a conclusion and focused on the problem of the friars' management of the economic affairs of the missions (*temporalidades*) (Leutenegger 1977, 227–54). What transpires from the arguments is the wish to continue missionary work in Texas but the need to free the Franciscans from the burden of managing the missions. Fr. Oliva understood the Franciscan mission not as the need to show numbers of converts but as the mandate to be steadfast and demonstrate conversion work even when no one was converted (*Y aunque sean mui pocas las almas, en quienes se propaga, no esta a cargo del Misionero, ni Dios [?] le dice, que convierta muchas almas, si no que trabaje en convertirlas, y no levante la mano de la labor, y mas que no convierta a ninguno*) (228).

Like all others, Fr. Oliva stated that the Natives were incapable of running the mission and that without the continuous intervention of the friars, the settlers would dispossess the Natives of everything they owned, including mission belongings and properties. While the second statement is certainly correct, as was witnessed when missions were secularized in the different provinces of New Spain, the first statement is debatable. The typical complement of two friars and two soldiers was not the ones who ran the daily activities of the missions. Native governors, fiscals, cowboys, shepherds, farm workers, cooks, and weavers ran the missions. There is no question that the missionaries supervised the overall schedule of tasks, although most of this on-site management was entrusted to Native officials. Whether or not Native officials could succeed in trade and dealings with the outside communities is another question. But there is no evidence that any such program was ever tried under the supervision of the missionaries in the Texas missions, although in some instances the friars entrusted the Natives with seed and animals to use as personal property.

Fr. Oliva did make three important points. First, he argued that missionaries were not taught how to be economic managers; their didactic and religious education was geared toward conversion activities (Leutenegger 1977, 233–34). He also noted that while some missionaries had been good stewards, others had not, but that status and power were attached to excellence in management as if those skills were intrinsic to Franciscan missionizing. Second, he stressed that economic conditions in Texas had changed (245–47). While the missions had formerly held a monopoly on corn and cattle products and could sell their surplus almost without any competition and at good prices, this was no longer the case. Faced with increasing difficulties, debts, and poor management, the friar recommended that the crown appoint honest stewards to take over the management of the missions. The problem was finding an honest steward.

Finally, Fr. Oliva addressed the essential issue and reminded his superiors of the old Franciscan debate between Conventuals and Spirituals (Leutenegger 1977, 243, 246). This time the rift was not about having an abode and books, though it was still about poverty and the appropriate role of the missionary. As Fr. Oliva saw it, the mission system required the missionary to be a worldly and efficient manager who made the mission a productive enterprise, but he, and others, wished to be poor again and return to the teaching of the Christian doctrine, the work of conversion, and the shelter of their cells and books. Referring to the management of economic affairs, Fr. Oliva stated, "How many poor missionaries in this world have given themselves to the path of an outside life, indulgent, secular and scandalous because they lacked the fervor obtained from religious retreat? Are we safe from such danger amidst this disorder?" (242) For Fr. Oliva, the security of the convent, a secluded corner in his cell, and immersion in theological works provided the mission and the missionary with the route to the path of conversion for which both were intended.

Fr. Oliva was not unique. Similar questions had been raised by Fr. Font in 1777, after the transfer of the Sonoran Jesuit missions to the Franciscans and in the wake of the plans to establish missions in the area of the Gila and Colorado Rivers. Fr. Font did not question the appropriateness of the role of the missionary as a mission manager but he questioned the need to demonstrate conversion by the number of baptisms performed. He did not equivocate; sustaining the missions and preserving "the faith in the Indians" was a continuous process and the purpose of missionary work (Brown 2006, 112).

Conclusion

The colonization of Texas started as a political and military reaction to French encroachment. Except for the Rio Grande missions that were part of Coahuila, the earliest period of mission-building was concentrated on the east Texas Caddoan-speaking groups and was a failure for the friars and a disappointment for the Caddoans. Despite multiple mission establishments throughout Texas, the San Antonio missions anchored the major settlement in Texas and remained viable throughout the eighteenth century.

Inspections and reports on the state of the missions emphasized the missionaries' constant preoccupation and special emphasis on the appearance of the mission, the mission's liturgical accoutrements and sacra, and on economic conditions. Comparatively little was said about the work of conversion or about Native housing and living conditions, except for totals of baptisms and burials and minimalist inventories of dwellings and furnishings.

By the 1760s, if not before, some of these missions were surrounded by walls which reflected as much defensive needs as the organization of the environment where Native neophytes resided. By the 1780s all the missions were surrounded by tall walls. It is often the case that defensive needs become the trigger for the exercise of power and social control. The architectural arrangement of the church-convent complex, Native housing, and other buildings structured the activities and the flow of people inside the compound, while sleeping arrangements and work assignments resulted in gender and age segregation, strategies that were part of the Texas method and that were perfected in Alta California. This architectural arrangement confined and monitored mission Natives. Once in a while, Natives were allowed to leave with permission of the friar, and the friars made annual trips to the "wild" to proselytize but mostly to bring back a new crop of potential neophytes. But the Natives were restless and cared little for Spanish juridical and mission boundaries, as the case of the Pamaque shows. A simple decision on the part of Natives to change their "ranchería" would engender questions of identity, possession, and labor that were always at the heart of the mission system but that were generally subsumed under a civilizing discourse of conversion.

A good mission was self-sustaining and profitable, but some missionaries found the work of managing the missions a distraction from the task of saving souls and the source of corruption and problems. Yearning for solitude, prayer, and apostolic works, discontented friars such as Fr. Oliva searched for a solution that finally came with the decline and closing of the Texas Franciscan missions. Alta California was to be the next experiment but one that would be rooted in the Jesuit work in Baja California.

Baja California

Jesuits and Franciscans

The Jesuits began their missionary work in Baja California in 1697 after Jesuit Fathers Eusebio Francisco Kino and Juan María de Salvatierra won permission to enter the peninsula. This was about a century after the Jesuits worked with the Calusa in Florida and seven years after the first Franciscan missions were established in central Texas. The authorization to missionize was made possible because the crown was not to spend any revenue for the enterprise, as all expenses were to be borne by the income from the Pious Fund.[1] This single fact affected the way the Jesuits approached conversion and how the crown and civil society viewed and evaluated Jesuit activities, and it may have been one of the underlying reasons for the expulsion of the Jesuits from the colonial world in December 1767. After the departure of the Jesuits, the Franciscans took over the management of the Baja California missions for a time.

The work of the Society of Jesus in Baja California was characterized by the adoption of several strategies quite possibly uniquely suited to the environmental and cultural conditions of the area (for a different analysis, see Jackson 2005, 55). Despite the fact that in the long run conversion results were little different from elsewhere, strategies such as the doctrinal rotational system sustained the financial health of the missions and had the potential to let Native populations retain their cultural moorings. Furthermore, the policy of not moving missionaries around and the existence of the Pious Fund enabled the society to be consistent in its on-site policies and permitted its members to retain considerable control over the management of the missions, the army, and the application of justice (Crosby 1994, 19, 158). Environmental factors, epidemics, attrition, resistance, and politics took their toll on the Native populations, on the material welfare of the missions, and on the work of conversion. Despite those problems and large population losses, when the Franciscans took over the Baja California missions in 1767, the missions were viable (263). The problems of mission growth versus mission sustainability and contraction due to attrition, population loss, and desertion were not compatible with the policies of the colonial empire. Sustaining a mission is a very different proposition than founding one, and the long-term management of the missions by the Jesuits established patterns and expectations with which neither the Natives nor the Franciscans could, or would, cope.

To begin it is useful to survey the interactions between Native populations and the Jesuits and analyze the strategies the Jesuits used to convert the hunter-gatherer groups in Baja California. To appraise the condition of the Baja California missionary program five years after the departure of the Jesuits and examine the decline of the missions, I use both a report made after the Franciscan takeover and before the missions were entrusted to the Dominicans in 1773 and sources that describe an event that led to a confrontation between Natives, Franciscans, and civil authorities.

The Jesuits: 1697–1767

As Father Burrus[2] noted, the viceroy's authorization letter is an essential document in understanding the extent of authority and responsibilities granted to, and assumed by, the Jesuits (1984, 22). The document privileged the Jesuits entering California as if they were "other superior commanders and soldiers of royal presidios and armies. The service in California will be reckoned as though it were given in time of actual war" (25). The Jesuits were God's soldiers, and as such, they were to provide for themselves, for the missions, and for the military protection they wished to have, and they were "to appoint, in the name of His Majesty, ministers of justice" (25). The full panoply of legislative and military controls was to be determined and financed by the Jesuits in consultation with the Spanish viceroyalty. Thus, until 1716, most of the soldiers in Baja California were supported by alms collected by the priests. These arrangements, which changed over time but established early patterns of conduct, permitted the Jesuits to have unusual control over soldiers and eliminated most of the acrimony between church and army that poisoned relations elsewhere.

As an example, for most of the 1690s to 1740s, Captain Esteban Rodrigues Lorenzo of Portugal was in command of the military and had a good and close relationship with the fathers (Crosby 1994, 68–70, 302–3). Lorenzo's large family was deeply involved in the Jesuit program of conversion. One of Lorenzo's sons, Bernardo, eventually took over command of the presidio, and Lorenzo's wife treated the sick and taught Native women to read, sew, and embroider (Burrus 1984, 92). The Jesuits were fully aware of the difference a good relationship and control over military issues made, as Father

Clemente Guillén clearly expressed in 1737: "It is less of a burden to have the Jesuit California treasurer pay the salaries and retain the presidio than to expose ourselves to the inconvenience of not having control over the government" (107). Father Sebastián de Sistiaga was more blunt: "A disgruntled captain in these far-away places is a veritable monster; or to put it better, a source of endless trouble" (133). Control over the military was beneficial to the missionaries and the soldiers and prevented contradictory policies. It also deprived the Natives of the room to maneuver they had in other places, where they manipulated hostilities between the two institutions.

From 1697 to 1768, the Jesuits established thirteen missions in Baja California (Burrus 1984, 60) among hunting and gathering populations. Unlike most Franciscans, Jesuit Fathers generally remained in the same mission or labored in different missions in the same area for decades, often until they died. This fact, coupled with innovative strategies, effective management of the order's finances, persistent efforts to disseminate conversion work, and the intellectual cosmopolitanism of the order, produced an unusual combination of faith, idealism, and pragmatics.

Generally, Native villages were located several hours away from the missions, and sometimes Native settlements aggregated with others or the Natives were persuaded to move to a location closer to the mission. The establishment of San José de Comondú is a case in point: the central mission pueblo had three dependent pueblos located respectively at half a league (1.3 miles), seven leagues (18.2 miles), and 10 leagues (26 miles) away. Father Sistiaga explained that "the numerous settlements, formerly widely scattered in every direction and inhabited by only a few persons, have been gathered into these towns" (Burrus 1984, 140). These relocations, which the fathers said were voluntary, likely agglomerated extended families into artificial social units, placed a premium on obtaining enough food to sustain larger settlements, and positioned enemy groups in proximity. Still, they provided Native groups with a modicum of independence and protected their ability to continue traditional practices that otherwise would have been under continuous scrutiny. Writing in 1744, Father Sistiaga saw the Natives' willingness to tolerate and mingle with their former enemies as proof of their conversion (142). That may have been the case, but the effectiveness of the soldiers in putting down revolts led groups to sue for peace, accept the imposed conditions, and, by inference, accede to conversion (99).

The Jesuits implemented a rotational system that had features in common with the European missions of the seventeenth century (Delumeau 1977, 192). This conversion system, whereby different Native rancherías visited the mission at different times, probably prevented confrontations between

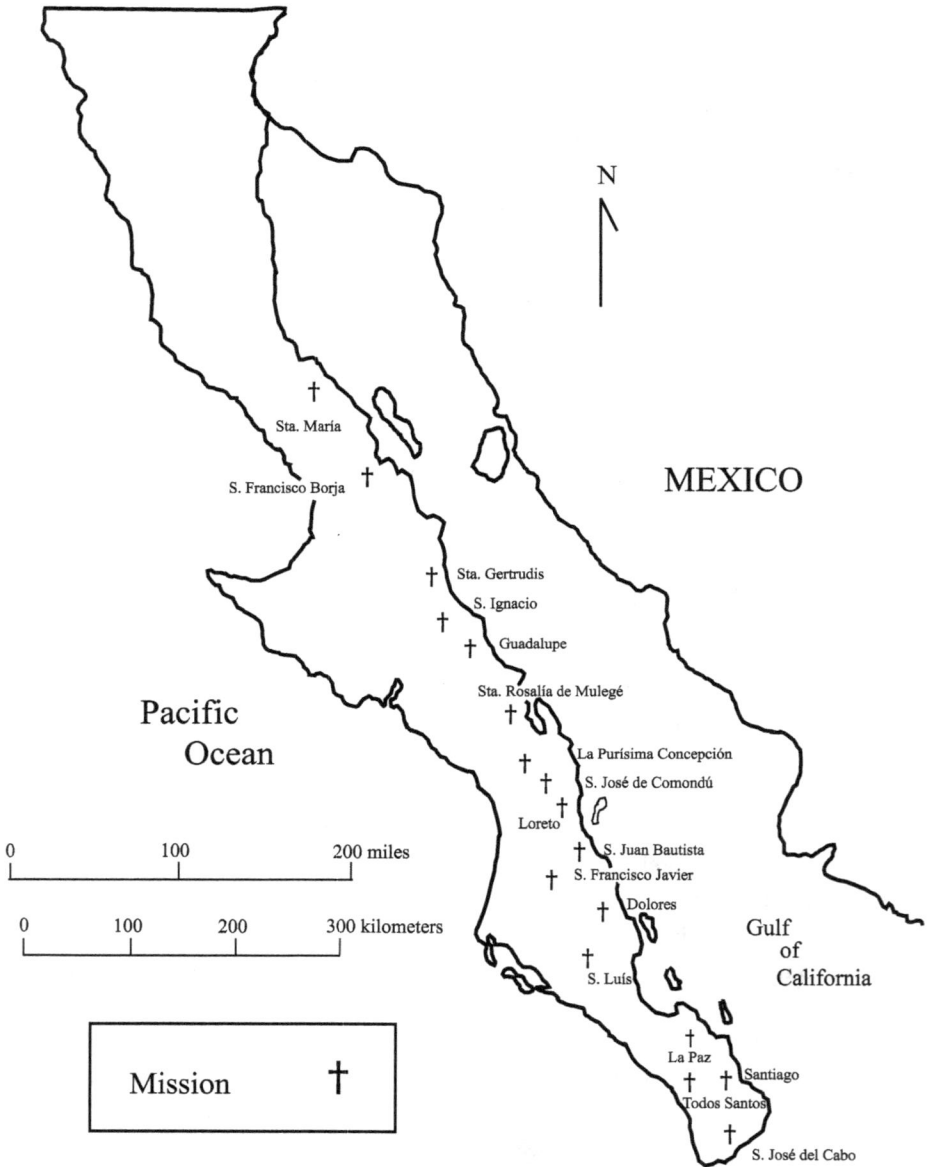

N

MEXICO

Pacific
Ocean

Gulf
of
California

Sta. María

S. Francisco Borja

Sta. Gertrudis
S. Ignacio
Guadalupe
Sta. Rosalía de Mulegé
La Purísima Concepción
S. José de Comondú
Loreto
S. Juan Bautista
S. Francisco Javier
Dolores
S. Luís
La Paz
Santiago
Todos Santos
S. José del Cabo

| 0 | 100 | 200 miles |

| 0 | 100 | 200 | 300 kilometers |

Mission   †

Map 8.1. Spanish missions in Baja California. Map prepared by Claire Huie and Don Wade.

groups about gifts and attention, minimized crowding, and certainly permitted the Natives to continue their lifestyles when away from the mission.

The Jesuit Johann Jakob Baegert, an Alsatian who came to California in 1750 and was assigned to Mission San Luís Gonzaga, described Loreto, the capital of the province and the main mission of Baja California. "The dwelling of the missionary, who was also the administrator and who had a lay brother to assist him, is a small, square, flat-roofed, one-storied structure of adobe brick thinly coated with lime. One wing is the church, and only this one is, in part, constructed of stone and mortar" (Baegert 1979, 117). Three other wings had six rooms each; the rooms measured about six yards wide by six yards long and had a window. These rooms were for the vestry; the kitchen; a small general store where soldiers, sailors, and visitors could buy merchandise; and a storage area for grain, beef, tallow, fat, and other goods. The priest's kitchen was equipped with a copper pan and a smaller copper vessel for preparing chocolate, both of which had been imported from Mexico; a few pots made of clay mixed with goat manure that were baked on coals in the open air; a spit; and a few cow bladders containing fat (125). A missionary's bedroom had a bed, two or three chairs, pictures, books, and a crucifix. Most missionaries kept a small garden next to the mission (117, 125). In 1769, Fr. Palóu commented that the Franciscans' rooms had only a table, a chair, a cot with a leather bottom, a lamp, and a bookshelf, but those furnishings appear to have been normal for a missionary's quarters (Palou 1994, 71). Dunne personalized Father Baegert's general statements by mentioning myriad items that belonged to specific friars, which varied from compasses and rulers to gloves, boots, and matches (1968, 440–41, 486–87). In addition, Dunne mentioned a selection of books that included the rules of the society and *Spiritual Exercises* (486). Indeed, from the beginning, Fr. Salvatierra made sure that the fathers joined together annually to perform the spiritual exercises (Crosby 1994, 186).

A bit farther from Mission Loreto's church was a small shed that served as the guardhouse and the barracks for unmarried soldiers. Usually six to eight soldiers were stationed at Loreto's presidio and fewer at other missions. To the west of these buildings were two rows of mud dwellings that housed 220 natives of all ages and sexes. Close by were forty-two single-room mud dwellings that housed married soldiers, sailors, carpenters, and others who might be living at the mission (Baegert 1979, 117).

The churches were eventually built of the best local materials, often with stone and wood brought from afar, and all churches were adorned with the best the religious could afford or was provided by wealthy donors. With the help of some master craftsmen and one or more supervisors, the local Natives built the churches and other mission buildings. Some churches, like that of Mission Santa Rosalía de Mulegé, had a reliquary with the bones of Santa Rosalía, a gift from Father Francisco María Piccolo (Dunne 1968, 439). All churches had bells and most had a Native choir and musicians.

In Baja California, all missions grew crops and raised livestock, but not all were equally successful. The lack of dependable water sources was one of the principal problems (Jackson 2005, 54, 122). "In some places water was brought half an hour's distance over irregular terrain through narrow channels or troughs carved out of the rock. . . . Nearly everywhere it was necessary to surround the water as well as the soil with retaining walls or bulwarks and to erect dams" (Baegert 1979, 129). A quick comparison of Baja California and Texas in terms of the number of mission livestock vis-à-vis the local population shows that any of the San Antonio missions owned more cattle per person than the missions in Baja California. For instance, Father Sistiaga's list of animals belonging to Mission Rosalía de Mulegé in the 1720s shows 210 head of cattle, 81 horses, and about 100 sheep and goats for about 100 people (Dunne 1968, 441, 496). In 1749, twenty-eight years after its founding, Mission San José in Texas had 2,000 head of cattle and 1,000 sheep for 200 Natives. In 1762, Mission Espada had 4,000 goats and 262 head of cattle for 207 people (Leutenegger 1985, 327–63). By the 1720s, Mulegé had been in existence for slightly over twenty years, while in the 1760s, Mission Espada had been located in San Antonio nearly thirty years. Obviously, different environmental conditions in Central Texas and Baja California, as well as the availability of water and pasture in the two areas, defy comparison and none is intended. The point is, however, that the success of a mission did not depend entirely on the numbers of livestock and that the Jesuits' rotational system permitted them to run a mission with far fewer resources.

Although the Baja California soil was poor, the Jesuits managed two maize crops a year, but crows, mice, and vermin often left little to be harvested. They also planted beans, chickpeas, squash, pumpkins, watermelons, melons, figs, oranges, lemons, pomegranates, bananas, and peaches. In some cases they planted sugar cane, cotton, and even rice. Vines grew well, and the missions were well provisioned with wine for mass and for sale (Crosby 1994, 113, 217, 227, 245–47).

Despite the fact that the missionaries touted their achievements and the harshness of their labors, all of which are undeniable, none of their work could have been brought to fruition without indigenous labor. Pelts and

skins were used for beds, furniture, bags, boats, ships, saddles, ropes, clothing, and shoes. Fat and tallow were essential for cooking, candles, and soap,
while wool from sheep was used to manufacture clothing and blankets. All
these items required Native labor and skills.

The Jesuits' discourse on the possessions and lifestyle of the Native populations is always ambivalent and frequently contradictory. They often marvel
at the Natives' contentment with the bareness of their surroundings, meager
possessions, and constant wandering in search of food. They perceived these
living conditions as liberating and worthy of admiration but extremely trying, yet they continuously derided the industriousness of the Natives, their
disregard for comfort, and their disdain for self-restraint regarding food
(Burrus 1984, 115; Nunis 1982, 91, 142).

The Jesuits produced a similar discourse about the intelligence of the Natives. They perceived them as "human beings, true children of Adam as we
are . . . endowed with reason as we are," but as "stupid, awkward, rude, un-
clean, insolent, ungrateful . . . an unreflecting people, without worries . . . a
people who follow their natural instincts" (Baegert 1979, 80). At the same
time, Jesuits described Natives as cunning and capable of planning and "reasoning when selfish interests or necessity demand it" (82). The disparaging
tone of this discourse is not as prevalent in the earlier periods when the
fathers continuously stressed patience, zeal, and compassion as the way to
overcome Native resistance to acculturation and Christianization. I suggest
that, despite the written claims of missionaries, there was a silent weariness
about the conversion project that privately acknowledged that the methodology of conversion rarely met its objectives. As is often the case, those
engaged in converting unwittingly blamed those being converted for failure
to measure up to expectations.

Despite the doctrinal rotational system the Jesuits adopted, hunter-gatherers posed special challenges. Father Sistiaga understood the difficulties of
the hunting and gathering lifestyle (Burrus 1984, 115–16), but Father Baegert
succinctly explained the psychological and pragmatic difference between
hunters and gatherers and horticulturists. He stated, "To work today in order to gather the fruit of their labor a quarter or half a year later seems un-
bearable to them" (Baegert 1979, 84). From the perspective of the missionaries, the concept of delayed reward was as essential to agriculture as it was to
Christianity: one labors today for future earthly and heavenly rewards. For
hunter-gatherers, both worlds were always intertwined and delayed gratifi-
cation simply made no sense.

Working at Conversion

Early contacts between Native populations and the fathers were generally amicable and emphasized curiosity and willingness to cooperate. Reports such as those from Father Piccolo, written in 1716 and 1721, demonstrate the Jesuits' process of familiarizing themselves with the landscape and prospecting for converts, while they afford a vision of the various Native groups as yet little affected by the pressure to convert (Burrus 1984, 78–92).

In 1716, on a trip northward from Mission Santa Rosalía, the Jesuits interacted with several groups that supplied the travelers with mescal (maguey plant) and pitahaya (the fleshy fruit of the cacti), cleared the trails for the fathers, and provided information on Native settlements (Burrus 1984, 78–83). Present in this and other reports is invaluable information about how Natives used resources and about conflict over boundaries. For instance, when Yejui, a Native leader who lived at the settlement of Temmanada and controlled a vast region, left his village to harvest pitahayas, he left instructions to notify him immediately if missionaries arrived. When Yejui came to see Father Piccolo, he explained that he had been detained in a dispute over resources and ended up involved in a conflict with another group (Burrus 1984, 84–85). Still, these were diplomatic interactions between the friars and the Natives that did not last after contact because of the spread of disease and the religious practices the Jesuits imposed.[3] In essence, contacts established with the intent to acquire knowledge were made on an equal footing between cultures and individuals and often convey a tone of equality lacking in later periods. In the early contact period, the Jesuits did not use the rhetoric of laziness and haughtiness; the Natives helped the fathers, but did not labor for them. It was not until later, after the Jesuits imposed Christianity on the region, that they adopted the discourse that described Native religious practices and shamanism as devilish.

As a result of an early contact, Father Piccolo described what he assumed, or was told, were shamanic rituals connected with a deer hunt ceremony and the manufacture of skin capes, and he stressed the large numbers of shamans and their authority. Piccolo commented, "They do not fight among themselves but only to defend their religion," although he noted that these Natives would kill over women (Burrus 1984, 87). Just as in Florida, and likely everywhere else, the Jesuits in Baja California knew that spiritual practices and autonomy over the choice of mates were two sensitive issues for Native groups.

Father Piccolo was given several hair capes by two Native captains from the area. Piccolo saw the capes as "the tribute the young natives pay to Satan in order to deck out the priestly shamans" (Burrus 1984, 87). These captains placed the capes and other "diabolic instruments" underneath the Christian altar built for religious ceremonies (87). The Native understanding of the missionary as a shaman, the Christian altar as a cultic place, and the clear equivalence between their shamanic objects of cult and Christian offerings are obvious. Still more telling are Father Piccolo's concluding remarks. He stated, "These are the objects I sent to Father Rector Juan María so that he would cast them as first fruits from the North at the feet of Our Lady, the *Conquistadora*" (87). Just as the Native shamans made offerings to the Christian God using their sacra, the Jesuit Fathers offered the Virgin Mary the same pagan objects previously offered by the Natives. The complex web of the work of conversion left no one untouched; objects and practices were often multipurpose, multivocal, and multispiritual.

But reactions varied. Faced with devastating smallpox and other epidemics, Father Taraval attributed the pestilence to the work of the devil that "made it appear that the fathers had brought about these calamities, that they had caused these many deaths, and that they were actually murderers" (Wilbur 1931/1972, 24). Likewise, when Natives withdrew from his mission and were decimated by disease, Father Taraval saw their flight as the work of the devil and their deaths as God's punishment (Jackson 1995, 121; Wilbur 1931/1972, 25). For the missionaries epidemics were the work of both God and the devil. In fact, according to Father Taraval, almost every event that contravened the work of conversion was the work of the devil. Overwhelmed by contagion they did not know how to control, the fathers sought relief and explanation in good and evil. Disease killed Native Americans, but it also injured the conscience of the missionaries.

The 1750 report of Father Lambert Hostell, who was stationed at Mission de Los Dolores, demonstrates that missionaries reacted differently to the spiritual practices of Natives and that Natives learned to construct explanations that assuaged the missionaries' qualms and permitted them to continue using shamanic symbols (Burrus 1984, 245–51). Father Hostell stated,

> Their paganism and superstition amounts to this: they believe in no divinity, but they do indulge in certain practices learned from their conjurers. The latter are no sorcerers in the real sense of the word used of those who have made a formal pact with the devil to the fulfillment of which they would consider themselves bound. In the beginning, we missionaries were of the opinion that they paid homage, as though to idols, to certain small wands, the tip of which contains the image of a

savage or bearded man; but the natives corrected our wrong interpretation, and informed us that they used these staffs merely to heighten their mirth on days of feasting and rejoicing. They call these wands "Tiyeicha" in their language, which means "He can talk." I thought that perchance the infernal spirit participated in their celebrations and even spoke to them through such objects; *but they assured me* that they have no dealings with the enemy of their souls, and that they have neither seen him at any time nor heard him speak. (Burrus 1984, 246–47, my emphasis)

Father Hostell described a rite of passage that included the piercing of children's ears and noses. In this celebration the shamans dressed in capes woven of human hair and carried the small staffs mentioned above as well as small "tablets into which they have scratched some rude figure. . . . Such figures have no idolatrous or superstitious meaning. They adorn themselves in the finery mentioned, but which as Christians they completely put aside and also throw away without reluctance their wands and tablets" (Burrus 1984, 247). Aside from the potential gullibility of the father, this example may well attest to how much the Natives actually understood of the nature of good and evil, particularly the ways they devised to circumvent and undo the connections between their practices and the devil. The Natives may well have "absorbed" Catholic teachings but not as the missionaries would have expected or wished. These reactions to Christianity, which were less strident than those of the Calusa and less final than those of the Hasinai, demonstrate the same efforts and keen ability to render neutral missionary prohibitions.

As missions were established and the conversion program began, confrontations between Native spiritual leaders over the imposition of Christian directives, particularly those about marriage, resulted in several Native revolts such as those in 1734–1735, during which several missions were attacked and civilians and missionaries were killed. These confrontations often led the missionaries to burn Native objects and ceremonial garments (Baegert 1979, 90). Conflicts between shamans and missionaries and the overt demotion of the former, regardless of gender, likely created transition problems in the performance of healing practices that were acceptable to Native populations.

As was the case at Mission San Ignacio, shamans (*guamas*)[4] often promoted revolts on the basis of the anger of Native gods as Native populations accepted Christianity. The shamans admonished that in retaliation for such acceptance, food would be scarce and the deer would vanish (Dunne 1968, 229), tactics similar to those used by the Calusa. The Natives faced intolerable spiritual conundrums: accept Christianity and face the wrath of their gods and shamans or reject Christianity and face the wrath of God and the missionaries. For the missionaries, obviously, the choice was between God and the devil, reducing the cosmic struggle to good and evil practices.

As conflict arose, the Jesuits devised a good-cop bad-cop routine whereby those arrested during revolts were tried by their brethren and sentenced to death. At this point the father would intervene and commute the sentence, setting the culprits free and sometimes even rewarding them with gifts (Dunne 1968, 230, 403). The pardon required a set period of confinement at the mission that would be lifted if those pardoned accepted Christianity and behaved accordingly. The goal of this choreography of punishment was conversion; it was also intended to show the merciful nature of the father and the compassionate characteristics of Christianity.

Foucault said that "the art of punishment . . . must rest on a whole technology of representation" and that it must obey certain principles (1979, 104). First it "must be as unarbitrary as possible" (104). In Baja California, as generally in New Spain, the destruction and killing resulting from Native revolts were punished with death and exile; the punishment emanated from the crime and the penalties "represented in their form the content of the crime" (105). The guilty were cut from the social fabric, just as they intended to cut off the social group from the source of good and of godliness. Second, the punishment "must reduce the desire that makes the crime attractive . . . so that the representation of the penalty and its disadvantages is more lively than that of the crime and its pleasures" (106). Foucault expanded on the various ways to achieve this objective: put the guilty individual to work, hurt his or her pride, subject him or her to ridicule and shame in front of spectators, and restore respect for property, freedom, and life. Public judgment, sentence, and punishment by Native group members, most often pueblo officials, achieved several of these objectives and rendered the crime unattractive, unpopular, and unrewarding. Third, "punishment can function only if it comes to an end" and if it permits the reform of the guilty (107). The period of punishment should facilitate the act of punishing and it should be phased out as it produces the desired results (108). The Jesuit fathers not only schemed to commute the sentence, they also established a period of confinement to the mission that was shortened if the culprits displayed remorseful behavior. Fourth, the punishment should aim less at those it punishes than at "all the potentially guilty" and "everyone must see punishment not only as natural but in his own interest" (109). The stated aims of missionary punishment were redeeming the guilty individual and making the crime less attractive to others. Fifth, punishment "is based on the lesson, the discourse, the decipherable sign, the representation of public morality" (109–10). The public nature of a missionary trial and sentencing plus the involvement of Natives in the judiciary proceedings implicated the Native social group in the process of punishing, rendered the act of revolt criminal in their eyes, and advertised the consequences of violating the social order as established by the missionaries. Finally, the discourse of crime had to be inverted and criminal actions devalued. How could missionaries prevent the revolt leader, the shaman, from being glorified and made a hero? It was the condemned who provided the final epitaph to the punishment procedures by acknowledging his crime, accepting his punishment, and above all by accepting the pardon offered by the missionary. Like the prodigal son, the Native was brought into the Christian fold through gentle punishment; the sinner was removed of revolt and redeemed. At least this is what the Jesuits expected to happen.

It is not my intent to equate Foucault's analysis of prison punishment to the system practiced in California by the Jesuits, yet there are clear indications that the Jesuits and Franciscans in the mission system used an orchestrated discourse of punishment as an "instrument and vector of power" produced by knowledge (Foucault 1979, 30).

The leaders of revolts who contravened the work of conversion were generally ladino headmen and shamans. The contests between Jesuit fathers and shamans for control of spiritual practices and the allegiance of Natives sometimes ended in a draw. At Mission San Ignacio, a rebellious shaman was appointed governor after he converted, but he reverted to his shamanic practices and was chastised and demoted. Later, when this shaman perished during an epidemic, Father Sistiaga saw divine intervention at work (Dunne 1968, 230 and note 22).

Some revolts late in the Jesuit period point to the increasing sophistication of the Natives at assessing their legal situation and power and negotiating the conditions of socialization and conversion. The Pericué revolts that began in the late 1740s and continued to 1766 are a case in point. Spanish miners in the southern region told the Pericué that Natives in Mexico were free to travel, owned plots of land, and sold their produce for profit. In light of this knowledge, the Pericué demanded that they be given the mission lands, be allowed to cultivate the land and sell their crops freely, and be provided with animals to transport their products to market and that the fathers continue feeding the women, the children, and the sick as they normally did. The Pericué demanded freedom to travel and to visit other missions and other provinces in New Spain, and they requested that the boat of Mission Santiago be made available to them (Clavijero 1789/2002, 351).

As Clavijero points out, the Jesuits considered the distribution of the mission lands a reasonable demand, but they objected to it because they argued that the Pericué were lazy and incapable of working the lands profitably (1789/2002, 351). An argument from silence is an argument that has not been proven because it has not been tested. Clavijero used an interesting argument to decry the Pericué demand for freedom of movement; he stated that as nomadic hunter-gatherers, the Pericué were actually limited in their freedom to travel before the arrival of the Jesuits, because they could not cross the lands of their neighbors, the Guaycura and the Cochimí (352). He added that even tribes of the same nation could not trespass on each other's territories (352). After the arrival of the missionaries, however, the Natives were free to travel through the extensive mission lands and could travel to other missions providing they made a request, had a reason to travel, and remained at the mission they intended to visit (352). These statements make clear that the establishment of mission lands and congregation or regrouping of Native rancherías involved serious disruption of traditional Native territories and resource allotment, issues that were crucial to Native identity and subsistence.

When the fathers rejected Pericué demands, twenty Pericué, presumably aided by others, boarded the mission boat in complete secrecy, crossed the Gulf, and reached Sinaloa. They planned to request that the Jesuits be removed and replaced with parish priests. Out of the income from the lands they were to cultivate, the Pericué were prepared to offer the parish priests who would replace the Jesuits room and board and to pay taxes to the king. While in Sinaloa, some of the Pericué presented their complaints to the deputy governor, who, at the behest of a Jesuit, did not act on the petition. The Pericué were brought back to Baja California, where they presented their claims to Father Lizasoáin, who had come to inspect the Jesuit missions. But he too declined their requests on the basis of the laws established by the viceroy and the king (Clavijero 1789/2002, 356).

Still the Pericué persisted. Again in complete secrecy and despite tighter security measures at the mission, they sailed off to Sinaloa. From there some went to Durango and others to Tepic. A delegation reached Guadalajara and its members submitted their claims to the colonial Supreme Court. According to Clavijero, the judge, who disliked the Jesuits, sent the Pericué claims to the Madrid court, thereby making the Pericué complaints a royal issue (1789/2002, 356–57). Two years later, apparently sick and hungry, the Pericué who had survived the adventure returned to the missions at Santiago and Dolores. Despite the fact that their claims had not been addressed, in 1766 the Pericué again presented their complaints to Father Carlos Rojas when he inspected the Jesuit missions (357–58). One year later the Jesuits left the peninsula.

Native resistance often may be masked as disinterest or laziness, but this was not the case with the Pericué. In the attempt to regain autonomy and control their future, the Pericué used several legal avenues, from local requests to the mission father to requests to Jesuit inspector generals, presidio commanders outside Baja California, provincial courts, and ultimately to the royal court at Madrid. They traveled far and wide and found the appropriate venues for delivering their complaints. For almost two decades the Pericué displayed uncanny ability and resourcefulness and enormous persistence. This is one occasion where Native enterprise might have led to autonomous management of missions had it been channeled and nurtured by the Jesuits. One wonders why the Pericué would not have been able to work the land profitably.

Practices of Conversion

The rotational conversion system the Jesuits followed brought different groups at different times to the mission, which certainly permitted the Natives to continue their own lifestyles when away from the mission. Despite that, once the Natives were baptized, they were to advance to other sacraments, and the Jesuits applied pressure for changes in social arrangements, particularly those regarding mating.

Young boys and girls who remained at the mission center were brought up separately from each other and from their parents, but this system did not apply to all adolescents. At least in some cases, young women were placed under the tutelage of an "upright woman of prudent judgment, *although an Indian*" (Burrus 1984, 140, my emphasis; see also Jackson 2005, 196). It is not clear if the young people were locked up and if this practice extended to women of marrying age.

Newborn children were brought to the priest for baptism; adults had to be convinced. Just as in Texas among the Caddoan-speaking groups, California Natives associated previously unknown diseases such as smallpox or measles with baptismal water and often refused baptism (Dunne 1968, 231). Missionaries gave males a piece of blue cloth, a blue woolen short shirt, and sometimes a pair of trousers and a long coat made of coarse cloth twice a year after they were baptized. Crosby also mentions linen shirts, cotton and silk hose, and hats (1994, 143). To the women and the girls they gave a thick cloak of wool that covered their bodies to the feet. Some missions also provided the women with jackets of flannel, woven cotton shirts, petticoats, and long and short silk stockings (143). As Father Baegert acknowledged, these garments were cumbersome and too hot for summer, and the Natives discarded them (1979, 62).

Girls who reached the age to marry apparently were not particularly submissive as marriage partners. Generally the prospective couple asked the consent of the missionary and he performed a Catholic marriage ceremony that included the placement of a ring on the fingers of the newlyweds. Baegert commented on how difficult it was to get a clear answer to a clear question that concerned marriage arrangements and kinship. He provided the following example:

> A missionary once begged me to find out whether a certain N. had been married to the sister of another N. before his baptism, which he received when he was a grown man. A simple "yes" or "no" would have decided the matter, but more than three quarters of an hour was spent with questions and answers without ever . . . finding the truth. I put the whole conversation down on paper and sent the protocol to the missionary, who was no more successful than I in finding out whether N. had been married to the sister or not. (Baegert 1979, 94)

Although missionaries attributed the situation to confused minds, quite likely it represented precisely the opposite because the question concerned potential bigamy, which the church prohibited. Native Americans exploited language differences in various ways that varied from the use of specialized oratory to leading the missionaries around the discursive bush. As the first generation that was born and reared among the missionaries came of age, ladinos came to predominate, and their influence with colonizers and colonized is noteworthy.

In the early mission period (1720s and 1730s), several Natives who lived in the villages surrounding Santa Rosalía Mulegé perished without confession mostly because word of their condition reached the missionary too late (Dunne 1968, 435–36). It was more typical for neophytes to confess more than once a year, and they generally did not die without confession, according to Father Miguel Barco, who ministered at San Francisco Xavier. Writing in 1762, Barco reported that the Natives no longer requested the presence of a shaman when they were dying, but he contended that such devotion might be due to the food the father provided to those who confessed (Dunne 1968, 393 and n. 15). Unlike neophytes in Sonora and Sinaloa, who often did not receive communion following confession, those in Baja California generally did. Most confessions and communions took place during Lent when the Natives fulfilled the precept of the Catholic church (395–96, 442).

The sacrament of confirmation was a privilege the Catholic church reserved to bishops, but in about 1756 the pope gave the Jesuits permission to administer the sacrament, and after that many Natives were confirmed. From 1756 to 1762, Dunne (1968, 395) shows a total of 3,030 confirmations for the Loreto, Comondú, San Ignacio, and Santa Gertrudis missions. Many others were confirmed during the inspection visit of Father Lizasoáin in 1762.

Catholic burials were a contentious issue and the Natives protested vehemently against them. Baegert once asked the reason for such reluctance and was told "that they considered it a mocking of the dead to bury them with the ringing of bells, chanting and other Catholic" practices (1979, 80). Native populations enjoyed music and singing, and that answer should have alerted the missionary to the powerful desire of Natives to be buried according to local custom, but Father Baegert dismissed Native customs as lacking ritual practices and as being a "mere ceremony" (79). It is also possible that mentioning the name of the deceased, which is part of Catholic funereal rites, would violate Native customs (see Geiger and Meighan 1976, 59–60). Last rites were seldom administered to the Natives, mostly because the fathers did not reach the dying in time.

Baegert (Nunis 1982, 168) found hearing confession the hardest of his priestly duties. He was preoccupied with whether or not the Natives actually understood the meaning of confession and the causal relationship between sin and confession, yet, he had to absolve the penitent; otherwise he would imperil his own soul, indeed a theological and moral dilemma. Baegert (1979, 81) mentioned that the Natives appeared not to count above six, which made confession very difficult because the missionaries always insisted on the precise number of sins committed and on the number of times they were committed. Also Natives did not confess "crimes" unless they were caught in the act.

Another problem with confession was the Natives' perception of time. For instance, Baegert (1979, 79; Nunis 1982, 147) notes that the Guaycura had a word for week that was the same as for "house" or "church" because they spent one week at the mission in its rotational system. For missionary purposes, the Guaycura "created" a word that signified both a period of time and space: a week at the house or mission. It might have been quite difficult for them to place sins in time—at least a time understood by a religious westerner (Geiger and Meighan 1976, 83). Confessional accuracy—when, where, what, and why—was most likely outside Native American hunter-gatherers' time reckoning and vocabulary (see Harrington 1934, 43–45). Likewise, the

Guaycura "counted" the years in reference to the pitahaya harvest season (Baegert 1979, 79; see also Geiger and Meighan 1976, 81–83 for other Native groups), which, again, might have made for very imprecise confessions.

The teaching of doctrine and the practice of confession were impaired by languages that were unyielding vis-à-vis each other. The nuanced aspects of the ceremonial and the natural Native world were lost on or misunderstood by the missionaries, while the religious concepts the priests espoused found no equivalence in the Native languages. Furthermore, Spanish loan words, which signified important religious concepts, such as *Dios* (God) and *alma* (soul), were often foreign to the missionary and to the Natives, yet priests used them to bridge the gap of incomprehension (Baegert 1979, 102). The concepts were alien, as was the language used to convey and teach them. Such multicultural-based teachings had to result in different rates and types of knowledge assimilation and were likely welded in various ways to traditional knowledge and custom. Unlike the majority of the Franciscans, the members of the Society of Jesus had strict rules about language learning and proficiency. Missionaries were compelled to pass language exams and were continuously admonished to study Native languages and write down their knowledge for the benefit of others (Burrus 1984, 115, 224–25). Nonetheless, for many missionaries, as for Baegert, Castilian Spanish was at best a second language and most Native interactions were labyrinths of potential misunderstandings.

Conversion was, and is, about words, and despite the languages the priests learned, words failed them because language is about culture. In 1752 Jacob Baegert wrote a letter to his brother George Baegert, also a Jesuit. Father Jacob discussed his frustration about trying to express and communicate Christian religious concepts. The language of the Guaycura had "no abstracts or even verbals. . . . There is no word that can express the nature of human feeling, of virtue, vice and passion, because they do not talk among themselves about anything else but what they can see and grasp" (Nunis 1982, 113–61). There were no words to express community, civil society, law, order, or quantities. They had past, present, and future tenses only. Their vocabulary lacked words such as "useful, pure, pious, moderate, kindly, virtue, envy, vice, mercy, decency, virgin, danger . . . place, cause, thing, opportunity, guilt, God, more, law, time, healthy, to say thanks, dead, punishment, to honor, the servant, to doubt, master, farmhand, the beginning, the end, to greet, limb, part, rich, poor, to buy, to redeem, to pity, house, year, 7, 8, 9, 10 and so on" (Nunis 1982, 146). Still, both parties made the Herculean effort to patch together meanings, and it is a wonder that conversion occurred. In this presence/absence of words and concepts may reside that indefinable realm that we have called syncretism. In most cases, conversion was not lost in translation; it remained incommunicado.

The Franciscans: 1768–1773

The expulsion of the Jesuits from Spanish America in 1767–1768 left the work of conversion of Baja California to the Mendicant Orders and, for the purpose of this book, principally to the Franciscans. As the *Purísima Concepción* unloaded its cargo of expelled Jesuits, it picked up the sixteen Franciscans who were to Christianize the Natives (Engelhardt 1929, 338). With the untimely departure of the Jesuits, old conflicts and rivalries were dissolved. It was a unique opportunity for the Franciscans, but one that came at the price of increased visibility and the stretching of resources and personnel.

Fr. Junípero Serra, a native of Mallorca and a seasoned missionary, was chosen to head the Franciscans in California. Serra's personality, commitment, and negotiating abilities were ideal qualities to make the enterprise a success, particularly when coupled with Fr. Francisco Palóu's intellectual capabilities and management skills. After landing, the friars proceeded to Mission Loreto to celebrate their arrival and the possibility of a resurrection: it was Easter Sunday.

Unlike the Jesuits, who, for the most part, had financial control of the missions they established, the Franciscans served at the discretion of the crown. Though they were given possession of all the churches and paraphernalia formerly possessed by the Jesuits, the control and administration of the properties and economic affairs of the missions (*temporalidades*) were, for a time, placed in the hands of secular authorities (Palou 1994, 34). The Franciscans were in charge of the Jesuit missions, but they lacked the financial autonomy the Jesuits had enjoyed and had to contend with the authority of secular managers and soldiers.

Fr. Serra assigned sixteen friars to the thirteen Baja California missions. The Native populations of these missions may well have been apprehensive about the rapid changes: Native populations were relocated, mission property was removed, and the distribution of goods disrupted. By August 1768, scarcely six months after the Jesuits had left, Don José de Gálvez, the king's inspector general, realized that secular management of the missions would quickly lead to their demise, so he gave the Franciscans control over the temporal affairs of the missions (Palou 1994, 35). Despite that, Gálvez micromanaged the affairs of the missions and injected his own vision of the mission project by displacing and redistributing Native populations and by immediately closing two of the southernmost missions, Nuestra Señora de los Dolores and San Luís Gonzaga. As Engelhardt points out, "The intention was to induce the natives everywhere to live together in communities rather than scattered over a large territory, so that they could be instructed systematically and habituated to a civilized manner of living" (1929, 350–51). Though there were other reasons for the displacement (Palou 1994, 73–78), the fact remains that the Jesuits had consistently resisted displacement, well aware that further disruption of the Native way of life was neither welcome nor productive. Over seventy years of toil among the Native populations of California had taught the Jesuits the limits of Native tolerance; Gálvez's arrogance and the Franciscans' acquiescence were bound to breed further discontent. Measures such as the forceful relocation and congregation of populations, the prohibition on gambling, the attempts to increase Spanish settlement and foster commercial ventures, and other issues created a state of unrest among the Native groups that not even the temporary panacea of gifts could assuage.

Either because of Gálvez's pressure, localized problems, and fear of criticism or because of the attraction of a fresh field of souls in Alta California, there seems to have been little reluctance to secularize missions in Baja California (Palou 1994, 112). With Fr. Serra's recommendation, Missions Santiago and San José del Cabo were entrusted to parish priests by the end of 1768. The secularization of these two mission-pueblos questions the usual contention that the Natives were unprepared to manage their own affairs (Palou 1994, 75). Not many Natives remained at those missions, and Palóu requested that they be exempted from paying a labor tribute to the king. He noted that the secular priest who had taken over Santiago had left under the pretext that he was sick but not without stating that "those pueblos were not for a secular priest (*curatos*), but for missionaries" (Palou 1998, 1:91–92). Either the Natives were able to take on the administration of the pueblos or the pueblos should have continued as missions. Obviously there were considerations other than the Natives' capabilities. Palóu further noted that the pueblos were in bad condition and said if the Franciscans were to continue administering them they would encounter problems and be accused of trading with sailors from the Manila fleet (Palou 1998, 1:84). The southernmost missions were poor, the Natives were uncooperative, the land was uninviting, and the missions were very distant from Alta California (Crosby 1994, 388). All of these were sound economic and political reasons to secularize them. But what did that have to do with the work of conversion? Like Fr. Manuel in Texas about one hundred years earlier, Fr. Palóu understood the pragmatics of conversion: cut your losses and move on.

Under Gálvez's leadership, the friars and the military collected an extensive list of goods from the southern missions to take to the missions that were to be founded in Alta California. Apart from a wealth of church paraphernalia, this list included horses, mules, and considerable amounts of victuals, including wine, raisins, wheat, ground corn, and animal fat (Engelhardt 1929, 381, 384–85). Amazingly, the list of sacra includes five consecrated altar stones, silver chalices, baptismal fonts, statues, and paintings (Engelhardt 1929, 385; Palou 1994, 98–101). While it is clear that some missions were located in more productive areas than others, it is less clear why the existence of surpluses that could be diverted to the founding of northern missions could not just as well have sustained the poorer missions in the south. The southern missions were steadily deprived of the meager but important resources they possessed in order to seed the Alta California mission project (Crosby 1994, 388; Palou 1994, 37).

Interestingly, Fr. Palóu, who was concerned with documenting the fate of the church property the Jesuits had acquired and accumulated, did not seem to realize the incongruence of the arrangement. Palóu states, "The Lord Inspector did nothing more than practice what the Jesuit Fathers had done when founding the missions; for the old ones assisted as far as possible those that were about to be founded. . . . In some manner he returned what had been taken; for he ordered that eight thousand pesos' worth of ordinary clothing should be distributed to the Indians of all missions, who in that year appeared very well clothed" (Engelhardt 1929, 386–87, 414). Clothing was part of the king's ration and the Jesuits had distributed it twice a year (Palou 1994, 115, 118). This gesture of pseudo-appeasement by a man who berated the Jesuits was made thanks to the Jesuit Pious Fund. In fact, the Pious Fund continued to pay for most of the missions' expenses (Engelhardt 1929, 430nn17, 18, and 20, 431, 437).

It is understandable but disingenuous to compare the procedure followed by Jesuits (and Franciscans) to what actually took place in Baja California. To seed a mission with the surplus of another was a logical practice, providing the procedure did not lead to the latter's unnecessary distress or closure. To deplete a mission's larder and lead to its closure raises the issue of what were the fundamental criteria behind expansion of the missionary program and conversion practices. Although the Natives might have been well clothed for a year with Gálvez's repayment, they were certainly struggling to survive, as Fr. Serra and Palóu acknowledged (1994, 89–93). In 1767–1768, the

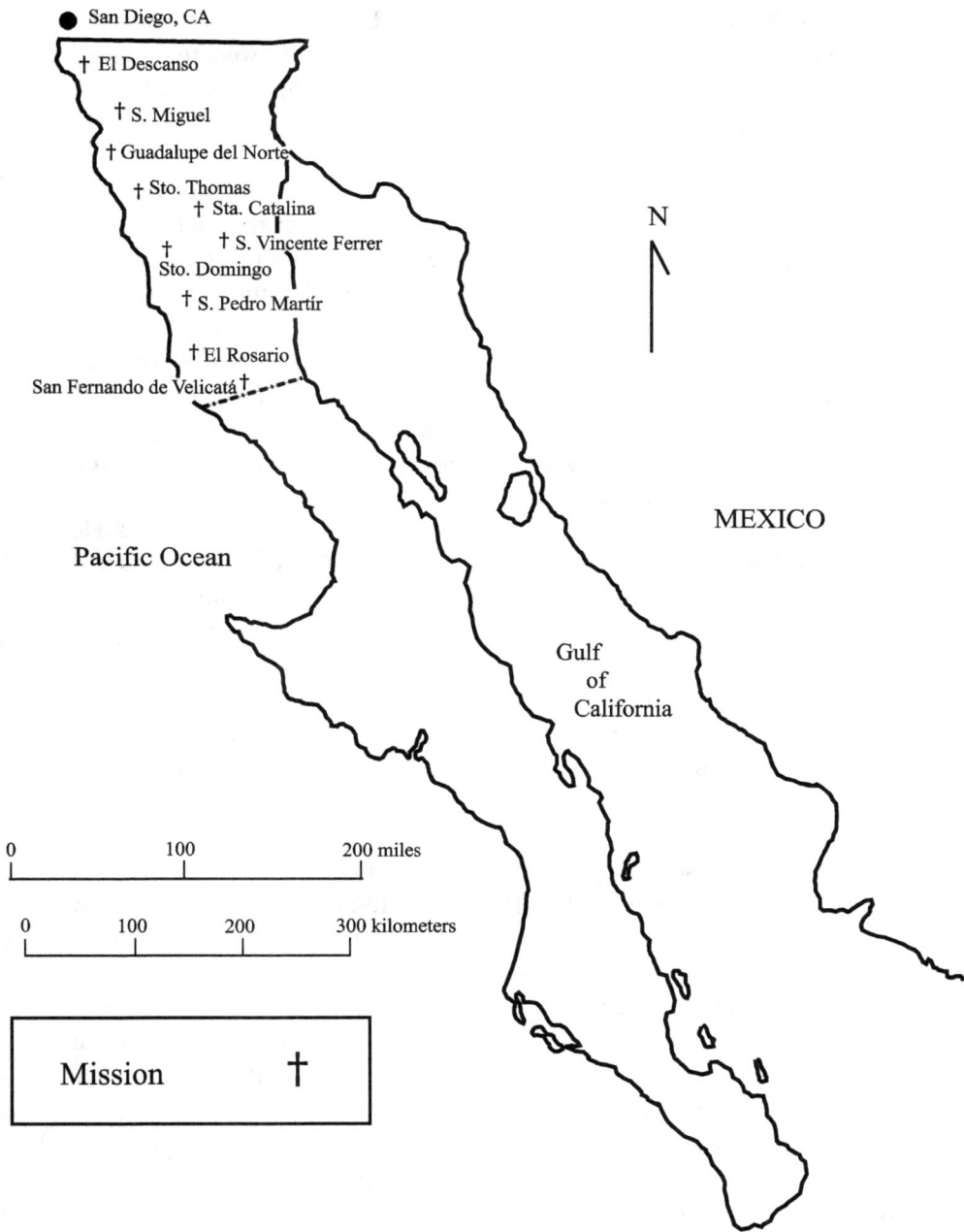

Map 8.2. Spanish missions in Upper Baja California. Map prepared by Claire Huie and Don Wade.

southern missions suffered locust plagues, and in 1769 the Natives of the Guadalupe mission and the mission station of San Miguel were told to fend for themselves because the friars could not feed them (Engelhardt 1929, 377, 391). These two missions were among the ones that in 1768 had provided foodstuffs bound for San Diego.

The establishment of Mission Velicatá, the first and only mission founded by the Franciscans in Baja California, leaves little doubt that the center of mission interest had shifted northward. There were no Natives around nor did any request baptism, but Velicatá linked the northernmost missions in Baja California to the new missions in Alta California. Fr. Serra was eager to meet some Natives, and eventually a group of males arrived to exchange gifts. Soon after that, the Natives began to congregate and asked for baptism. The relationship established between the Franciscans and the Native chief at Velicatá proved fruitful until Velicatá (Mission San Fernando) was delivered to the Dominicans four years later.

By May 1769, Fr. Palóu was in charge of the Baja California missions. He quickly realized that due to the economic measures Gálvez had enacted and the state of the missions, many soon would have to close. Missions Santiago de los Coras and San José del Cabo had already been secularized, and the other missions were not doing well. Forceful relocation of populations in mission-pueblos led to Native revolts. Furthermore, Gálvez stipulated that the Natives were to extract salt for the crown without a salary, though the missions were to provide for the Native families when the males were away (Palou 1994, 94, 103). In addition, Gálvez ordered that the Natives of the southern missions cultivate one fanega of corn (1.6 bushels) as tribute to the king, while those in the northern part of Baja California were to pay this tribute in the form of wine or figs (Palou 1998, 1:91–92). The missions could not be maintained without Native labor. In all conversion models and arrangements, ultimately the issue of Native labor became central, even when sublimated under the discourse of Native laziness.

By the middle of 1770, the Franciscans had been placed in an intolerable position. They were in control of the economic affairs of the missions, but the bureaucratic and legislative measures enacted by the crown rendered that control almost meaningless. Nonetheless, they had to manage the affairs of the missions and proceed with the work of conversion. As if the problems with the existing missions were not serious enough, the crown ordered the founding of five new missions in the north. As Fr. Rafael Verger, then *guardián* of the San Fernando College, acknowledged, "There is nothing, neither in the old ones [missions] nor in the new ones, yet we will be responsible for the expenses made, and we shall be blamed as careless and incapable. The old missions have been ransacked; the new ones are missions in name only" (Engelhardt 1929, 436). How well the Franciscans came to understand the plight of the Jesuits, and how ironic that while the Franciscans in California were seeking control of the economic affairs of the missions, the Franciscans in Texas were trying to be relieved from them.

Pressed by the crown, and despite the misgivings of the Franciscan leadership, the college did send thirty friars for the California missions. Fifteen friars were distributed between eleven Baja missions: Velicatá, Santa Maria, Santa Gertrudis, San Ignacio, Santa Rosalía de Mulegé, Guadalupe, Purísima Concepción, San José de Comundú, San Javier, Loreto, and Todos Santos.

In January 1772, three years after the Franciscans took over the management of the Baja California missions, Fr. Palóu prepared a report on the state of the missions in response to a request from Fr. Rafael Verger and as required before the Baja California missions were officially delivered to the Dominicans (Palou 1998, 1:121). The lengthy document, which was produced at the same time as other reports from Texas previously discussed and under the same Franciscan leadership, provides an internal assessment of the state of the missions. Because the honesty of the friars is not an issue, these reports contain the best information for gauging the living conditions of the Native populations and the missionaries' work of conversion. The economic state of the missions in the years following the Franciscan takeover, the effect of epidemics, the hasty administrative decisions, and the conflicts between the military and the church show the disruption that followed the departure of the Jesuits that led to closings, congregation of groups, and Native dislocations. One of the things that became apparent from the reforms was a move to limit the population of each mission to about 200 people per mission, with very few exceptions.

Mission San José del Cabo came under the purview of the Franciscans in April 1768, as did most of the other missions. Fourteen months later, Fr. Juan Morán, who ministered to the mission, died during an epidemic that killed all but fifty of its Native residents (Palou 1998, 1:131). Some of those killed were from Mission Todos Santos. The Natives of Mission Santiago de los Coras were afflicted with venereal disease, as were the Natives of Todos Santos. Inspector-General Gálvez moved the latter population to Mission Santiago in October 1768 (Palou 1998, 1:132). He also transferred one Native ranchería from San Xavier to San José, but of the forty-four people (12 families, or an average of 3.6 people per family) who were moved, only three remained after the epidemics of 1769 (Palou 1994, 75; 1998, 1:131). In April 1769, Mission Santiago was secularized and Mission San José was made a *visita*[5] of Mission Santiago, but the priest left and the Franciscans retook possession of the missiíons. At the time of the report, only sixty people were left at Mission Santiago, who survived on the cattle still remaining.

The seven hundred members of the Guaycura tribe, which had resided at Missions La Pasión and San Luís Gonzaga, were moved in 1768 to Mission Nuestra Señora del Pilar (also known as Todos Santos) when Missions La Pasión and San Luís closed. Despite threats and punishments, the Guaycura adapted poorly to the new surroundings and apparently refused to work. To maintain the mission, which was located in good, well-irrigated land, the friars hired Natives from other areas as laborers. The epidemic of 1769 reduced the Guaycura to 170 people, a number that included about thirty people who had fled from the mission to the mountains (Palou 1998, 1:133). The mission was turned over to the Spanish governor in 1771. Thus, by 1771 four missions had been secularized or closed, many Natives had perished from disease, and several Native groups had been displaced, facts that could not be conducive to the Franciscan work of conversion.

Mission San Francisco Xavier was clearly in better economic and religious condition than the ones previously discussed. From April 1768 to November 1771, although the friars had actually baptized 83 children, 115 people old and young had perished. Fourteen couples had contracted marriage. The missionary of San Xavier had formerly ministered to three outlying pueblos, but Gálvez ordered the people in the outlying areas to relocate at the mission. Then he realized that the mission lands could not support the incoming population, so he ordered twelve families to move to Mission San José del Cabo and twenty-five families to settle at Loreto, thus reducing the population of Mission San Xavier to sixty families (205 people, for an average of 3.4 people per family) and seven widows, a total of 212 people. The mission still had farming implements and some cattle and it was producing wine and fruit from several orchards, but it had suffered devastating crop losses because of locust plagues followed by drought, which had killed not only the locusts but also the crops and animals (Palou 1998, 1:135–36).

Mission Nuestra Señora de Loreto was located near the presidio of the same name and therefore enjoyed a special position. From April 1768 to December 1771, the friars baptized 76 children, Spanish and Native, while 131 persons died and 20 couples married. When the inspector general visited the mission, the Natives had abandoned it except for nineteen families. Gálvez determined that the mission should house 100 families, but only twenty-five families were brought in from San Xavier because Fr. Palóu did not think more people could be maintained with the resources of the mission. At the writing of the report the mission had 40 families for a total of

160 people (an average of 4.0 people per family). In addition to wild cattle, the mission had eighty-six horses and seven mules (Palou 1998, 1:137–38).

Mission San José de Comundú was one of the most prosperous. It grew sugar cane, corn, wheat, cotton, olives, grapes, and several fruits. From April 8, 1768, through December 1771, the friars baptized 94 children, married 28 couples, and buried 241 children and adults. All the 82 families, which amounted to 216 people, an average of 2.6 people per family, resided at the mission. The mission had large herds of wild cattle but only 25 oxen, some cows and calves, and good herds of horses, sheep, and goats (Palou 1998, 1:139–40).

From the time the Franciscans took over Mission Purísima Concepción de Cadegomó until December 1771, the friars baptized 39 children, married 15 couples, and buried 120 children and adults. All 168 Natives were congregated at the mission (158 married people and seven widows and widowers). The mission grew corn, wheat, grapes, and pomegranates in good quantities. Despite the locusts, the mission grew 300 arrobas of figs (about 16,530 lbs., as an arroba equals 25 kg.), which is not a negligible crop for a bad year, but there were other years when the fig crop reached 900 arrobas (49,500 lbs.). The mission produced a lot of cotton and had some tame cattle but much more wild cattle. Like Mission Comundú, it had good herds of horses, mules, sheep, and goats (Palou 1998, 1:140–41).

At Mission Nuestra Señora de Guadalupe, the friars baptized 53 children, performed 28 marriages, and buried 130 people, young and old, from April 1768 to September 1771. The relocations Gálvez ordered, whereby Natives were moved to San José and Purísima, coupled with the many deaths left only 39 families composed of 142 Natives at the mission, an average of 3.6 people per family. The mission had two outlying settlements where a variety of crops and fruits were grown. In 1770, the mission suffered a locust plague that affected all crops and fruits. The mission had large and very good pasturelands that supported horses, mules, sheep, goats, and 212 cows, from whose milk Natives made good cheese (Palou 1998, 1:142–43).

From April 1768 to August 1771, the friars at Mission Santa Rosalía de Mulegé baptized 48 children, married 17 couples, and buried 113 children and adults. All 180 people lived at the mission (46 families, an average of 3.9 per family), but they were not doing well because the 1770 floods had washed away a dam and eroded the planting soil. The mission was poor; it had 34 head of cattle, 1,111 sheep and goats, a small number of horses and mules, and many wild mustangs and cattle. The Natives had expressed a desire to move to a nearby place called La Magdalena, which was located near the beach, where they could easily continue their fishing traditions (Palou 1998, 1:143–44).

At Mission San Ignacio, the friars baptized 115 children, married 68 couples, and buried 293 children and adults from April 1768 to August 1771. At the time of the report, the mission had 136 families for a total of 558 people (an average of four people per family), all residing at the mission as they were ordered to by Inspector-General Gálvez. This resulted in the largest Native population of all the old missions, though they did not remain together long. In August, at the time of Fr. Palóu's inspection, the locusts had destroyed the corn and other crops, but the crops had been replanted and there was a chance they might survive. Normally the mission grew wheat, corn and olives, grapes, and other fruits as well as cotton. The mission had wild and tame cattle and good herds of horses, mules, sheep, and goats.

San Ignacio was a prosperous mission by comparison and by Fr. Palóu's account. When the locust plague devastated the crops, the Natives were given permission to leave to procure their own sustenance. Since these were hunter-gatherer groups who were being taught to become farmers, one wonders what they would have thought about farming as a reliable way of making a living. Indeed, Palóu (1998, 1:145) states that the Natives were killing and surviving on the mission's sheep and goats (*ganado menor*). As in Texas one hundred years earlier, Natives resorted to using the products of the mission to supplement or enhance their subsistence rounds.

From April 1768 through August 1771, the Franciscans at Mission Santa Gertrudis baptized 254 children, buried 403 children and adults, and married 102 couples. The mission counted on its rolls 1,138 persons (357 families, an average of 3.1 per family), who lived in seven surrounding rancherías and subsisted by hunting and gathering. Only 174 people lived at the mission (40 families, an average of 4.4 people per family). The Franciscans acknowledged that they could not support them on what the mission produced, nor could they fulfill Gálvez's orders to relocate them because the people strongly resisted moving and warned that if the friars tried to relocate them, they would leave (Palou 1998, 1:146). The friars had finished the construction of a series of adobe dwellings for the mission Natives. The mission grew wheat, corn, barley, and grapes and other fruits, but it too had suffered the devastation caused by the locusts. It had 113 head of cattle, a large herd of horses, 25 mules, 140 sheep, and 470 goats.

The difference in the size of families that resided at the rancherías (3.1 per family) and those that resided at the mission (4.1 per family) is noteworthy, although it is hard to decide what it means. Were hunter-gatherer families smaller because of the difficulty of obtaining food? Is this discrepancy just

Figure 8.1. Diegueño Indians, 1849. Drawn by John Woodhouse Audubon. Courtesy of the Braun Research Library, Autry National Center, Los Angeles, California.

accidental? Does this difference reflect the inclusion at the mission of some individuals who normally would not be considered family members?

At Mission San Francisco de Borja, the Franciscans had baptized 401 persons, including 26 adults, and performed 273 marriages from April 1768 to August 1771. They had buried 499 children and adults, a number very close to the number of those they had baptized, but Fr. Palóu states that all the population of the region had been Christianized. At the mission lived 184 people, or 44 families and three widowers, an average of 4.0 people per family. The mission covered five outlying rancherías with a total population of 970 people; thus, in total, the mission served 1,479 people. Fr. Palóu again acknowledged that San Francisco de Borja could not support the neophyte population and that the Natives who lived in the rancherías survived by hunting and gathering, although they also planted crops at San Francisco Regis and at a locale called El Paraíso. They grew corn, wheat, barley, grapes, figs, pomegranates, and abundant cotton, but in 1771 the locusts devastated the corn crop. The mission had 500 head of cattle, 1,700 sheep, 930 goats, 215 horses, 43 mules, and three asses (Palou 1998, 1:147–48).

Mission Santa María de los Ángeles was taken over by the Franciscans in May 1768. At the time, the mission did not have a church yet because the Jesuits had founded it only in October 1766. The Franciscans built an adobe church and a two-room dwelling for the friars as well as a storehouse. From May 1768 to September 1771, the Franciscans baptized 199 adults and married 120. They buried 108 children and adults. As of September 1771, the mission had 186 families composed of 523 people (2.8 people per family) who lived in *rancherías* in the environs of the mission; only five families and four young males resided at the mission. The mission had poor agricultural land and pastures and grew a scant amount of corn and wheat. It had only twelve head of cattle, seven horses, and twenty-six mules. The poor location of the mission led to the suggestion that it should be moved to the new mission of Velicatá, but no final decision had been made (Palou 1998, 1:148–49).

The report concludes that the missions served a total of 5,094 Natives; when the Franciscans had received the missions from the Jesuits, there had been 7,149 mission residents. The population decline of 2,055 persons was attributed to the epidemics that had occurred in the preceding three years and four months. These numbers, like all others, are problematic, as Jackson has eloquently shown (1995; 2005, 275–77). But if we accept the loss of 2,055 people in three years, we obtain a yearly average of 685 deaths, though we do not know how many neophytes ran away. Fr. Palóu stated that the Indians were contented and that these missions could not, nor could they ever, be secularized, because "the land is so poor that it does not help its indigenous (*naturales*) inhabitants to maintain a priest (*cura*)" (Palou 1998, 1:150). It is noteworthy that Fr. Palóu did not state that the Natives were not prepared to take care of themselves, but he did state that "it seemed convenient to leave those ancient missions" (Palou 1998, 1:151).

Apart from the observations made above regarding the disruption caused by disease and administrative decisions, the Franciscan report on Baja California highlights one major shift resulting from the loss of Native population. Most missions could house and support their neophytes, generally eliminating the need for the rotational system the Jesuits had devised. This also meant that in most cases, the remaining Native population was farther ahead in the process of Christianization, socialization, and acculturation. This is not a negligible point because attention and concentration on these "ancient" mission populations, regardless of the numbers, could result in the long-term Christian communities envisioned by the missionaries. The issue of demonstrating conversion with baptismal numbers and showing economic progress, which required new converts and a larger labor force, precluded such a bold move, yet that was basically what Fr. Oliva and Fr. Font advocated.

On the other hand, at Santa Gertrudis and at San Francisco de Borja, which registered larger populations, most of the Natives remained in their *rancherías*, and at San Ignacio the Natives had been told to procure their own food and were using the mission flocks as a resource without permission. In fact, at San Ignacio in 1771 most Natives were simply gathering and hunting. Apparently, if the Native residents procured their own food, established missions with smaller populations could remain stable even in years with poor crop yields, while missions with larger populations could survive if most of the neophytes lived in *rancherías* or were told to leave. Certainly the friars did not have a choice, but the fact remains that when crops failed or when the mission could not feed its neophytes, the Natives had to resort to their traditional methods of hunting and gathering.

Fr. Palóu also reported on Mission San Fernando de Velicatá, the Baja California mission the Franciscans had established. From May 1769 to September 1771, the Franciscans had baptized 306 adults and 74 children, 12 people had died, and 86 had married. Compared to the baptism and burial numbers recorded for the other missions, the "newness" of the population of this mission is noteworthy, particularly considering that only twelve families resided at the mission. This was because the friars could not yet support all the neophytes; the rest lived in *rancherías* nearby. At Velicatá the Franciscans maintained the rotational system the Jesuits had used; each week the people from a specific *ranchería* came to the mission to receive Catholic instruction. The Franciscans appointed a captain and catechists (*temastians*) for each *ranchería*; these instructors gathered the people every day to recite the Christian doctrine. As they had for the Jesuits, the *temastians* kept an eye on the people for the friars and informed them of any problems that occurred while the people were in the *rancherías*. The lands of the mission proved to be poor for cultivation and although Natives planted corn, wheat, and trees, the yields were dismal. Still, the animals brought from San Francisco de Borja had multiplied and the mission had 49 head of cattle, 40 sheep, 44 goats, and 12 horses. As of September 1771, the church paraphernalia had not arrived, but the mission had some vestments and a bell previously taken from the old missions (Palou 1998, 1:153–54). Velicatá was surrounded by *rancherías* of "pagans" and needed soldiers so the missionaries could go through the *rancherías* to search for gentiles and bring them to the mission. Fr. Palóu also stressed that concern about security prevented the friars from establishing the five missions between Velicatá and San Diego that the crown had ordered. The same was certainly true for the eight missions that the crown ordered established farther north between San Diego and San Francisco (Palou 1998, 1:154–55).

Fr. Palóu included a document in his report that stated the amounts and provenances of the funds belonging to the Jesuit Pious Fund. He requested that these funds be used to sustain the extant missions and the ones yet to be established and that they be used to clothe the Natives on a regular basis. He also explained part of the Jesuits' investment practices: they would buy rentable properties and use the proceeds to finance the missions protecting the returns and avoiding financial downturns (Palou 1998, 1:157–59).

Palóu's report and the transfer of the Baja California missions from the Jesuits to the Franciscans raise one last point. It seems that while in Texas the threshold of sustainability and success of a mission hinged primarily on the labor force, in Baja California it depended on maintaining a small resident population at the mission and using a rotational system of teaching that presumably facilitated conversion without providing outright economic support of the neophytes. Still, as Leandro's case shows, labor and control were always part of the equation.

The Case of the Mayordomo

In August 1771, the Guaycura of Todos Santos complained to Spanish governor Barri about the mayordomo (overseer) of the mission because he overworked the people, flogged them, and starved them to death. Palóu dismissed the complaints as the usual ploys of the Guaycura. He cited the troubles the Guaycura had caused the Jesuits and recounted a recent episode when a Native had lodged a similar complaint (Palou 1998, 1:110). Fr. Palóu stressed that the mayordomo did not administer punishments but instead informed the resident friar of any problem with the Natives. As Engelhardt explains, the friar, "like a father, ordered some whipping to be administered in his presence, seeing to it that the chastisement was that for sons" (1929, 445). Palóu stated that the Guaycura were up to their old tricks and that they destroyed and stole everything. Indeed, the friars had to hire someone to fetch wood for the Guaycura because if they were sent to get wood they would not return, a statement that demonstrates how eager the Guaycura were to get away from the mission. Be that as it may, Governor Barri did not accept Fr. Palóu's explanations and sent the complaints to the viceroy.

The case of the Guaycura affords a glimpse at the changes in the mission system after the departure of the Jesuits. While the Guaycura often chose to rebel against the instructions of the Jesuit fathers, they continued to maintain a good deal of autonomy because of the rotational system the Jesuits used. Once the Franciscans took over and Inspector-General Gálvez relocated the Guaycura to Todos Santos, they were forced to congregate in pueblos (Palou 1998, 1:111). Thus began a vicious circle whereby some Guaycura chose to flee and were brought back by the soldiers. A Guaycura chief by the name of Leandro helped the soldiers bring back the fugitives, but so many fled that Leandro was gone all the time. The friar made sure that Leandro had mules with which to pursue the fugitives and good clothing and that his plot of land was sown and harvested so that Leandro would not waste time with other chores. As Leandro and his family received weekly food rations, he was able to sell produce from his private plot of land. Leandro was playing a double game; while he delivered fugitives who were not his friends to the mission, he made sure that his friends and the women he preferred remained at large. Once Leandro's maneuvers were discovered, the friar chastised him, dispensed with his services, and ordered him to remain at the mission. Leandro planned revenge. A few days later, he asked permission to go to Santa Ana, a nearby mining pueblo, to conduct some business. When Fr. Ramos, the mission friar, consented, Leandro rushed to the presidio to report that the mission was in revolt because of the cruelty of the mayordomo, Juan Crisóstomo de Castro, a Spaniard, who Leandro said mistreated the Natives and even had killed one person. Although Fr. Ramos was aware of Leandro's intentions, he let him go, but apparently he said that Governor Barri had no authority within the mission and that he could not remove the mayordomo, who served at the friar's discretion. Leandro succeeded in presenting his complaint to Governor Barri. He accused the friar of not hearing the Natives in confession and made sure the governor was aware of Fr. Ramos's comment on the authority of the governor over mission affairs (Palou 1998, 1:112–13).

The story meanders in this game of "governor said, friar said, Native said"; each party used miscommunication, innuendo, impressions, and egos to maneuver for maximum advantage. Regardless of the veracity of any particular account or even the reputation of the Guaycura, Leandro, like any ladino, knew well how to play both sides of the situation and which buttons to press to elicit the desired reaction: that was precisely why he had been useful to both the friar and his friends. In the end, no one received satisfactory resolution. From this case issued a long-term enmity between Governor Barri and the Franciscans and an erosive relationship between Barri and Palóu. According to Fr. Palóu (1998, 1:114), Governor Barri became the defender of any Native who complained against the friars. The Natives lost respect for the friars, failed to attend prayers and catechism, stole, and felt free to rebel. Indeed, Palóu (1994, 272) confided to his superior "The situation is frightful" [*Esto está malísimo*]. In response to Governor Barri's statements that the friars' control extended solely to "preaching, hearing confessions and saying Mass," Fr. Palóu retorted that the friars were in charge of all spiritual and temporal matters related to the missions except for the elections of the village governors and the criminal cases which were the purview of the governor (Palou 1998, 1:114).

The yearly election of Native officials mandated by the crown was a sore point between the civilian authorities and the Franciscans and one Governor Barri used to exasperate Fr. Palóu. The election of Native officials was to involve civil and religious authorities, because it aimed at preparing the Natives for the Spanish model of governance. For the friars, however, the elections had immediate pragmatic results because these officials were crucial to the administration and running of the missions. Regardless of the frictions brought about by the elections, without the avowed support of the governor and the military, the friars could do little to control the Natives.

In Leandro's case, the governor would not allow the Natives to return to the mission unless the mayordomo was removed and the friars would not remove the mayordomo. Palóu finally blinked, but did it in such an intelligent way that he got rid of several problems at once: he surrendered the mission to the governor. In effect, he proposed that the mission be closed and that the remaining Guaycura families residing at Todos Santos be relocated to other missions. This parochial conflict precipitated a decision that affected the Baja California missions (Palou 1998, 1:121–23). By 1773, the Dominicans officially took charge of all the remaining Baja California missions, except for San José de Comundú, San Ignacio, Santa Gertrudis, and San Francisco de Borja.

The case of the mayordomo sheds some light on aspects of the mission system. As a middleman between friars and Natives, the mayordomo's position of power was a magnet for conflict that tested the limits of missionary tolerance. Leandro used his knowledge to acquire power and play double games and to explore the space of conflict always latent between church and civil authorities. For his services, he received economic rewards that were translated into power and prestige. Despite the fact that Leandro and his family received mission food rations, he was given his own land plot for cultivation and helpers to farm it and was able to sell the produce of his land. He also received clothing and transportation and enjoyed nearly complete freedom of movement. As Palóu (1998, 1:111) recognized, he was treated differently from all others. Most of all, Leandro's word and the innuendos he made carried enough weight to poison the relationship between the Franciscans and the military. This case also demonstrates how Natives accrued positions of power within missions because the missionaries relied on the information they provided. Jesuits and Franciscans institutionalized a system of control that used Natives to control mission populations. To serve the mission's needs, missionaries empowered Natives, particularly ladinos, to exert control over their brethren, but ladinos had multiple agendas and spoke for several interests, not least their own. The same occurred with Antonio Arcón, who used his knowledge and influence to parley leadership among Native Texas northern groups. As Foucault pointed out, "Suddenly, what made power strong, becomes used to attack it" (quoted in Gordon 1980, 56). Maneuvering around in the colonial murk, ladinos subverted the short-term plans of many and the long-term plans of a few, but often their actions had unintended consequences.

In July 1769, Fr. Serra and his entourage crossed to Alta California and reached San Diego. For the next several decades Fr. Serra was on a sacred mission to establish missions, and the imprint of Fr. Serra's religious fervor and radicalism marked the Alta California mission enterprise.

Conclusion

The Jesuit missionary work in Baja California benefited from geographic and economic factors and specific conversion practices. The isolation of the peninsula, the Pious Fund, and wise management and control of the army, at least for some of the time, gave the Jesuits measures of autonomy not available to the Franciscans. Furthermore, the doctrinal rotational system the Jesuits used made it possible to run the missions with fewer resources and, more important, provided the Native populations with some freedom to continue their cultural practices and maintain social networks. The Franciscans did not covet Baja California, but the expulsion of the Jesuits made the Baja missions a Franciscan problem. These Natives were children of other fathers tossed suddenly and anew into relationships and practices they thought they had mastered. The Jesuits had become outcasts and the Franciscans had to demonstrate progress in their missionary endeavors. Soon the Franciscans found a way out of the problem of converting the Natives of Baja California: they took to the north.

Alta California

Franciscans

Missions, my Lord, missions—that is what this country needs. They will not only provide it with what is most important—the light of the Holy Gospel—but they will also be the means of supplying foodstuffs for themselves and for the Royal Presidios.

Fr. Junípero Serra to Teodoro de Croix, August 22, 1778 (Serra 1956, 3: 255)

When the Franciscans moved into Alta California, Florida was almost a memory (Bushnell 1994, 204–6) and their missionary program in northern Mexico and Texas was winding down. The Franciscans in Texas and Coahuila were in the midst of a soul-searching period about their methods of socializing Natives and the appropriateness of juggling mission economics (*temporalidades*) and the work of conversion. By the 1790s, all Texas missions in the San Antonio cluster had been secularized and only two Spanish missions established in Texas remained.

The movement to Alta California was predictable, but the economic and strategic interests of the Russians in the territories to the south put the Spanish on notice and sped up the colonization of the northern California region. In 1768, Viceroy De Croix instructed Inspector-General José de Gálvez to locate the ports of San Diego and Monterey and he asked Franciscan friar Junípero Serra to Christianize the province. As it had in Texas about a century before, evangelization provided an innocuous foreground for political and strategic maneuvers in the background. Once more, battles of good and evil cloaked international power plays. Ironically, the Pious Fund, which Jesuits carefully constructed to subsidize the work of conversion, was used to jump-start the whole California enterprise, reemphasizing the political aspect of missionization as well as the incongruence of the expulsion of the Jesuits (Serra 1956, 3: 475n182). Similarly, a century earlier, the crown had relied on the Urdiñola-Aguayo fortune to help colonize Texas and check French expansion.

There are interesting connections between California and Texas. Like Fr. Antonio de Jesús Margil, a powerful influence on the early Texas missions, over a century later Fr. Serra was influenced by the Spanish nun María de Jésus de Agreda, who is presumed to have traveled to the Americas in spirit and who wrote about her mystic experiences (Colaphan 1999; Palou 1913, 118, 120, 123; Sandos 2004, 38; Weber 1992, 99–100). Both friars found incentive and justification for conversion of Native populations in Agreda's visionary experiences, as her writings and visionary testimony provided "divine approval" of the continuation of the Franciscan missionary practices (Colaphan 1999, 157; Geiger and Meighan 1976, 60, 145). Also, after the attack on the San Sabá mission in Texas, Fr. Serra and Fr. Palóu were to be assigned to San Sabá, but at the last minute they were sent to Sierra Gorda instead (Weber 1992, 243). Had Fr. Serra been sent to Texas, he might have made a great deal of difference to the future of the Texas missions.

Like Texas, the Alta California mission field was the exclusive purview of the Franciscan Order and that made it possible for the Franciscans to continue and perfect a model of missionization they had tried and used in Texas and that in Alta California aimed at greater control over the nomadic Native populations. As built environments, the Alta California missions integrated architectural elements common to the haciendas, with which they shared objectives and concerns. Unlike in Texas, in Alta California the absence of well-armed groups such as the Apache, the Comanche, and the Wichita-speaking groups that continuously harassed the Texas missions in the late period removed the need for fortified mission compounds. In California, Native threats originated from within the missions, reinforcing the Franciscan tendency to control Native populations from within the missions.

As the last colonial attempt at Franciscan mission-building, Alta California provides the end point of mission trajectory and modeling. Missionaries and Natives assessed and negotiated positions at the same time that missionaries were required to respond to harsh criticism of their methodologies and practices.

Go North

The historical conjuncture that brought together José de Gálvez and Fr. Junípero Serra was fortuitous. Both were extreme, passionate men. Despite profound differences, in the end they were enablers of each other's worldviews. Gálvez envisioned prosperous Native communities that became self-sufficient by raising crops and livestock. Fr. Serra subscribed to the same basic ideas but was obsessed with harvesting souls. In July 1769, Fr. Serra founded Mission San Diego de Alcalá for the Diegueño on the day of the commemoration of the Spanish battle of Navas de Tolosa against the Moors in 1212. At the end of the eighteenth century, amid Bourbon reforms and tentative Enlightenment excursus, Spanish missionaries were still fighting the "infernal armies" and the infidel and equating religious conflicts in the Old World with those in the New World (Engelhardt 1930, 44–46). Fr. Serra, in particular, harbored deep concerns about sorcery and devil worship and informed on people while he was a friar in Sierra Gorda. Fr. Palóu, his companion and biographer, was commissary for the Holy Office (Serra 1955, 1:19–21, 43). It can be argued that Fr. Serra's attitudes toward conversion represented a reactionary turn to a medieval paradigm (Sandos 2004, 40–45; Weber 1992, 243). I suggest that his choice as father president of the California missions asserts that his views still represented the mainstream of Franciscan missionary thinking and practice.

From 1769 to 1823, the Franciscans established twenty-one missions along the coast of Alta California. Often the missions did not result from requests of the Native populations, but the Franciscans were not always unwelcome. One of the worst receptions took place at Mission San Diego de Alcalá, the closest one to the missions previously established in Baja California. It is evident that the Natives would have attacked the friars from the start except for the presence of the army. Finally in August 1769, they did attack (Priestley 1937, 9). One year later, attempts to baptize children still proved futile and no converts had been made (Serra 1955, 1:149–53, 209).

The so-called sacred expedition of 1769 to Alta California, which was commanded by Gaspar de Portolá, enabled the military to inspect the country and permitted the friars to reconnoiter appropriate places for missions. Unfortunately, the assets of the Baja California missions were extensively used for this expedition and for other efforts to colonize Alta California (Jackson 2005, 116). Among the many items the army and the friars requisitioned were 142 mules that were essential for transportation between the southern missions (Palou 1994, 96–98).

North of San Diego, the Spanish on the "sacred expedition" generally encountered friendlier Natives who brought offerings of food whenever the friars stopped. Presumably in the area where Mission San Juan Capistrano later was erected, Fr. Juan Crespí, the diarist of the expedition, met some Natives and made them recite the acts of faith, hope, and charity. The Natives repeated his words with great fervor and tenderness though they did not understand a single word they uttered (Engelhardt 1930, 54). These statements or others that indicate that the Natives "devoutly venerated the cruci-

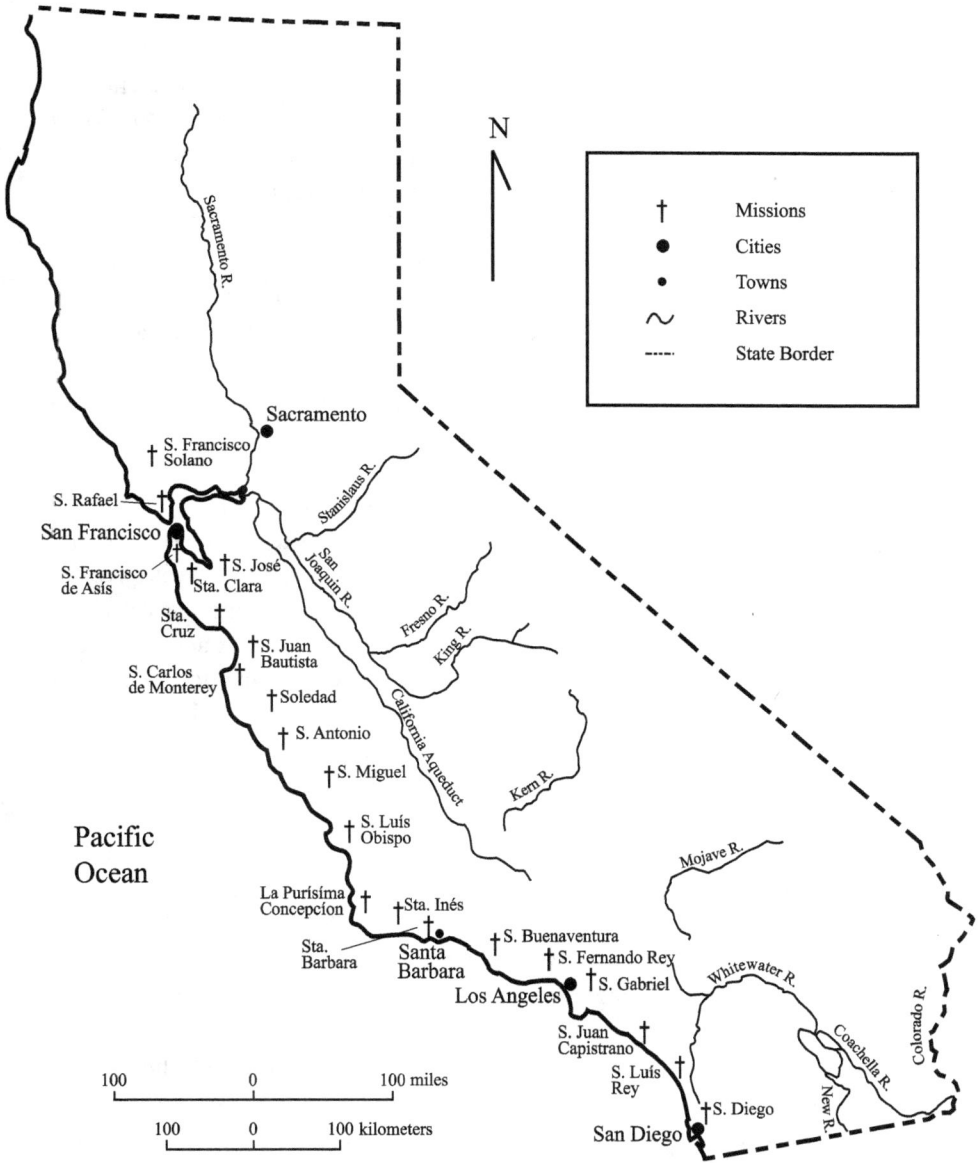

Map 9.1. Spanish missions in Alta California. Map prepared by Claire Huie and Don Wade.

fix" (54) have to be reconsidered and recast by separating the actions of the Natives from the words that characterize such actions. Hospitable behavior and proficient mimicry created illusions in the minds of the friars, who saw with their ethnocentric eyes what they wished to see. Likewise, the friars perceived instances where Native women at Mission San Gabriel made offerings to a painting of the Virgin Mary as acts to honor the Catholic mother of Jesus and not as acts embedded in Native spiritual traditions (Palou 1913, 127; Serra 1955, 1:359). There are exceptions to this pattern. Fr. Gerónimo Boscana (Robinson 1969, 227–341), a Mallorcan who ministered at Mission San Juan Capistrano late in the mission period (1814–1826), made an effort to record and understand Native traditions even though he searched for Christian justifications for what he saw and attributed all things sexual to the work of the devil.

In a memorandum written on June 22, 1774, Fr. Serra (Serra 1956, 2:89, 113) reported a conversation he had with a Native Rumsen from San Carlos Mission who stated that in the beginning the Natives had believed that the friars were the sons of the mules they rode. Apparently, the Natives believed that the friars were the souls of Native ancestors who came to visit them from below ground disguised as mules. If Serra's report is accurate, it is noteworthy that these were reappearances of non-Christian ancestors. Serra questioned the Native about why the Natives had placed small fish, pieces of deer meat, and bird feathers on the arms of the Christian cross when the Spanish arrived and why they had placed broken arrows at the foot of the cross.[1] The Native responded they had done this so the cross, named *porpor*, would not be angry with them, and he added that shamans saw the cross at night rising to the sky, not made of wood, as it was, but "resplendent with light, and beautiful to behold" (Serra 1956, 2:89, 113; see also Hackel 2005, 163). For that reason they offered the cross all they possessed and had great respect for it. Through another interpreter, Fr. Serra ascertained that when the friars arrived, the Natives saw the crucifixes they carried on their chests shining bright and very large. As the friars approached, the crosses had become progressively smaller. Sometimes the Natives also saw flocks of birds they had never seen before that appeared to fly to greet and accompany the Spaniards.[2] While the Franciscans, and Serra in particular, interpreted Native understandings as signs that confirmed the righteousness of the missionary enterprise, they refused to contemplate unmistakable acts of rebellion as repudiation of conversion practices. As a result, Native revolts dealt crushing blows to the friars' feelings and created a climate of fear. But instead of causing the missionaries to desist, armed resistance emboldened them to persevere and try harder, at least during the early period of conversion.

Regarding the way Natives perceived the Europeans, Pedro Fages made some interesting comments. In a discussion of the advantages and possibilities of establishing colonies in Alta California, he volunteered that the Natives saw the settlers as "exiles from our own lands who have come here in quest of their women; for they would then see coming here to settle men who had their own wives, instead of noting, as at present, that we have come neither to oppose them in arms nor to settle the country, since only men have come" (Priestley 1937, 43–44). In fact, "no Hispanic women came to Alta California before 1774" (Hackel 2005, 60). These reactions to colonization were quite similar to those of the Hasinai in Texas eighty years earlier and expressed Native perceptions of the Europeans' motives. For the Natives to commandeer a country and its people without outright conflict and settlement was illogical, a point to keep in mind when trying to make sense of revolts and other forms of Native resistance.

Despite previous missionary experience, the move into Alta California was made with little, if any, advance planning. It must be remembered, however, that the Franciscans had little to do with the political agenda that determined the timing. The Natives did not understand Spanish and the Franciscans did not know the local Native languages. Further, the Franciscans had difficulty procuring Native interpreters and had to rely on Native Americans to learn Spanish in order to communicate (Engelhardt 1930, 126). Yet it was during this initial period of contact, when neither party possessed the ability to communicate, that conversion work was initiated, often in a feverish rush to save souls. For instance, one year after the founding of the mission at San Carlos and its move to Carmel, the friars still did not have an interpreter (Serra 1955, 1:257). Two years later they were still training boys to be interpreters and using ladinos such as Cypriano Ribera, who came with the Franciscans from Baja California, learned the local Rumsen language, and was proficient enough to serve as interpreter (Hackel 2005, 138). Lack of interpreters also led to curtailment of baptism in some cases (Serra 1956, 2:139). The role of the ladino interpreter-catechist was key in translating and interpreting doctrine and in the religious discourse that came to be used by Native American populations (Serra 1955, 1:209, 225, 241, 267). By 1775, Fr. Luís Jayme, who ministered at Mission San Diego, had translated the entire catechism in the Diegueño language (Yuman language group), undoubtedly with the help of Native interpreters. This mission had a Native choir, acolytes for Mass, and catechists who led question-and-answer sessions on doctrine and who worked at the missions and at each ranchería (Serra 1956, 3, 71). In November 1775, though, the Natives at San Diego staged a major revolt during which Fr. Jayme was slain, challenging the view that communication improved the chances of conversion and raising the issue of what factors influenced revolts.

Clearly the willingness or ability of Natives to learn Spanish affected the processes of socialization and conversion or, at least, a friar's perception of his success. As late as the early 1800s, most friars stated that Natives born at the missions were proficient in Spanish while the contact generation retained their Native languages (Geiger and Meighan 1976, 20–21). The friars of Mission Soledad reported that the Natives continued to speak their own languages until they were baptized (20). The friars at Mission San Francisco reported that Natives thirty years old or older did not learn a second language, while at Mission San Gabriel, Fr. Martín and Fr. Cabot stated that women spoke less Spanish than men (20–21).

During the early period, all mission buildings were simple, flimsy structures constructed of reeds (tule) or wood poles that were enclosed by a stockade to prevent outside Natives from attacking and to try to keep mission Natives within the compound (Jackson and Castillo 1997, 82; Palou 1913, 127, 240, 250; Priestley 1937, 11, 19, 44). These stockades were often equipped with locks and keys, effective symbols of control (Serra 1955, 1:351). Mission structures included a chapel, dwellings for the friars, a cemetery, and at least a storehouse. Sometimes a jail or other building served as a chapel until a proper church could be built (Serra 1955, 1:237, 255). Just as in Texas, the flimsy constructions were replaced later with sturdier wooden or adobe buildings (Priestley 1937, 56, 63), and the friars' cells were plastered, whitewashed with lime, and fitted with doors, locks, bolts, and crossbars. At San Carlos, for instance, there were rooms for the mission soldiers and two kitchens—one for the soldiers and another for the friars. A third building was divided into three areas: one for the "Christian girls," another for the chickens, and another "for no particular use" (Serra 1955, 1:257). In 1775, at San Carlos, a Native muleteer had sexual intercourse with a Christian Native woman. The friars asked that the man be arrested and the woman was locked up at the mission (Serra 1956, 4:421). Thus, it is apparent that the practice of locking up women for sexual "misconduct" or to prevent such occurrences was put in place early.

From the start, the mission compound conformed to the quadrangle arrangement and "the cloister or quadrangle" (Serra 1955, 1:385) and was isolated with the buildings, army barracks, and other secular constructions placed outside of the mission stockade. At the time of the visit of Jean François

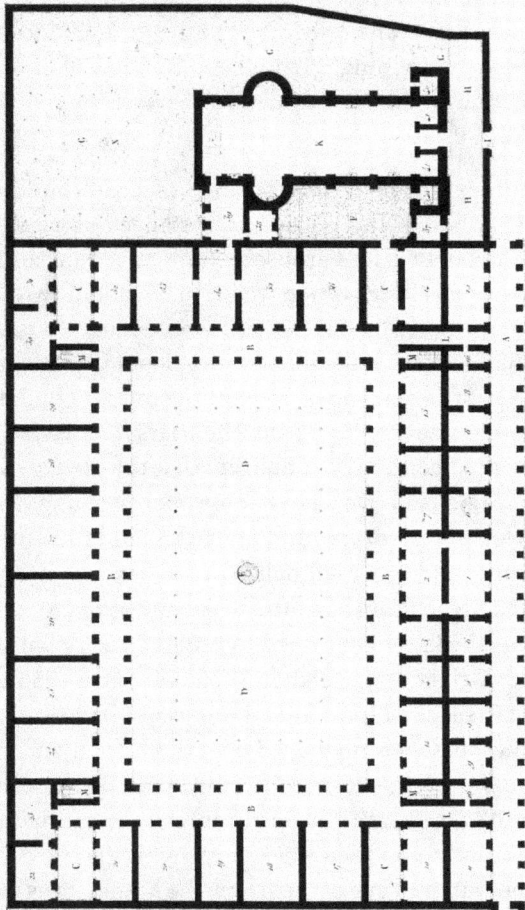

Figure 9.1. Plan of Mission San Luis Rey, Santa Margarita Valley, California, 18?. Engraving by Charles Avril. C. Robert B. Honeyman Jr. Collection of Early Californian and Western American Pictorial Material. Courtesy of Bancroft Library, University of California, Berkeley.

de La Pérouse in 1786, the mission at San Carlos was already designed with the church facing a square and the missionary residence and storehouses located opposite the church. La Pérouse described the arrangement:

> The Indian village stands on the right, consisting of about fifty huts which served for seven hundred and forty persons of both sexes, including their children. . . . These huts are the most wretched anywhere. They are round and about six feet in diameter and four in height. Some stakes, the thickness of a man's arm, stuck in the ground and meeting at the top, compose the framing. Eight or ten bundles of straw, ill arranged over these stakes, are the only defense against the rain or wind. (Margolin 1989, 77, 79–80)

When the inhabitants left their dwellings, they placed a bundle of straw across the entrance, although there were no instances of theft (Margolin 1989, 90). Margolin notes that La Pérouse's numbers mean "an average of about fifteen people per dwelling" which would mean about two square feet per person (80n9)! In the best of scenarios that would mean considerable acrobatics. It is likely that several of the inhabitants slept outside while others, especially the children and young boys, slept in the mission buildings. Also, given the average family size obtained from the friars' reports, which range from three to four people per family, it appears that the Native dwellings at San Carlos might have housed over five families per dwelling. In time, the friars built various workshops, ovens, and granaries, and the missions were well supplied with cattle and other animals.

During the first years, the friars had little to eat and relied mostly on what the Natives offered, as the latter continued to procure their own sustenance (Palou 1913, 133, 135; Geiger and Meighan 1976, 44; Serra 1955, 1:191, 241, 257, 265, 269, 357). The lack of food forced the friars to deemphasize baptism because "finding ourselves unable to give them food and keep them with us, we baptized very few, except when necessity demanded" (Geiger 1970, 32; Serra 1955, 1:347). Despite Fr. Serra's intense disinclination toward the Jesuit system because it provided the Natives with the freedom to wander off and escape the watchful eye of the friars, the Franciscans were forced to adopt some sort of temporary rotational system (Geiger 1959, 58). Serra recognized that the Natives learned the doctrine in the *rancherías* and came back on their own, but "they came back to us from the gentiles so changed we could hardly recognize them" (Serra 1955, 1:347). Fr. Luís Jayme, for instance, was of the opinion that "it is better for them to be gentiles than bad Christians" (Geiger 1970, 33). In 1773, five years after the establishment of Mission San Diego, the Natives were still coming to the mission from far-off

rancherías; they set up "their little huts outside, but near the mission pali-
sade" (Serra 1955, 1:369). The dwellings remained despite the objections of
the military commander, Captain Pedro Fages, who feared that a gathering
of Natives nearby could facilitate attacks. This means that although there
was a mission community, most of the neophytes were nonresidents who
built temporary housing and procured their own sustenance. Some of the
Natives had been baptized and most were under instruction, except for the
traditional reticent old men. As late as 1815, these elders insisted on continuing Native traditions and were responsible for transmitting cultural knowledge through storytelling (Geiger and Meighan 1976, 26, 48). In fact, the
friars continued to stress that conversion would be eased "if the old people
and young ones did not live together for the former are the ones who mis-
lead the young" (57). Five years later, when Fr. Serra came to administer the
sacrament of confirmation, the people at San Diego were still scattered and
typically came to the mission only on Sundays (Serra 1956, 3: 261). Thus, in
the beginning the Franciscans were forced to use some version of the Jesuit
rotational system, as they did in Baja California in some cases.

By 1774, the condition of the established missions had improved considerably and the crops were doing well (Serra 1956, 2:41, 65). Food rations
could be a maximum of one almude (0.13 bushels) of corn for eight days,
depending on the harvest, and the rations were supplemented with meat
and beans. In his writings, Fr. Serra often emphasizes the use of cow's milk as
essential to the diet of both the friars and the Natives (Palou 1913, 133, 155;
Serra 1956, 2:55). An 1813–1815 questionnaire completed by the Franciscans
also mentions the use of milk and cheese (Geiger and Meighan 1976, 85). As
far as I could determine, references to milk in the mission diet are few except
for at Alta California.[3] The Jesuits in Baja California made cheese at Mission
Guadalupe, and Father Baegert once asked for a recipe to cook rice in milk
(Nunis 1982, 187). The use of milk was probably normal at other missions,
but I have found no such references for Texas or Coahuila.

As Serra put it succinctly, "Three times a day they eat from what we provide them; they pray, sing and work; and from the labor of their hands we
can boast of fields of wheat, corn, beans, peas and a garden chock-full of
cabbage, lettuce and all kinds of vegetables" (Serra 1956, 2:79). Nevertheless,
unbaptized Natives were still supplying the missions with meat (Serra 1956,
2:115), and Natives sometimes left the mission to hunt, fish, and gather specific wild foods such as acorns (Hackel 2005, 244–45; Serra 1956, 2:207).

In 1775, Fr. Serra made a detailed report on the five missions that had
been established. San Diego had a brushwood church, an adobe house
where the friars lived that was divided into rooms, an adobe storehouse, a

thatched-roof barn for the horses and mules, an adobe building for the forge, a log building with a thatched roof for the servants, a corral for the cattle, another corral for the mares and horses, and thirteen dwellings for the Natives. These dwellings were made of logs and had thatched roofs. Serra included measurements for all buildings except for the Native dwellings (Serra 1956, 2:225). Although Serra's report provides a lot of detail about church paraphernalia, animal husbandry and crops, and even about some dwellings built for mixed-marriage couples, it mentions no other details about Native dwellings. As other missionaries did, he emphasized the appearance of the church buildings and the economic state of the missions. There are three possible explanations for the silence about Native housing: the dwellings provided by the missionaries varied little, these structures were taken for granted, or little concern was attached to them. This general absence of information on Native dwellings continued into the late mission period (see Allen 1998, 29; Farris 1991; Williams and Cohen-Williams 2007, 103–10).

At the San Diego mission, 116 people had been baptized, 19 had contracted matrimony, and 19 had perished since 1774. The mission had 97 people in its compound (*bajo de campana*) divided into 19 families for an average of 5.1 people per family (Serra 1956, 2:227–28). Requests for needles to sew leather, thimbles, and cards for carding wool indicate that hides and animal fibers were being processed for local use and that some weaving was done, but the quantities were small. Fr. Serra's memorandum of July 3, 1775, asked for shoemakers' needles, skeins for sewing leather, thread, six bolts of coarse cotton cloth, and flannel and Querétaro cloth for a mission yet to be founded. Serra specified that the needles were to be used by the Native women. The report also asked for pottery or metal plates and other dinnerware (Serra 1956, 2:279).

As Native women married sailors and non-Native mission laborers, they built their dwellings in the mission compound facing the friars' dwellings and the church. Fr. Serra envisioned that this would be the beginning of towns and that these couples would serve as example for other neophytes (Serra 1956, 2:151). Serra's reluctance to include soldiers in this idyllic settlement plan might have stemmed from the disinclination of local women to move out of the community once they married or from Serra's unwillingness to let Native women leave the fold of the mission (Serra 1956, 2:151). While Fr. Serra supported the formation of secular enclaves made up of mixed couples within the mission compound, he did not countenance the establishment of pueblos composed of "settlers" near the missions.

In the 1780s, Felipe de Neve established a pueblo near Mission Santa Clara. The Franciscans objected, to no avail. They moved Mission Santa

Clara to higher ground because of flooding, but it remained close enough to the pueblo to be exposed to the problems caused by the settlers (Skowronek 1999). When boundaries were established between the mission and the pueblo, the friars complained that the land and the water belonged to the Natives. Fr. Serra also commented that Neve wanted to establish a pueblo "composed of people, as they say, de razón—just as if the Indians did not have the use of reason too" (Serra 1956, 4:169). Apart from the Franciscan insistence that Natives should have no intercourse with the Spanish settlers and military and their need to delimit encroaching settlements, Serra's statement epitomizes two continuous problems with the missions. First, Natives were to be socialized in Spanish cultural ways, but only those of which the friars approved: the land and its produce belonged to them but only under the terms and conditions of Franciscan teachings. The Franciscans believed that the Natives were endowed with reason but never enough to control their future. Second, the necessary presence of the army was always a mixed blessing, particularly in California where the incidence of abuse and rape of Native women by soldiers is well documented (Castillo 1994, 67–93; Geiger 1970; Weber 1992, 247, 261). In addition, secular frontier settlements resulted primarily from army families or from establishments that supported the army, a situation that placed soldiers, settlers, and Natives in permanent contact as workers in a labor economy that characterized colonial encounters. These troubles and the attitudes of missionaries continued into the late period, although the 1813–1815 questionnaire indicates that Natives had a good deal of autonomy in acquiring and preparing food (Geiger and Meighan 1976, 86–88, 110–11).

By 1784, most mission buildings were being built of adobe and the missions were doing well (Palou 1913, 166). At Mission San Carlos de Monterey, the missionaries had built a separate building 30 varas (82.5 feet) long that was divided into a storeroom at one end and a dormitory for the young women at the other end. In the middle there was a "large room with two barred windows and doors which was to be divided into two rooms and was to serve for the ship's officers and other guests" (Serra 1956, 4:275). Sketches of Mission Carmel made in 1791 by José Cordero and reproduced in Margolin still show Native dwellings that fit La Pérouse's 1786 description (1989, 88–89). At this mission, there were two granaries, a carpenter's shop, a blacksmith shop, and corrals. In addition, there was another building where the women ground corn and made cheese. No information is given about Native housing (Serra 1956, 4:275).

In 1773, Fr. Serra became involved in a power struggle with military commander Pedro Fages. To resolve the dispute and clarify the issues, Fr. Serra wrote a memorial to the viceroy that provides some information about the running of the missions in Alta California, the conflicts with the army and civil authorities, and the administration of justice. First, there were serious problems concerning the sexual behavior of the soldiers with the Native women. Second, aside from crimes that involved capital punishment, Serra requested that only the friars be allowed to control and punish the Native population, continuing the previous practices. Third, the Franciscans requested ten to fifteen soldiers for each mission. While in Texas the crown had reduced the number of mission soldiers, in Alta California each mission had at least four to six soldiers and sometimes more (Serra 1955, 1:347–49). Combined with the geographic location of California and its physiographic characteristics, the increased presence of soldiers might have diminished the need for the walled compounds that were prevalent in Texas in the late period. In both geopolitical and religious terms, the focus of the crown had shifted to California. Fr. Serra also requested several hired laborers to help cultivate the land and specialized laborers such as carpenters and cattle herders; the practice of hiring laborers became common in the late mission period (Jackson 2005, 94, 127). Fr. Serra appealed to ancient custom to have a soldier serve as mayordomo of each mission and asserted his right to choose and maintain the mayordomo, which they called the soldier-missionary (*"que llamaban el soldado missionero"*) (Serra 1955, 1:310; 1956, 2:107–9). The issue, which already had festered in Baja California, remained unresolved and resurfaced later.

The Baja California missions were still the source of cattle for the northern missions, but other supplies were being imported from the mainland (Jackson 2005, 116, 166–69). Fr. Serra asked for mules, horses, and cattle so that the missionaries could provide the neophytes with meat and milk. Fr. Serra demanded that the military stop opening correspondence between the friars and their superiors. This problem was certainly not unique to California, and it underscores the lack of trust and the conflicts between the two institutions.

To create incentives for mixed marriages and possibly to legitimize pre-existing unions, Fr. Serra asked that soldiers who married Native women be given a bonus, such as a mule, at marriage. If the husband remained married after one year, he was to receive a pair of cattle, a mule, and "later a piece of land for private cultivation" (Engelhardt 1930, 137–38; Serra 1955, 1:379–87; 1956, 2:31, 149–51, 153). These requests demonstrate an effort to legitimize miscegenation or to bring the military into the missionary fold. The time frame of one year underscores the ephemeral character of marriages between soldiers and Native women. Many of Fr. Serra's requests were granted,

Figure 9.2. Church, buildings, and ruins of the Mission of San Antonio de Padua, Monterey County, California, 1873. Etching by John Edward Borein. Courtesy of the Bancroft Library, University of California, Berkeley.

but not the request for rewards to soldiers who married Native women. In 1801, Fr. Lasuén, who by then presided over the California missions, stated that twenty-four Native women had married non-Natives, although the friars did not look kindly on marriages that took neophyte Native women away from the mission (Kenneally 1965, 1:205–6; 1965, 2:212). In spite of attempts by secular officials such as Pedro Fages to loosen the power of the friars over the Natives, the memorial continued to emphasize the control of the friars. From the friars' point of view, they were the fathers of the Native neophytes and as such were responsible for their well-being, education, and punishment.

In November 1775, neophytes and gentiles from forty to sixty rancherías sacked and burned Mission San Diego, killed several people, and beat to death Fr. Luís Jayme (Geiger 1959, 59–60; Palou 1913, 171–76). The revolt plan included the destruction of the San Diego presidio, but confusion at the start of the attack led the Natives to forgo that part of the plan. Fr. Serra compared that event to the 1758 destruction in San Sabá in Texas, where Fr. Serra and Fr. Palóu had been destined to go. The events at San Sabá certainly distressed the Franciscan community and marked a change of policy in Texas. The two revolts had similar short-term effects but very different causes. San Sabá was a geopolitical revolt intended to deliver a message about incoherent Spanish political policies, opposing alliances, and territorial control between Native groups, while in San Diego the revolt was about land occupation by colonizers and Catholic religious rule. Unlike the San Diego revolt, the San Sabá revolt was organized and led by non-mission Natives.

For the Franciscans, the martyrdom of their brethren was the essential connection between the two revolts. Unlike the reaction in Texas where the culprits were not mission Natives and were not easily reached, the reaction of the military in California against the Natives was harsh and provoked further unrest. Several Natives were involved in the revolt, including Carlos, who was leader of a Christian *ranchería*, and his brother Francisco. Carlos and others traveled from *ranchería* to *ranchería* to organize the uprising. In October, mission Natives attended a ceremonial dance at a *ranchería* and were flogged by Fr. Fuster. This incident caused many neophytes to join the revolt. Just as at San Sabá, the friars were warned of the impending danger but discounted the reports (Geiger 1959, 60).

In California, however, the friars tended to attribute the anger of the Natives to the soldiers' sexual misconduct (Geiger 1959, 60). There is no question that the actions and cruelty of the soldiers aroused the anger of Natives, but so did prohibitions set by the friars about Native ceremonial practices. Serra's reaction regarding the guilt and punishment of the culprits was the epitome of the pragmatic Christian. It was indeed an act to convert. He asked that the murderers be permitted to live so they could be saved (Serra 1956, 2:407). In 1778, Fr. Serra administered the sacrament of confirmation to three of the Christian ladinos who had presumably masterminded the revolt. A fourth leader had since died, and the fifth member had disappeared (Serra 1956, 3: 263). The organization and leadership of this revolt movement exemplified the intimate relationships between mission and nonmission Natives.

The killing of Fr. Luís Jayme was a message of spiritual anger. The friar was found in an arroyo, stripped of his robes and of the undergarments around his lower body. He had been stabbed multiple times in the chest and other parts of the body, and his face had been clubbed beyond recognition. Interestingly, Fr. Jayme probably had a closer connection with the Native community than other missionaries because he had just completed a Diegueño vocabulary. For a while the revolt and killing created a siege mentality among the friars. Fr. Fuster, Fr. Jayme's companion, was deeply affected by the sight of Fr. Jayme's body and the realization that the killing was a communal act of violence.

In a discussion of ritual violence and revitalization movements, Lepowsky (2004, 3–5) notes that during the so-called Toypurina revolt of 1785, the Natives at San Gabriel mission were angry because the Spanish were living on their lands and prevented the Native population from performing ritual dances. In its territorial scope, strategic planning, ritualized acts, and stated grievances, the San Diego revolt was certainly meant to unite and revivify an ailing people. At San Diego, the ritual act of beating and spilling the blood of Fr. Jayme implicated the many by the blows of the few. Though no mention is made of sexual mutilation of the friar, the disrobing of lower body and removal of undergarments were probably public ritual responses to Christian repression of Native sexuality. On the other hand, the well-known killing of Fr. Quintana in 1812, which involved Natives from missions Santa Cruz and Santa Clara (Asisara 1991, 3–11), had overt sexual connotations both in the commission of the crime and in the actions of the Natives after the murder. All the people involved were neophytes familiar with the mission routine. The killers removed the testicles of Fr. Quintana and buried them in the outhouse (Asisara 1991, 8). If the first act is significant, the second is probably even more so because it compared the male essence of the friar to excrement.[4] Between the removal of one testicle and the removal of the other the Natives obtained the keys to the storehouse and to the women's and single men's dormitories. Freed women and men proceeded to the orchard where the friar had been killed and "had their pleasure" (Asisara 1991, 8). Though the immediate motive for the killing might have been redress for punishments suffered, the ritualized aspects of the killing and its aftermath mark it as a message against sexual repression. Still, the fundamental issue was one of power and control over the lives and labor of missionized Natives, as the continued references to possession of the keys that opened the doors to storage rooms, chests, and dormitories clearly emphasize. The killing opened doors to sites that were forbidden and were controlled by the friar: it was a release.

The attack on San Sabá in March 1758, on the other hand, involved a very large coalition of different Native groups. But the killing of the two friars, Fr. Alonso de Terreros and Fr. Santiesteban, did not involve sexual mutilation, although both friars were disrobed and the latter friar was decapitated (Nathan and Simpson 1959; Wade 2003, 188–90). While the killings of Fr. Jayme and Fr. Quintana carried explicit messages against conversion practices, the attack on San Sabá did not. I agree with Lepowsky's (2004, 45, 49) suggestion that revolts are sensitive to phases of colonial domination. I would add that revolts were responses to local and regional colonial historical conjunctures, as was the case of the attack on San Sabá Mission or

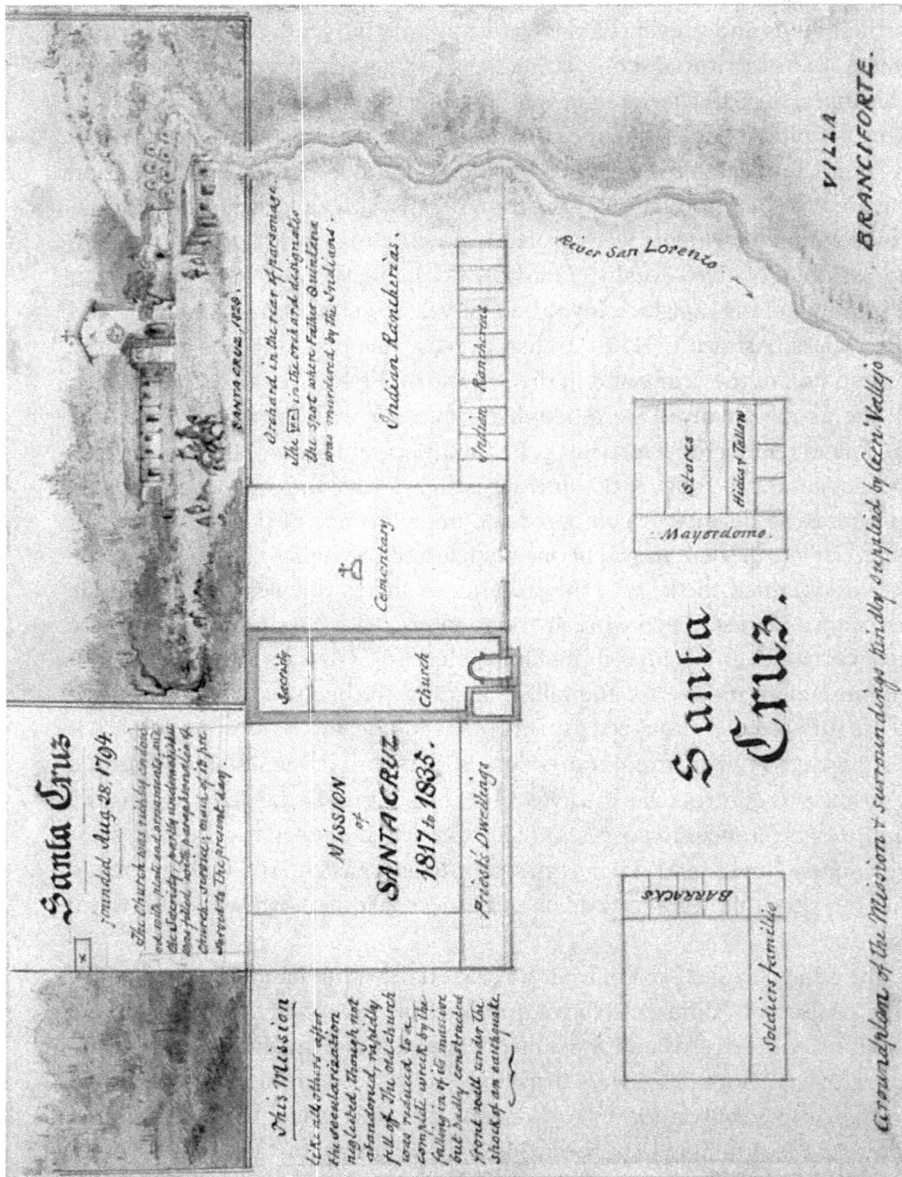

Figure 9.3. Ground plan of Santa Cruz Mission, Santa Cruz, California, in 1825. Courtesy of the Bancroft Library, University of California, Berkeley.

even the case of the Pericué. Revolts responded to multiple grievances that resulted from occupation and domination and emphasized "the connection between religious practice and political autonomy" (46).

The law required that mission-pueblos elect Native officials every year, yet Alta California had evaded the requirement with the argument that the missions were not pueblos (or *doctrinas*) and that therefore the Laws of the Indias did not apply. The friars understood that electing Native mission officials either was just a pro forma attempt to empower those Natives whom the friars' deemed reliable and compliant or was an instance of instruction about civil and legal procedures and duties. They did not see them as actual elections whereby those chosen were invested with the power of their respective offices (Kenneally 1965, 1:75). As the king's edict made clear, that was not the letter or the intent of the law. Thus, when Felipe de Neve took office as governor in 1777, he made sure that the law was put into effect and implicitly used that legal requirement to curb the authority of the friars and diminish their power over the Natives. Fr. Serra, who had zero tolerance for the military, had admitted little interference in mission affairs, and had circumvented most problems resulting from the Bourbon reforms, had to comply with the legal commandment this time. Wisely, Serra disguised his contempt for the legislation and his dread of a loss of power by trying to rig the elections and place certain Natives in office. His concern that the Natives might have "a less exalted opinion of the Fathers" apparently was shared by other Franciscans who worried that Native leaders would be emboldened to start rebellions or that Natives would be made to work for the presidios and exposed to pernicious influences (Serra 1956, 3: 297, 303). Fr. Serra saw the elections as disruptive to the uniformity of the organization of the missions, which Fr. Lasuén later disputed vehemently as not being a mission system (Kenneally 1965, 2:212–13). Serra primed the Franciscans' response by suggesting that they use as objections that "no Indian has authority to dispose of his people without the consent of the Fathers," or that they could not comply because their president (Fr. Serra) did not agree with the decree. Serra figured he could handle the backlash as he normally did.

To counter Governor Neve's legal authority, Fr. Serra ordered the several volumes of the *Recopilación de Leyes de Indias* so he could brush up on legal arguments and play for time (Serra 1956, 3: 353, 365–67). In his response, Serra expanded on problems that had arisen after the first elections and emphatically reiterated that while the friars allowed the Natives the titles of governor, alcalde,[5] or fiscal, these individuals were to be punished as any other Native. According to Serra, fear of punishment made those elected to office fulfill their duties religiously. He said that this was the tradition in the New World and that even the early saints, like S. Francisco Solano, had used this kind of punishment (Serra 1956, 3: 413, 415). His comments reveal that the issue was not the elections; the issue was the possibility that Native officials could be beyond punishment and therefore beyond coercion. The issue was finally settled with the appointment of Fr. Fermín Francisco de Lasuén, who faced a very different set of circumstances and was a far better diplomat than either Fr. Serra or Fr. Palóu. Fernando Librado's recollections from Mission San Buenaventura indicate that the election system continued through the nineteenth century; mission residents continued to elect alcades, mayordomos, and corporals (1979, 13). Librado (1979, 14) also noted that one alcalde was opposed to the practice of Native "mysteries"; this observation implies that others were not and that Native spiritual practices continued into the late mission period. Conflicts about the power of Native elected officials seem to have become more acute in the late mission period; Natives may have become more aware of the possibilities available to Native officials as they acquired knowledge of the power of their positions and learned to use it.

When Natives rebelled, either abandoning the missions and taking to the hills or shooting cattle, the friars pressed the military and Governor Neve about the need to reverse the appointments of elected Native officials and punish the culprits. Unlike Fr. Serra, Fr. Lasuén understood that the "neophytes have not yet acquired much love for our way of life; and they see and meet their pagan relatives in the forest, fat and robust and enjoying complete liberty. They will go with them, then, when they no longer have any fear and respect for the force, such as it is, which restrains them. They are still much addicted to the pagan way of life which they led, and which they see continually in many of their own people" (Kenneally 1965, 2:6). This statement is intriguing at two levels. First, he noted that Natives outside the mission not only had complete liberty, a fact well known, but also were fat and robust. Why would any Natives remain in the mission when the quality of life was so much better outside it? Second, the friars' clear awareness that despite years of socialization and conversion work, the Natives continued to prefer their "pagan way of life" remains a continuous thread from Florida to California, and yet the friars remained deaf to such loud cries. Only the friars' unambiguous belief in the righteousness of their work can explain such deafness; they stayed the course.

After Serra: An Apologia

In August 1784, Fr. Serra died and was soon after replaced with Fr. Lasuén. Before Fr. Serra's death there had been hints that the Franciscans were to be replaced by the Dominicans, as had been the case in Baja California (Kenneally 1965, 1:xxv). During his tenure as president of the California missions, Fr. Lasuén faced some of the same issues as Fr. Serra, but while Fr. Serra had been combative and had a dictatorial style of governance, Fr. Lasuén generally led by consensus and used a lighter touch with his brethren and the bureaucrats.

The 1790s were a time of continuous personal problems with the friars and difficulties in recruitment. Several of the Franciscans who had been in California for many years retired, some died, and some who came to replace the retired and deceased friars did not stay. From issues of health due to climate to Fr. Hilario's and Fr. Barcenilla's disturbed behaviors or Fr. Antonio Concepción's presumed madness (Kenneally 1965, 2:41–42, 58, 83, 95–99, 103–4, 120–21, 144), Fr. Lasuén felt "like one caught under a mill stone which never ceases to grind, and evidently never will cease" (Kenneally 1965, 2:167). As Fr. Serra's tenure was awash with problems in provisioning the missions and in keeping military interference at bay, Fr. Lasuén was plagued with ill or discontented friars who sometimes lacked "patience with the Indians" or were incompatible with their companions (Kenneally 1965, 2:149).

With great difficulty but with tact, Lasuén was able to deal with most personnel problems. The affair of Fr. Antonio Concepción, however, had repercussions. His presumed unstable mental behavior led to his departure from California and although Fr. Concepción departed voluntarily, he later became disgruntled and made some accusations about the organization and practices of the mission. Fr. Concepción's claims opened the door for a barrage of complaints from army personnel that fueled fires that had been smoldering for years. The fact that the initial charges originated with a Franciscan made the whole affair all the more painful and distasteful and lent credence to charges others made. Fr. Lasuén's response to the charges provides information about the mission system or, as the friar would have it, about their conduct and administration (Kenneally 1965, 2:197). Fr. Lasuén's text was written in spurts, follows the sequence of questions posed to him, and has its own logic. I have changed the order in which he presented material and I have grouped the material by subject matter and practices. I do not discuss the defense mounted by Fr. Lasuén. I focus my discussion on issues that deal with the work of conversion and the administration of the missions as related to Native Americans.

According to Fr. Lasuén, the mission Natives were supplied with a blanket, two loincloths for the men and two tunics each year. Presumably the tunics were for the women. Those who lost or gambled their clothing could get replacements if they asked for them. After looms were introduced, most missions also distributed skirts to the women. Vaqueros were given pantaloons and boots, a hat and shoes, and sometimes leather jackets made of buckskin. Mothers were given a new cotton blanket and some clean old garment that could be used for the newborns. Old clothing was also used for the sick; for extra bedcovers, shrouds, and handkerchiefs; and for the poor (Kenneally 1965, 2:198–99, 204–5). Mission attire differed for people who lived in *rancherías* or shunned western clothing. For instance, Pedro Fages reported that male Natives who lived between the San Diego and San Francisco Solano missions wore "a sleeveless doublet made of undressed strips of rabbit or otter skins twisted and put together with some degree of skill," while "women cover[ed] themselves with aprons made of leaves of reeds softened by beating and gathered at one end into a belt" (Priestley 1937, 13). Over this garment they wore a skirt made of two tanned deerskins in warm weather. In cold weather the women protected their backs with another deerskin. The friars' answers to the 1813–1815 questionnaire confirm that clothing continued to be given each year, but they often distinguished between traditional dress and regular mission attire (Geiger and Meighan 1976, 147–53).

The work schedule of pregnant women was reduced so they did not have to grind corn, and nursing mothers were generally released from work altogether and were not punished for any misdeeds. They were generally employed at spinning, sewing garments for the sick, repairing rags for reuse, cleaning wheat, or in light domestic chores. Although pregnant women did not have to work at the mission, Fr. Lasuén affirmed that they were often seen coming from the woods or the beach burdened with loads of wood, leaves, seeds, shellfish, or fish (Kenneally 1965, 2:210). These remarks leave little doubt that Natives continued to procure foods and other needed supplies on their own, which is confirmed by the answers given to the 1813–1815 questionnaire (Geiger and Meighan 1976, 85–86, 107).

The friars kept a watchful eye on pregnant and nursing mothers to prevent abortions, particularly among the women of the San Luís Obispo and San Buenaventura missions. These and other statements indicate that the friars were concerned about high mortality and low birth rates, a worry amply demonstrated in their responses to the 1813–1815 questionnaire, although the friars attributed disease and low birth rates to moral laxity (Geiger and Meighan 1976, 71–80, 105–6). Fr. Lasuén stated that the Natives often ridiculed the friar's precautions with pregnant women; they said that non-Christian Native women continued to work as usual during pregnancy and after childbirth (Jackson and Castillo 1997, 82; Kenneally 1965, 2:210). The missionaries also saw new mothers as a problem because they were so obliging with their offspring. Even two years after birth the women would stop working every time the child cried, wanted to nurse, or pointed to the part of his or her body where he or she was hurting (Kenneally 1965, 2:209–10).

Everyone got three daily meals, generally atole or pozole.[6] Those on the sick list got atole morning and evening, were served a meat stew at noon, and got over two pints of milk a day. When a Native took a fancy to the friar's meal, that person would get a meal from the friar's table that included bread. This indicates that, at least in some cases, the friars ate with some of the Natives in a communal refectory and that bread or tortillas were not normal fare, which is confirmed by the responses to the 1813–1815 questionnaire (Geiger and Meighan 1976, 130). According to Fr. Lasuén, Natives were given plenty of time to harvest wild foods, but they liked the abundance, quality, and certainty of the crops available at the missions and apparently preferred barley to any forest seed. The mission Natives sold a measure (a fanega, or 1.6 bushels) of wheat, corn, and other produce for four strings of beads and bought forest seeds for two strings of beads. The Natives had established those rates of exchange and had created equivalencies between western weights and measures and indigenous exchange rates (Kenneally 1965, 2:201–4). The 1813–1815 questionnaire provides some information about exchange practices. Gambling and "stealing" were quite common, taken as forms of exchange. Lending was ubiquitous as another form of exchange, particularly between kinfolk and friends (Geiger and Meighan 1976, 105–6). Beads and seeds were lent and used as currency; wives were exchanged at San Gabriel and San Fernando; fish quantities were exchanged for agreed-upon quantities of acorns at San Luís Rey (107), and at San Carlos the Natives sold wood and bought and exchanged small items (20). It is very likely that the friars understood hospitality rules of exchange as outright lending (107), providing the reader with a narrower and distorted cultural context for exchange practices. Though little is said about such mission practices, trade in goods and services must have been lively.

Fr. Lasuén offered little information about Native housing except to say that their dwellings were just like those of the non-Christian Natives "in material and style" but were cleaner because the missionaries made sure the Natives kept them neat (Kenneally 1965, 2:206). He added that the Natives constantly improved on their housing and that at the San Francisco and Santa Clara missions the dwellings of neophytes had "grinding stones, pans, pots, stew-pots" and in some cases ovens for baking bread (2:206). Some of the upgraded dwellings had been built at San Luís Obispo and Santa Barbara and more were planned. These new houses were equipped with windows and doors (2:206), features common in Texas by the 1770s. Once again, we encounter the bifurcated discourse in which missionaries stated that Natives constantly improved their dwellings yet at the same time complained about the laziness and lack of cleanliness of Natives.

Girls and spinsters slept in a dormitory and were locked up at night. In 1786, La Pérouse reported that "an hour after supper, [the friars] take care to secure all the women whose husbands are absent, as well as the young girls above the age of nine years, by locking them up, and during the day they entrust them to the care of elderly women" (Margolin 1989, 91). Fr. Lasuén commented that the friars took care that the women's stay in the dormitories did not affect their health and that it had "been determined that death" occurred "but rarely among those who observe this rule of life" (Kenneally 1965, 2:206). The missionaries believed that secluding women and segregating the genders were healthy rules of life. The friars had enlarged the dormitories and made sure they were well ventilated and clean, as was the case at San Carlos. At the time of the report (June 19, 1801), Fr. Lasuén stated that the women's dormitory (*monjerío*) was the best room of the mission except for the church. It was 16 varas (44 feet) long and over six varas (16.5 feet) in width and height, and its walls were constructed of one-and-a-half adobes and whitewashed. A platform along the sides of the building was used for sleeping and the toilets were separate. The room had three windows on one wall and four on the other. Single women and widows could stay outside the mission and during the day go about their daily chores, but they were locked up at night. At the San Buenaventura mission the women were permitted more freedom, but unlike women in other missions, they were said to keep to themselves (Kenneally 1965, 2:206–7). Comments such as these, or comments made about the incidence of abortions among the women at San Buenaventura, San Luís Obispo, Santa Clara, and San José (Geiger and Meighan 1976, 106) reveal that the friars were aware of and preoccupied with women's sexual and reproductive behavior and wanted to control it.

Single men from Santa Barbara or San Buenaventura were not compelled to sleep together in the mission buildings such as the kitchen or other places. Although single men were locked up at night at some missions, Fr. Lasuén recognized that this precaution was not needed in most missions because the single women were secured under lock and key (Kenneally 1965, 2:207). The friars focused on the women in their efforts to prevent sexual contact. La Pérouse, however, witnessed "men in stocks and women in irons for having eluded the vigilance" of the female chaperones and the friars (Margolin 1989, 91). Julio César (1930), a Native born at Mission San Luís Rey in 1824, confirmed that there was a dormitory for women and a "department" for bachelors.

Mission Natives worked five to six hours daily during the summer and four to five in winter (Kenneally 1965, 2:207). Field labor was segregated by gender and age. Generally one friar would supervise the men, another would supervise the women, and another the children (Serra 1956, 2:307). Because a certain number of Natives would always be absent or sick or had run away, it was rare to have more than half of the mission population at work on any given day. While they worked in the fields, some Natives would leave and come back or rest for a while if they so wished (Kenneally 1965, 2:212–13). Most work, however, was assigned as specific individual tasks to be performed during working hours; the friars considered these to be very moderate tasks. Native people were employed as "cooks, laundrymen, millers, water-carriers and woodcutters" and as shoemakers, tanners, and deerskin workers (2:212). Women and young girls were employed for household chores or as wet nurses and babysitters and often received only their daily food as payment. Men and women sometimes asked for a day off, but they typically did not return for several days.

In response to disingenuous comments of army personnel that were included in the questionnaire sent to Fr. Lasuén, the friar asserted that the army treated the Native laborers as "mere Indians" when it came to rations and wages, but when it came to the work to be performed they made sure that the Natives worked a tight schedule from early morning to noon and that after a short rest they resumed work till nightfall (Kenneally 1965, 2:208). In fact, Lasuén claimed that the Natives intensely disliked being forced to go to the presidios to work, despite the good working conditions the friars negotiated with the presidio commanders (Kenneally 1965, 2:208–9, 210–11). As for the mission, the friars tried their best to lighten the workload, particularly for women. Heavy loads, such as adobes and tiles, were transported by wagon. Boys and girls were kept busy with light chores to make sure they grew up accustomed to work and not to idleness. In their responses to the 1813–1815 questionnaire the Franciscans readily recognized that the missions needed "a thousand little things which it would be impossible for us to accomplish without the hands and feet of the boys" (Geiger and Meighan 1976, 130). One assumes that grinding corn for the mission population, a task accomplished by Native females, was one of those "little things."

All traditional games were permitted, except for those that were contrary to religious teachings. La Pérouse mentioned that the Natives played two games: a hoop and stick game called *takersia* and another game called *toussi* that involved four players and consisted of hiding a piece of wood in one hand and having players guess which hand held the wood (Margolin 1989, 95–96). The winner got glass beads or "with the independent Indians, the favors of their women" (96). Natives had learned card games from the Spanish and excelled at them. The friars forbade all contact with people who played cards, but the settlers sold card sets to the Natives at exorbitant prices. As Lasuén pointed out, it was expected that fathers who cared for their children would prevent contact between the Spanish and the Natives in order to curtail the pernicious influence of the former (Kenneally 1965, 2:211–12, 214). Except for those who were vicious or malicious, no Native had been punished for maintaining contact with a soldier, he said. The friars encouraged contacts between a "better class of people" and the Natives. Fr. Lasuén made clear that it was common knowledge that Natives who wished to work for private individuals were allowed to do so, although the Natives profited little from such engagements.

The friars understood their mission as "provid[ing] the neophytes with all the education and instruction" they could receive (Kenneally 1965, 2:216). For their efforts, they felt that they "should have the authority, the right, and the opportunity to correct and discipline them for their own good" (2:216), particularly when they committed "crimes against religion, against approved customs, against the peace of the community, against public and private security" (2:220). They punished Native men by putting them in prison, flogging them, or putting them in shackles or in the stocks, practices that were ordered removed from Texas missions in 1748. The men were generally incarcerated in the guardhouse, in the men's dormitory if available, or in other rooms within the mission compound where other Natives could supervise them. Women were imprisoned in the women's dormitory and were also flogged, but the flogging was administered by women to instill "into them the modesty, delicacy, and virtue belonging to their sex" (2:217). At the Santa Barbara mission, they were placed in the stocks located in the women's dormitory (2:217). La Pérouse confirmed these practices in 1786 (Margolin 1989, 88–89). Fr. Lasuén admitted that the friars sometimes "disciplined" Native workers who abandoned assigned tasks at the mission only to go to the presidio to perform the same work (Kenneally 1965, 2:213). As the friar explained, such irresponsible behavior had to be corrected so the Natives understood that "charity begins at home" (2:218). This statement is contradictory, because in the same document Fr. Lasuén also stated that Natives disliked being made to work at the presidio, unless one assumes that the Natives' dislike resulted from the fact that their wages were handed over to the friars.

As to the harshness of most punishments, Fr. Lasuén quoted a colleague who commented that "in an average school a person would receive more punishment for not knowing his lesson than he would receive here for living in concubinage" (2:218). Despite the fact that today we find the application of corporal punishment repugnant, the friar was correct. Corporal punishment remained in effect in many beneficent and public institutions all over the world for many years to come.

Fr. Lasuén provided the Franciscan view and criteria for punishment. Barbarous and ignorant folk needed penalties that were different from penalties for cultured and enlightened people. The punishment should fit the crime, should not be useless or counterproductive, and should be harsher for repeat offenders. These were Platonic notions of justice that were still engrained in the penitentiary system of justice, but the friars did not follow those criteria with the Natives (Le Goff 1984, 22). Instead, they used patience with the Natives because they were "poor and miserable creatures who deserve better treatment" (Kenneally 1965, 2:221). A friar would exhaust all possible ways to elicit correct behavior, as the father of a family would. Punishment should be used as "an effective method of correcting, never as an instrument to harass the offender" (2:221). The rules were that "no matter how grave or enormous the offense, they are never to be given even one stroke more than twenty-one, and the instruments used should never bring blood, or cause any notable bruise" (2:221). Prisoners who suffered an "accident" were released, and those who ran away or committed offenses while absent were pardoned if they returned voluntarily. All punishments were to be corrective even when the offender was deemed inveterate (2:221).

Notwithstanding the army's statements that Natives rebelled because of lack of food, Fr. Lasuén was likely correct in stating that the principal reason for Native revolts was their attachment to their traditional lifeways or, as the friar put it, their love for freedom and "the call of the wild" (Kenneally 1965, 2:204, 215). This is certainly true, particularly if one considers that the friars' teachings against Native traditions and spiritual practices created cultural stress that could only be alleviated by the very practices the friars wished to eliminate. I shall return to this subject.

Baptism was generally administered after a period of fifteen to thirty days of instruction (depending on the aptitude of the neophytes), and only rarely was it given with less instruction. Friars were very careful not to rebaptize any Native; in 27,000 baptisms only two females and one male infant were rebaptized, and in each of these cases the circumstances were very unusual. In each mission, at least one friar taught the catechism to the Natives in the local Native language. The responses to the 1813–1815 questionnaire make clear that by that time, most missions had translated the catechism into the most prevalent local Native language (Geiger and Meighan 1976, 53–55). The catechism was taught morning and evening, alternately in Spanish and in the Native language. To the charge that the missionaries neglected instruction in the Spanish language, Fr. Lasuén stressed that this was not the case and that Natives were given gifts as encouragement to speak Spanish and were often reprimanded for not doing so (Kenneally 1965, 2:199–201). One of the friars at San Buenaventura mission never learned the Native language and always spoke in Spanish to the neophytes. A few Natives replied in Spanish but most responded in their own language, thus maintaining long conversations in the two languages. Fr. Lasuén (2:199–201) confirmed the Native ability to learn languages; that California Natives learned Spanish quickly and liked the language.

Fr. Lasuén's heartfelt response is an invaluable document of a time and a worldview and must be treated with respect. It is as honest and logical as it is sad. Religious men spent their lives attempting to change the culture of men and women who fought to retain their cultures. All was done ostensibly in the name of religion, and some of the friars' efforts gave a bad name to religion. Fr. Lasuén understood well that the effort to procure "sustenance from the open spaces is incomparably greater" than efforts to enjoin the Natives to work at the mission and that while "the former is free and according to their liking," mission labor was "prescribed, and not according to their liking" (Kenneally 1965, 2:203). Lasuén knew that this was the crux of the problem and the battleground. The friar said, "Here, then (and it cannot be otherwise), lies all the loss and harm which can be imagined or said to have befallen these natives through Christianity" (2:202, parentheses in original). Painfully aware of criticism, Fr. Lasuén stated the missionary's task transparently: he had to "'denaturalize'" the Native "to transform a savage race . . . into a society that is human, Christian, civil and industrious" and that required the Natives "to act against nature" (2:202; Sandos 2004, 92–93). In fact, Fr. Lasuén and the missionaries saw Native culture as a contagious disease from which the Natives would recover if the friars exhibited patience and endless effort and the Natives avoided their "savage" brethren. Their culture was a stage the Natives would surpass when they "gently submit themselves to rational restraint, something they had not known before" (Kenneally 1965, 2:202). For the friars, Christian teachings, a steady supply of food, and hard work would finally win over the Natives to the value of Christianity and civilization and lead them to be deaf to the "almost invincible 'call of the wild'" (2:215). Therein lay the ultimate battleground, which by the end of the mission period would be strewn with the corpses of a few friars and those of thousands of Native Americans.

Conclusion

California was a land of promise; it promised a field of converts and a place in heaven. The Franciscans invested their efforts and their experience in what would be the last stage of the colonial Spanish mission venture in New Spain. After a time, Alta California missions became profitable enterprises with architectural features and practices that further enforced gender segregation. The friars brought potential new converts to the missions in the usual pattern of forays or Natives joined either because a mission was established in their territory or because Native group leaders agreed to bring in their followers. As in Texas, the Franciscans tackled an ever-increasing degree of meddling by a military determined to decrease missionary control over the Native population and increase its own influence.

Native revolts and revitalization movements, often spurred by the demands of the friars or by epidemics, demonstrate that, as elsewhere, conversion practices in California were ill received. While the friars in Texas were contemplating a restructuring of the mission system that would free them from the responsibilities of managing the economic affairs of the missions, in Alta California the Franciscan leadership wrestled with the problems caused by the resident friars but saw little conflict between religion and economics. The fundamental battle, however, was with a change in culture that questioned the concept and existence of the missions, especially their practices. By the end of the eighteenth century, it was no longer a matter of the friars sustaining conversion; they needed to justify conversion. The next three chapters gather and discuss religious and economic practices employed in the process of conversion.

Daily Schedules and Yearly Calendars

Native Americans who entered voluntarily or were brought forcibly to missions were made to follow routines; these were the strategies of socialization and Christianization the missionaries followed. These routines were intended to reset and regulate the internal clocks of the neophytes and instill habits of work, cleanliness, orderliness, and restrained behavior. This was nothing short of a complete overhaul of all conscious and unconscious behavior. Native life courses were disrupted and the cultural expectations of the social group and the individuals who made up the group were irremediably altered as their statuses and roles became irrelevant, were phased out, or were demoted. Missions rearranged the social order and privileged young males, those who learned Spanish, and those who were (or appeared to be) compliant.

Groups that had hunted and gathered for a living before entering the missions had a difficult time adapting to routines, confined spaces, regimented behaviors, and specific foods. Life in a mission cannot be reduced to the enacted routines, but the repetitive nature of these practices produced behavioral patterns that affected the way Native peoples perceived their physical and social environment. The preoccupation of scholars with the importance and impact of these routines and behavioral patterns is not new (Almaráz 1979; Campbell 1988; Campbell and Campbell 1985, 20; Fox 1989, 29–32; Webb 1952), but not much has been done to compile, contrast, and analyze the archival information.

This chapter is divided in two parts: an examination of daily schedules and a review of the yearly liturgical and civic calendar. The first part has two objectives: to describe the basic mission daily routine as compiled mostly from the Texas Franciscan archival records and to compare and contrast the relevant differences between the general daily practices adopted by the Franciscans and by the Jesuits. Similarly, I shall discuss the significant differences between the Franciscans' and the Jesuits' approaches to the implementation of the annual liturgical and civic calendar.

Daily and Weekly Practices

In the Franciscan missions in Texas, the day began with divided families. Couples lived in small housing units of about five to six varas long by four varas wide (14 to 17 feet by 11 feet), while young boys lived with the friar until they were considered grown, probably between five and ten years of age (Habig 1978, 144). Young unmarried females remained with the household unit, unless segregated in unique compounds established for females. These spaces, mislabeled *monjeríos*[1] (nunneries) in Alta California, were not created until the later mission period, and there is no mention of them in the Texas missions (Ettinger 2004, 37; Jackson 2005, 191–92).

On a typical morning, the mission bell rang at sunrise calling all Natives to Mass. Everyone was required to attend and the children served as acolytes (Garcia 1745, 40).[2] To ensure that no one faltered, an elderly Native, a crier, would go through the pueblo to call people to Mass. After Mass the neophytes recited the Christian doctrine in Castilian. A mission report from 1745 (Xavier Ortiz 1745) stated that the teaching of the doctrine was uniform for all missions and it was the same used by the early missionaries, including icons such as Fr. Margil, Fr. Vergara, and Fr. Hidalgo. Nonetheless, a report from 1727 indicates that prior to that date they had used Fr. Bartolomé Castaño's catechism but had switched to the catechism of Father Jerónimo Ripalda, a Jesuit (Almaráz 1979, 14; Polzer 1976, 51–52). Despite possible variations, Texas doctrinal manuals indicate that at least one Native language was used to teach the doctrine, but that may not have been generalized. In fact, Fr. Xavier Ortiz (1745) explained that the friars who studied any of the Native languages affirmed they could not teach the catechism in the Native languages because these lacked the necessary terms, a remark also made by the Jesuits. Thus, Castilian-speaking Natives explained the mysteries of the Faith to their gentile brethren in what Fr. Xavier Ortiz called "a special catechism" (14). Later, in Alta California and possibly as a result of criticism (Hackel 2005, 130–31), the Franciscans alternated the teaching of the catechism in Spanish and in the most prevalent Native language.

In 1745, Fr. Garcia's manual affirmed that the catechism should be taught at sunrise to make sure everyone attended and that after that the work of the day began (Leutenegger 1977, 32). This also avoided the complaint that the friars made the Natives get up at midnight, an interesting remark considering that nowhere do we get information about nocturnal practices, although Matins prayers started at midnight as they were combined with

Vigils, the nocturnal liturgical office.[3] After the morning prayers, each group attended to their assigned chores: most young and middle-aged male adults went to the fields while the women remained in the mission compound. The youngest boys stayed at the friary where they received daily instruction, often administered by the Native fiscal, but as soon as they were capable of working in the fields, they were replaced with the next youngest group (de los Dolores et al. 1762). The boys who lived in the convent rang the bells for afternoon and evening prayers, and they were to make sure that those who lived outside of the convent attended prayers (García 1745, 40). The explications of the doctrine and the question-and-answer sessions were to be done every other day, but the catechism was taught every day (de los Dolores et al. 1762; Leutenegger 1977, 32; Lopez 1786; Xavier Ortiz 1745). Because the Natives were lax, the friars used "force of fear and respect" to ensure that people attended religious services and did the work required. As discussed below, punishment was to be meted by the fiscal always with the friar's knowledge and in his presence to avoid excesses (Leutenegger 1977, 40–41). Young men, who might be sleepy in the morning, were gathered at the end of the day to learn the doctrine (32). Fr. García also suggested that adults be excused from the afternoon prayers because the males rested during the short siesta period and the women who had just returned from their chores needed time to prepare the tortillas for the family.

The main meal took place at noon. Women prepared the meal for their male folk and often delivered the meals to those working in the fields. At sunset the church bell was rung to assemble the mission population for catechism and prayers recited in Castilian at the church door. The boys set up the oil lamp and sounded a clapper to assemble the widowers and single males to sing the Alabado and the Salve hymns at the door of the friar's cell, concluding the evening prayers. Apparently women did not attend the evening prayers, at least by the time Fr. Garcia's manual was prepared. On Sundays and holy days the Natives attended Mass with clean clothes and combed hair. The type of prayers and recitations changed according to the day of the week and the liturgical calendar, but most religious services were accompanied by music and singing. The musicians were generally young men who enjoyed playing musical instruments and who became quite proficient. Sunday Mass was accompanied by musicians who played harp and violin and by male and female choir singers. The 1755 inventory of Mission San José, in Texas, includes a violin, a lute (guitar?), and a lyre (Habig 1978, 122).

On Mondays and Wednesdays the catechism was recited. A boy posed a question and everyone responded aloud. The catechism addressed the basic

Figure 10.1. Mission San Francisco de la Espada, San Antonio, Texas. Robert Runyon Photograph Collection, image number 04146. Courtesy of the Center for American History, University of Texas at Austin.

tenets of the Catholic church, from the nature of the Holy Trinity to the description of hell. After the question-and-answer session, the Act of Contrition was chanted aloud, and the friar addressed the catechumen to expand on specific parts of the doctrine. On Tuesdays and Thursdays, the Natives recited prayers beginning with the Lord's Prayer, followed by the sacraments and the Act of Contrition. The service ended with the Salve hymn. On Fridays the whole congregation followed the Way of the Cross in the church, generally with a young male leading the prayers. During Lent, everyone abstained from eating meat and the friar read the prayers by the light of an oil lamp. On Saturdays, they recited the Rosary and ended the prayers with the Alabado. On Sundays, after the reading of the gospel, the friar would inform the congregation of the upcoming events and note which ones they were obliged to attend. Sunday ceremonies were tied to the weekly distribution of meat, an event of great significance for groups that had previously hunted and gathered for a living, as they were generally prevented from hunting on their own and depended on the friar for meat supplies. The distribution of other rations was also tied to church work and festivities (Xavier Ortiz, 1745).

Fr. García's manual stipulated that the kitchen of the friary should be staffed with boys assigned to weekly duty, a practice the Jesuits also followed (Leutenegger 1977, 40; Polzer 1976, 51). Outside of the friary, women were to make tortillas and atole for the missionary and for the boys who lived at the convent. The fiscal made sure that the boys did not collect the tortillas or the atole from the women. Control over interactions between females and males extended even to occasional contacts that took place in day-to-day living. These prohibitions, which were certainly violated, nonetheless conveyed a message of illicit contact and provoked deviant, "sinful" behavior. Interactions with family members or between prospective mates that were necessary for healthy relationships were stigmatized as wrongdoing. This message was put across not only to people of mating age but also to mothers and fathers and their male offspring (Ettinger 2004, 39).

Pablo Tac's narrative illustrates practices in use late in the Alta California mission period (Hewes and Hewes 1991, 158). The "old man," as Pablo Tac refers to his father, hunted and fished, presumably daily, to feed the members of the household, while the "old woman" prepared the meals for the family group (157). Tac's shorthand description accords well with the information provided in the responses to the 1813–1815 Franciscan questionnaire (Geiger and Meighan 1976, 85–88). Pablo's recollection of daily chores according to age and gender indicates that family members were isolated from each other but that female and male family members ate the noon and evening meals together, after which those who had to attend to specific chores left. Tac's description of the family leave-taking is idiomatic and charged with longing. He said, "The father leaves his son, the son leaves his sister, the sister the brother, the brother the mother, the mother her husband with cheer, until the afternoon" (Hewes and Hewes 1991, 158).

Every morning and on Saturday after Mass, the women swept the church, the sacristy, and the patios of the friary (García 1745, 40). Once they finished this task the women received their soap ration. Fr. García stated that the fiscal was to make sure that the women swept their houses every day and that each week or fortnight they swept the entire pueblo so they could learn to live in physical and spiritual cleanliness and be free from the pernicious effects of humidity and garbage (Leutenegger 1977, 41). This seems to have been the general procedure in the Texas missions, but these practices probably did not vary much from mission to mission, and Fr. García's recommendations worked mostly as guidelines.

Each week the friar made sure that the host maker made enough hosts for communion. Apparently the male assigned to this task was a Native, and the friars took great care to ensure that he performed this task cleanly. Two

Native women were assigned to clean the glass lamp and the church candlesticks, but the church linens were sent to the presidio to be cleaned and mended by Spanish women. In California, however, Native women generally were the laundresses and seamstresses (Palou 1998, 1:118–19). Fr. García admonished his readers not to give Natives the key to the place where sacred implements were stored (Leutenegger 1977, 39). Inquiries resulting from the murder of Fr. Andrés Quintana in 1812 at Mission Santa Cruz in California emphasize how keys to containers and rooms were used to control and exclude Natives from the activities related to such places. Such policies provoked deviant behavior and offered sites of resistance. They likely conveyed the message that the mission was for the Natives but that nothing belonged to them. The same inquiries disclosed that Native women sometimes washed the church linens and were summoned to cut and sew clothing for the missions (Asisara 1991, 10). The responses to the 1813–1815 questionnaire confirm this assignment of chores and add that Native women often washed the friar's garments (Geiger and Meighan 1976, 129–30). Women's access to church cloths and to the friar's garments (undergarments?) provided them with tangible contact with ritual objects and with an intrinsic closeness to the privacy of the friar's most intimate acts. Although I have found no evidence of the potential of this intimacy with ritual objects or with the persona of the friar, the fact remains that such closeness could elicit ritual responses, *malleficio*, an acute awareness of the friar's human condition, and attraction or repugnance.

Failure to comply with the rules and schedules brought about punishment. In 1740, the Santa Cruz de Querétaro *discretorio* issued a set of guidelines related to the punishment of infractions. The list of punishments emphasizes the interconnectedness between religious and civic practices. Friars were not to punish neophytes personally; that was to be done by the fiscal and the alcalde (*que por propria mano de ningun modo castiguen los Padres a los Yndios, pues para esse fin se les ponen fiscals, y Alcaldes*) (Santa Ana 1748). A Native who renounced the Catholic faith and ran away in order to enjoy a life of laziness received no more than twenty-five lashes, but one who renounced the faith to practice any kind of idolatry received up to fifty lashes; this rule, of course, applied to shamans. Those who lived together without matrimony received up to thirty lashes. Those who stole items from the mission were given ten lashes, but if the item belonged to someone else they were to get fifteen lashes. If they traded items received as gifts they were given eight lashes, but if the culprit was a Spaniard or a foreigner he would get fourteen lashes. Those who missed the teaching of the doctrine or ate meat on meatless days were given eight to ten lashes, and if they missed work, they were given six lashes. If they showed disrespect to the mayor-domo or any Spaniard they were to get fifteen lashes, but punishment was not to be applied until the circumstances of the event were ascertained and culpability was established. Those who caused trouble in the mission or committed serious offenses were given between forty and fifty lashes. These penalties applied only to Christianized Natives; the non-Christians were to be treated with greater tenderness. All punishments were to be adminis-tered with great charity and it was ordered that, without exception, stocks, irons, and any other instruments of punishment be removed from all mis-sions (Santa Ana 1748).

Fr. Garcia's manual, however, stipulates other punishments, often harsher than those postulated by the *discretorio* (1745, 80–81). Natives who lived together as man and wife but were not married or those who being married abandoned their spouses were to get fifty lashes (as opposed to 30 lashes stipulated by the *discretorio*). Those who did not confess during Lent were to get forty-four lashes for the first offense and fifty for the second. Those who normally did not attend Mass on Sundays or feast days were to get twenty-four lashes the first time and fifty lashes the second time. Those who ate meat on Fridays were publicly punished with twenty-four lashes for the first offense and fifty for the second offense. The fiscal who did not inform on and instead covered up the sins of the Natives would get twenty-four lashes for the first offense in the hope that he would take heed. This punishment was to be administered in public and if the fiscal committed a second offense he was to get fifty lashes. These punishments had been agreed upon at the Synod of Quito, Peru, and were to be applied with extreme charity (80–81). In addition, the friar recommended that missionaries "talk to [the offender] alone, encourage him, give him positive advice, show him you feel his pain and you want his welfare, just as Saint Paul did" (81). But across the cultural divide, punishment became aggression, and no words could mitigate the incomprehension. Moreover, Native public officials, usually the fiscal, who was often from a rival group, administered the punishments while ladino interpreters mouthed expressions of consolation and Christian love!

To reckon the possible cumulative effect of infractions resulting from a single act, let us consider the hypothetical case of a male who ran away from the mission during Lent, stole items of food for the journey, and missed at least one working day, a day of doctrine, Sunday Mass, or confession. In this hypothetical case, running away could result in a minimum of 122 lashes. This punishment accounting may be the reason for the 450 lashes to which Governor Barri condemned a Native by the name of Osorio, one of the examples of maltreatment Fr. Palóu used during his acerbic interchange with the governor (Palou 1988, 262).

In addition to the daily and weekly religious schedule, Natives who had not received baptism underwent special instruction, which could be conducted in church or in the friar's cell. Sometimes persons who had received baptism were also required to attend these sessions, as they were considered ignorant of the basic doctrine. These people probably had been baptized when they were sick; such individuals had to receive the appropriate Catholic instruction after they recovered. Those who were proficient in the Catholic faith assisted the friar. These ladino Natives were called *temastians* (catechists), and the roles they performed were essential to the missions, although some friars were wary of them. Fr. Martin García thought that they bungled or abridged translations (1745, 57). *Temastians* not only taught the Christian doctrine but also translated doctrinal concepts, modulating and mediating the language of conversion. Their role is still poorly understood, but it is possible that the particular tone that came to characterize Catholicism in Latin America acquired its modality as *temastians* struggled to voice the incommensurable or refashioned Catholic concepts to make them acceptable.

Twice a day the neophytes recited the Rosary, and every evening the whole congregation prayed for all the souls in purgatory while one Native tolled the bell and other Native males sang. After the evening prayers and ceremonies, the young males returned to the friary to sleep, while the rest of the family huddled in their assigned dwelling inside the mission compound.

California

Franciscan daily and weekly routines and practices did not differ much between Texas and Alta California (Hackel 2005, 147). In 1786, La Pérouse described the daily routine and added some information about Native life at the missions in Alta California.

> The Indians as well as the missionaries rise with the sun, and immediately go to prayers and Mass, which last for an hour. During this time three large boilers are set on the fire for cooking a kind of soup, made of barley meal, the grain of which has been roasted previous to its being ground. This sort of food, of which the Indians are extremely fond, is called atole. They eat it without either butter or salt. . . . Each hut sends for the allowance of all its inhabitants in a vessel made of the bark of a tree. There is neither confusion nor disorder in the distribution, and

when the boilers are nearly emptied, the thicker portion at the bottom is distributed to those children who have said their catechism the best. The time of repast is three quarters of an hour, after which they all go to work, some to till the ground with oxen, some to dig in the garden, while others are employed in domestic chores, all under the eye of one or two missionaries. The women have no other employment than their household affairs, the care of their children, and the roasting and grinding of corn. (Margolin 1989, 85–86)

La Pérouse continued:

At noon the bells give notice of the time of dinner. The Indians then quit their work, and send for their allowance in the same vessel as at breakfast. But this second soup is thicker than the former, and contains a mixture of wheat, maize, peas, and beans; the Indians call it pozole. They return to work from two to four or five o'clock, when they re-pair to evening prayer, which lasts nearly an hour and is followed by a distribution of atole, the same as at breakfast. These three distribu-tions are sufficient for the subsistence of the greater number of these Indians. (87–88)

Schedules and practices had not changed much by the end of the mission period in Alta California, as indicated by the responses to the 1813–1815 Franciscan questionnaire (Geiger and Meighan 1976). The recollections of Fernando Librado, a Chumash from Mission San Buenaventura, and those of Julio César, a Native from Mission San Luís Rey, also confirmed the sta-bility of the daily schedule but Librado's comments indicate that the fri-ars were more lax, or relaxed, about Native spiritual practices (César 1930; Librado 1979, 47, 51). Neither Librado nor César mentioned the teaching of catechism, but Librado mentioned the daily morning prayers and both emphasized attendance at Mass and other religious ceremonies. They also mentioned the punishments meted out for infractions and gender segrega-tion in dormitories (Librado 1979, 47–48). Both also emphasized the com-merce in hide and tallow and the importance and power of Native elected officials (Jackson 2005, 134–35; Jackson and Castillo 1997, 23). Lorenzo Asisara's recollections of his father's eyewitness account of the slaying of Fr. Quintana in 1821 appear to indicate that the daily regime of prayers and labor was still essentially the same as it had been for decades (Asisara 1991, 6–10). It is likely, however, that visual liturgical art played a greater role in the Californias than it did in Florida, Texas, or northeastern Mexico, not so

Figure 10.2. San Luis Rey Mission, California. Etching by John Edward Borein. Robert B. Honeyman Jr. Collection of Early Californian and Western American Pictorial Material. Courtesy of the Bancroft Library, University of California, Berkeley.

much because of its use as a conceptual tool but because of its abundance as a conversion tool (Hackel 2005, 148–51).

Pablo Tac's narrative indicated that only the young males attended school and learned the catechism. Older members of the family provided for and attended to the household, and all the other members were engaged in mission work assignments (Hewes and Hewes 1991, 157–58). Tac's narrative provides a glimpse of moments of commensality and intimacy at the Franciscan Mission San Luís Rey in Alta California in the 1800s. He states,

At twelve o'clock they eat together and leave the old man his share, their cups of clay, their vessels of well-woven fiber which water cannot leak out [of], except when it is held before the face of the sun, their frying pans of clay, their grills of wood made for that day, and their pitchers of water also made of clay. Seated around the fire they are talking and eating. Too bad for them if at that time they close the door. Then the smoke rising, being much, and the opening which serves as a window being small, it turns below, trying to go out by the door, remains in the middle of the house, and they eat, then speaking, laughing

and weeping without wishing to. The meal finished they return to their
work. (Hewes and Hewes 1991, 157–158)

The vivid description of objects and people trapped in drafted smoke freezes
the tableau of daily life. Interestingly, Pablo Tac "saw" the cooking and serving vessels and placed them in functional settings, but he did not identify the
food. They eat, laugh, and weep; smoke gets in their eyes.

Baja California

Although the methods and doctrinal schedule the Jesuits and Franciscans
used were quite different, the religious teachings were obviously quite
similar. Clavijero provides a generalized schedule for the Jesuit missions in
Baja California, while the writings of other Jesuits personalize the mission
schedule (1789/2002, 376). For the Natives at the mission, the day started
at sunrise with the ringing of the bells and Mass, which was followed by
the ritual singing of the Alabado. During Mass the neophytes recited the
Rosary, and before and after the service, they were "taught the Christian
doctrine by being asked questions in their own language" for about thirty
to forty-five minutes (Baegert 1979, 121). Clavijero said that after Mass the
fathers distributed a breakfast of atole and then everyone went to their daily
chores, but Baegert also stated that the missionary distributed cooked wheat
and maize to the blind, the aged, the weak, and women who were pregnant
(Clavijero 1789/2002, 376; Baegert 1979, 122). Those whom the missionaries could not provide with food procured their own. At noon the workers returned for a meal of pozole, sometimes supplemented by meat and
vegetables, and those who were sick received a second meat ration. After a
period of rest, Native workers returned to work until sunset. At sunset the
bells were rung and everyone assembled in the church to recite the Rosary
and a litany to the Virgin Mary, and on Sundays and holidays the neophytes
gathered to sing. Once the religious ceremonies were over the Natives had
dinner and returned to their dwellings. If there was no fieldwork to be done,
everyone attended to their assigned chores or to private business (Clavijero
1789/2002, 376).

In Baja California the Jesuits segregated some mission neophytes by age,
gender, and status. "The older boys and bachelors have a room apart where
they sleep; married couples have their own little houses because it is customary, when any of the mission flock marry, to build them a house" (Fr.
Tamaral quoted in Crosby 1994, 239). Men and women and boys and girls
were always segregated during religious ceremonies and the teaching of cat-

echism, and men and women had different catechists. After the evening prayers men and women were taught the catechism again and finally retired for the day.

From July until late October the evening prayers were often said outside in front of the church because of the heat. When the week was over, the Natives who were on the rotational system "returned to their native land, some three, others six, others fifteen and twenty hours from the mission" (Baegert 1979, 121). Presumably the people living in Native villages met in the morning for prayers and singing and then attended to the task of finding sustenance. In the afternoon they returned to sing the litany to the Virgin. A chosen catechist (*temastian*) helped the missionaries teach the doctrine at the mission station. Once the Natives returned to their villages, a Native *temastian* also supervised the religious practices (Clavijero 1789/2002, 376). All the Native groups came to the mission center for major religious festivities, and the missionary preached sermons on Sundays and feast days (376).

Yearly Schedule

The Catholic liturgical calendar was varied and included many feasts, ceremonies, and performances that also had civic and economic implications. In Texas, as generally throughout New Spain, on January 1, the Feast of the Circumcision, the mission pueblo residents elected their Native officials. In Texas, after Mass, all the men in the pueblo assembled in the corridor facing the friar's cell to cast their votes for the governor and the alcalde of the mission pueblo. The friar wrote each vote on a piece of paper and the voter stated his agreement with a cross.[4] Since there were different Native groups in the missions, it was customary to alternate these positions of authority between the two most prominent groups. For instance, at Mission Concepción in San Antonio, where the Pajalate and the Tacame were the most prominent Native groups, one year a Pajalate governor and a Tacame alcalde would be elected and the following year the reverse would take place. Similarly, at San José Mission in Texas, the three principal Native groups, the Pampopa, Pastia, and Suliajame, alternated leadership positions (Habig 1978, 36). Smaller Native groups were incorporated into one of the major ones and were represented through it. This arrangement, which was necessary to balance power and create a fairly predictable outcome, must have resulted in frictions and discontent among smaller groups, whose loss of numbers was translated into loss of power and representation. This inequality is often an overlooked result of epidemics and absenteeism. Likewise, this style of governance and power distribution probably resulted in linguistic uniformity. Indeed, Fr. Francisco Lopez reported that at Mission Concepción the various groups had adopted the Pajalate language (*y el ydioma de estos es el mas usado y general*) (Lopez 1786). While language diversity increased with the admixture of Native groups in Alta California (Hackel 2005, 136), the evidence in Texas indicates a long-term trend toward uniformity in language and worked as a mechanism of what might be perceived today by archaeologists as part of mission culture patterning. Also, the use of catechisms translated into the most prevalent Native language at each Alta California mission likely resulted in long-term language uniformity (2005, 136).

Once the votes were cast, the friar announced the name of the elected officials. The governor and the alcalde knelt before the friar and the governor was given his staff of office. The friar chose the fiscal and gave him the booklet of rules that was the symbol of his office. The ceremonies ended with the singing of the Alabado. The friar, if he so wished, opened a bottle of wine to be shared among the voters. The mayordomo (overseer) and the caporal (vaquero or cowboy) were elected for life and at the discretion of the friar. Their roles and assignments will be discussed later. This procedure guaranteed that the friar selected three out of the five pueblo mission officials.

The election of pueblo-mission officials was seldom practiced in Alta California until late in the mission period and was a source of endless friction between crown officials, Franciscans, and Native populations. In the midst of conflicts with Governor Barri, Fr. Palóu commented on the procedure (Palou 1994, 301–2). The Natives would be summoned and would gather behind the church to vote. The local missionary would propose three people whom the friar considered capable of governing. Apparently they were to know Spanish. The fiscals were considered church officials and were not elected in the same fashion. The tensions surrounding these elections are indicative of power struggles between church and civilian authorities. Palóu conceded that "from the good governance of an Indian governor results the peace, calm, and spiritual and economic progress of a mission, while a bad leader (*cabecilla*) will sway all others and risk the loss of the mission" (307). Pablo Tac stated that there were seven alcaldes (pueblo officials) "with rods as a symbol that they could judge the others" and that the chief of the alcaldes supervised all tasks in coordination with the orders of the local missionary (Hewes and Hewes 1991, 155).

In Baja California, the different Native groups elected officials who were responsible for proper attendance at the catechism and religious ceremonies of all groups, including those that lived far away from the mission. These Native officials were in charge of leading the reciting of the catechism in the morning and the evening, supervising the reciting of the Rosary, and making sure that the Natives behaved properly and kept silent when in church. They led and supervised the daily reciting of the Rosary by those who lived away from the mission. They also policed the area, prevented disorder, punished offenders, reported crimes, and aided the sick, bringing them to the mission if necessary. The insignia of their office was a staff, sometimes adorned with a silver knob. In reality, their duties incorporated those of the governor, mayordomo, and fiscal, although their religious responsibilities included the role of catechist, which went beyond those of the traditional Native cadres, as dictated by the crown. Some soldiers who exercised the functions of mayordomo trained and supervised the Natives, and their duties incorporated some of the tasks of the fiscal. Crosby noted that some soldiers were assigned to the missions "as mayordomos, vaqueros, or regular soldiers on full pay" (1994, 190–91).

In Texas, on Mardi Gras Sunday, the Natives attended Mass in honor of Jesus of Nazareth. The statue of Jesus was removed from its niche and placed on the high altar where it remained throughout Lent. Every day during Lent the whole congregation performed the Way of the Cross. During this period, everyone was to confess to fulfill the annual precept. To avoid confusion and make sure everyone complied, the friar assigned specific days and times for each person to confess. Regardless of the pragmatic reasons for this arrangement, it provided the friar with a good deal of power over people who had to perform a ritual that was likely confusing and intensely invasive because of the questions and the answers it elicited. Unlike people from central Mexico (Greenleaf 1961, 45; Ricard 1933/1982, 32), there is no indication that the indigenous groups in the regions under discussion ever had any cultural mechanism that could be associated with the act of confessing. Indeed, boasting about one's achievements appears more culturally consistent with hunting-and-gathering societies than the volunteer admission of one's foibles, assuming that foibles were not seen as achievements. It is likely that reluctance to confess stemmed from a fear of diminished prestige that could result from presenting achievements as failures. During Holy Week, the Natives also took communion. They had to fast after midnight on the eve of communion, and the friar gave a sugar cone (*piloncillo*) or a bar of chocolate for breakfast to those who received the Holy Host. The instruction manuals indicate that confession and communion outside of the Lenten season were neither expected nor required (de los Dolores et al. 1762). During Lent everyone seven years and older abstained from eating meat: the friar ate fish and the Natives ate beans, and sometimes squash, at the noon meal.

The rituals of Holy Week were important and were celebrated everywhere in the mission system. In San Antonio, on Palm Sunday the friar ordered the fiscal to get palms from the spring where they grew to be used in the procession. On the eve of Ash Wednesday, the fiscal burned the palms; the following day, the ashes were blessed and distributed. After this ceremony the friar said Mass. During Lent the friar ordered the mayordomo to select twelve men to symbolize the twelve Apostles at the washing of the feet. On the evening of Holy Thursday, some Natives carried the altar of Jesus of Nazareth bearing the cross and another of the Lady of Sorrows, while other Natives carried crosses on their shoulders. During the procession everyone sang and recited the Rosary; after the procession, the friar preached on the passion of Christ and the mystery of reincarnation (Leutenegger 1977, 34).

On Good Friday there was another procession in which some Natives carried the image of a naked Christ tied to the cross and others shouldered an altar with the Virgin Mary dressed in black. During the procession the community performed the Stations of the Cross, and when the procession entered the church, the friar preached a sermon on the passion of Christ. While the Sacred Host was in the church, four armed soldiers remained on guard; two at the tabernacle and two at the door of the church. These soldiers, who were relieved in shifts, stayed at their posts day and night until the Saturday morning church service. During Holy Week the congregation did not recite the doctrine, but they recited the Rosary on Holy Saturday.

During Holy Week in California, Texas, and Sinaloa and Sonora in Mexico, local Native populations built elaborate arches decorated with greenery and flowers for the procession, which was accompanied by bells, drums, and trumpets. For the duration of Holy Week and during the celebrations of Corpus Christi, many Natives remained in the church day and night and "they prayed on their knees with rosaries and in great order" (Pérez de Ribas 1645/1999, 251). In Sonora and Sinaloa, the Jesuits held three processions during Holy Week and at Corpus Christi: one for men, one for women, and another for boys and girls. The first procession was called "a blood procession," during which both men and women flagellated themselves. In the church, men were separated from women and mothers took great care that their small children did not cry during the ceremonies (250–51, 449). This type of ritual gender segregation continued to be practiced by the Jesuits in Nueva Vizcaya (Deeds 2003, 19). I should note that flagellation was a common practice in Europe among church officials and the common folk (Delumeau 1977, 46–48).

In Baja California, the Jesuits used a rotational system to catechize, but on the important Catholic holidays and during Holy Week, the whole congregation assembled at the mission for religious ceremonies. On that occasion they received their meat rations, a few bushels of maize, some dried fruit, and items of clothing. These religious celebrations included games and shooting contests, just as they would in Europe where fairs were associated with religious holidays (Baegert 1979, 121; Crosby 1994, 215).

The movable feast of Corpus Christi took place in May or June and was celebrated everywhere with great solemnity (Deeds 2003, 68; Polzer 1976, 31, 71, and 78; Kapitzke 2001, 19; Taylor 1996, 254–55). In the days immediately before the feast, the friar ordered scaffolds to be built and decorated with tree branches and greenery and other decorations; these practices were also common in Nueva Vizcaya (Deeds 2003, 80). It appears that the feast rituals were similar to those of later times because branches of greenery and other vegetal materials were strewn throughout the procession path, as it is the custom still in many places around the world, including Italy, Portugal, and Spain. The ciborium and the altars were carried in procession over the prepared path. People from other missions were invited, and during the festivity the Natives performed the Matachines[5] and, at least in Texas, the people who performed and danced often dressed in women's clothing. At an earlier time these celebrations may have included *gigantones*[6] instead of the Matachines, but the friars endeavored to replace the *gigantones* with the Matachines (Leutenegger 1976, 39–40).

The feasts of St. Anthony, St. Paul, St. Peter, St. James,[7] and St. Anne took place in June and July. The extent of these celebrations depended on the mission, the economic difficulties the mission was experiencing at the time, and the number of Natives present. Some of these celebrations, particularly the feast of St. James, were very dear to the Natives because for some, these were the only days when they were allowed to ride horses. There were other celebrations such as the Ember Days, which were four days of fasting and prayer that marked the beginning of a new season. Ember Days were traditionally "days of cosmic danger" that were celebrated in many European nations. What meaning traditional hunter-gatherers assigned to these celebrations is not known.

The evidence from Texas shows that each mission celebrated its patron saint and invited the friars and residents of other missions to the celebration. In the case of Mission Concepción in San Antonio, the Feast of the Immaculate Conception was celebrated with the slaughter of a cow, which provided the festive noon meal. Depending on the financial condition of the mission, the Natives might also be given sugar cones. Generally the festivities included a procession held in the mission plaza as well as singing and firecrackers. Oil lamps and candles were placed in the friary and sometimes in the houses of the Natives. The ceremony ended with the Salve hymn. During the feast, a young bull was brought to the mission plaza and the Native population chased and ran the bull with great merriment.

On November 2, the missions celebrated All Souls Day with three masses, but the Natives attended only the third Mass. After Mass, the friar led a procession that ended at the cemetery. The church bell tolled from Vespers until the hour when the friar began leading the prayers for the deceased and for the priests buried at the mission. Although the records are not explicit, it appears that the participants brought offerings either for the deceased or for the church, because after the procession, the friar collected all the offerings and prayed over them (Leutenegger 1976, 13–14). The following day the church bell tolled from dawn to evening until prayers were concluded.

Little is said about the festivities around the Christmas season, though it was celebrated throughout New Spain (Taylor 1996, 252–53; Webb 1952, 263). On Christmas Eve, the Natives were given beans, sweet potatoes, fried sweet bread, and other sweets and possibly chocolate. On that day, the Natives performed the Matachines in front of the friary, and in the following days they repeated the performance for the Spanish governor and the presidio personnel. In California, Christmas was celebrated with midnight Mass, singing, and nativity plays and pageants (Skowronek and Thompson 2006, 221). All the rituals and festivities discussed above were punctuated by merriment and the distribution of unusual foods and amenities such as meat, sweets, and tobacco. These occasions were memorialized and associated with specific demonstrations and foods and entered the religious secular traditions that are reflected today in Catholic and Native celebrations.

Conclusion

The establishment of missions in New Spain introduced the week as a Christian time unit of prayer and labor. Daily schedules changed all behaviors taken for granted. They refashioned fears, expectations, and desires and subjected them to a schedule. Conversion was about the cumulative effect of practices such as daily prayers, sacraments, and religious festivities that fused with western clothing, non-Native foods, and agricultural chores. Most of all, conversion aimed to forcefully modify behaviors that ranged from what a Native dreamed or thought about to how, when, and with whom she copulated. In time, these practices marked a Native's life course, blurring ancient traditions and becoming the nexus of memory. The aim was to produce a "civilized" Christian Native who, like the European peasant, labored for daily bread, received the sacraments, married and produced offspring within the fold of matrimony, prayed daily, went to church on Sunday and festive days, knew his or her place in society, and died a Christian. This was the program of conversion and socialization. It was simple, inflexible, and, for most Native Americans, culturally distasteful.

Part 3

The City of God

Religious Practices

The most important task of the apostolic worker is to provide his flock with spiritual sustenance and the second is to make sure they labor so that united and congregated in pueblos [the friars] can provide them with spiritual nourishment.

(Fr. Diego Martín García 1745, 33)

A friar's duty and mission was to convert, and conversion was a lifelong process. Religious practices framed the lives of the Native Americans who entered missions in what could be called a sacramental life course—that is, an individual life course with life changes marked by specific sacraments. Adults from the generation of colonial contact were unlikely to reference life changes by the reception of sacraments because in general they would have undergone Native rites of passage before entering the missions. Not so with those born into the missions or brought in as infants or toddlers; those would be in the middle, fractioned between old and new, marooned between conflicting cultural expectations and social traditions. If it survived, this "middle generation" was torn between conceptual worlds and likely lost its traditional and comforting place in a genealogy of kin and culture.

A fervor to convert souls and the arrogance of conviction blinded the missionaries to the enormity of the changes they asked of Native peoples: longstanding cultures were shorn of people and traditional practices. Mission religious practices had important social and individual implications for Native Americans, and the sacraments they received marked their life courses. Similarly, the administration of sacraments was pivotal to evaluating the success of a mission. The discussion that follows considers how the friars provided neophytes with spiritual nourishment and what the repercussions of a sacramental life course were and asks how the missionaries measured conversion and what the modern historical problems are in defining and assessing conversion.

Sacraments: Life-Course Markers

The administration of church sacraments did not always follow the same precept, nor was there always agreement about who should be permitted to receive specific sacraments or when a neophyte was ready for a particular sacrament. The reforms enacted by the Council of Trent took hold very slowly, and the administration of most sacraments was not standardized until the middle of the seventeenth century (Armstrong 2004, 18; Delumeau 1977, 196). In fact, "reform was about reclaiming past perfection, not creating something new" (Armstrong 2004, 20). Nevertheless, official mission reports generally agree on sacramental policy (de los Dolores et al. 1762; Lopez 1786; Xavier Ortiz 1745). What follows is a discussion of each sacrament that missionaries normally administered to Native neophytes.

Baptism

The sacrament of baptism marked the transformation of a Native into a Christian, at least in name. The number of baptisms in effect measured the number of conversions and the success of a mission. Baptismal registers confirmed apostolic work, justified the existence of the missions and missionary work, and were the measure and proofs the missionaries used to assess and demonstrate their work. Baptisms were religious, legal, and economic records that verified that a Native had been instructed in Catholic doctrine and had entered the Catholic faith and that the missionaries were complying with the mandate from the crown and were due the crown stipend (*sínodo*) for their work. Baptism was ideally administered no more than three days after a child was born, upon request, or if the child was in danger of dying. Children less than nine years of age could be baptized without being instructed in doctrine (Hackel 2005, 135n16). This means that children judged to be younger than nine years of age could be baptized when they entered a mission. Children who appear on the same date in the baptismal registry likely entered the mission at the same time and were less than nine years old.

Sometimes adults also received baptism with relatively little instruction in doctrine or in *artículo mortis*. Thus, the administration of the sacrament often did not require the consent of the Native to whom the sacrament was given. Reception of the sacrament did not produce "visible" results nor did it necessarily imply changes in cultural practices except for the process of naming; baptized individuals were given a Christian-European name. The records make it difficult to evaluate the cultural significance of that change and whether or not retention of Native names together with Christian names is time sensitive. It is possible that when that a Native name was recorded at the time of baptism, this implied that the person had undergone a naming ceremony. Also, the fact that the same Christian names were often given to different Natives may have canceled out the significance of the new name. Still, renaming is possessing anew, and one should not discount the importance of the act of christening; its purpose was to sever the neophyte from his or her previous spiritual life and relationships. In addition to being the central legal document for any mission Native, the baptismal record was a statement of ethnicity and proof of possession of mission lands and property. The cases of the Pamaque and the Pampopa demonstrate the cultural and economic significance of the document (see Chapter 7).

Missionaries referred to the reluctance of Natives to be baptized and their association of baptismal water with death many times. Father Pérez de Ribas (1645/1999, 96, 241) cites some instances of Native resistance to baptism in Sinaloa and Sonora, and there is relevant evidence from Baja California and Alta California (Clavijero 1789/2002, 264, 270; Dunne 1968, 229, 231; Hackel 2005, 170). The Hasinai and other east Texas groups clearly associated baptism with death and generally refused to be baptized (Leutenegger 1979, 24, 51, 53; Xavier Ortiz 1745). A thorough analysis of the historical record would probably find this attitude toward the sacrament to be widespread and possibly connected to epidemics (see Metcalf 2005, 203). Indeed, there may be a link between baptism and transmission of disease, because during the ceremony the priest would apply his saliva on the foreheads of those receiving the sacrament (Delumeau 1977, 92).[1] The ceremony also included blowing into the face of those being baptized, which could be associated with "evil breath" (Delumeau 1977, 166). On the other hand, Mendieta reports that the Natives in the central basin of Mexico "had great faith in holy water" and drank it when they were sick to cure illness (Habig 1978, 27).

Confession (Penance)

Baptism is a precondition for the sacrament of confession, and confession of all sins is a precondition for communion and all other sacraments. Still, as Dunne noted, communion did not necessarily follow confession (1968, 395). While baptism was a sacrament done to the Native and was often administered without the person's consent, confession and all other sacraments required the consent and active participation of the neophyte. This is an important distinction because the performance of confession and acts of contrition imply a different level of participation on the part of Natives and different stages of cultural engagement with Christian doctrine. Indeed, they can be seen as manifestations of belief among Native Americans. Had it not been for the punishment of and sanctions against those who did not confess, participating in this sacrament could be seen as an indication of conversion.

Fr. Mariano pointed out that "all those who acquired [doctrinal] competence confessed and received communion (de los Dolores et al. 1762, 58). The act of confessing requires recognition, if not acceptance, of what constitutes a sin, and it cannot be validated without verbal acceptance of guilt and contrition. Guilt and contrition can be faked, but although faking them can be read as resistance, it also means that Native Americans understood and had internalized Christian teachings well enough to find ways to subvert them. Gurzinski notes such patterns among "civilized" agriculturists, but the same was true among hunter-gatherers (1989, 105). Such mechanisms of evasion would not be necessary or visible until some time after the onset of missionary work. The invasive nature of confession and the very notion of ordering in time (sequencing), reclassifying, and describing one's deeds as faults may have been utterly foreign to some groups but acceptable or commensurable to others. We have little information to evaluate the cultural impact of this sacrament, which constituted a prerequisite for access to other sacraments. Gurzinski notes that confession imposed an "order of enunciation" on the neophytes that subverted "systems of multiple references, varying according to their ethnic group, location, social group, and ritual context" (1989, 97). This was particularly true for Catholic prohibitions regarding relationships between kinfolk, whether the relationship was fictive or established by blood (101). Intrinsically social practices became individual practices that were judged and sentenced under notions of free will that "must have perplexed the Indians as much as that [concept] of the soul" (97–98). Confession was as much a Christian sacrament of redemption as it was a form of control over the innermost thoughts, dreams, and practices of Native Americans, and in a sense its effects may have been maximized among hunter-gatherers whose lifeways were so enmeshed with, and dependent on, kin networks (see Radding 1998b, 186–87).

During Lent all Catholics were to confess (Xavier Ortiz 1745). The *El Cuadernillo de la Lengua de los Indios Pajalates* composed by Fr. Gabriel Vergara in 1732 includes several questions that were asked of the Natives during confession (Vergara 1732/1965). Most of the questions in the extant published version of this manual relate to sexual behavior. Below are the Spanish original and the translation of some of the questions.

Did you fornicate with married women? With how many? With how many women related by blood? With these how many times? [*¿Con otras casadas fornicaste? ¿Con cuantas casadas? ¿Cuantas parientas? ¿Con las parientas cuantas veces?*]
Did you fornicate with single women? With how many? With those related by blood how many times? [*¿Con otras solteras fornicaste? ¿Cuantas eran? ¿Con unas parientas cuantas veces?*] (83)

Afterward the confessor would tell the penitent to pray or perform some good deed to wipe away the sins the penitent had confessed (84–85). The missionary explained that the penitence had to be done in this world; otherwise the confessant would remain in purgatory until expiation of the sins was completed. When people died, they were sent to purgatory to pay for the sins they had committed, even those who abided by God's laws and confessed. Purgatory was described as a house of fire located beneath the earth. Unlike hell, which had a big fire, purgatory had a small fire. There were no demons in purgatory, just souls paying for the sins they had committed. Once the sins were expiated, God removed the souls from purgatory and took them to heaven. As the friar explained, God would not send the sinner to hell, and he forgave all sins if the sinner made a good confession. To obtain such pardon Christians had to pray, attend Mass, and pray for the dead to ensure that God freed their souls from purgatory and transported them to heaven. Those who performed good deeds on this earth paid for their sins while on earth and did not need to go to purgatory. Pérez de Ribas told the story of a Native who watched a field burn and decided to confess to avoid the fire of hell (1645/1999, 664). But to what did he confess? It is anyone's guess how this system of debits and credits was perceived and internalized by the neophytes.

Vergara's manual instructed the friar to repeatedly admonish the confessant, "To pay for your sins I now order you to pray, etc. . . . And every time you go to mass, and all the masses you attend and all the good deeds you perform until your next confession I order you to offer them to God to wipe away your sins. Do you want to give all these [good deeds and prayers] to God to wipe away your sins? And will you say the prayers according to my orders? The prayers I told you to say are etc. . . . I also command you to confess again in one, two or three moons etc." (Vergara 1732/1965, 84–85). Likewise the instructions for confession used in Alta California stressed the punishment by fire and the desolation and isolation suffered by those who died in sin or made bad confessions (Hackel 2005, 159–60). Ostracism, social isolation, and consuming fires would convey profound messages to hunter-gatherers, who were intrinsically social beings and who depended deeply on pyrotechnology.

In 1760, Fr. Bartholomé García published an instruction manual for the administration of the sacraments. The manual includes doctrinal instructions in Spanish and in the Pajalate language, apparently the most common Native language in at least some of the San Antonio missions in Texas (Lopez 1786). The manual guides confessor and confessant through the traditional ritual of confession, from genuflection before the missionary and prayers to the questions and conclusion. The manual starts by stating that if the confessor wanted to ask doctrinal questions, he should refer to the catechism, indicating that the manual's instructions were geared toward practices and not concepts. The manual said that the confessor should ascertain whether the penitent had confessed and taken communion the previous Lent and then should ask if the male or female was married and if he or she had recalled all his or her sins [*¿has pensado todos tus pecados?*]. "Tell me all the sins you committed; don't lie to me: if you lie to me, and if you do not tell me all your sins, you will make a bad confession, and the Devil will take you to hell; do not fear me; do not be embarrassed with me" (García 1760, 3). The questions span the Ten Commandments, but they are slanted toward telling preoccupations. The questions related to the first commandment include, "Did you call on the devil? Are you a shaman? Did the devil teach you to bewitch? For how many years have you been a shaman? How many [people] did you bewitch? How many of those died? Did you teach others how to bewitch? How many? And what things did you use to bewitch? Bring me the thing that you used; go [and] bring it to me and I will confess you then" [*Has llamado á el demonio? Eres echizero? Eres echizera? El demonio te enseño a echizar? Quantos años ha que eres echizero? A quantos echizaste? Quantos de los que echizaste murieron? Has enseñado á alguno á echizar? A quantos has enseñado? Y con que cosas echizas? Traeme essa cosa con que echizas: vete, traeme-la, y despues te confessarè*] (7, 9). These constitute almost all the questions regarding belief and faith in God, indicating that evidence of belief consisted mostly of the absence of shamanic practices. Still, as late as 1760, questions of shamanism were central to the process of conversion. The abandonment of Mission Rosario and the case of Antonio Arcón may indicate increased shamanic influence in the late mission period as revitalization movements served to bring together varied groups and harness their power at times of greater stress. Such was the case among the Apache in 1764, when they saw a vision man who told them to refuse baptism and promised them a paradise where they would be reunited with their kin (Wade 2003, 198).

Many of the questions regarding several of the commandments center on sexual behavior between close family members. For instance, in the fourth commandment, the confessant is asked if "his or her children have watched when he, or she, fornicated with his wife or husband" (García 1760, 12). The manual's instructions to the confessor about questions to ask regarding the sixth commandment included about thirty-eight questions on sexual intercourse; three of the eighteen questions for the fourth commandment are also about sexual behavior. The manual includes mostly questions about sexual relations between people in various grades of kinship, but it also asks questions about touching, masturbation, sex in church, homosexuality, bestiality, and sexual speech (15–24). The same holds true for the *Ventureño Confesionario* of Fr. José Señán, who was stationed at Mission San Buenaventura in Alta California (1797–1823). Fr. Señán's confessional manual asked Native men and women numerous questions about sexual conduct, but it pried even more intensely into kinship relations to make sense of "inappropriate" sexual behavior (Señán 1967, 39–59).

In addition to the friars' intense preoccupation with sexual behavior and their piercing study of "deviant" customs, the issue of sex between kinfolk is central to the attempt to control and modify Native traditional behavior to comply with Catholic doctrine. The details educed in the confessional questions also show that the friars were trying to identify specific kin relationships and locate and prevent contact between kinfolk. Likely, segregating women from men was not so much the result of observed behaviors as it was the result of information obtained through confession, which served as an ethnographic tool for learning about sociocultural mores. Moreover, as Robert Jackson has noted, confessional disclosures also contributed to perceptions about women (personal communication 2005). Obviously, two friars could not physically observe the behavior of two to three hundred Natives, nor could they supervise the diverse daily tasks. Gossip, information from pueblo officials, and confession had to be prime ways to gather information. The need to acquire information (knowledge) in order to exert repression (power) and achieve modification of behavior (knowledge/power) is overtly displayed in the confessional questions. In addition, the questions in Fr. García's and Fr. Señán's manuals about touching, voyeurism, homosexuality, masturbation, or bestiality, and whether those practices were common or not, would have marked behaviors that were sanctioned as normal in Native culture as deviant and sinful. Conversely, these questions might have introduced these behaviors.

Fr. Señán's manual includes several questions about avoiding pregnancy and methods of inducing abortion, acknowledging the friars' preoccupation with population loss and making clear how the act of confession was used to acquire information (1967, 37–38). The questions are not just about sins of commission but also about the methods of commission. Certainly from the Catholic perspective, abortion was a mortal sin, but if the missionaries could know how Natives were terminating pregnancies they could perhaps learn who was copulating with whom and could try to control the behavior.

Like Fr. García's instructions, Fr. Señán's instructions show that shamanism continued to attract the attention of the friars. In the Ventureño case, confessional queries regarded rainmaking and propitiatory rites, such as the scattering of seeds connected with hunting and fishing, practices also mentioned in the 1813–1815 questionnaire (Geiger and Meighan 1976, 47–50).

Fr. Bartholomé García suggested that the missionary exhort the penitent at the end of the confession by asking, "Why don't you fear God? Why don't you fear hell? You should be careful: you should not annoy God with your sins; if you annoy him much, maybe he will tell the Devil to take you immediately to hell; maybe he will suddenly take your life so you will sin no more, and God will throw you in hell for the Devils to burn you" [*Porquè no tienes miedo à Dios? Porquè no tienes miedo al Infierno? Pues anda con cuidado: à Dios no lo has de enojar con los pecados: si enojas mucho à Dios, quizas le dirà al Demonio, que te lleve presto al Infierno; quizas de repente te quitarà Dios la vida, para que no buelvas hazer pecados, y te echarà Dios al Infierno, para que te quemen los Demonios*] (García 1760, 27–28). The combined emphasis on a punishing God, fear of hell, and eternal damnation had to produce conversion through fear if it produced conversion at all. There was nothing out of the ordinary about this approach to conversion; it would be maintained for many centuries throughout the Catholic world.

As Father Ribas described it, the routine the Jesuits used was not much different (1645/1999, 250). During the period of general confession, the converts prepared by attending church for two hours in the morning and another two in the afternoon. The men and women were separated: the men remained in the choir loft and the women in the nave of the church, a clear hierarchical message. Those who confessed and who visibly corrected their sins within a given period received communion and were obligated to receive the sacrament again on the principal feast of the Virgin Mary. Failure to receive communion was equal to a statement of prior sin. Thus, confession and communion were sacraments that allowed friars to monitor the neophyte community.

The need of missionaries to verify that the behavior of neophytes was not sinful implies that perhaps they personally inspected household arrangements and monitored dances and other visible practices deemed pagan; otherwise the missionaries would have had to rely on personal observations, the reports of the *temastians*, or gossip. This system implied that pagan Native practices were shielded from the missionaries and moved underground. The role of the *temastians* and other mission pueblo officials became central to the continuation of Native practices, and their complicity with shamans and revolt leaders was essential.

Jesuit Jacob Baegert, who was stationed at Mission San Luís Gonzaga in Baja California from 1749 to 1761, discussed the teaching of doctrine to the Natives. Baegert stated, "Most of them, even if they have heard it hundreds and hundreds of times, are not able to answer the necessary questions at all or by memory, never sufficient for salvation" (Nunis 1982, 154). Baegert's specific comments on the sacraments of confession and communion show how Native lifestyles and cultural practices and the requirements of conversion clashed in pragmatic ways that had little to do with comprehension. "The three hundred sixty heads which I have as parishioners are not many, but it would be much less trouble to hear daily the farmers from Alsace . . . than two hundred eighty of my parishioners in my mission only once a year. If one listens to two of them a day, it is a great achievement" (155). Preoccupied with the difficulty of explaining dogma to the Natives, the presumed incomprehension of the Natives, and the need to administer communion to the Natives despite their ignorance, the Jesuit tackled the problem of requiring confession before communion. He could not deny confession to those who were dying or to those who had been exposed to danger and might die without the assistance of the priest; if he did, he would imperil his own soul. Thus, he had to provide them with temporary absolution in confession, knowing that their knowledge of the doctrine was insufficient for the administration of the sacrament. "How can one then let such a being only have communion once in a while? If they only would give up committing adultery and worse things, I would not refuse them communion, because of their ignorance" (155). It would be shortsighted to dismiss a missionary's ambivalence and anguish about these matters; daily decisions about religious precepts and administering sacraments imperiled his soul as well as those of his Native wards.

Still, if one takes at face value the principal reasons that the missionaries found the administration of the sacraments of confession and communion difficult and problematic, they can be reduced to two issues. First, Natives could not memorize the questions posed in confession and therefore did not supply the appropriate answers. Second, each confession was a laborious and time-consuming exercise for the friar, who had to elaborate on the questions and guide the confessant.

These complaints are baffling because they emphasize a Native problem with memorization, which resulted in protracted and "bad" confessions. Given that the Native groups discussed relied on the oral transmission of information, the presumed difficulty with memorization leaves the researcher with two obvious conclusions: either the questions posed in confession were so foreign to the cultures that people shunned them from consciousness and memory or the "faulty" memorization was a strategy to circumvent confession and wear out the missionary. No doubt different groups at different times employed different strategies. Since Natives did not have difficulties with memory in other areas, we can postulate that their so-called difficulty with the memory tasks confession required was a strategy of resistance. In their responses to the 1813–1815 questionnaire, the friars at Mission San Antonio de Padua stated that the Natives had such good memories that "some can explain things exactly when they are questioned about business matters, which we [the friars] would have to note down in order to remember" (Geiger and Meighan 1976, 36). Rare statements such as this indicate the complexity of an issue that was central to conversion.

The Jesuit perspective on confession was deeply rooted in the rules and practices of the Society of Jesus. In *Spiritual Exercises*, the fundamental manual of Jesuit spiritual renewal, repetition was not just a didactic tool but also the spiritual instrument to facilitate deeper and growing understanding and modification of behavior (Barthes 1976, 60). The *Exercises* also provided a paradigmatic structure that was inserted in the work of conversion. As Barthes points out:

The accountancy is obsessional not only because it is infinite, but above all because it engenders its own errors; being a matter of accounting for his sins . . . the fact of accounting for them in a faulty way will in turn become an error that must be added on to the original list; this list is thus made infinite, the redeeming accounting of errors calling up per contra the very errors of the account; for example, the particular Examination of the first Week [in the Exercises] is above all designed to make an accounting of the lapses committed with regard to prayer. . . . Thus we see Ignatius, in his Journal, requesting a sign from God, God delaying in giving it, Ignatius growing impatient, accusing himself for being impatient and recommencing the circuit: one prays, one regrets praying badly, one adds to the faulty prayer a supplementary prayer for forgiveness, etc. (Barthes 1976, 70)

The limitlessness of the sinful condition immersed the convert in a labyrinth of guilt. We do not know how Native Americans comprehended the essence of this conundrum. We do know that saints and Catholics all over the world wrestled continuously with such problems. As Hackel has stated, "In essence, missionaries taught Indians only the rudiments of Catholicism but required of them a deep and enduring faith" (2005, 128). One could make a case, however, that being found "guilty" of being pagan, and being trapped in a maze of guilt, Natives exited the moral trap through revolts and revitalization movements that often incorporated themes and practices from Christianity as those elements became essential to a collective memory shattered and fragmented by population loss. Native life courses were disrupted by mission life and by sets of events and practices such as epidemics and religious requirements that altered the social structure of the groups, the place of each individual in the group, and his or her expected roles and statuses. Generation gaps become noticeable in conflicts. The fact that pre- and post-contact people of different ages, backgrounds, and knowledges lived together made conversion difficult, and their differences found expression in revolts. If indeed epidemic diseases were especially severe among the very young (the first post-contact generation) and among the very old (the last pre-contact generation of elders). The generation in the middle was neither fully acculturated nor steeped in the ancient traditions. Instead it wavered in cultural vacillation, alternately swayed by episodes of assertiveness and anger and by times of enduring half-hearted accommodation. But it was mostly this generation of ladinos that questioned conversion with the voice of revolt; the acts of those who revolted and the symbols they used exemplify the position of the ladinos astride the cultural divide. In 1815, Fr. Señán demonstrated this cleavage perfectly: "The son counts eighteen years as a Christian but the father is an obstinate savage still enamored of his brutal liberty and perpetual idleness. The granddaughter is a Christian but the grandmother is a pagan. Two brothers may be Christians but the sister stays in the mountains. A neophyte twenty years a Christian marries a woman but recently baptized. Such is the situation" (Geiger and Meighan 1976, 61).

Eucharist (Communion)

While baptism signified membership in the Catholic faith, the Eucharist marked a neophyte's graduation into full knowledge of the mysteries of Catholicism. To receive communion, the neophyte needed to demonstrate adequate knowledge of Christian teachings, including an understanding of the doctrine of the Holy Trinity and the mystery of the transubstantiation of Christ—his living presence in the holy wafer. Missionaries were often perturbed by what they perceived as Native incomprehension of these fundamental mysteries (Clavijero 1789/2002, 377). Without comprehension and acceptance of those truths of the Catholic faith, confession and especially communion were meaningless and actually sacrilegious. The ability to recite these "truths" did not demonstrate comprehension or acceptance. Obviously the essential problem was one of faith, as nothing is comprehensible about the mystery of the Holy Trinity if you are not a believer—that is why it is a mystery. Although the missionaries' discourse was about comprehension, what perturbed them was the neophyte's lack of faith. This is a crucial point for scholars who analyze conversion and the processes of "assimilation" of religious teachings that have been grouped under the shorthand notion of syncretism. Quite likely a slowly acquired habitus of practices was folded into a substratum of more ancient traditions and beliefs. Whether faith would have entered into such folding is entirely unclear.

Confirmation (Chrism)

The sacrament of confirmation is meant to confirm and fortify a neophyte's faith. This sacrament, which requires baptism and entails the laying on of hands and anointing with sacred oils, was even more controversial than others. As a result of the Council of Trent, in 1565 the church decreed that only bishops were authorized to confirm believers (Habig 1978, 19). The Papal Bull of 1755 finally permitted the sacrament of confirmation to be administered to Native Americans (Nunis 1982, 176). The Jesuits were permitted to administer confirmation around 1756, and the Franciscans obtained permission to administer the sacrament in 1777 (Geiger 1959, 151).

Matrimony

The sacraments of communion and confession required the consent and engagement of the convert, but their effects were not necessarily visible within Native societies. These sacraments did not necessarily imply a realignment of social and kinship relations. However, the sacrament of "marriage" did just that. Prohibitions regarding mating with certain members of Native society and the requirement that each person have only one single partner had far-reaching implications for the entire fabric of kinship relations and altered innumerable statuses, positions, roles, cooperative actions, trade relations, partnerships, and the like. While other sacraments could be dismissed or forgotten and were only "real" on certain occasions and at certain times of the year, matrimony affected each and every daily practice and relationship. One cannot divorce the sacrament of matrimony from other sacraments, particularly that of confession.

As with the sacrament of confirmation, controversy surrounded the application of the sacrament of matrimony to Native populations. After several decades, Pope Paul III determined that Native men should be given their first wives as their legitimate wives, if missionaries could determine who the first wife was (Habig 1978, 20). The policy the missionaries adopted was to ratify the unions of all Natives who married before entering the mission, but each man could have his union ratified with only one woman (de los Dolores et al. 1762, 58–59). There was a margin of arbitrariness in applying the rules that no doubt eased a missionary's qualms and was exploited effectively by Natives. However, it was only after the Council of Trent that "marriages performed by a cleric legitimized sexual relations," and it was much later before uniform marriage rules became the norm (Twinam 1999, 37). Some of the important changes were the prohibition of sexual intercourse prior to the ceremony of betrothal, the requirement that a priest be present to sanction the marriage, and the requirement that Native people produced children only within wedlock. If the new church rules were problematic for Christendom, they were devastating for Christianized Native populations in New Spain. Such rules deeply compromised social and kinship networks and injected a new class of prejudice toward the offspring of Native couples, marking them ethnically and racially. We cannot evaluate the consequences of Christian requirements for the coupling practices of Native populations, largely because of the death toll caused by epidemics and the consequent sex and gender imbalances. We do know that the children of mixed marriages became known by a social class system that emphasized grades of color.

Extreme Unction (Last Rites)

The sacrament of extreme unction was often not given to the Natives because priests were not available and because Natives seldom asked for it (Xavier Ortiz 1745). Extreme unction is an elaborate ceremony that includes confession, contrition, communion, recitation of the creed, and anointing with holy oils (García 1745; Mitchell 1990, 24). These rituals were generally abridged because friars on the frontier had to administer the sacrament in inhospitable places and under difficult conditions. The missionaries often lacked the sacred oils they needed to perform the sacrament, but they visited the sick daily and most Natives died with a friar at their bedside (de los Dolores et al. 1762, 62; Xavier Ortiz 1745). In Coahuila, Bishop Gavarito chastised the Franciscans for not having recently consecrated oils, and the account of Fr. Quintana's killing demonstrates that the friars were administering last rites to the Natives. Julián, one of the participants in the plot, complained that he was going to die because he had been given last rites

(Asisara 1991, 7). This indicates that the Natives not only associated the sacrament with death but may have expected it to cause death.

One issue related to the provision of spiritual nourishment was the shortage of missionaries, and although there were exceptions, the church generally refused to admit Natives who were fourth-generation descendents from "pagans" to the religious orders (Habig 1978, 20). The lack of secular priests in many areas of the northern frontier was also a result of the control the Jesuits and Mendicant Orders had over the Christianization of the Native populations and their reluctance to secularize the missions.

Doctrinal Reforms

In 1786, Fr. Oliva, who was president of the Texas missions, commented that after the missionaries from the College of Zacatecas took over from the Querétaro friars, the teachings of the Christian doctrine and prayers were conducted in a different manner (Leutenegger 1977, 37–39). Beforehand, the Natives had recited prayers and doctrine every morning and evening. The friars explained doctrine on Mondays, Wednesdays, and Fridays, except when feast days fell on one of those days. This system was maintained during the first year after the missions were transferred to Zacatecas in 1773, but then each friar decided to follow the system he considered best, and most taught doctrine only on Sundays and sometimes not even then. Given the changes in the mission system, Fr. Oliva suggested that morning prayers be dispensed with and that all missions adopt the schedule the friars at Mission San José y San Miguel de Aguayo in Texas used. Fr. Oliva suggested the following schedule (Leutenegger 1977, 38–39, retranslated by the author). On Monday, Tuesday, Wednesday, and Thursday, prayers were to be recited. On Monday the Natives were to recite the catechism, and on Wednesday missionaries were to give a talk or explanation of doctrine. On Friday the Natives were to do the Stations of the Cross with comments on the passion of Christ, and on Saturday they were to celebrate the crown of Mary[2] and the friar or catechist would talk a bit about the Virgin Mary. On all feast days and on Saturdays, there was to be a Mass for the pueblo, and if the missionary wished, he could celebrate a Mass on the day of the feast of the patron saint of the mission. In light of the changes in the system, Fr. Oliva considered that such schedule would not tax Natives or friars and that Natives would continue to receive the instruction to which they had grown accustomed. All friars in charge of missions were obliged, as a matter of conscience, to say Mass for the congregation, and Mass continued to be obligatory for the Natives.

Conversion Practices and Strategies

The Franciscans and the Jesuits who labored in Mexico's northeastern frontier in the early period used different strategies for converting hunting and gathering populations. In places where Franciscans missionized, local groups requested mission-pueblos and congregated within missions temporarily but did not adapt to a settled and horticultural lifestyle and dispersed once local food supplies were exhausted. Thus, the Natives eventually abandoned or only nominally occupied the missions the Franciscan established in east Texas from 1690 to 1721. Although the Hasinai groups expelled the friars in 1693, the missionaries returned in 1715 under conditions that prevented what any missionary would consider fruitful conversion work. By the late 1720s, the only active mission in east Texas was San Miguel de Los Adaes, in modern Robeline, Louisiana.

The San Antonio missions brought together hunters and gatherers belonging to different ethnic groups, often groups that had little contact with each other before entering the mission, harbored deep enmities against each other, spoke different languages, and had different cultural-social backgrounds (Campbell and Campbell 1985, 18–21). The friars tried to accommodate the differences between these groups, but diseases and the lack of alternative facilities often frustrated those efforts. With time, the result was an apparent (but misleading) cultural and linguistic uniformity that, as Fr. Francisco Lopez noted, reflected the values and traditions of the most powerful or numerous group or group of groups (1786). A 1740 report from Fr. Benito de Santa Ana pointed out that despite the great variety of Native groups in the San Antonio missions, four principal languages were used. But the friars had almost no interpreters and communicated largely through sign language, which made teaching doctrine and administering sacraments difficult (Habig 1978, 59–60).

By the middle of the eighteenth century, the missions in the San Antonio River area were behind walled compounds. These walls had a dual purpose: to prevent the residents from fleeing the mission and to protect them against attackers, particularly Apache groups. Conversion work took place in the mission, but each year the friars went to the "wild" to bring back gentiles to be Christianized (Santa Ana 1748). Soldiers kept guard and friars and soldiers systematically journeyed to the hinterland and to the coast to bring back deserters and willing, or unwilling, prospective converts by force. Similar practices of "recruitment" were used in most areas of New Spain.

Unlike in Baja California, there were few instances of overt organized resistance or revolts in the Texas missions (Clavijero 1789/2002, 148, 151,

162, 173, 180, 183, 219–20). Instead, the Natives resisted the colonial system by fleeing, which forced missionaries to hunt for the deserters or gather new potential neophytes. Both solutions hampered the work of conversion, although the latter provided a set of new baptisms that provided written proof of new conversions. In the mission reports, new baptisms seemed to demonstrate progress, but in reality they often revealed precisely the opposite.

Native desertion and revolts are indications of rejection of conversion practices, though they may not point to rejection of conversion. In Texas, attacks on missions generally originated with non-mission Natives and attacks were motivated by complex territorial and power struggles between several Native groups and the colonizers. The attack on Mission San Sabá in 1758 is the obvious example, but the Apache attacks on the San Antonio missions or the debacle of the San Xavier River mission complex illustrate well the difference between violent confrontations to address issues peripheral or external to conversion versus violent actions to contest conversion. In the Californias and northeastern Mexico the revolts can be understood as rejection of the practices of conversion, but the same cannot be assumed for Texas.

In the northern frontier, specifically in the Laguna-Parras areas, the Jesuits used different strategies in their work with settled horticulturists, particularly with the nomadic hunter-gatherers who lived very far apart and in sparsely populated areas (Alegre 1956, 420–22; 1958, 106–9; Pérez de Ribas 1645/1999, 134, 662, 666). At contact, the Jesuits practiced a wilderness model, following the Native groups as they procured their daily subsistence. But, like the Franciscans, the Jesuits ended up establishing missions and pueblos in the Laguna and Parras areas, although apparently they continued to follow a schedule whereby the children attended the doctrine every day while the adults came in only on Sundays or feast days. By 1599, the mission included a school for the children, but except for the children it seems that most neophytes came to the mission only to learn doctrine and attend religious ceremonies; they did not live at the mission.

In Baja California, the Jesuits worked with nomadic groups that hunted, fished, and gathered wild foods for a living. Fr. Sebastián de Sistiaga, who was stationed in Baja California at Mission San Ignacio in 1744, stated:

It is only with great effort and ceaseless exertion that they support themselves. In order to overcome their hunger, they must be continually on the move, forced to traverse vast distances to gather from their sterile lands the bit of fruit some of the trees produce, and even then not always reliable. In the summer and autumn their hunger is stilled with less effort because, during these two seasons, provided it has previously rained, they gather from some thorny bushes a fruit called by the natives of the opposite shore pitahayas, the softest and sweetest of all. In the hills there are prickly pears. . . . This scarcity explains why a settlement, even when small, must roam over an extensive territory for sustenance. . . . This doubles the effort and exertion needed to search for and find them in order to preach to them and convert them to our Holy Faith. (Sistiaga 2001, 94)

In Baja California the missions were located far apart from each other. Unable to follow the Natives throughout the countryside, again the Jesuits convinced or compelled the Natives to resettle closer to the mission center. The fathers established a rotational system whereby each settlement came to the mission for religious instruction. Natives in newly established missions came to the mission center according to a weekly rotation system, while those in well-established missions came in on Saturday, remained for the Sunday celebrations, and left on Monday (Clavijero 1789/2002, 376). Father Sistiaga stated that "after such instruction and practice, the catechist asks some few chosen ones to repeat what has been said. This is done every day until all in each town have been called on. This continuous cycle in the teaching of the catechism does away with the danger of forgetting or ignoring what is necessary in knowing and understanding the essentials for eternal salvation" (Sistiaga 2001, 95). During the week spent at the mission, the Natives followed a strict routine of religious practices. The Jesuits divided their converts in groups that consisted of several tribes or tribelets and lived in distinct geographical areas and pueblos. Discussing his local "brigades," as Father Baegert called them, the father stated,

The Indians have the greatest advantage because they come to the mission every three or four weeks with "sack and pack, tall and small." After fourteen days they return from whence they came and the camp of San Luis is reoccupied with another brigade. During the time when they are here, one says Mass early in the morning; then one lets them say the main prayer of Christian dogma; then I explain to them some of these dogmas, and afterwards I let them go. From the church they run helter-skelter as fast as possible into the woods to look for some food. In the evening they come back if they do not forget about it and say the same Christian dogma as in the morning. That is a pitiful life. If they work, one gives them food to eat. And what is it? One grinds some corn, fills a kettle with water, cooks it and gives each compulsory serviceman his ration, unsalted and ungreased, also full of thousands of uncleanliness, for each one brings an unwashed turtleshell bowl in which he carried before earth or manure; another brings a cow horn; the third waits til his comrade empties his plate. (Nunis 1982, 153–54)

From the point of view of the Natives, the Jesuits' rotational system kept people in their settlements, caused less disruption of family units, and permitted continuation of Native cultural and social practices. And if it did not minimize the effect of epidemics, it surely afforded those affected the comfort of their kinfolk. From the point of view of the missionaries, the system meant that they did not need to travel with the Native groups and that priests did not need to provide Natives with regular meals, except for those who lived at the mission center, those who were in the mission for the weekly teachings, and those who performed chores (Clavijero 1789/2002, 237). These strategies minimized the number of situations where Natives would become disappointed and disillusioned when the mission's food ran out and permitted the fathers to manipulate the timing of the visits of the different *rancherías* to make sure they could provide adequate food.

Commenting on the conversion progress of the Natives, Father Sistiaga said, "What is most amazing is that, alone and far away from the missionary, they observe the same schedule in their towns and even away from them" (2001, 95). It seems that the friar's perception of the Natives' compliance with the doctrinal schedule was illusory, but we have no way of assessing if indeed the Natives were faithful to their doctrinal pledges. Regardless of these well-conceived strategies and the friars' perception that the natives remained faithful to the Catholic teachings when away from the mission, widespread, well-organized Native revolts suggest that some Natives rejected the Jesuits' teachings (Clavijero 1789/2002, 274, 288, 294, 297, 303, 305–8.) The conundrum is that because we rarely have Native voices stating their intentions, historians and anthropologists are compelled to read the actions of Natives as evidence that they rejected conversion practices, if not conversion itself. Despite the revolts, mission methodology did not change much, although the Jesuits cut their losses, abandoned certain missions, increased security when possible, and became less trusting of the Natives.

The evidence appears to indicate that most of the revolts in the Parras-Laguna areas were driven mostly by deadly epidemics, while the revolts in Baja California resulted more from clashes between the fathers and shamans, who could not accept the religious practices taught or imposed by the missionaries and were determined to terminate the missionaries' teachings, either by forcing them out or by killing them (Clavijero 1789/2002, 288). One of the most contentious issues was the missionaries' insistence that Natives have only one wife (Baegert 1979, 151–52; Clavijero 1789/2002, 279; Guest 1989, 7). On the other hand, attributing the rebellions of the Córa, the Pericúe, or others simply to the practice of maintaining multiple wives is myopic.

The missionaries understood the revolts as the work of the devil, reducing Native choice to western diabolism (Clavijero 2002, 259–61; Pérez de Ribas 1645/1999, 124, 657, 673–74). The revolts likely had deeper meanings. Torn between missionaries and shamans, the Natives made accommodating and temporary choices, only to realize they could not continue dual practices without damaging the self and losing prestige. These daily cultural contests compromised Native customs that were intrinsically spiritual and had decisive outcomes. Wives meant kinship connections, and kinship connections meant spiritual connections. Also, as Clavijero surmised from the writings of the Jesuit fathers, in groups where the wives did most of the food gathering, fewer wives meant less food and less prestige (Clavijero 2002, 87–88; Castillo 1994). For instance, among the Pericúe groups, the accumulation of food resources had important repercussions for communal ceremonies and the redistribution of deer pelts that affected mainly women. Wives who had been "discarded" by their husbands because of Catholic teachings were hard pressed to find other husbands in groups where females outnumbered males. Quite possibly such imbalance resulted in a loss of status for the female gender and created groups of unattached females cut off from kinship networks (Clavijero 2002, 274). This situation might have been aggravated by the fact that the Jesuits often kept the children, particularly the males, at the mission center. These issues likely were more distressing for the generation sandwiched between the precontact generation of elders that rejected Christianity and the generation born after contact that was more amenable to Christian teachings; the cultural stability of this "middle generation" was in shreds and its members had no appropriate role models. There were other consequences of violating the restrictions the Catholic faith imposed. When missionaries withdrew the sacrament of communion from those who did not "repent" of the sin of having more than one wife, those individuals stood to lose face, power, goods, and gifts.

In Texas and in Alta California, the Franciscans used essentially the same approaches to conversion and the same sacramental policies and schedules. In both mission provinces, Native populations complied with the annual precept, and although we have no statistics for Texas, the numbers for Alta California from 1814 to 1819 indicate a great variation in the percentage of

Natives who complied with the confession precept. The highest percentage computed by Hackel indicates that at Mission San Carlos, 229 people out of 326 adults took communion, while at Mission San Luis Rey no one did (2005, 176). Franciscans and Jesuits struggled with the notion of administering communion to neophytes who were considered doctrinally unprepared or unfit because of their lifestyle. Withdrawal of communion was a tremendous responsibility that imperiled the soul of the missionary, an issue Father Baegert struggled with. No responsible missionary would take such an issue lightly, which means that the numbers presented by Hackel are significant.

Still, there were noteworthy differences between California and Texas: in California, the number of neophytes was larger; the missions were commercial centers, particularly for the long-distance hide-and-tallow trade, which required a large labor force; and the missionaries segregated the genders much more frequently. There are two other significant differences between Texas and California; the incidence of reported sexual assault of female neophytes, which might well explain the absence of *monjeríos* in Texas, as well as the occurrence of missionary slayings with clear sexual messages or overtones in California.

Measures of Conversion

Native populations had to become aware of the existence of God, and knowledge of His existence was measured by how fast and how well the Natives learned the basic prayers and rituals of the Catholic church. The ability of a Native person to memorize and recite such prayers as the Hail Mary, the Our Father, and the Creed was central to how missionaries assessed that person's learning in the process of becoming a good Christian. The missionaries also interpreted prompt attendance, proper attire and demeanor, and appropriate body movements and emotional responses during religious ceremonies as proof of learning and proficiency as a Christian. Christian discourse generally did not require or imply comprehension of the rituals and their profound doctrinal relationships. This does not mean that some missionaries were not conscious of and disturbed by the perceptible gap between acceptance of sacraments and comprehension of their theological meaning. In that respect, the situation in New Spain differed little from that of coeval populations in rural Europe or in other colonized parts of the Americas (Delumeau 1977, 161, 175).

As important as the enunciation and performance of what a neophyte learned was what the neophyte did or did not do. Renunciation of Native ritual practices, traditions, foods, clothing, and certainly language, was rewarded and understood as progress. Ladinos excelled at this evidence of acculturation, this balance of unlearning with learning, and it was this that brought them to positions of leadership and power among both their people and the missionaries. The best and the brightest pueblo officials and catechists were ladino males, as gender segregation privileged males. Catechists translated and interpreted Christian doctrine to their brethren, and I suggest that they were critical to the particular tone Christianity acquired among the Native populations of colonized America. Native pueblo officials also interpreted for and imposed on their brethren European rules of governance and administered mission justice: punishments stipulated by the missionaries were predicated on a moral and religious system that had to be interpreted for the offender. Conversion was not just about religion; it sought to reset the moral compass of Native Americans.

Ladino expediency was not lost on the friars. Fr. Martin García warned of the problems that ladino Spanish proficiency could create in light of the friars' deficiency in Native languages (1745, 59). He noted that the more ladino (acculturated) the Natives became, the more they were indomitable and the more problems they caused. Indeed, the leaders of almost every revolt or serious event that affected the missions spoke Castilian.

Most missionaries were deeply committed to the Christianization of the Natives; otherwise they would not have spent their lives trying to achieve that goal. Missionaries followed strict rules of behavior and vowed to follow the directives of their superiors. They measured the success of their work by the number of baptisms and they measured the progress of the neophytes by whether they lived permanently at the mission and chose to partake of other sacraments, particularly those that marked a change of status or termination of life, such as marriage and last rites. Unlike the sacraments of confession and communion, which were noted but not registered, church records of baptism, marriage, and last rites were also bureaucratic documents that provided secular officials with information about colonial subjects and the state of the missions and monitored the missionaries' performance. What meaning Native Americans attributed to sacraments and the fact that baptism does not a Christian make are altogether different questions and are largely rhetorical.

At a deeper level the problems with the work of conversion were more pedagogic and didactic than religious. To be or to appear to be Catholic rested on ritual ability and proficiency in performance. It was often parody, not comprehension, that provided the measure of how well the Natives were doing. The emphasis on rote learning facilitated by symbiotic rituals sedated the need for comprehension or introspection. The pedagogical method missionaries used produced false readings of their success. But apart from statistical measures based on baptismal records that more often than not counted those who had perished rather than those who had survived, how does one measure conversion? And should we disengage evidence of comprehension and learning from acceptance? These questions are particularly relevant because without addressing them we conflate single events (baptism) with short-term evidence (historical records that reflect individual life-course histories and specific mission histories). Also, we tend to evaluate the long-term results of colonial missionization in terms of modern interpretations and the expansion of Catholicism in the Americas, establishing a cause-and-effect relationship that stops short of addressing longer histories of postcolonial conversion practices.

The evidence discussed for the Calusa unquestionably indicates that they comprehended and learned Catholic doctrine but chose not to accept it. The Calusa are certainly not the only well-documented example of this dialogic tension, but the evidence is far sketchier for hunter-gatherer populations. Dorsey showed that in Québec, the Huron "could ask difficult questions issuing from what they saw as inconsistencies in Catholic theology" (1998, 403). If the missionaries ever asked the Natives what they thought of religious practices, they neglected to record it, though insults, desecrations, killings, and desertions may speak louder than words. Still, not every Native reacted in that fashion, and we seldom hear from those who adopted Christianity. When we do, it is through the voices of the missionaries, a fact that renders the evidence problematic.

Native individuals reworked rituals and doctrine into their cosmological views if and when Catholic rituals could be grafted into them and made cultural sense. The evidence that Native populations adopted or reworked the symbol of the cross is considerable (Mello e Souza 2003, 62–64; Hackel 2005, 163; Wade 2003, 77–78, 238–39), as are intriguing cases of empathy for or identification with the crucified Christ or with the Virgin Mary feeding the baby Jesus (Serra 1955, 1:359; Wade 2003, 12). It is also quite clear that the prescribed, highly choreographed nature of Catholic rituals appealed to many Native American groups. Rituals such as Mass, Easter passion plays, Christmas, Corpus Christi, and other special religious feasts and processions fascinated and resonated with Native populations (Deeds 2003, 68; Kapitzke 2001, 18–20; Pérez de Ribas 1645/1999, 291–92, 511). On such occasions, Native performances and dramatic displays of fervor provided mixed messages to the missionaries. There is no question that throughout New Spain, ritual and instrumental music were particularly pleasing to Native populations and that they willingly learned to play and sing and often excelled at both (Cayward 2006, 13–15, 23–26; Dunne 1968, 397; Geiger and Meighan 1976, 133–37; Habig 1978, 221; Piccolo 2001, 84; Sandos 2004, 128–53). For instance, Fernando Librado, a Chumash from Mission San Buenaventura, stated that he sang the Catalan Mass and that he performed at different missions during Mass and other religious ceremonies (1979, 48). The Catalan Mass was taught by Fr. Durán, who ministered at Mission San José in Alta California (Geiger and Meighan 1976, 169n90). Settlers also hired Native singers and players for celebrations such as baptisms (Librado 1979, 50). Librado mentioned a variety of instruments Natives played as well as a play called *Star of Bethlehem* and other celebrations on Christmas Eve (Librado 1979, 49; Flores 1995, 36–44). As Sandos has demonstrated, passion plays and ritual singing were important didactic tools in the work of conversion (2004, 128–53). For the friars, Native people rose to the grandeur of the festive but failed the test of the quotidian.

Another measure of how Christian a Native had become was how "appropriate" his or her sexual behavior was. Those groups whose social organization required a sole partner were seen as more civilized, and the friars viewed this "moral" behavior as closer to the Christian model to which all converts needed to aspire. Western moral and dress codes were overt outward signs of conversion, as was the use of the Castilian language. For missionaries, the model Native was the farmer who tended the crops, ate frugally, and provided for future planting; in sum, one who planned his life around agricultural cycles, toiled daily, and had the future in mind. Those were Christian and civilized behaviors that the friars readily understood and accepted as the behaviors of God-fearing people who led clean and profitable lives. Missionaries made no allowance for what was perceived as excess, such as inebriation, all-night dancing, and particularly unrestrained food consumption, though the friars often understood that these were ritual practices. They expected Natives to respond to nature's excesses such as plagues and floods with fortitude and balance them with adherence to daily rituals that provided a measure of control over a temperamental environment and the harshness of frontier life.

The problem of gauging how conversion affected Native populations is how to go beyond sacramental records and avoid the inferences, and logical pitfalls, of the numbers recorded. If more people died than were baptized, the net gain in terms of converts might not be negligible. If, in turn, many of those baptized had the sacrament administered to them precisely because they were dying, the result might be negligible because they would not propagate the faith. Demographically all these numbers are significant, but they lose relevance in terms of assessing conversion. More relevant, from my point of view, are the mission reports that describe the state of the missions in terms of the physical conditions of the buildings and furnishings and the economic status of the missions regarding crops and other supplies. Mission reports sometimes comment on the practices of conversion but seldom on the results of conversion. What the reports stress are the actions of the friars: they administered sacraments, visited the sick, supervised the work of the Natives, did the accounting, collected debts, traded and monitored mission elections . . . all for the welfare of the Natives (de los Dolores at al. 1762). In addition, the reports assess the state of "conversion" of the Natives on the basis of their performance as workers and their disinterest in all things civilized. Thus, the state of their spiritual conversion was conflated with their behavior as "civilized" human beings." For the friars, being a Christian could only be understood as being a civilized Christian. As Fr. Xavier Ortiz explained, "If these Indians were like those from other missions who, as Infidels, know how to govern and keep themselves by raising cattle, farming the lands and by trading like people . . . but instead they are slightly more than animals until they learn some civility and skills in the missions" (Xavier Ortiz 1745). Conversion was to be born again, but few Natives tolerated the change.

The exception to the steady litanies about the reluctance of Natives to work and their permanent wish to return to their "wild ways" is the occasional affirmation that those who acquired doctrinal proficiency confessed and received communion (de los Dolores et al. 1762). This would indeed be a measure of conversion, but neither confession nor communion was generally recorded. The obvious conclusion is that while the management of the affairs of the mission caused moral problems for the missionaries, it also affected the way conversion was perceived.

Conclusion

It is hard or even impossible to determine the results of conversion practices and their effects on Native populations because the archival records seldom include Native voices and because the measures of conversion the missionaries used are laden with pitfalls.

If we assume, and that is a dangerous path, that refusal to work and disinterest in the affairs of the mission and its properties were indicators of a negative attitude toward what the mission had to offer, or wanted to offer, we might be reading the spiritual through the temporal. If we dismiss the vehement wish of the Natives to return to their previous way of life, a wish recorded continuously by the majority of the missionaries, we might be disregarding the few clues the Natives left of their rejection of mission life. Different postcontact generations acted out different desires and fears, and many sacramental registries simply mark the end of a life. In fact, a friar at San Fernando stated in his response to the 1813–1815 questionnaire that "a great change is noticed in those who were born of Christian parents" (Geiger and Meighan 1976, 93).

Conversion was offered as a package deal: to be a Christian was to be civilized. (Or was it the other way around?) You were not converted unless you behaved like a convert. While the wilderness model gave primacy to the Natives' environment and operated within a relative balance of power, the mission model and its permutations worked with a kept audience with little power. In the short term, the first model failed because neither party could sustain its demands and the second failed because the power imbalance left the Natives with little room to choose.

The City of Man

Economic Practices

The work of conversion was the heart of the concept of missionizing, but the lifeblood of the mission was its economic health. I have discussed the concept of mission, but it is wise to consider the different meanings of mission. First, there was the mission of the missionary—his charge to bring salvation to those unaware of God's existence. The second meaning of mission, intrinsic to the first, was the act of converting and civilizing. Despite being different referents, both imply active engagement with the other, at the deepest levels of cultural change that affected the body and the soul. The third meaning of mission denotes the set of buildings and spaces, sacred and secular, where religious and economic practices took place and often stood for those same practices. This last connotation, which sustained and harmonized the possibility of the other two, often soiled the image of the missionary as it questioned his involvement in economic and political affairs. The natural but insidious cohabitation of these varied meanings of mission resulted in uneasy feelings for the friars and sometimes made them question which city they served, God's or Man's. Like the preceding chapter, what follows is a rendering of the economic practices to contextualize their importance in the process of conversion and its effects on Native Americans.

A mission without Natives did not exist; without Natives, the physical buildings constituting the architectural compound designated as a mission lacked a raison d'être—a population to be converted. Fr. Martin García stated it eloquently: "And the mission is made, as I said, not by the abundance of things but by the people, and [a mission] with the first and without the second is like a body without a soul" (1745, 131).

The missions that existed from the late seventeenth century onward in Texas, Florida, California, and northeastern Mexico could not survive without a great deal of manpower. The Native population was essential to the functioning of a mission even at its most precarious. The complex structure of roles, assignments, and tasks that had to be performed every day and throughout the year entailed specific ritual and workspaces and required a substantial population with considerable and varied skills. Like the hacienda, the mission was an economic enterprise that incorporated the full spectrum of activities to sustain a large population that was generally reticent and often rebellious. A friar could do little to manage and supervise the running of a mission without the help of Natives as supervisors and as laborers. Without the consent and active participation of Natives, little could be accomplished. How that consent and participation was elicited and what that consent meant were the cruxes of conflict. The mission provided the necessities of life as the crown and the church understood them, but life as Natives understood it often took place elsewhere.

Work: Spaces and Time

The ideal mission layout was the quadrangle, either enclosed or open on one side.[1] The mission layout in the regions discussed in this work was often a lopsided quadrangle that was produced by rebuilding, or relocation of mission buildings, or opportunistic add-ons. Regardless of local and geographic conditions, the spatial plan of the buildings radiated from a central square of which the church and convent were the keystones. In addition to the church, the complex typically included a sacristy, cells for the friars and visitors, dormitories for young male neophytes, a kitchen, and workspaces for the friars. When Native housing was included in the mission compound it was often placed at one of the sides of the quadrangle. All missions had a complex of workspaces that followed various arrangements and changed over time. These included workshops for carpentry, blacksmithing, and weaving. There were also kitchens, granaries, toolsheds, water wells, ovens, stables, grinding and sugar-cane mills, tanneries, and water tanks. The spatial arrangement of ritual places, dwellings, and workplaces varied from mission to mission and often tracked changes in commerce and the economic development of the mission.

Entry into a mission altered the rhythm of life of Native Americans and introduced them to a seasonality of activities and scheduled daily practices that were foreign to their sociocultural systems. These changes had profound implications for hunter-gatherers. Bourdieu shook our thinking habits when he made us aware of all those insignificant "out of mind" practices that move us through a day that have more meaning than we know (Bourdieu 1977, 79). It is often the diminution of the capacity to "do without thinking" that brings to painful attention how much thinking goes into doing. It is the nexus of taken-for-granted practices that organizes one's world and it follows, as Bourdieu explained, that the "orchestration of habitus cre-

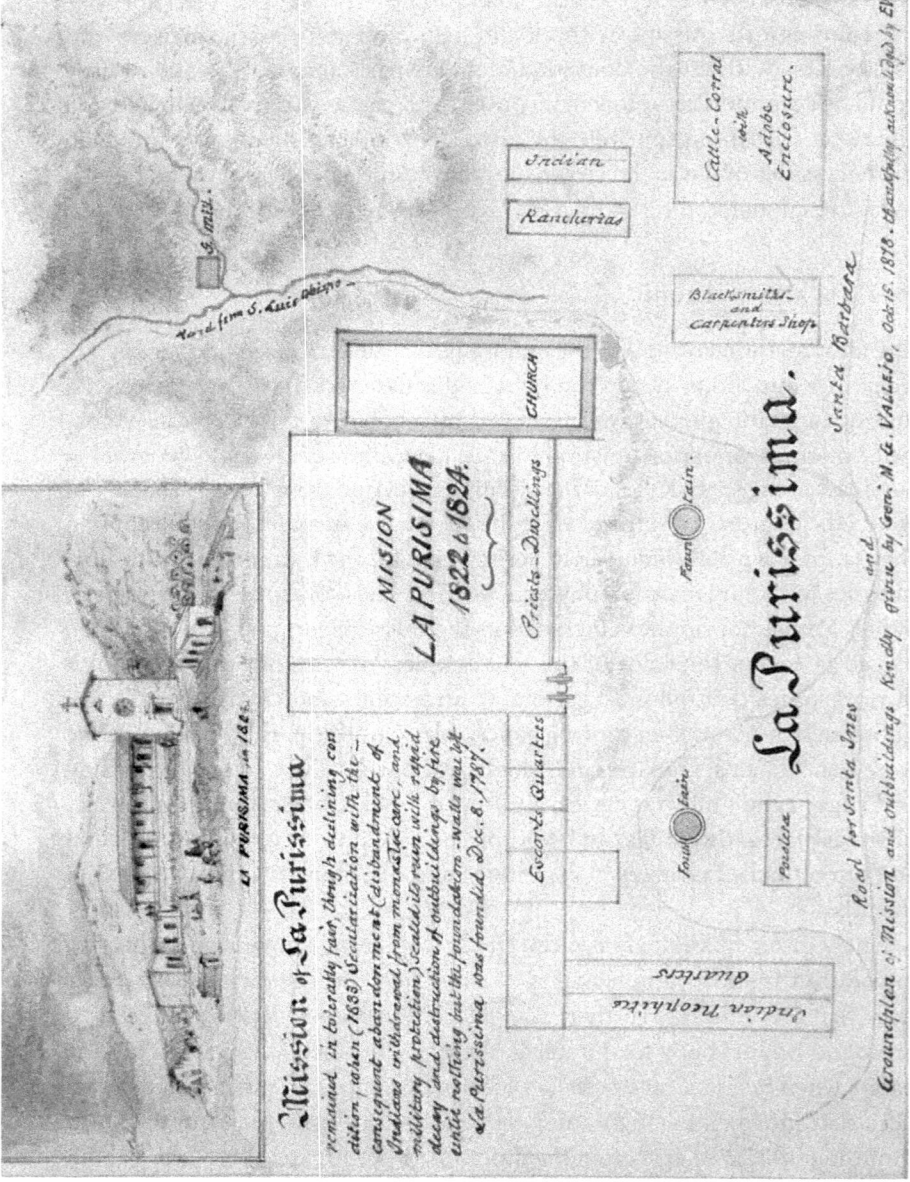

Figure 12.1. Ground plan of La Purisima Mission and outbuildings with sketch of mission in 1824. Courtesy of the Bancroft Library, University of California, Berkeley.

ates a commonsense world" whereby the members of a group, for instance, automatically understand and receive reinforcement of their cultural competence (1977, 80). These "habits" are acquired in the course of a particular history, genealogy, and cultural-environmental setting. The "competent" habitus is "laid down in each agent by his [or her] earliest upbringing which is the precondition not only for the co-ordination of practices but also for the practices of co-ordination" (1977, 81). Hunter-gatherers who entered a mission had to acquire and master a nexus of practices foreign to their previous life. They needed to sever themselves from automatic "insignificant" practices that established their cultural competence and made sense of the social world they had inhabited before. The homogeneity of a group's conditions of existence and the intelligible practices of a group, particularly a hunting-gathering group, were harmonized "as two clocks or watches in perfect agreement as to the time" (Leibnitz quoted in Bourdieu 1977, 80). Mission schedules shaped the calendric "co-ordination of practices," while the long-term "practices of co-ordination" were left to the individual.

Effective and long-term cultural change is change of deep-seated habitus, and it has profound implications regarding Leibnitz's clocks or what Luckmann called Inner Time, or body time, and Intersubjective Time, or social time. Body time is individual time, "the present in which we are immersed with our bodies" (Luckmann 1991, 153). Social time is experienced in face-to-face interactions to achieve synchronization of consciousness and practices whereby "they can form a unitary course of social interaction" (156). The time of everyday life is social time experienced according to pre-established social categories that can take the form of rites of passage, resource or harvest cycles, solar or moon cycles, or the calendar. In hunter-gatherer societies the enmeshing of body time with social time is perceived as far more embedded in the rhythmic flow of daily life and the acquisition of wild resources than it is in literate societies. The remarks Franciscans made in their responses to the 1813–1815 questionnaire demonstrate this enmeshing. For instance, at missions at San Diego, San Luís Rey, and elsewhere, Natives reckoned time by the sun, the moon, and specific harvest seasons named after the respective resources (Geiger and Meighan 1976, 81). At Santa Barbara, however, the friar proudly noted that "now the Christians govern their lives in regard to work, meals and the rest by the sound of the bell" (82). Offhand remarks included in the questionnaire point to deeper levels of conflict and resentment with western time as it confronted and affronted ritual. As an example, Natives at Mission San Carlos were extremely displeased when asked how long had it been since the death of a relative (56–60, 83).

Native people who entered the mission had to have experienced shock regarding personal and social time until they adapted (if they adapted) to the mission schedule and rearranged body time and social time in order to "govern their lives . . . by the sound of the bell" (Geiger and Meighan 1976, 82). It is possible that tight, compulsory time schedules (interactive social time) facilitated the retooling of some aspects of body time (individual time). Compulsory changes in body time, as translated into sets of new practices (habitus), would produce a body time that was always arthritically and convulsively fighting itself as "old" practices interfered with the acquisition of new ones. In addition, that acquisition required conscious thought and effort, which means that much time was needed before new practices would be taken for granted. Indeed, missionized Natives could be said to have been out of time.

Economic activities are sociocultural practices that have specific social consequences. Redefining how Native Americans made a living changed their priorities, modified their life cycles, and altered social interactions such as when to eat or when to copulate. Mission life and its time schedules required Natives to acquire new knowledge that put a premium on discarding lifelong skills and acquiring others that they often understood imperfectly or even considered irrelevant. The skills they had to leave behind varied from using their Native language to ritual singing and dancing, fishing and hunting, manufacturing weapons, or selecting appropriate herbs (Geiger and Meighan 1976, 19–21, 24–26, 40). Mission Natives who retained a Native compass and some traditional standards had to attain considerable social plasticity to develop their roles as missionized Natives while retaining attachments and skills that permitted them to navigate old and new conceptual worlds. Just as they became bilingual, they became bicultural, in some cases retaining their traditions while in others needing to discard them. Such is the case of the manufacture of bows and arrows, which persisted because Natives continued to procure their own food and because the missionaries needed them as warriors. Conversely, ritual singing and dancing went underground or were forcefully discarded. At stake were ethnic survival and the avoidance of schizophrenic group entities and individual identities.

Natives rose before sunrise, put on their uncomfortable abrasive garments, and followed the regimented practices described in chapter 10. Their work was rewarded with daily or weekly rations whose distribution was mostly out of their control. Each person's contribution to the communal economic pool was anonymous, and many individual roles became group roles. Native positions of power and status had important economic and social effects. Mission-pueblo governors, mayordomos, fiscals, and sacristans benefited from preferential treatment in housing, clothing, gifts, and food choices. Regardless of prior Native social arrangements in terms of gender and age, within the mission social network no power positions were given to females. In fact, the sexual fears of the friars, stemming from their vulnerability to temptation and innuendo and their fears of "illicit" contact between indigenous females and males, worked to ostracize women and segregate their economic roles. Likely women held covert power positions, but the historical dread of Native voices makes it difficult to uncover where such power foci were located. The evidence for female shamans is more abundant for California and northern Mexico and is negligible for Texas (see Behar 1987; Geiger and Meighan 1976, 49; Lepowsky 2004), but without a doubt the influence of women went beyond shamanistic events that caught the attention of the friars and merited recording (see Asisara 1991 and the role of women in the events). Still, a patriarchal social regime was installed and sanctioned at the missions, leaving out the coherence of Native checks and balances as well as the mechanisms that had been worked out in European social structures. Adaptation entailed adopting such solutions and in time they were put into practice, but many Natives did not live long enough to benefit from them. Also, flight and high mortality rates led to continual replacement of Native groups in the missions, causing a stuttering in the development of social structures that might have facilitated cultural transitions between hunting-and-gathering modes of living and social arrangements and a sedentary and regimented mission life.

Just as the economic life of the mission was embedded into its mission to convert, so were its economic practices folded into religious activities. In Texas, before Sunday Mass, the cattle were slaughtered for the weekly distribution of meat rations, and after Mass, males received their tobacco ration. Likewise, after Monday Mass, the friar distributed corn rations to the women according to family size, season of the year, and availability of supplies. Salt rations were given once a week, possibly on Monday. On Thursday, the vaqueros traveled to the mission ranches to get the cattle to be slaughtered on Sunday. On Saturday, the women swept the courtyard of the mission, the church, and the sacristy, and when they finished, they received a soap ration according to family size.

Hunting-and-gathering populations that reckoned time according to the seasonal harvest of wild resources and herd movements had to mark time by weekly events punctuated by religious activities tied to food rations. The friars sandwiched weekly distribution of important foods such as meat, corn, and salt between religious practices to ensure Native attendance and penalize absence. These covert economic sanctions were, in effect, also religious punishments that had sociocultural consequences. Resistance to religious practices by absence resulted in less food, which hampered an individual's ability to survive and maintain physical fitness and likely caused loss of status. In Baja California, where the Jesuits followed a rotation system, food rations were not given to those who did not attend religious practices and refused baptism. In fact, Dunne suggests that the Jesuit practice of distributing food only to those who came to the mission for religious instruction may have resulted in less resistance to disease in times of food shortages (1968, 232, 403).

In Texas and Alta California young and adult males took to the fields every day to prepare the ground, sow, and harvest. Adult women and probably adolescent girls also worked in the fields, but by the mid-1750s, the friars in Texas had stopped that practice because of the disruptions their presence caused. Women were still allowed to work in the fields when there was an urgent need and sometimes after they had prepared and brought the noon meal to their male kinfolk. In the mission a woman's appropriate place was in the house grinding corn to supply her household and the people living at the convent.

In 1786, while visiting Alta California, La Pérouse noted that the women used a metate and a long round mano to grind corn (Margolin 1989, 86–87 and n15). A member of La Pérouse's expedition gave the friars a manual grinding mill that would have saved labor and increased productivity because with the mill, four women could do the work of one hundred, but another visitor to Carmel in 1792 made no mention of the mill and noted that the women were grinding corn using metates and manos. In Alta California, Fernando Librado noted that on Saturdays, old men brought two types of brooms for the sweepers. *Juncus* (rush) brooms were delivered to the "nuns, some for the department where they had twelve metates . . . going all the time, some for the kitchen, the church, the padres' room, the wine cellar, and for the loom room" (1979, 15). In Texas, the mission at San José had a water-powered grinding mill that supplied flour locally and to the other San Antonio missions (Wade 1993). It is not clear to what extent that device eased the labor of women.

A Friar's Calendar: Cyclical Chores

The yearly cyclical chores connected with the running of the mission were vast. The following narrative has been compiled from several historical sources but principally from *Guidelines for a Texas Mission* (Leutenegger 1976), the *Report of Fr. Ignacio Antonio Ciprián* (Leutenegger 1979), and several mission inspection reports (de los Dolores et al. 1762; Lopez 1786; Xavier Ortiz 1745).

In early spring before planting began, the whole community was engaged with cleaning and repairing the irrigation ditches and dams. Bridges and fences were repaired annually, and the cane and the stubble from the last crops were burned. At least by the 1780s all fields had strong wooden fences (Lopez 1786). The fields were weeded and the soil was tilled and plowed in preparation for the new crops. In Texas, corn was planted in May or June, depending on the weather conditions. If the corn crop had been insufficient in the previous season and it was thought that the same problem would arise again, corn was also planted in February or March. Once the corn matured, the fiscal assigned men to guard the fields so that neither human nor beast could feast on it. At harvest time the corn was brought to the mission in wooden carts and unloaded by the women and children (Leutenegger 1976, 37). Normally only a small amount of corn was shelled: most of the crop was dried and stored in the husk. Weekly corn rations were given to each household and females ground the daily corn using metates and manos (20).

In Texas, cotton was planted around April, depending on the timing of the last frost, and in August or September children picked the cotton. If there were not enough children to do the job, the women would help. The cotton crop was brought to the missions, where the women placed it on hides to dry. These hides had to be prepared beforehand and kept for this purpose. Afterward young and adult females cleaned the cotton and set it again to dry. Every day the cotton crop was taken out to be placed in the sun until it was completely dry and put away in the loft of the barn where it was stored (Leutenegger 1976, 37–38). In the 1750s, Mission San José in Texas expected a cotton crop of about 100 arrobas, or about 5,500 pounds (Habig 1978, 124).

Fruit trees were planted and tended accordingly, and chiles were planted around March or April, depending on the weather. Beans of more than one kind were planted in June in designated areas. Although the records tell us little about this horticulture, fruit, chiles, squash, pumpkins, and beans had to be picked, prepared, or shelled for storage, and apparently women and children did most of these chores. Chiles were essential for seasoning, and the other crops provided variety in the diet and alternatives to meat protein during Lent. Mission San José had a good herb garden, and apparently its fruit orchard was famous for the biggest and best peaches available in the area (Habig 1978, 145, 221). Unlike other areas in New Spain such as California, grapes and olives were rarely cultivated in Texas and wheat was hardly worth the effort. The mission diet in Texas reflected its New World roots. Between crops, the soil was weeded, hoed, and irrigated. Melons and watermelons were harvested and the seed was collected for future plantings. Because Natives were quite fond of these fruits, their distribution was rationed. One or two gardeners were assigned to each orchard, and when the fruit was ripe the gardeners harvested it and brought the daily crop to the friary. The availability of these and other crops was thought to keep Natives from leaving the mission to search for food elsewhere (Leutenegger 1976, 53). There are frequent mentions of women who liked to leave the mission to gather wild food resources, and although the friars did not outlaw the practice, they discouraged it (49). In Baja California, missionized Native populations continued to resort to traditional foods, although their diet was often supplemented by rations the Jesuits provided. In Texas, Natives could leave the mission to hunt (Santa Ana 1748, 189), and in Alta California some Native men were allowed to hunt and fish and offered some of their catch to the friars (Hewes and Hewes 1991, 157; Margolin 1989, 90) or they gathered wild resources to comply with the friars' demands (Hackel 2005, 245). Moreover, the responses to the 1813–1815 questionnaire indicate that local natives hunted and fished; gathered acorns, nuts, and seeds; kept private garden plots; and prepared many meals in their dwellings (Geiger and Meighan 1976, 85–88).

Not much is said about the planting and processing of sugar cane in Texas, but Fr. Mariano stated that each mission planted sugar cane annually because Natives prized sugar cones (*piloncillo*) over most other foods (de los Dolores et al. 1762, 61–62). At Mission San José in Texas, the sugar cane grown was from Castile, and most years it yielded the equivalent of 500 pesos' worth of sugar cones and enough molasses for local needs. This mission had a hut for the sugar cane and a sugar mill, furnaces, vats, a trough, and molds for *piloncillo* cones (Habig 1978, 123–26). The Natives collected seasonal nuts and berries as they had always done, but it is likely that the friars organized seasonal harvesting parties. Tobacco must have been grown also because it was distributed regularly, but nothing is said about its cultivation. The accounting records of Mission San Francisco de Espada in Texas show the importation of tobacco (Jackson 2000, 12).

During March and April the sheep were sheared. Missions kept large numbers of sheep, which were an essential source of income and were used at the mission for their milk and their wool. Shepherds, often Native Americans, served one month at a time and were to inform the friar about the number of sheep, ewes, and lambs the mission owned. The animals were branded and castrated at the missions or at the ranches owned by the missions. In Texas, many of the castrated animals were driven annually to the

Rio Grande to be sold in the local markets; the revenue accrued to the mission. In 1756, Mission Concepción had a flock of 1,800 sheep, and in 1772 it had 3,840 (Leutenegger 1976, 42n). In 1755, San José had 3,500 sheep and expected a healthy increase in the flock (Habig 1978, 125). Sheep were seldom slaughtered at the mission, and then only for friars and the sick. Goats were certainly used for meat, but if the missionaries made goat cheese, the records are silent on the matter. In Alta California, however, milk was part of the diet and women were employed to make cheese.

Most missions had weaving rooms supervised by an adult male who was chosen with care because everyone, especially young males, had to respect and obey him. An expert weaver supervised the weaving and selected other weavers, but adult females and children carded and spun the cotton and the wool. From cotton they made white homespun cloth for the shirts and pants that were distributed to the males annually, and from the wool they made blankets that were worn in cold weather. For this reason, blanket work had to be finished by the end of summer. The cotton weaving was done in two widths, wider and narrower. The narrower homespun was used for pants and shirts for the boys. The weavers also made wool blankets of two widths. Needles were imported for the seamstresses, and the women sewed all the garments for males and females (Habig 1978, 112). At San José, Natives had heavy cotton bed sheets that were woven in the mission (149).

Every day the boys went to the *acequia* (irrigation ditch) to wash the wool and they left it to soak in kettles. This job had been performed by women, who had washed the wool in the river, but by 1760 the Texas friars had determined that too much of the wool was lost and that the males did a better job. It is not clear that this reassignment of workers was actually due to loss of material. As time went on, the friars in Texas seemed to segregate the women more and more, preventing them from performing chores outside the mission compound and restricting their movements to the dwellings and mission quarters in efforts to prevent them from having contact with males. This gender segregation policy culminated in the female dormitories in California where women were locked up at night.

The wool was washed and left to dry in the mission patio. Once it dried, both women and children were employed to prepare cotton and wool for weaving. The overseer weighted the skeins to make sure that all the material was accounted for. Every day the overseer took the skeins to the friar's cell for safekeeping, and only the amount needed daily for weaving was taken from the friar's cell to the workshop. Such zeal and control over cotton and wool was to prevent anyone from stealing yarn and to avoid any collusion between the overseer and the spinners. These operations were also supervised by the fiscal, who made sure the work was properly done and completed on time.

The work assignments for wool and cotton were very similar. The women were given one to two ounces of cotton or wool to be cleaned and spun at the distaff. As they cleaned the cotton, they picked and saved the seeds for planting. The women took the work home, and the following morning they delivered to the friar the skeins of cleaned cotton or wool. Each morning the overseer distributed three ounces of carded cotton to each child, and each evening the children delivered the yarn to the missionary. The children disentangled the yarn, wound it in skeins, and cut it as necessary for weaving. The friar accumulated the material prepared by the women and children and supplied the expert weaver with the exact weight (20 ounces) of yarn for each blanket (Leutenegger 1976, 41–46). As the blankets were finished the friar began distributing them. When all the people had been provided for, the friar could choose to have some coarse wool overcoats (*cotones*) made for those who needed them most during the winter.

If they asked for it, women were given cloth for shirts, and they sewed their own garments. However, unlike males, women were supplied with ready-made undershirts imported from Mexico. The Native mission officials and others selected by the friar were given cloth from Puebla (Leutenegger 1976, 25–26). Generally the mission population was provided with only one set of garments, but the friar could elect to provide an extra set of garments to those he considered worthy: a set of clothing of lightweight fabric and another of heavy weight. For instance, normally at Mission Concepción two women got linen shifts and another set of shifts from Puebla to provide them with a change of clothing, but this did not happen every year. We are not told who these women were, but it is possible they were related to or married to pueblo government officials. This practice distinguished persons in authority as well as those favored by the friar. Such distinctions in clothing rewarded what the friar considered appropriate behavior, conferred prestige, and were tools to ensure compliance. In the Californias, the Jesuits provided clothes to the neophytes twice a year and the Franciscans imported cloth and clothing (Palou 1994, 57–58, 118). At San José de Comundú in Baja California, women wove the blankets, at least during the Franciscan period (Palou 1994, 92).

Cattle was raised and kept in the ranches of the missions, supplying meat, tallow, fat (*manteca*), hides, and glue. When the population of the mission was small, four to six animals were killed each week for meat and by-products. These numbers probably did not vary much. In 1758, Mission San José had a population of 281 Natives; and they slaughtered seven beef cattle each week: four for the mission, one for the shepherds, one for the cowboys, and one to be made into jerky and used for the sick (Habig 1978, 130–31). The records are silent about how entrails and other animal parts were used as food resources. It is likely, however, that the entrails were kept and that sausage-like products were prepared, given the traditional Mediterranean diets and background of most of the friars. The hides were used for clothing, shoes, saddles, rope, bed frames, furniture, pictures, chair seats, book covers, and other items (149). The rendered fat was essential for cooking and making soap and candles, and the hooves were used for buttons, glue, and other essential items. In Baja California, the cattle were driven from mission to mission for pasture, and poor missions or those that had recently been established were provided with animals from other missions to supplement or start their herds.

This picture contrasts sharply with the practices in Alta California in the late mission period. At Mission San Diego, for instance, twenty-four animals were slaughtered every fifteen days (Geiger and Meighan 1976, 85), while at San Buenaventura at least forty-five head of cattle were slaughtered every week (86). At that mission, "in the season when the cattle are very fat, the slaughter of sixty cattle takes place twice a week in order to increase the amount of tallow for sale so that necessary goods may be procured. Large portions of the meat are taken in carts to the field and burned because there is no one to take it away. The neophytes in their houses have plenty of fresh and dried meat" (86). While in northern Mexico, Baja California, and Texas the slaughter of mission cattle to feed the Native populations was tightly controlled and even deserved royal attention, in Alta California during the late period the needs of the commerce in hides and tallow determined how many animals would be slaughtered, permitting excess and waste.

Dispersed references show that the Texas missions raised chickens destined for meals given to the sick (Habig 1978, 131). Obviously they also used eggs in their diets and these could be used to make sweets. In the Alta California missions women raised chickens and gave the eggs to their children. The Natives owned clothing, some furnishings and hunting tools, and the fowl they tended (Margolin 1989, 90).

In Texas, October and November were the months to brand cattle. The friar told the other missions and the settlers to remove their cattle from the lands that belonged to each mission. Many conflicts arose at this time because privately owned animals would be mixed with the mission herds. Each evening Native vaqueros made sure that cattle kept at the mission were corralled and let out to pasture in the morning. Most missions had ranches with vaqueros who lived at the ranch with their families and cared for the animals (Leutenegger 1976, 32). The horses raised were used at the mission, were traded or sold to the presidios, or were taken to northern Mexico for sale. Mules and donkeys were kept by the missions and were essential for the mule trains that transported people and goods between missions and brought imported items from supply posts south of the Rio Grande. The saddle maker was generally a Spaniard who was contracted as needed; he was paid in corn and meat. In Alta California, mission muleteers transported goods between missions and presidios and in the 1800s were actively engaged in the extensive hide and tallow trade (Librado 1979, 16–17).

At the end of the Texas summer, young males began to cut the quelite (*Atriplex matamorensis*, cenizo, or *Atriplex texana*, saltbrush) from the patio and from around the mission to burn it (Richardson 1995, 60–61). The ash was then mixed with fat (*sebo*) and lye and the mixture was boiled in kettles to make soap used throughout the year. The soapmaker knew the proportions of ashes to fat, how much lye to mix, and how long to boil the mixture. If there was no one knowledgeable enough to perform the job, the friar would instruct the fiscal, who took care of the task. Limestone blocks were collected and brought to the mission. The rocks were burned in an oven to make lime that was kept in a specified room to be used for soap and for food preparation, especially for corn. The wood for the oven was brought to the mission in carts. These carts were made and repaired at the mission by the carpenters. "Dark soap" was distributed to Natives, while "white soap" was presumably kept for the friar and the convent (Habig 1978, 230).

Another cold-weather task was candlemaking. If the mission did not have a candlemaker, the friars called one from the presidio who would be assisted by a mission boy. The friar supplied the fat and the wicks for the candles (Leutenegger 1976, 35). In Texas, most candles were made with cattle fat, but the friars also traded for bear fat to make candles that burned cleaner and were much preferred. Missions needed a substantial supply of candles for lighting the friar's quarters and shops and especially for all religious ceremonies. In Alta California they also imported wax for candles and olive oil for the lamps (Palou 1994, 57–58, 131).

Other work was necessary for the running of a mission. The cook was always a married male because mission rules did not permit female cooks and the friars had problems with single men (Leutenegger 1976, 21). These problems are not specified but they may have been related, as they generally were, to relations with female staff. Although each week the fiscal appointed Native women to grind the corn and make tortillas for the friar, in Texas, women from the presidio prepared the friar's bread (wheat bread?) but Native women prepared the meals for their male relatives. In Texas, salt was either obtained from the presidio, which sent people out to collect it, or the missions contracted with the muleteer to bring some. There are few references to salt, but the San José mission kept salt in storage (Habig 1978, 113) and apparently so did other missions (de los Dolores et al. 1762, 60). In California, Natives often extracted and transported salt for the missions and for the presidio, despite the friars' objections (Palou 1994, 94, 103). It is clear that the muleteers, who were often Natives, transported many items either from nearby places or from south of the Rio Grande (Habig 1978, 146). The continuous need for supply convoys that brought many of the products the missions and the settlers needed to San Antonio and east Texas gave rise to a thriving business that employed Natives and non-Natives, who were paid in kind. For instance, Mission San José supplied cattle to San Sabá in the 1750s as well as other products to other missions and presidios (127, 145). In Texas, Missions Rosario and Espíritu Santo raised large herds of cattle which they sold to presidios, settlers, and other missions (Lopez 1786). In California, where the missions were the principal source of agricultural products for the presidios, a good supply of pack animals was essential for transportation (Costansó 2001, 117; Jackson 2005, 137; Palou 1994, 93).

Elderly males who were chosen by the mayordomo or the fiscal brought wood for the kitchen and hay for the friar's horses and mules. The carpenters were also older males; they worked on the plow yokes, made carts and furniture, cut planks, and did other woodwork with the assistance of young male apprentices. Each mission had a blacksmith who was either a Native or a Spaniard. This person was paid by the task or was contracted annually to make and repair metal tools and objects such as plowshares, hatchets, and like items (Leutenegger 1976, 33). Also, each presidio or mission had a barber who was contracted annually, or by task, to shave the friar every week, usually on Saturday. The barber was also the person who performed incisions or bleeding (phlebotomy) whenever these procedures were deemed necessary for medical reasons. Writing about Baja California, Crosby (1994, 288) notes the important role of midwives and the telling absence of information on this issue.

In Alta California, cupping glasses (*ventosas de vidrio*) were imported, which indicates that bleeding was still practiced (Perissinotto 1998, 28). The friar kept a supply of medicines from herbs to chocolate for healing the sick (Palou 1994, 57–58). The inventory of the mission at San José lists some of the medications used as well as books on medicinal and surgical practices (Habig 1978, 242). The list includes incense, *alucema* (lavender), rosemary, *cassia fistula* (the golden shower tree), copper sulfate, lead, mercuric sulfide, ginger, and hemp. Lists from the Santa Barbara Presidio in California show anise, nutmeg, blue vitriol (copper sulfate), sweet mercury, cassia, and sweet almond oil, among other items (Perissinotto 1998, 28). At San José, the medical treatises available were written by the famous court physician Dionisio Daza y Chacón, by Juan Vigo, and possibly by Bartolomé Hidalgo de Agüero (Habig 1978, 234). The Jesuits in Baja California as well as missionaries in other areas consulted Father Johann Steinheffer's *Florilegio Medicinal*, published in Mexico in 1712 (Dunne 1968, 441; Skowronek and Thompson 2006, 38).

While it is possible to generalize about the economic calendar of the San Antonio missions because they shared physiographic and climatic conditions, the same is not true for Baja or Alta California. Still, regardless of the mission's location, planting, harvest, and related chores followed precise schedules. At San Barbara, barley was planted in December; in December and January, Natives sowed wheat. In February they planted garbanzo beans, peas, and favas (broad beans), while by March they had planted corn, followed by kidney beans in April. The harvest season began in June with barley, followed by the harvest of the wheat crop in June and July and finally by corn in August and September. In April and June shepherds and cowboys sheared the sheep and castrated and branded the cattle (Hackel 2005, 282). Interspersed with agricultural and animal husbandry chores, Native workers performed a variety of seasonal chores just as they did in Texas. For instance, from March to October they carded, spun, and wove wool and cloth (Hackel 2005, 284). The mission records of Alta California, unlike those of Texas, provide information about making tiles and adobe bricks and the products of tanneries (Hackel 2005, 284–85, 305–7).

Mission economy was rooted in a labor economy that produced a surplus. Natives supplied the labor force and the surplus was invested—not necessarily in the mission that produced it but in the mission network of specific orders or colleges. The wealth and health of each mission determined its ability to feed and clothe the Native population. To this equation were added the contributions from the crown in start-up funds, missionary salaries, and subsidies in the form of soldiers' wages. Other factors in the equation were the private donations and endowments that provided extra funds in cash or goods to the missions and the funds raised by the missionaries in payment for religious services to the civilian population. This combination of economic factors makes a strict Marxist reading of the mission economy impossible.

To this communal economic panorama, one must add a local system of redistribution that created an underground economy fueled by individual interests and social customs. Doubtless people passed on goods from the mission to family members and friends and others in need, and doubtless the friars were unaware of most of these exchanges. In addition, goods were exchanged due to gambling and game-playing despite mission-mandated punishments and the friars' efforts to stop it (Leutenegger 1976, 40). This underground exchange system extended beyond each mission and included presidio officials, settlers, and other missions. Clothing and items of personal adornment were the things the friars noticed—items that were given to Natives at annual or seasonal distributions. Exchange for services such as those the shamans provided was common (Nunis 1982, 145; Pérez de Ribas 1645/1999, 494), though sometimes it was the friars who were on the receiving end of such exchanges (Pérez de Ribas, 248).

In Baja California the Jesuits allowed, or closed their eyes to, the development of small industries and trade. Natives procured and tanned deerskins, made shoes and carrying bags of rawhide, used the produce of their garden private plots for barter, braided the hair of cattle into halters, made pottery, traded turtle shells on the mainland, made cotton blankets and hose, wove baskets and hats out of cane and palm fronds, and even made a popular "sweet preserve by roasting hearts of mezcales" (Crosby 1994, 218–19). Several of these items, particularly blankets, hosiery, and basketry, were manufactured by women and were possibly also traded by them. As domestic employees and babysitters, women had a different kind of access to non-Native households and likely could barter their goods on an individual basis. In Texas, the friars' tight control over spun wool and cotton indicates that a viable underground economy was thriving and was of concern to the friars (see below).

After Texas supply convoys arrived from Saltillo or Boca de Leones, the friars apportioned the goods to be given out and began distributing goods to the Native population. These items are often called "gifts," but most were part of the required provision of clothing. The items were generally purchased with available resources created by a combination of the stipend the crown paid each friar (*sínodo*), the income generated by the work of Natives, and the friars' conservative management of financial resources. The friar would make a list and call males and females at different times to distribute baskets containing goods to be used throughout the year. The baskets destined for the women contained three or four strings of beads, a necklace, some ribbon, straps, a waistband, a rosary, a small brush, an underskirt, a camisole, and a piece of linen to line the skirt. Sometimes the baskets also included a shawl and two pieces of flannel for skirts. Older women did not receive cloth to line the skirts. Young females received a similar basket of goods if the friar had enough materials. Young women were also given "tape" that was likely used as part of the apparatus for menstrual pads (Leutenegger 1976, 27–30). Although most of these items were imported, the baskets appear to have been made locally. We are not told who the basket weavers were or where they obtained the materials for the baskets, although the inventory of the mission at San José mentions thread made from the agave plant (*media libra de pita*), fruit baskets, and sacks (*costales*) (Habig 1978, 113–14).

Archaeological evidence in Texas demonstrates that pottery was used at the missions and likely was made there (Hester 1989a, 1989b, 80–84; Perttula et al. 1995; Ricklis 1999; Walter 2007, 8–88). Despite that evidence, no mention of pottery-making or the identity of the potters has been found. Fr. Mariano (de los Dolores et al. 1762, 61) stated that income generated from the mission's surplus and from the friars' *sínodo* was used to buy clay vessels (*ollas y barros*) and the San José mission's inventory includes china cups, pitchers from Patamba, and plates from Puebla (Habig 1978, 114, 122). Nevertheless, in one of San José's mission workshops, where a variety of items were stored, there were six old vessels, three jugs, and one pot made of clay that were not identified as imports (Habig 1978, 122). More perplexing is the large amount of kitchen implements and dinnerware made of copper and iron. The Native pueblo is listed as having sixty-nine large copper kettles, forty-six iron griddles (*comales*), and thirty-eight copper pots (*ollas*) (115). The convent kitchenware also had copper pots, a brass mortar, pitchers, skillets, and dinner plates; spoons and forks were all made of metal and some of them were from "China" (113, 122). In California, earthenware from Puebla was imported for the missions and for the Santa Barbara presidio, as were clay pots, skillets, and pans from Guadalajara (Perissinotto 1998, 31). The invoices from the Santa Barbara presidio also demonstrate that some imported items, such as honey and syrup, were supplied in specific earthenware jugs (25–26). Unlike in Texas, several Alta California missions had kilns, and there is ample evidence of pottery production (see for instance Skowronek and Thompson 2006, 170–73). Pablo Tac also mentioned pottery vessels being used in his family's dwelling (Hewes and Hewes 1991, 158). Likewise, in Baja California, Fr. Baegert mentioned pottery being made locally and fired in earth ovens (1979, 117).

In the annual distribution of goods in Texas, males received a knife and shoes. The pueblo governor got a hat every year while everyone else received one only if he needed it. A tailor was called to cut the clothing for the males, and the cut pieces were distributed to the women to sew. The alcalde and the fiscal were given knee-length coats and lined trousers with buttonholes; everyone else got plain trousers. The evidence is mixed regarding how the Natives felt about this clothing. There is considerable evidence that Native groups prized European clothing but not necessarily the clothing the friars provided. Actually, the evidence seems to indicate that certain colors of clothing were coveted and were associated with specific positions and statuses; these items were used for dressing up and had a performance function. Cotton and wool garments manufactured at the mission were rough and scratchy and in Texas, they were certainly hot. Native people who previously had gone about naked would have been doubly uncomfortable working in such garments. Some of the evidence indicates that Natives, particularly males, continued to wear loincloths and avoided wearing mission garments. For instance, in Alta California the friars distributed breechcloths and blankets. When they went to Sunday Mass, males wore a breechcloth and a blanket (a wrap); sometimes they wore clean cotton overshirts. The Natives were given leather shoes that they were required to wear to Mass, but when there were too many Natives and not enough shoes, one group attended the first half of the Mass and departed, leaving the shoes behind to be used by the second group (Librado 1979, 48–49). In Texas, once or twice a year all Natives were given a pair of shoes imported from Saltillo if they asked for them. Men, women, and children could get woolen stockings and even silken hose if the friar decided to pay for them. The friars decided which people would get better clothing and accessories.

The fact that wearing these garments was obligatory and that the friars equated looking civilized with being civilized raises other issues related to body functions and habitus for males and females. Aside from western notions of privacy, which are likely not pertinent, western garments impeded and changed habits of the body, some of which may have had considerable sociocultural consequences, as would be the case with blood taboos and the cultural treatment of menstruation and the afterbirth. Nonfertile and menopausal females were treated differently in terms of clothing and the assignment of chores. Older women were not supplied with lining for their underskirts, possibly because they no longer had menses (Leutenegger 1976, 28). Little is said about sexuality, but sexual practices and childrearing practices certainly changed after the sexes were segregated and monogamy was imposed.

However, Fr. Martin García admonished (1745, 118) that males should not be given tasks that kept them away from their wives because that was against the objectives of matrimony and against procreation. Fr. García added that the population decrease was not so much due to epidemics, disease, or the harshness of the labor schedule but to the little time the males had with their wives. The answers to the 1813–1815 questionnaire are quite ambiguous about relationships between couples. At the mission at Santa Barbara the friar commented that local Natives loved their wives unconditionally after they were over forty years of age, a possible change of affective status related to age and fertility (Geiger and Meighan 1976, 24).

Another issue to be considered was whether there were appropriate role models, female or male, for novel situations. Were there enough surviving members in any mission and of any group to serve as mentors for the next generation? Did the high rate of turnover among mission residents due to runaways, disease, and conflict allow a cadre of old-timers to acculturate the newcomers? The environment of the mission promoted acculturation, but especially for females acculturation came from their peers.

The mission work schedule left little time for amusement, and few activities were acceptable to the friars. Festive occasions permitted dances and music, but most of the activities that Native Americans had been accustomed to were not allowed. In Texas, Native men and women liked to play *palillo*, a game played with small pins; *patole*, a game played with four sticks; and *chueca*, a ball game that may have been similar to lacrosse. The friars did not allow women to play *chueca*, which they considered too strenuous and unbecoming to females, although they permitted them to play *palillo* and possibly *palote*. Sometimes the friar would let them play these games, but he would not allow groups from the presidio or other missions to play the home team for fear the players would gamble away their clothing or possessions. Men would bet anything they owned, while women often bet their beads (Leutenegger 1976, 40; Santa Ana 1748). As in Alta California, game playing and betting spurred trade. The information from Baja California, the tight supervision of the friars of stores of cotton and wool in Texas, and the punishment stipulated for this type of trade indicate that there was an active underground exchange economy based not only on mission "gifts" but also on manufactured products that demanded special skills.

The *mitote* was the principal ritual celebration of the Native American groups in northeastern Mexico and Texas. The word *mitote* has been used to indicate a variety of celebrations accompanied by dancing and drinking and performed for different reasons; thus the word offers little information to help us identify specific celebrations. *Mitotes* were often permitted and if they were not, Natives stole away for the celebrations (Habig 1978, 149).

It is worthwhile to speculate about what Natives drank at *mitotes*, if anything, and where they prepared their concoctions when the friars permitted them. The responses to the 1813–1815 questionnaire mention ritual dancing and some beverages, but in general the Alta California Native populations were said not to use ritual intoxicating drinks (Geiger and Meighan 1976, 47–48, 50, 89). Ethnographic information collected in the late nineteenth century and afterward clearly indicates ritual dancing, singing, and the ceremonial imbibing of some intoxicating beverages (DuBois 1908, 72–79; Kroeber 1908, 62–65; Sparkman 1908, 221).

Failure to perform religious or economic practices could result in punishment. Not much changed in the application of corporal punishment throughout the mission period, and the evidence is mixed about the use of irons and stocks as instruments of punishment (Guest 1989). The friars continued to see Natives, young and old, as children frozen in time and space, unable to comprehend or evolve beyond a child's age and intellect (23, 28–29). The friars considered it their lawful task and God-given right to reprimand and physically punish their wards. The use of the irons, whippings, and confinement were some of the most frequent punishments the friars implemented. When La Pérouse visited Alta California in 1786, he saw Natives in irons and in stocks, and the friars told him that Native men and women were punished when they "neglected the exercises of piety" and when they committed sins (Margolin 1989, 82). At Mission San Buenaventura there were two types of stocks. One type resembled weighted wooden shoes, which the priests would require men and women to wear while they worked in the fields as a punishment (Librado 1979, 17). The killing of Fr. Quintana was spurred by punishment meted out to Natives (Asisara 1991, 6–7). These were not unusual practices for the friars because they used the same methods with their wards in Europe and saw punishment of the body as intrinsic to redemption. Researchers react with abhorrence to the notion of corporal punishment, but for the friars and the Catholic ethos of the time (and much later) corporal punishment was needed to discipline and subjugate the body. Friars commonly used the cilice[2] under their garments to mortify the flesh, and the discipline was openly used for flagellation during processions.[3] For instance, referring to the good character of Fr. Zalvidea, who was at San Luís Rey, Julio César stated that he had "trance-like states—having continuous battles with the devil whom he accused of threatening to conquer him. He gave himself many beatings, he used silicios" (1930, 15).

Jesuits and Franciscans did not seem to be bothered by their own postulations that they could not entrust the running of missions to their resident Natives, while the rules the missionaries made and their allocation of labor make it obvious that the friar could not conceivably maintain the mission without Natives. In daily contact with Natives the friars witnessed their industrious and often very imaginative ways of dealing with problems, yet they continued to talk about them as savages and children.

As Fr. Martin García explained, "After caring for the fields, all the attention and care should be given to the house of God" (1745, 125). It was the missionary's duty to preserve the mission not only by governing it in economic terms but also (and principally) by guaranteeing that there were souls to convert. When the numbers of mission residents dwindled through flight or disease, friars took trips to the hinterland and to the coast to round up new converts and bring back Natives who had escaped. Without Natives to convert, the missionary could not missionize; without Natives to labor, the missionary did not have a mission.

Conclusion

The colonial conversion program was holistic and aimed at re-forming body and soul to produce a civilized hardworking Christian. The royal mandate and the objectives of the missionaries wedded the civic and the economic to the spiritual, and the mission became the arena where these perspectives and often-conflicting purposes were played out. Conversion became the sum of civilized behaviors: the body mirrored the soul, and thus was conversion measured.

As early as the 1740s the Franciscans acknowledged the burden that management of the missions placed on them as well as its corroding and corrupting influence. As the mission entrapped the Native in its controlling layout, it trapped the missionary in the web of its premises. A friar's labors were his reward and his penance; the Natives' labor was their value and their tether.

Conclusion

A Summa of Many Parts

Missions are memory sites for many descendants of colonial populations and for colonized Native Americans. Spanish missions enshrine complex and contested memories for those whose long-term histories are implicated in the process of mission-building and conversion. But there is a difference, and that difference resides in the colonial program. There were those who willingly came to colonize and those who unwillingly were colonized.

The missionaries who traveled to New Spain were prepared to wage a battle against evil. They had honed their conversion skills in the trials of the Inquisition against heresy and witchcraft and in the tribulations of the European folk afflicted with disease, poverty, and famine. Defining the boundaries between good and evil was vital to the religious combat they engaged. This duty engendered countless conflicts and in the process changed both missionaries and Natives. The task proved particularly trying with the hunter-gatherer populations in the frontier regions discussed in this work because missionaries generally encountered Native spiritual practices that did not fit idolatrous definitions. Missionaries should have understood vows, offerings, appeals to the supernatural, and curing practices with herbs and potions in context and perceived them as more incongruous than threatening. Similar traditions existed among European country folk and most missionaries had grown up surrounded by them, and if they fought such traditions they also dismissed them. Missionaries failed to see the connection between their saintly bone relics and the sticks, stones, and bones in shamans' pouches. They saw only what they were prepared to see. In the end, because of their fear of erring and zealous fervor, they rendered all that was incomprehensible evil and the work of the devil.

The introduction in the New World of heretic and Inquisition discourses and proscriptions influenced the creation of stereotypes about women, Muslims, Jews, and racialized others whose bodies, traditions, and practices became associated with evil deeds. Hunter-gatherer populations already linked with the wild and perceived as untamed and dangerous by New

World settled indigenous people were further stigmatized by the connections missionaries made between the devil and their environment, mode of living, and the foods they collected.

The devil had a central role in the process of conversion and his malevolent presence was proof of the trials of conversion. Each victory against the devil validated the work of the missionary. According to the friars, the devil inhabited the "temples" of the Calusa, advised the Hasinai, and battled for the souls of those dying from devastating epidemics in Parras. Shamans perished because they did the bidding of the devil in Baja California or because they led revolts in Alta California. And if the devil was in people, things, and the land, he also sustained the anguish of the missionaries in their intimate personal struggles.

Most of the conversion efforts discussed in this work targeted hunter-gatherer populations that lived off the land. These groups relied on hunting, fishing, and the collection of wild foods and scheduled their movements about the landscape to profit from those resources. Their dwellings were impermanent and their sojourns short. But the Calusa and the Hasinai were different, and they presented specific challenges to the Jesuits and the Franciscans.

The Calusa and the Hasinai lived in settlements, but while the Calusa were mostly fishermen and hunter-gatherers, the Hasinai were proficient horticulturists. The persistent refusal of these groups to accept conversion probably had its roots in complex social arrangements that linked the social to the numinous and admitted limited compromise. The Calusa dissuaded the Jesuits mostly by argument and the Franciscans by outright expulsion. The Hasinai, on the other hand, threatened, expelled, but later again welcomed the missionaries, only to be uncooperative and cause them to leave. In both cases, the Natives refused to congregate in mission pueblos. This hampered the ability of missionaries to use their customary didactic methods; the friars could not make the Natives attend religious ceremonies and were unable to establish a schedule of practices that, as they saw it, would result in conversion. It is possible that the dispersed settlement pattern of the Hasinai groups was a factor in their rejection of the Christian practices and doctrine, but that does not seem to have been the case with the Calusa. The ability to induce Native groups to live within or near missions and maintain a kept audience, so to speak, was vital to missionary work.

Northeastern Mexico was a difficult field of conversion for other reasons. Agricultural haciendas, cattle ranches, and mines coupled with the *encomienda* and *repartamiento* systems created an insatiable demand for

Native labor that implicated and corrupted all levels of society. If it did not corrupt the missionaries, it forced them into compliance. The region's physiographic characteristics and specific economic development led to the adoption of models of conversion that reflected those conditions as much as they did the background and religious ideals of the missionaries. The Jesuits' work in the Parras-Laguna areas was marred by epidemics and revolts despite the missionaries' optimistic reports. For a spell, the Jesuits tried the wilderness model by following the nomadic populations on their subsistence rounds, but that model of conversion proved unworkable and they established open mission-pueblos. In Coahuila, Fr. Larios also followed a wilderness model, but he too had to resort to establishing mission-pueblos because the goal of missionaries and crown officials was a settlement of Christian subsistence farmers.

The high demand for labor placed most Native people either in urban households and businesses or in the rural haciendas and mines. Natives in the urbanized areas could learn doctrine and attend religious ceremonies in the town church if their owners permitted (and often owners refused permission). Natives working in the haciendas or mines, mostly under some version of the *encomienda* system, were to be ministered by the friars at the *encomenderos'* expense. Indeed, the defining characteristics of the wilderness and the urban-rural models are the location of the Native population and its condition as a labor force. The wilderness model accommodated the realities of Native hunter-gatherer lifeways but was not feasible because its ultimate goal was rapid settlement, while the urban-rural model of conversion accommodated and reflected the conditions created by the colonizers' labor requirements but produced dismal conversion results.

With the help of the Franciscans, and to fulfill its civilizing mission, the crown established mission-pueblos that included both Tlaxcalan farmers and local hunter-gatherer groups. The Tlaxcalans were given incentives to teach the nomadic groups to be good productive Christians, but aside from the Tlaxcalans, the results were very meager in terms of socialization and conversion. Some of the conversion efforts in Coahuila and Nuevo León, however, were based on gathering Natives in pueblos (*congregas*) that, as Fr. Santa María pointed out, were little more than labor pools.

The 1715 King's Edict together with the various requests and complaints from *encomenderos*, settlers, soldiers, nomadic groups, Tlaxcalans, and Franciscans show that the crown knew well the extent of the problems and how they affected Native populations and that the laws did little to resolve the issues. Laws mean little when they can be thwarted by self-interest and collusion of interests. Northeastern Mexico is an example of the extreme importance of Native labor in the frontier, but Native labor was equally vital to the missions in Texas and elsewhere.

The conversion of Texas Natives spanned a century, but my analysis is restricted mostly to the early conversion attempts among the Hasinai, the Rio Grande missions, and the five missions located along the San Antonio River. Unlike the missions in east Texas, all the San Antonio missions were founded for hunter-gatherer groups, and they were profitable and long lasting. They began as simple mission-pueblos protected by a nearby presidio, but by the 1760s, if not earlier, all missions had become walled precincts. These walls were built as much to keep neophytes inside the mission and make flight difficult as they were to defend against outside attacks by groups such as the Apache. It is generally accepted that the principal foes of the San Antonio missions were the Apache. No doubt Apache groups were a serious threat to mission residents and settlers, but the Apache menace began in earnest in the 1720s and the massive mission walls were not constructed until the 1760s. In fact, the 1758 attack on San Sabá mission may have been the catalyst for an enhanced defense posture.

The Texas missions faced a permanent problem with Native desertion, and the friars, accompanied by soldiers, took trips to the hinterland and the coast to replenish the mission population. By the late 1750s, the military was far less cooperative and the friars had to postpone or forego those trips. This implied fewer baptisms to show conversion and heralded a decline in the religious and economic vitality of the Texas missions. Fewer neophytes implied fewer baptisms and labor shortages as evidenced by the cases of the Pamaque and the Pampopa and by unfinished construction projects. A Native labor force was essential to sustain a mission so that the missionary could work at converting. In other words, Natives labored to maintain the system that most of them wished to abandon. This evidence underlines the intricate relationship and interdependency between the religious and the economic conditions of the missions. On the other hand, and even though the number of neophytes in the Texas missions was generally low, by the 1770s in Texas and by the time the Franciscans delivered Baja California to the Dominicans, older missions housed around 200 Natives, a number that allowed the missions to remain viable, despite a shrinking Native labor force.

The Franciscans always segregated young males from their families to minimize contact with their fathers and elders because such contact was considered detrimental to their conversion and education. Young males were reared and educated to be acolytes and interpreters and to perform various tasks in the mission. By the 1740s, the Franciscans in Texas were segregating women with the chores they assigned them and by prohibiting them from working in the fields or washing yarn in the *acequía*. I interpret the progressive restrictions on the movement of females and the construction of walls surrounding the Natives' quarters or the mission as attempts to monitor and control the Natives in general and females in particular. This pattern continued in Alta California.

In 1788, Fr. Oliva argued eloquently for the need to disengage the economic management of the missions from conversion work. There had been other similar requests, but Fr. Oliva's exposition of the problem shows that the friars were well aware of the perils and collusion that resulted from the economic management of the missions. Religious practices and economic practices constituted a structured web that aimed at converting while civilizing, and decoupling them was not possible. These concepts and objectives were embedded in each other and constituted a practice with a single final outcome. The solution, as Fr. Oliva suggested, was to hand over the management of the missions to an honest agent. Alternatively, the Franciscans could entrust the missions to the Native residents. Apparently it was as difficult to find an honest manager as it was for the friars to accept entrusting the missions to the Natives.

Baja California was missionized by the Jesuits and, after the Jesuits were expelled, by the Franciscans. The Jesuits enjoyed a good measure of autonomy over the administration of their missions, mostly because of the Pious Fund that helped finance the missions and obtain other necessary goods and services. Faced with environmental conditions that were less than ideal for agriculture and with hunter-gatherer populations that were dispersed over large territories, the Jesuits devised conversion strategies that were helpful to the friars and, I argue, also beneficial to the Natives. In some cases the Jesuits congregated different *rancherías* and moved them closer to the mission, but most Natives continued living in the *rancherías*. These Natives came to the mission to receive instruction in doctrine according to a rotational schedule; while they were living in the *rancherías*, chosen catechists led them in prayer. It is debatable whether the Natives actually learned doctrine or prayed when they were not at the mission. That is a moot point, as we cannot measure the conversion progress of those who participated in the rotational system versus those who remained at the mission. What is relevant is that the rotational system allowed the Jesuits to run missions with fewer resources and that the system had the potential to allow Native Americans to retain their cultural practices.

Cultural change did not impact all neophytes equally nor did they respond to missionary work in the same fashion. The contact generation benefited from initial enticements but also endured the brunt of repression. Their behavior had been shaped by their own sociocultural systems, and resilient shamans and elders kept group traditions alive despite the onslaught of missionary measures. A significant aspect of the gap between the contact generation and subsequent generations was how each generation experienced rights of passage, cultural signposts in a Native's life course. The first generation born or reared within the mission's fold should have experienced neither the persuasion nor the repression of the contact generation, and their life courses would have been marked by the reception of sacraments. The ladinos came from this generation: they had been baptized, they spoke Castilian, and they were familiar with Spanish customs. Acculturated ladino Natives exploited both sides of the cultural divide and were generally the leaders of revolts.

Nevertheless, both the contact generation and later generations subverted conversion in different ways. Like the Calusa, the protracted case of the Pericué shows the extent to which Native groups learned to outmaneuver the missionaries and explore a multitude of avenues for expressing their discontent and bargaining for their rights. In spite of those efforts, in Baja California, as elsewhere, the missionaries continuously expressed the opinion that the Natives were children incapable of taking care of their own affairs and could not be trusted to run the missions. Surprisingly, they considered Natives to be capable of acquiring and understanding Christian knowledge and even entrusted some with teaching doctrine to other neophytes. But when it came to managing economic property, missionaries persisted in seeing them as inept.

The Jesuits were expelled from New Spain in 1767–1768 and the Franciscans were asked to take over the Baja California missions, which they did for around five years. The departure of the Jesuits had to be distressing for the Native populations, mainly because it disrupted relationships, schedules, and food supplies. The civil and religious decisions that followed and the power struggles between military and religious officials undoubtedly accelerated the decline of most Baja California missions. Despite these changes, the remaining "old" missions retained about 200 people and were economically viable.

Mission reports and assessments written by the missionaries or by other entities are useful documents for evaluating the condition of each mission. What these documents mention and emphasize is as important as what they omit. Such reports are particularly significant during periods when missions were being conveyed from one party to another because the accuracy of the reports could be questioned by the receiving party. Consistent recording of the economic aspects of a mission's affairs, unfailing emphasis on the material and sacral wealth of the mission, and repeated omission of information on the neophytes' religious progress and on their material conditions of living indicates how lopsided the goals of the colonial mission had become, or at least how the assessment of its goals was portrayed in a distorted way. True, a mission's sacramental registers provided a "progress" report; but what did that mean in terms of conversion? I shall return to that issue at the end.

The conversion work of the Franciscans in Alta California provides a useful contrast to their work in Texas. In a sense, Alta California was the mission field where all lessons learned could be applied, and as in Texas the Franciscans were solely in charge. Patterns of control and segregation that began in Texas were perfected in Alta California with dormitories for females and sometimes for males and with missions that typically formed an enclosed quadrangle, though California missions were rarely walled.

During the early period, the Franciscans struggled to garner enough funds to keep the missions on a sure footing and to keep the military at bay. By the time financial worries declined, Fr. Serra had died and Fr. Lasuén was in charge of the missions. Lasuén's tenure was plagued with personnel problems. In Texas, Fr. Oliva questioned the appropriateness of closing the Texas missions and of liberating the friars from the responsibility for financial management of the missions; in Alta California, Fr. Lasuén strove to keep control of the affairs of missions and had to respond to a questionnaire that challenged Franciscan methodologies, practices, and authority. Fr. Lasuén's response is a valuable source of information about Franciscan missionary practices, but it is also valuable because in it Lasuén acknowledged that after many years of attempts to convert them, the Natives continued to yearn for their life in the wild.

A mission was about conversion and conversion was about practices that effectively denaturalized Native populations. In order to convert hunter-gatherer populations the missionary needed not only to congregate them but also to keep them tethered. The outlining of the mission's daily schedules, the calendar of religious ceremonies and festivities, and the discussion of a sacramental life course serve to trace the trajectory of planned practices whose cumulative effects were meant to produce conversion and socialization over the course of a life. Indeed, although Christianization aimed to conquer masses, conversion was counted by the individual—a grain of sand on the heavenly shores. While yearly calendars and the sequential administration of sacraments were to produce a refurbished ritual register, daily routines were meant to change a neophyte's habitus by forcing a rearrange-ment of the inner workings of a neophyte's body time and synchronize it with the time of social interactions and with mission schedules. But long-term changes in the habitus of hunters and gatherers required other points of intervention.

The living strategies of hunter-gatherers fall along a continuum that reflects choices about movement, dwelling, and food collection. All these choices are sensitive to concepts of time, but food collection depends almost entirely on timing. Missionary conversion strategies sandwiched religious practices between key economic practices, such as meat distribution. This linked access to food with religious compliance; in addition, those who did not comply faced physical punishment. Similarly, kin and gender segrega-tion practices were often tied to power and higher-status positions associ-ated with food distribution, labor assignments, and religious activities.

Jesuits and Franciscans used gender segregation to control the Natives' sexual activities principally for religious reasons. Segregation was accom-plished through practical measures such as selectively assigning daily chores, arranging mission buildings into male and female areas, and confin-ing women under lock and key. In their zeal to monitor and ascertain sin, the passive measures women took to avoid procreation, the active measures women took to promote abortion, and sexual relations between kinfolk, mis-sionaries sought and benefited from the information disclosed in confession; otherwise the number, detail, and persistence of questions they asked about these matters during confession makes little sense. In fact, the questionnaire format of the confessionary manual worked as an ethnographic instrument of research.

Conversely, the missionaries' practice of wedding religious practices to civic and economic practices likely accorded well with Native American cos-mologies, but it did violence to Native Americans with its specific Catholic demands. From afar, we can follow the mission's routine of daily tasks and find it normal or taxing. We know that festivities were welcomed and that Natives enjoyed the music and ceremonies attached to the Catholic liturgy. We can evaluate the possible effects of confession and the pragmatic out-comes of matrimony. But we do not know the impact of all those practices taken together. We can say, however, that these were the practices that were implemented in order to bring about conversion.

Both church and crown required evidence that missionaries were propa-gating the Catholic faith. The missionaries measured conversion by the num-ber of baptisms they administered even though most of those they baptized were moribund and later died. At best, many of these were souls in Heaven and names on a registry and were not the people who would become good, productive Christians for years to come and who would spread the word of God and manage the affairs of the mission. Few faithful Natives remained after disease had taken most and the desire for freedom had taken many. When only a small number of converted Natives remained, the missions were considered to be in decline. I think Fr. Oliva was right. As he understood it, God's mandate to the missionary worker was to be steadfast and demonstrate conversion work even when no one was converted.

The spiritual conquest of New Spain took place on a battleground between good and evil that had European roots and New World actors. Missionaries demonized Native American spiritual practices and debased and branded as sinful Native practices that had counterparts in European folk traditions and, more importantly, in the Catholic church. The obvious parallels between the shaman's sacra and Catholic sacra such as bone relics were not lost on the missionaries, but they chose to demonize Native sacra nonetheless. That brings us full circle to the issues of transmission of knowledge, cultural change, and the results of conversion. If one measures conversion by the effort and commitment of the missionaries, their achievements were momentous. By the measurement standards of the missionaries, there is little question that Native Americans converted. If we consider transmission of knowledge and cultural change as results of the work of conversion it is unquestionable that both occurred. It is true that they left behind festering wounds and scars, but it is also true that they left behind valued traditions and markers of identity. Today, the presence of Native Catholic populations in the Americas leaves no doubt that Native Americans converted. The question is: to what did they convert?

Notes

Introduction. One Stone Throw and Many Ripples

1. The concept of the life course refers to the various stages and rites of passage during the span of an individual's life, from birth to death. As Harlow and Lawrence explained, "It is culturally constructed and need not exactly follow biological or mental development in humans" (2002, 3). In this work, the concept is used to include important events in the lives of Native Americans. Instead of traditional Native rites of passage and associated roles and statuses, the life course of missionized Natives was marked by the sacraments. The reception of these sacraments together with what was considered appropriate social behavior determined their status and many of their roles within the mission.

Chapter 1. Good and Evil: A Battleground

1. Throughout the text, the word "Native" is capitalized because it is used with the same grammatical and lexical value as "Spanish" or "English" to denote membership in an ethnic group.

2. The Patronato Real was a set of privileges the pope gave to the crowns of Portugal and Spain as discoverers of New Worlds that could be Christianized. These privileges gave the Iberian crowns a great deal of control over the church in the New World.

3. See Chapter 3 for more about the Spirituals and Conventuals.

4. Unless otherwise noted, all English translations from Spanish or French are the responsibility of the author.

5. For a complete discussion of the concepts of doxa and heterodoxy as used by Pierre Bourdieu, see his *Outline of a Theory of Practice*.

6. See Chapter 5 for more about Rogel's dealings with the Calusa.

7. Baudot noted in his text that he was referring to 1 Corinthians 2 in the New Testament.

Chapter 2. The Religious and the Spiritual: Europe and the Americas

1. The questionnaire, titled *Preguntas y Respuestas*, was sent to the Spanish colonies by Don Ciríaco González Carvajal, secretary of the Department of Overseas Colonies, on October 6, 1812. This document falls slightly beyond the main time period considered in this work, but it was included because of its relevance to the matters discussed.

2. The Agnus Dei (the Lamb of God) scapular is a small pouch that contains a wax disc with the figure of a lamb impressed on it that has been blessed by the pope.

Chapter 3. The Franciscans: Men of the Cloth

1. The concept of a proper is part of a theory of practice Michel de Certeau elaborated and is related to the relationship between subject, object, and discourse (1988, 35–37).

2. The history of the development of the Franciscan Order is exceedingly complex. For a good study of the early period see David Burr, *The Spiritual Franciscans*.

3. Cardinal Ximénez Cisneros (1436–1517), a Franciscan, was appointed confessor to Queen Isabella in 1492. In that post and as Archbishop of Toledo he was a man of great influence.

Chapter 4. The Jesuits: Diversity of Spirits

1. The theory of habitus, as developed by Pierre Bourdieu, posits that the habitus produces practices while being produced, at least partially, by the very social and historical conditions that engender the habitus. Bourdieu stated that the habitus is "laid down in each agent by his earliest upbringing, which is the precondition not only for the co-ordination of practices but also for practices of co-ordination" (1977, 81).

2. Roland Barthes defines "discern" as to distinguish, to separate, to part, to limit, and to recognize the founding function of difference. This last meaning is crucial to the understanding of St. Ignatius experiences; whence the title of the chapter (1976, 53).

3. Some authors, such as de Aldama (1990, 79), show September 14, 1540 as the official date.

4. A rite of passage, characteristic of the Great Plains groups, during which an individual sought spiritual guidance.

Chapter 5. Southern Florida: Jesuits and Franciscans

1. By contact generation, I mean Native Americans who not only had early contacts with the colonizers but who also entered the missions late in adolescence or in adulthood.

2. The Spanish military and political leader of a province.

3. The notion that a soul is connected with reflections on a mirror or on a pool of water seems to relate to a shaman's capability to see future events in a reflective surface. An example of this practice is the episode during the Coronado expedition when the "Turk" is presumed to be talking with the devil in a vessel filled with water—a reflective surface (Castañeda 2002, 182–83).

4. A chalice-like vessel used to keep and transport the Holy Host.

Chapter 6. Northeastern Mexico: Franciscans and Jesuits

1. The *encomienda* was essentially a grant of Native laborers that was generally connected to a land grant. Susan Deeds offered one of the best defining explanations of *repartimiento*: "In this system of forced labor, work crews were drafted from villages and given fixed-term assignments for which they were meagerly paid in kind" (1998, 25).

2. Urdiñola settled in and traded in the mining town of Avino in 1578. The mines were discovered by Francisco de Ibarra and Diego de Ibarra was governor of the area.

In 1585, Urdiñola had already acquired several properties in the area (Alessio Robles 1978, 110).

3. The concept of *reducción* implied congregation of Natives in a mission pueblo where they would be catechized and acculturated to Spanish language and customs.

4. Catholic missionaries called anyone who had not been baptized a gentile. The term as they used it is synonymous with "non-Christian."

5. John Ingham cites a similar belief in Tlayacapan, Morelos, whereby high winds and whirlwinds were associated with or represented the devil (1986, 106, 116). Likewise Cynthia Radding notes the belief in destructive winds among the O'odham of Sonora (2005, 205).

6. Spanish colonizers used the term *ladino* for Native Americans who spoke or understood Spanish and were acculturated to Spanish customs.

7. An unofficial foray into unknown territory.

8. Captain Alonso de León the elder was one of the first colonizers of Nuevo León. His son, also named Alonso de León, was governor of Nuevo León and was the leader of several expeditions to Texas in the last decades of the seventeenth century.

9. Generally a *doctrina* was an incipient parish administered by regular clergy. The term, however, was very loosely applied, and members of religious orders cared for many *doctrinas* in the frontier.

10. One of the many names often applied to Native groups by the Spanish. Sometimes "Borrados" designated a specific ethnic group; other times it simply meant that the members of the group painted or tattooed their bodies.

11. Although I often refer to the crown to mean the body of royal officials who prepared and promulgated the laws, Native populations did not know nor did they relate to the crown. Spanish official discourse connected the king to his subjects, the Natives, and it was to the king that they owed allegiance, whether willingly or not.

12. The Alabado and Salve were religious hymns.

13. A vara is an old Spanish and Portuguese unit of measurement whose value varied through time and according to place of use. The Spanish vara is generally accepted to be 33 inches. In Texas the vara is generally accepted as being about 33.3 inches.

14. This could result in a payment of about 91.25 pesos for each Native female or male employee.

15. Mixed-race offspring of an Indian woman and a mulatto male.

Chapter 7. Texas: The Franciscans and Their Method

1. Fray Benedict Leutenegger selected, transcribed, and translated Spanish mission documents, which are housed in several collections. With the help of several other people, particularly Catholic sisters, Father Leutenegger published seven volumes of a documentary series. The quality of the translations varies, but the volumes provide transcripts of the original documents. In some cases I used the transcriptions in these volumes, while in others I also consulted the original documents, but I am solely responsible for all translated materials.

2. The *xinesí* was the Tejas Caddoan spiritual leader.

3. For instance, this document states that the so-called nation of the Tenipajuya was simply a family of the Pausane.

4. For a study of Texas missions' censuses and sacramental registers see Robert Jackson 2004.

5. Alegre y Capetillo signed this document simply as Fr. Joseph Ygnacio María Alegre, but he is referenced under Alegre y Capetillo in order to avoid the impression that these were two different people.

6. The report issued by Fr. Mariano de los Dolores is the same report Fr. Leutenegger transcribed and translated. I have provided references because I consulted and used both documents.

7. Mission Rosario was closed in 1777 and remained closed for about a decade. For a comprehensive review of Mission Rosario's history, see Kathleen Gilmore 1984.

Chapter 8. Baja California: Jesuits and Franciscans

1. A financial arrangement whereby the Society of Jesus used the income accrued from donated properties and gifts to subsidize the missions in California.

2. Modern Jesuit historians have translated and transcribed many important documents, among which are official and personal letters of the Jesuit fathers who worked in New Spain. Whenever possible I used primary sources that have been translated and are available to any reader.

3. For a comprehensive discussion of disease, epidemics, and demography during the mission period see Robert Jackson 1995 and 2005.

4. According to Dunne, *guama* or *wama* was one of the Native words for shaman (1968, 13–15, 459).

5. In this context, a *visita* was a settlement that lacked a resident missionary but was associated with a specific mission and served by its missionary.

Chapter 9. Alta California: Franciscans

1. In 1813, Fr. Felipe Arroyo de la Cuesta reported similar beliefs among the Natives of San Juan Bautista (Geiger and Meighan 1976, 145).

2. Fr. Espinosa reported that some of the Hasinai believed that the appearance of little birds, presumably under certain circumstances, was "a sign that the absent ones" were near (Swanton 1942, 222).

3. The use of milk in the diet is important for its economic implications and because many Native American populations are known to be lactose intolerant.

4. For the use of animal excrement as medicine, see Geiger and Meighan 1976, 72.

5. One of several public officers in a pueblo.

6. Atole is a gruel made from corn flour; pozole is a corn-meal mush prepared as a thick soup-like stew.

Chapter 10. Daily Schedules and Yearly Calendars

1. *Monjeríos* were convents for nuns, but obviously these *monjeríos* were not destined to nuns. In fact, the word *monjerío* does not appear in the Real Academia Dictionary until 1984 (Real Academia Española 1984, 923, 2).

2. As far as I can determine this is not the same document Leutenegger published in 1977, but it likely was the source for the document he published. Leutenegger also

states that this *Metodo* was written in 1787, probably by Fr. Joseph María García who was in charge of Mission Concepción in 1787 (Leutenegger 1977, 38 note 4). This document was written and signed by Fr. Ygnacio Martin García, not Joseph María García. As yet I have been unable to clarify the historiography of both documents, and since they are clearly different, I used and cited both.

3. Catholic liturgical prayers said at dawn.

4. The European custom of signing with a cross also attributed legal significance to the sign of the cross.

5. Normally, Matachines are Native dancers who wear elaborate costumes and masks and often use wooden swords in their performances. For a discussion of the differences between specific Native ceremonies accompanied by rhythmic movements, see Alberro (1999, 40–50). Matachine celebrations and dances were also traditional among the Tarahumara (Deeds 2003, 68) and among the Yaqui and Mayo (Radding 1998a, 194).

6. *Gigantones*, as the word implies, are oversized cardboard or papier-mâché figures displayed at fairs and dances.

7. For a discussion of the importance of St. James in ritual and secular activities, see de la Teja (2001). The feast of St. James (Santiago) was celebrated throughout New Spain (Pérez de Ribas 1999, 65).

Chapter 11. The City of God: Religious Practices

1. The application of saliva could well have been a vehicle of contagion, although not necessarily of an epidemic disease.

2. The Crown of Mary is a rosary that consists of seven decades celebrating the seven joys of the Virgin Mary. These seven joys are: the annunciation by the angel Gabriel, the visitation of Mary to her cousin Elizabeth, the birth of Jesus, the adoration of the Magi, the presentation of Jesus in the temple, the resurrection of Jesus, and Mary's assumption to heaven and her coronation there.

Chapter 12. The City of Man: Economic Practices

1. For a thorough discussion of various types of mission buildings and their construction cycles, see Jackson (2005).

2. The *cilice* is a spiked chain worn under clothing on the upper thigh or at the waist as mortification.

3. The discipline is a multistrand rope that is knotted at the ends or has metal spikes at the ends (or sometimes a metal chain) that is used to flagellate the body as mortification of the flesh.

References Cited

Abassolo, Juan Antonio. 1750. Letter to the Discretorio of the College of Santa Cruz de Querétaro. Archivo del Convento de Santa Cruz, Convento de San Francisco, Celaya, Roll 9:1400–401, Old Spanish Missions Research Library, Our Lady of the Lake University, San Antonio, Texas.

Alberro, Solange. 1999. *El águila y la cruz, Orígenes religiosos de la conciencia criolla. México, siglos XVI–XVII*. Mexico City: Fondo de Cultura Económica.

Alegre, Javier F. 1956. *Historia de la Província de la Compañia de Jesus de Nueva España Tomo I*. Ed. Ernest J. Burrus and Félix Zubillaga, Rome: Institutum Historicum.

———. 1958. *Historia de la Província de la Compañia de Jesus de Nueva España Tomo II*. Rome: Institutum Historicum.

Alegre y Capetillo, Joseph Ygnacio Maria. n.d. "Report of the Procurador Apostolico y Procurador del Colegio de Santa Cruz de Querétaro." Archivo del Convento de Santa Cruz, Convento de San Francisco, Celaya, Roll 9:1516–37, Spanish Missions Research Library, Our Lady of the Lake University, San Antonio, Texas.

———. 1759. "Autos de visita." Archivo del Convento de Santa Cruz, Convento de San Francisco, Celaya, Roll 9:1470–504, Spanish Missions Research Library, Our Lady of the Lake University, Texas.

Alessio Robles, Vito. 1978. *Coahuila y Texas en la época colonial*. Mexico City: Editorial Porrúa.

Allen, Rebecca. 1998. *Native Americans at Mission Santa Cruz, 1791–1834*. Los Angeles: Institute of Archaeology, University of California.

Almaráz, Felix D. Jr. 1979. *Crossroads of Empire: The Church and the State on the Rio Grande Frontier of Coahuila and Texas, 1700–1821*. San Antonio: Center for Archaeological Research, University of Texas at San Antonio.

———. 1989. *The San Antonio Missions and Their System of Land Tenure*. Austin: University of Texas Press.

Anonymous. n.d.a. "Apologia de Sn. Juan Bautista que se reduce â dos puntos." Archivo del Convento de Santa Cruz, Convento de San Francisco, Celaya, Roll 9, Old Spanish Missions Research Library, Our Lady of the Lake University, San Antonio, Texas.

———. n.d.b. "Manifesto en nos. Puntos." Archivo del Convento de Santa Cruz, Convento de San Francisco, Celaya, Roll 9:1445–49, Old Spanish Missions Research Library, Our Lady of the Lake University, San Antonio, Texas.

———. 1756. "Manifesto en que se examina y prueba el Drto de las missiones â diversos Yndios." Archivo del Convento de Santa Cruz, Celaya, Roll 9:1400–1409, Old Spanish Missions Research Library, Our Lady of the Lake University, San Antonio, Texas.

Armstrong, Megan C. 2004. *The Politics of Piety: Franciscan Preachers during the Wars of Religion, 1560–1600*. Rochester, N.Y.: University of Rochester Press.

Asisara, Lorenzo. 1991. The Assassination of Padres Andrés Quintana by the Indians of Mission Santa Cruz in 1812: The Narrative of Lorenzo Asisara. In *Native American Perspectives on the Hispanic Colonization of Alta California*, ed. Edward D. Castillo, 26:3–11. New York: Garland.

Baegert, Johann J., 1979. *Observations in Lower California*. Trans. M. M. Brandenburgh and Carl L. Baumann. Berkeley: University of California Press.

Bakhtin, M. M. 1986. *Speech Genres and Other Late Essays*. Trans. Vern W. McGee. Ed. Caryl Emerson and Michael Holquist. Austin: University of Texas Press.

Bangert, William V. 1972. *A History of the Society of Jesus*. St. Louis, Mo.: Institute of Jesuit Sources.

Barthes, Roland. 1976. *Sade, Fourier, Loyola*. Trans. Richard Miller. New York: Hill and Wang.

Baudot, Georges. 1553/1979. *Tratado de Hechicerias y Sortilegios de Fray Andrés de Olmos*. Mexico City: Estudios MesoAmericanos.

———. 1990. *La Pugna Franciscana por México*. Mexico City, D.F.: Alianza Editorial Mexicana.

Bean, Lowell J. 1974/1991. "California Indian Shamanism and Folk Curing." In *Ethnology of the Alta California Indians*, Vol. 1, *Precontact*, ed. Lowell J. Bean and Sylvia Brakke Vane. New York: Garland.

Bean, Lowell J., and Sylvia Brakke Vane. 1974/1991. "Shamanism: An Introduction." In *Ethnology of the Alta California Indians*, Vol. 1, *Precontact*, ed. Lowell J. Bean and Sylvia Brakke Vane. New York: Garland.

Behar, Ruth. 1987. "Sex and Sin: Witchcraft and the Devil in Late-Colonial Mexico." *American Ethnologist* 14, no. 1:34–54.

Benavides, Adán. 2001. "Genealogy." In *Reassessing Cultural Extinction: Change and Survival at Mission San Juan Capistrano, Texas*, ed. Alstom V. Thoms, Dawn A. J. Alexander, and Adán Benavides. College Station: Texas A&M University, Center for Ecological Archaeology.

Blaine, Martha R. 2000. "Native Voices: 'They Say He Was Witched.'" *American Indian Quarterly* 24, no. 4:615–34.

Bolton, Herbert E. 1917. "The Mission as a Frontier Institution in the Spanish-American Colonies." *American Historical Review* 23, no. 1:42–61.

Bourdieu, Pierre. 1977. *Outline of a Theory of Practice*. Cambridge: Cambridge University Press.

Braudel, Fernand. 1972. *The Mediterranean and the Mediterranean World in the Age of Phillip II*. Trans. Sian Reynolds. New York: Harper & Row.

Brown, Alan K. 2006. "Three Letters from the Pen of Fray Pedro Font." *Journal of the California Missions Studies Association* 23, no. 1:85–118.

Bureau of Indian Affairs. 2003. "Receipt of Petitions for Federal Acknowledgment of Existence as an Indian Tribe." *Federal Register* 68, no. 54 (March 20). Available online at http://a257.g.akamaitech.net/7/257/2422/14mar20010800/edocket.access.gpo.gov/2003/03–6659.htm.

Burkhart, Louise M. 1989. *The Slippery Earth: Nahua-Christian Moral Dialogue in Sixteenth-Century Mexico*. Tucson: University of Arizona Press.

———. 2001. *Before Guadalupe: The Virgin Mary in Early Colonial Nahuatl Literature*. Albany, N.Y.: Institute for Mesoamerican Studies, University at Albany.

Burr, David. 2001. *The Spiritual Franciscans: From Protest to Persecution in the Century after Saint Francis*. University Park: Pennsylvania State University Press.

Burrus, Ernest J., ed. and trans. 1984. *Jesuit Relations: Baja California, 1716–1762*. Los Angeles: Dawson's Book Shop.

Bushnell, Amy T. 1994. *Situado and Sabana: Spain's Support System for the Presidio and Mission Provinces of Florida*. Athens: University of Georgia Press.

Butzer, Elisabeth. 2001. *Historia Social de Una Comunidad Tlaxcalteca: San Miguel de Aguayo (Bustamante, N.L.) 1680–1820*. Saltillo: Archivo Municipal de Saltillo.

Cabeza de Vaca, Álvar N. 1993. *The Account: Álvar Núñez Cabeza de Vaca's Relación*. Trans. by Martin A. Favata and José B. Fernández. Houston: Arte Público Press.

Campbell, Thomas N. 1988. "Indians of San Antonio Missions." In *The Indians of Southern Texas and Northeastern Mexico: Selected Writings of Thomas Nolan Campbell*. Austin: Texas Archaeological Research Laboratory, University of Texas at Austin.

Campbell, Thomas N., and T. J. Campbell. 1985. *Indian Groups Associated with Spanish Missions of San Antonio Missions National Historical Park*. San Antonio: Center for Archaeological Research, University of Texas at San Antonio.

Casañas, Francisco de Jesus María. 1691. *Relacion*, 103–23. Box 2B141, Spanish Material from Various Sources, 1600–1921, Center for American History, University of Texas at Austin.

Castañeda, Carmen. 1984. *La Educación en Guadalajara durante la Colonia 1552–1821*. Guadalajara: El Colegio de Jalisco, and Mexico City: El Colegio de México.

Castañeda, Pedro de Nájera. 2002. *Relación de la Jornada de Cíbola*. Ed. John Miller Morris, Spanish ed. Mariah Wade. Chicago: Lakeside Press.

Castillo, Edward D. 1994. "Gender Status Decline, Resistance, and Accommodation among Female Neophytes in the Missions of California: A San Gabriel Case Study." *American Indian Culture and Research Journal* 18, no. 1:67–93.

Cavazos Garza, I. 1994. *Breve Historia de Nuevo León*. Mexico City: El Colegio de México, Fundo de Cultura Económica.

Cayward, Margaret L. 2006. *Musical Life at Mission Santa Clara de Asís, 1777–1836*. Santa Clara, Calif.: Santa Clara University.

Cervantes, Fernando. 1994. *The Devil in the New World: The Impact of Diabolism in New Spain*. New Haven, Conn.: Yale University Press.

César, J. 1930. "Recollections of My Youth at San Luís Rey Mission." *Touring Topics* 22:42–43.

Chapa, Juan B. 1997. *Texas & Northeastern Mexico, 1630–1690*. Ed. William C. Foster. Austin: University of Texas Press.

Chauvet, Fidel de Jesus. 1981. *Los Franciscanos en Mexico (1523–1980)*. Mexico City: Editorial Tradicion, S.A.

Chipman, Donald E. 1967. *Nuno de Guzman and the Province of Panuco in New Spain, 1518–1533*. Glendale, Calif.: Arthur H. Clark.

Christian, William A., Jr. 1989a. *Local Religion in Sixteenth-Century Spain*. Princeton, N.J.: Princeton University Press.

———. 1989b. *Apparitions in Late Medieval and Renaissance Spain*. Princeton, N.J.: Princeton University Press.

Clavijero, Francisco Xavier. 1789/2002. *Historia de la Antigua o Baja California*. Ed. and trans. Feliz Jay. New York: Edwin Mellen Press.

Colaphan, Clark. 1999. "María de Jesús de Agreda, the Sweetheart of the Holy Office." In *Women in the Inquisition: Spain and the New World*, ed. Mary E. Giles. Baltimore, Md.: Johns Hopkins University Press.

Conklin, Beth A. 2001. *Consuming Grief: Compassionate Cannibalism in an Amazon Society*. Austin: University of Texas Press.

Cortinas, Manuel. 1745. "Autos de Visita." Archivo San Francisco, vol. 33, pp. 69–74, Box 2Q258, Spanish Material from Various Sources, 1600–1921, Center for American History, University of Texas at Austin.

Costansó, M. 2001. "A Beachhead at San Diego." In *Lands of Promise and Despair*, ed. Rose Marie Bebe and Robert M. Senkewicz. Santa Clara, Calif.: Santa Clara University.

Crosby, Harry W. 1994. *Antigua California: Mission and Colony on the Peninsular Frontier, 1697–1768*. Albuquerque: University of New Mexico Press.

Curley, Michael J. 1940. *Church and State in the Spanish Floridas (1783–1822)*. Washington, D.C.: Catholic University of America Press.

Cutter, Charles R. 1986. *The Protector de Indios in Colonial New Mexico, 1659–1821*. Albuquerque: University of New Mexico Press.

de Aldama, Antonio M. 1990. *The Formula of the Institute: Notes for a Commentary*. Trans. Ignacio Echániz. St. Louis: Institute of Jesuit Resources.

de Certeau, Michel. 1988. *The Practice of Everyday Life*. Berkeley: University of California Press.

———. 2000. *The Possession at Loudun*. Trans. Michael B. Smith. Chicago: University of Chicago Press.

Deeds, Susan M. 2003. *Defiance and Deference in Mexico's Colonial North*. Austin: University of Texas Press.

de Guadalupe, Joseph. 1754a. Letter to Tomas de Uribe. Archivo del Convento de Santa Cruz, Convento de San Francisco, Celaya, Roll 9:1417–19, Old Spanish Missions Research Library, Our Lady of the Lake University, San Antonio, Texas.

———. 1754b. "Querella, y tiernos lamentos que da San Juan Capistrano, a Ntro. R. Pe. Comisario Genl. quejandose de Viçarron." Archivo del Convento de Santa Cruz, Convento de San Francisco, Celaya, Roll 9:1443–59, Old Spanish Missions Research Library, Our Lady of the Lake University, San Antonio, Texas.

de la Teja, Jesús F. 1991. "Forgotten Founders: The Military Settlers of Eighteenth-Century San Antonio de Béxar." In *Tejano Origins in Eighteenth-Century San Antonio*, ed. Gerald E. Poyo and Gilberto M. Hinojosa. Austin: University of Texas, Austin.

———. 2001. "St. James at the Fair: Religious Ceremony, Civic Boosterism, and Commercial Development on the Colonial Mexican Frontier." *The Americas* 57, no. 3: 395–416.

de León, Alonso, Juan Bautista Chapa, and Fernando Sánchez de Zamora. 1961. *Histo-*

ria de Nuevo León con noticias sobre Coahuila, Taumalipas, Texas y Nuevo México, escrita en el siglo XVII. Monterrey: Gobierno del Estado de Nuevo León, Centro de Estudos Humanísticos de la Universidad de Nuevo León.

de los Dolores, Mariano. 1758. Archivo del Convento de Santa Cruz, Convento de San Francisco, Celaya Collection, Microfilm Roll 9:2719–22, Old Spanish Missions Research Library, Our Lady of the Lake University, San Antonio, Texas.

de los Dolores, Mariano, Joseph Guadalupe, Joseph Lopez, Juan de los Angeles, Pedro Parras, Joseph Ygnacio Maria Alegre, Benito Varelas, and Manuel Rolan. 1762. "Report to the Guardian Francisco Xavier Ortiz." Archivo San Francisco el Grande, vol. 27, pp. 38–76, Box 2Q256, Spanish Material from Various Sources, 1600–1921, Center for American History, University of Texas at Austin.

Delumeau, Jean. 1977. *Catholicism between Luther and Voltaire: A New View of the Counter-Reformation.* Trans. Jeremy Moiser. Philadelphia: Westminster Press.

de Nicolas, Antonio T. 1986. *Powers of Imagining: Ignatius de Loyola.* New York: State University of New York Press.

Dorsey, Peter A. 1998. "Going to School with Savages: Authorship and Authority among the Jesuits of New France." *William and Mary Quarterly* 55, no. 3: 399–420.

DuBois, Constance G. 1908. "The Religion of the Luiseño Indians of Southern California." *University of California Publications in American Archaeology and Ethnology* 8, no. 3: 69–186.

Duby, Georges. 1980. *The Three Orders: Feudal Society Imagined.* Trans. Arthur Goldhammer. Chicago: University of Chicago Press.

Dunne, Peter M., 1968. *Black Robes in Lower California.* Berkeley: University of California Press.

Engelhardt, Zephyrin. 1929. *The Missions and Missionaries of California.* Vol. 1. Santa Barbara, Calif.: Mission Santa Barbara.

———. 1930. *The Missions and Missionaries of California.* Vol. 2. Santa Barbara, Calif.: Mission Santa Barbara.

Ettinger, Catherine R. 2004. "Spaces of Change: Architecture and Creation of a New Society in the Californian Missions." *Boletín: The Journal of the Californian Mission Studies Association* 21, no. 1: 23–44.

Eymeric, Nicholas. 1595. *Directorium inquisitorum.* Venetiis: Apud Marcum Antonium Zalterium.

Farris, Glenn. 1991. *Archaeological Testing in the Neophyte Family Housing Area at Mission San Juan Bautista, California.* Sacramento, Calif.: Resource Protection Division, California Department of Parks and Recreation.

Febvre, Lucien. 1982. *The Problem of Unbelief in the Sixteenth Century.* Trans. Beatrice Gottlieb. Cambridge: Harvard University Press.

Few, Martha. 2004. *Women Who Live Evil Lives: Gender, Religion, and the Politics of Power in Colonial Guatemala.* Austin: University of Texas.

Fletcher, Alice C., and Francis La Flesche. 1972. *The Omaha Tribe.* 2 vols. Lincoln: University of Nebraska Press.

Flint, Richard, and Shirley Cushing Flint, ed. 2005. *Documents of the Coronado Expedition, 1539–1542.* Dallas: Southern Methodist University Press.

Flores, Francisco J. A. 1976. *El Diablo y los Espanoles.* Spain: Universidad de Murcia.

Flores, Richard R. 1995. *Los Pastores: History and Performance in the Mexican Shepherds' Play of South Texas*. Washington, D.C.: Smithsonian Institution Press.

Florescano, Enrique. 1997. *Memory, Myth, and Time in Mexico from the Aztecs to Independence*. Trans. Albert G. Bork with the assistance of Kathryn R. Bork. Austin: University of Texas Press.

Foucault, Michel. 1979. *Discipline & Punish: The Birth of the Prison*. New York: Random House.

———. 1990. *The History of Sexuality*. Vol. 1. *An Introduction*. New York: Vintage Books.

Fox, Ann. 1989. "Food and Nutrition among the Inhabitants of the San Antonio Missions." In *Selected Essays from the 1986 and 1987 San Antonio Missions Research Conferences*, ed. Arthur R. Goméz. San Antonio: San Antonio Missions National Historical Park.

Frugoni, Chiara. 1996. "Saint Francis: A Saint in Progress." In *Saints: Studies in Hagiography*, ed. Sandro Sticca. Binghamton, N.Y.: Medieval & Renaissance Texts & Studies.

Ganss, George E., ed. 1991. *Ignatius of Loyola: The Spiritual Exercises and Selected Works*. New York: Paulist Press.

García, Bartholomé. 1760. *Manual para Administrar Los Santos Sacramentos de Penitencia, Eucharistia, Extrema-Uncion, y Matrimonio*. Imprenta de los Heredereros de Doña Maria de Rivera, en la calle de San Bernardo y esquinas de la Plazuela de el Volador.

García, Diego Martin. 1745. *Breve y Legal Noticia de las Calidades, y Costumbres de los Yndios: Metodo, Que Han de Observar con Ellos, y Consigo Mismos Los Obreros Evangelicos Que Quieren Ganar Sus Almas Para Dios*. Berkeley, Calif.: Bancroft Library, University of California.

García, Rubial A. 2006. "Icons of Devotion: The Appropriation and Use of Saints in New Spain." In *Local Religion in Colonial Mexico*, ed. Martin Austin Nesvig. Albuquerque: University of New Mexico.

Geiger, Maynard J., trans. and ed. 1959. *The Life and Times of Fray Junípero Serra*. 2 vols. Washington, D.C.: Academy of American Franciscan History.

———. 1970. *Letter of Luís Jayme*. Los Angeles: Dawson's Book Shop.

Geiger, Maynard J., and Clement W. Meighan. 1976. *As the Padres Saw Them: California Indian Life and Customs as Reported by the Franciscan Missionaries, 1813–1815*. Santa Barbara, Calif.: Santa Barbara Mission Archive Library.

Gil, Eusebio, Carmen Labrador, A. Diez Escanciano, and Jose Martinez de la Escalera, eds. 1992. *El Sistema Educativo de la Compania de Jesus, La "Ratio Studiorum."* Madrid: Universidad Pontificia Comillas.

Gilmore, Kathleen. 1984. "The Indians of Mission Rosario." In *The Scope of Historical Archaeology: Essays in Honor of John L. Cotter*, ed. David G. Orr and Daniel G. Crozier. Philadelphia, Pa.: Department of Anthropology, Temple University.

Ginzburg, Carlo. 1991. *Ecstasies: Deciphering the Witches' Sabbath*. Trans. Raymond Rosenthal. New York: Pantheon Books.

———. 1992. *The Night Battles: Witchcraft and Agrarian Cults in the Sixteenth and Sev-*

enteenth Centuries. Trans. John and Anne Tedeschi. Baltimore, Md.: Johns Hopkins University Press.

Goggin, John M., and William C. Sturtevant. 1964. "The Calusa: A Stratified Nonagricultural Society (with Notes on Sibling Marriage)." In *Explorations in Cultural Anthropology: Essays in Honor of George Peter Murdock*, ed. Ward H. Goodenough. New York: McGraw-Hill.

Gordon, Colin, ed. 1980. *Power/Knowledge: Selected Interviews and Other Writings, 1972–1977.* New York: Pantheon Books.

Green, Julien. 1987. *God's Fool: The Life and Times of Francis of Assisi.* Trans. Peter Heinegg. San Francisco, Calif.: Harper and Row.

Greenleaf, Richard E. 1961. *Zumárraga and the Mexican Inquisition, 1536–1543.* Washington, D.C.: Academy of Franciscan History.

Griffen, William B. 1979/1991. "Indian Assimilation in the Franciscan Area of Nueva Vizcaya." In *The Franciscan Missions of Northern Mexico*, ed. Thomas E. Sheridan, Charles W. Polzer, Thomas H. Naylor, and Diana W. Hadley. New York: Garland.

Guardian y Discretorio, El. N.d. Letter to the Commissario General. Archivo del Convento de Santa Cruz, Convento de San Francisco, Celaya, Roll 9:1403–14, Old Spanish Missions Research Library, Our Lady of the Lake University, San Antonio, Texas.

Guest, Francis F. 1989. "An Inquiry into the Role of the Discipline in California Mission Life." *Southern California Quarterly* 71, nos. 1–4: 1–68.

Gurzinski, Serge. 1989. "Individualization and Acculturation: Confession among the Nahuas of Mexico from the Sixteenth to the Eighteenth Century." In *Sexuality and Marriage in Colonial Latin America*, ed. Asunción Lavrin. Lincoln: University of Nebraska Press.

Habig, Marion A., comp. 1978. *The San José Papers, Part I: 1719–1791.* Trans. from the Spanish by Fr. Benedict Leutenegger et al. San Antonio: Old Spanish Missions Historical Research Library at Our Lady of the Lake University.

Hackel, Steven W. 2005. *Children of Coyote: Missionaries of Saint Francis.* Chapel Hill: University of North Carolina Press.

Hall, Linda B. 2004. *Mary, Mother and Warrior: The Virgin in Spain and in the Americas.* Austin: University of Texas Press.

Hann, John H. 2003. *Indians of Central and South Florida, 1513–1763.* Gainesville: University Press of Florida.

———, ed. and trans. 1991. *Missions to the Calusa.* Gainesville: University Press of Florida.

Harlow, Mary, and Ray Lawrence. 2002. *Growing Up and Growing Old in Ancient Rome: A Life Course Approach.* New York: Routledge.

Harrington, John P. 1934. "A New Original Version of Boscana's Historical Account of the San Juan Capistrano Indians of Southern California." In *Smithsonian Miscellaneous Collections* 92, no. 4. Washington, D.C.: The Smithsonian Institution.

Hester, Thomas R. 1989a. "Texas and Northeastern Mexico: An Overview." In *Columbian Consequences*, vol. 1, ed. David Hurst Thomas. Washington, D.C.: Smithsonian Institution Press.

———. 1989b. "Historic Native American Populations." In *From the Gulf to the Rio*

Grande: Human Adaptation in Central, South, and Lower Pecos, Texas. Fayetteville: Arkansas Archaeological Survey.

Heusinger, Edward W. 1936. *Early Explorations and Mission Establishments in Texas.* San Antonio: The Naylor Company.

Hewes, Minna, and Gordon Hewes. 1958/1991. "Indian Life and Customs at Mission San Luis Rey." In *Ethnology of the Alta California Indians,* vol. II, *Postcontact,* ed. Lowell John Bean and Sylvia Brakke Vane. New York: Garland.

Hoyo, Eugenio del. 1985. *Indios, Frailes y Encomenderos en el Nuevo Reino de León Siglos XVII y XVIII.* Archivo General del Estado de Nuevo León.

———. 1990. *Triptico de la Colonia.* Cuadernos del Archivo No. 49. Monterrey: Archivo del Estado de Nuevo León.

Ingham, John M. 1986. *Mary, Michael, and Lucifer: Folk Catholicism in Central Mexico.* Austin: University of Texas Press.

Jackson, Robert H. 1995. *Indian Population Decline: The Missions of Northwestern New Spain, 1687–1840.* Albuquerque: University of New Mexico Press.

———. 2000. *From Savages to Subjects: Missions in the History of the American Southwest.* Armonk, N.Y.: M. E. Sharpe Inc.

———. 2004. "Congregation and Depopulation: Demographic Patterns in Texas Missions." *Journal of South Texas* 17, no. 2:6–50.

———. 2005. *Missions and the Frontiers of Spanish America: A Comparative Study of the Missions in the Rio de la Plata Region and the Northern Frontier of New Spain.* Scottsdale, Ariz.: Pentacle Press.

Jackson, Robert H., and Edward Castillo. 1997. *Indians, Franciscans, and Spanish Colonization: The Impact of the Mission System on California Indians.* Albuquerque: University of New Mexico Press.

Kapitzke, Robert L. 2001. *Religion, Power, and Politics in Colonial St. Augustine.* Gainesville: University Press of Florida.

Kenneally, Finbar, ed. and trans. 1965. *Writings of Fermín Francisco de Lasuén.* 2 vols. Washington, D.C.: Academy of American Franciscan History.

Kramer, Heinrich, and James Sprenger. 1928/1971. *The Malleus Maleficarum.* Trans. with introduction and bibliography and notes by Montague Summers. New York: Dover Publications.

Kroeber, A. L. 1908. "Ethnography of the Cahuilla Indians." *University of California Publications in American Archaeology and Ethnology* 8, no. 2:29–68.

Lacouture, Jean. 1993. *Os Jesuítas, 1. A Conquista.* Lisbon: Editorial Estampa.

Lambert, Malcom D. 1961. *Franciscan Poverty: The Doctrine of the Absolute Poverty of Christ and the Apostles in the Franciscan Order, 1210–1323.* London: S.P.C.K.

Le Goff, Jacques. 1984. *The Birth of Purgatory.* Trans. Arthur Goldhammer. Chicago: University of Chicago Press.

———. 2000. *S. Francisco de Assis.* Trans. Telma Costa. Lisbon: Editorial Teorema.

———. 2004. *Saint Francis of Assisi.* Trans. Christine Rhone. New York: Routledge.

Lepowsky, Maria. 2004. "Indian Revolts and Cargo Cults." In *Reassessing Revitalization Movements: Perspectives from North America and the Pacific Islands,* ed. Michael Eugene Harkin. Lincoln: University of Nebraska Press.

Leutenegger, Benedict, ed. and trans. 1976. *Guidelines for a Texas Mission: Instructions for the Missionary of Mission Concepción in San Antonio ca. 1760.* San Antonio, Texas: Old Spanish Missions Historical Research Library at Our Lady of the Lake University.

———. 1977. *Management of the Missions in Texas: Fr. Jose Rafael Oliva's Views concerning the Problem of the Temporalities in 1788.* San Antonio, Texas: Old Spanish Missions Historical Research Library at Our Lady of the Lake University.

———. 1979. *The Texas Missions of the College of Zacatecas in 1749–1750.* San Antonio, Texas: Old Spanish Missions Historical Research Library at Our Lady of the Lake University.

———. 1985. *Letters and Memorials of Fray Mariano de los Dolores y Viana.* San Antonio, Texas: Old Spanish Missions Historical Research Library at Our Lady of the Lake University.

Lewis, Laura A. 2003. *Hall of Mirrors: Power, Witchcraft, and Caste in Colonial Mexico.* London: Duke University Press.

Lewy, Guenter. 1960. "The Struggle for Constitutional Government in the Early Years of the Society of Jesus." *Church History* 29, no. 2:141–60.

Librado, Fernando. 1979. *Breath of the Sun: Life in Early California as Told by a Chumash Indian, Fernando Librado, to John P. Harrington.* Ed. and anno. Travis Hudson. Banning, Calif.: Malki Museum Press.

Lopez, Francisco. 1786. "Puesto è Ynforme que el Padre Presidente de las Misiones de la Provincia de Texas ò Nuevas Filipinas, remite al Yllmo Sor Fr. Rafael José Verger." Vol. 764. Box 2Q237, Spanish Material from Various Sources, 1600–1921, Center for American History, University of Texas at Austin.

Lopez, Rosalva Loreto. 2002. "The Devil, Women, and the Body in Seventeenth-Century Puebla Convents." Trans. Sonya Lipsett-Rivera. *The Americas* 59, no. 2:181–99.

Losada, Juan. 1730. "Autos de Visita." Archivo San Francisco el Grande, vol. 33, pp. 11–18, Box 2Q258, Spanish Material from Various Sources, 1600–1921, Center for American History, University of Texas at Austin.

Luckmann, Thomas. 1991. "The Constitution of Human Life in Time." In *Chronotypes: The Construction of Time,* ed. John Bender and David E. Wellbery. Stanford, Calif.: Stanford University Press.

MacCormack, Sabine. 1991. "Demons, Imagination, and the Incas." *Representations* 33, Special issue, *The New World*: 121–46.

MacMahon, Darcie A., and William H. Marquardt. 2004. *The Calusa and Their Legacy: South Florida People and Their Environments.* Gainesville: University Press of Florida.

Margolin, Malcolm. 1989. *Monterey in 1786: The Journals of Jean François de la Pérouse.* Berkeley, Calif.: Heyday Books.

Martin, J. Jeffries. 2002. *Venice's Hidden Enemies: Italian Heretics in a Renaissance City.* Ann Arbor: University of Michigan.

Matson, Daniel S., and Bernard L. Fontana, trans. and ed. 1977. *Friar Bringas Reports to the King: Methods of Indoctrination on the Frontier of New Spain 1796–97.* Tucson: University of Arizona Press.

McGrade, Arthur S. 1999. "The Medieval Idea of Heresy: What Are We to Make of It?" In *The Medieval Church: Universities, Heresy, and the Religious Life: Essays in*

Honour of Gordon Leff, ed. Peter Miller and Barrie Dobson. Rochester, N.Y.: Boydell Press.

McNeill, John T., and Helena M. Gamer. 1938. *Medieval Handbooks of Penance: A Translation of the Principal Libri Poenitentiales and Selections from Related Documents*. New York: Columbia University.

Medgyessy, Laszlo. 2004. "Mission or Proselytism? Temptations, Tensions and Missiological Perspectives in Eastern European Christianity: A Case Study of Hungary." In *Contextuality in Reformed Europe: The Mission of the Church in the Transformation of European Culture*, ed. Christine Lienemann-Perrin, Hendrik M. Vroom, and Michael Weinrich. Amsterdam: Rodopi.

Mello e Souza, Laura de. 2003. *The Devil and the Land of the Holy Cross: Witchcraft, Slavery, and Popular Religion in Colonial Brazil*. Trans. Diane Grosklaus Whitty. Austin: University of Texas Press.

Metcalf, Alida C. 2005. *Go-Betweens and the Colonization of Brazil, 1500–1600*. Austin: University of Texas Press.

Milanich, Jerald T. 1998. *Florida's Indians from Ancient Times to the Present*. Gainesville: University Press of Florida.

Mitchell, Jon P. 2001. "The Devil, Satanism, and the Evil Eye in Contemporary Malta." In *Powers of Good and Evil: Social Transformation and Popular Belief*, ed. Paul Clough and Jon P. Mitchell. New York: Berghahn Books.

Mitchell, Timothy. 1990. *Passional Culture: Emotion, Religion, and Society in Southern Spain*. Philadelphia: University of Pennsylvania Press.

Moorman, John. 1988. *A History of the Franciscan Order from Its Origins to the Year 1517*. Chicago, Ill.: Franciscan Herald Press.

Nathan, Paul D., trans., and L. B. Simpson, ed. 1959. *The San Saba Papers*. San Francisco: John Howell Books.

Nunis, Doyce B., Jr. 1982. *The Letters of Jacob Baegert, 1749–1761, Jesuit Missionary in Baja California*. Trans. Elsbeth Schulz Bishof. Los Angeles: Dawson's Book Shop.

Olin, John C., ed. 1974. *The Autobiography of St. Ignatius Loyola*. Trans. Joseph F. O'Callaghan. New York: Harper Torchbooks.

O'Malley, John W. 2000. *Trent and All That: Renaming Catholicism in the Early Modern Era*. Cambridge: Harvard University Press.

Padden, Robert C. 1956. "The Ordenanza del Patronazgo, 1574: An Interpretative Essay." *The Americas* 12, no. 4: 333–54.

Palou, Francisco. 1913. *Life and Apostolic Labors of the Venerable Father Junípero Serra*. Introduction and notes by George Wharton James. Trans. C. Scott Williams. Pasadena, Calif.: George Wharton James.

———. 1994. *Cartas Desde La Península de California (1768–1773)*. Transcritas y Editadas con Algunas Notas y Cuatro Apéndices Documentales por José Luis Soto Pérez. Mexico City: Editorial Porrúa.

———. 1998. *Recopilación de Noticias de la Antigua y de la Nueva California, 1767–1783*. Nueva edición con notas por José Luis Soto Pérez. Tomos I and II. Mexico City: Editorial Porrúa.

Peláez, A. C., Héctor Barraza, Ana Maria E. Serrato, and Mayela Sakanassi. 1991. *El Sur de Coahuila Antiguo Indigena y Negro*. Saltillo: Universidad IberoAmericana.

Pérez de Ribas, Andrés. 1645/1999. *History of the Triumphs of Our Holy Faith amongst the Most Barbarous and Fierce Peoples of the New World*. Trans. Daniel T. Reff, Maureen Ahern, and Richard K. Danford. Tucson: University of Arizona Press.

Perissinotto, Giorgio, ed. 1998. *Documenting Everyday Life in Early Spanish California*. Santa Barbara: Santa Barbara Trust for Historic Preservation.

Perttula, T. K., M. R. Miller, R. A. Ricklis, R. D. Prikryl, and C. Lintz. 1995. "Prehistoric and Historic Aboriginal Ceramics in Texas." *Bulletin of the Texas Archeological Society* 66:175–235.

Phelan, John L. 1956. *The Millennial Kingdom of the Franciscans in the New World: A Study of the Writings of Gerónimo de Mendieta (1525–1604)*. Berkeley: University of California Press.

Piccolo, Francisco M. 2001. "A Foray in the Wilderness." In *Lands of Promise and Despair*, ed. Rose Marie Beebe and Robert M. Senkewicz. Santa Clara: Santa Clara University.

Pilling, James C. 1895. "The Writings of Padre Andres de Olmos in the Languages of Mexico." *American Anthropologist* 8, no. 2:43–60.

Polzer, Charles W. 1976. *Rules and Precepts of the Jesuit Missions of Northwestern New Spain*. Tucson: University of Arizona Press.

Priestley, Herbert I., trans. 1937. *A Historical, Political, and Natural Description of California by Pedro Fages, Soldier of Spain*. Berkeley: University of California Press.

Rabago y Theran. 1754. "Declaration." Archivo del Convento de Santa Cruz, Convento de San Francisco, Celaya, Roll 9:2400–2401, Old Spanish Missions Research Library, Our Lady of the Lake University, San Antonio, Texas.

Radding, Cynthia. 1998a. "The Colonial Pact and Changing Ethnic Frontiers in Highland Sonora, 1740–1840." In *Contested Ground: Comparative Frontiers on the Northern and Southern Edges of the Spanish Empire*, ed. Donna J. Guy and Thomas E. Sheridan, 52–60. Tucson: University of Arizona Press.

———. 1998b. "Crosses, Caves, and Matachinis: Divergent Appropriations of Catholic Discourse in Northwestern New Spain." *The Americas* 55, no. 2:177–203.

———. 2005. *Landscapes of Power and Identity: Comparative Histories in the Sonoran Desert and the Forests of Amazonia from Colony to Republic*. Durham, N.C.: Duke University Press.

Real Academia Española. 1984. *Diccionario de la lengua española. Vigésima edición*. Madrid: Espasa-Calpe.

Reff, Daniel T. 1998. "The Jesuit Mission Frontier in Comparative Perspective: The Reductions of the Rio de la Plata and the Missions of Northwestern Mexico, 1588–1700." In *Contested Ground: Comparative Frontiers on the Northern and Southern Edges of the Spanish Empire*, ed. Donna J. Guy and Thomas E. Sheridan. Tucson: University of Arizona Press.

Reid, Charles J., Jr. 2004. *Power over the Body: Equality in the Family*. Grand Rapids, Mich.: William B. Eerdmans Publishing Company.

Ricard, Robert. 1933/1982. *The Spiritual Conquest of Mexico: An Essay on the Apostolate and the Evangelizing Methods of the Mendicant Orders in New Spain, 1523–1572*. Trans. Lesley Byrd Simpson. Berkeley: University of California Press.

Richardson, Alfred. 1995. *Plants of the Rio Grande Delta*. Austin: University of Texas Press.

Ricklis, Robert A. 1999. Spanish Colonial Missions of Espíritu Santo and Nuestra Señora del Rosario. *Bulletin of the Texas Archeological Society* 70:133–68.

Robinson, Alfred. 1969. *Life in California during a Residence of Several Years in That Territory, to Which Is Annexed a Historical Account of the Origin, Customs, and Traditions of the Indians of Alta-California by Fray Boscana*. New York: Da Capo Press.

Rodríguez-Sala, Maria Luisa, Maria Eugenia Cué, e Ignacio Gómezgil. 1995. *Exploradores en el Septentrión Novohispano*. Mexico City: Miguel Ángel Porrua, Grupo Editorial.

Roest, Bert. 2000. "Converting the Other and Converting the Self: Double Objectives in Franciscan Educational Writings." In *Christianizing Peoples and Converting Individuals*, ed. Guyda Armstrong and Ian N. Wood. Turnhout, Belgium: Brepols Publishers.

Sabo, George, III. 1998. "The Structure of Caddo Leadership in the Colonial Era." In *The Native History of the Caddo*, ed. Timothy K. Perttula and James E. Bruseth. Austin: Texas Archaeological Research Laboratory, University of Texas at Austin.

Sandos, James A. 2004. *Converting California: Indians and Franciscans in the Missions*. New Haven, Conn.: Yale University Press.

Santa Ana, Benito Fernandez. 1748. "Patente del R.o P Guard.n y V. Discretorio expedida en el año de 1748 para el govierno de las Missiones." Vol. 766, Box 2Q237, Spanish Material from Various Sources, 1600–1921, Center for American History, University of Texas at Austin.

Saranyana, Josep-Ignasi. 1991. *Teología Profética Americana*. Pamplona: Ediciones Universidade de Navarra.

Schneider, Tsim D. 2007. "The Role of Archived Photographs in Native California Archaeology." *Journal of Social Archaeology* 7, no. 1:49–71.

Señán, José. 1967. *The Ventureño Confesionario of José Señán*. Ed. Madison S. Beeler. Berkeley: University of California Press.

Serra, Junípero. 1955. *Writings*. Vol. 1. Ed. Antonine Tibesar. Washington, D.C.: Academy of American Franciscan History.

———. 1956. *Writings*. Vols. 2 to 4. Ed. Antonine Tibesar. Washington, D.C.: Academy of American Franciscan History.

Silverblatt, Irene. 2004. *Modern Inquisitions: Peru and the Colonial Origins of the Civilized World*. Durham, N.C.: Duke University Press.

Sistiaga, Sebastián. 2001. "Life in the Missions." In *Lands of Promise and Despair*, ed. Rose Marie Beebe and Robert M. Senkewicz. Santa Clara: Santa Clara University.

Skowronek, Russell K. 1999. *Identifying the First Pueblo de San José de Guadalupe: Some Archaeological, Historical, and Geographical Considerations*. California Mission Studies Association Occasional Paper 2. Santa Clara: California Missions Association.

Skowronek, Russell K., and Elizabeth Thompson. 2006. *Situating Mission Santa Clara de Asís: 1776–1851: Documentary and Material Evidence of Life on the Alta California Frontier: A Timeline*. Berkeley: Academy of American Franciscan History.

Sneed, Patricia. 1992. "Taking Possession and Reading Texts: Establishing the Authority of Overseas Empires." *William and Mary Quarterly*, 3rd ser., 49, no. 2:183–209.

Sousa, Lisa. 2002. "The Devil and Deviance in Native Criminal Narratives from Early Mexico." Trans. Sonia Lipsett-Rivera. *The Americas* 59, no. 2:161–79.

Sparkman, Philip S. 1908. "The Culture of the Luiseño Indians." *University of California Publications in American Archaeology and Ethnology* 8, no. 4:187–234.

Swanton, John R. 1942. *Source Material on the History and Ethnology of the Caddo Indians*. Bureau of American Ethnology Bulletin 132. Washington, D.C.: Smithsonian Institution.

Sweet, David. 1995. "The Ibero-American Frontier Mission in Native American History." In *The New Latin American Mission History*, ed. Erick Langer and Robert H. Jackson. Lincoln: University of Nebraska Press.

Taussig, Michael. 1987. *Shamanism, Colonialism, and the Wild Man: A Study in Terror and Healing*. Chicago: University of Chicago Press.

Taylor, William B. 1996. *Magistrates of the Sacred: Priests and Parishioners in Eighteenth-Century Mexico*. Stanford, Calif.: Stanford University Press.

———. 2003. "Our Lady in the Kernel of Corn, 1774." *The Americas* 59, no. 4:559–70.

Thoms, Alstom V., Dawn Alexander, and Adán Benavides. 2001. *Reassessing Cultural Extinction: Change and Survival at Mission San Juan Capistrano, Texas*. College Station: Center for Ecological Archaeology, Texas A&M University.

Turner, Victor, and Edith Turner. 1978. *Image and Pilgrimage in Christian Culture*. New York: Columbia University Press.

Twinam, Ann. 1999. *Public Lives, Private Secrets: Gender, Honor, Sexuality, and Illegitimacy in Colonial Spanish America*. Stanford, Calif.: Stanford University Press.

Valdés, Carlos Manuel. 1995. *Historia de los pueblos indígenas de México. La Gente del mezquite*. Juárez, Mexico: Centro de Investigaciones y Estudios Superiores en Antropología Social.

Verbeke, G. 1976. "Philosophy and Heresy: Some Conflicts between Reason and Faith." In *The Concept of Heresy in the Middle Ages: Proceedings of the International Conference, Louvain, May 13–16, 1973*, ed. W. Lourdaux and D. Verhelst. The Hague: Leuven University Press.

Vergara, Gabriel. 1732/1965. *El Cuadernillo de la Lengua de los Indios Pajalates*. Ed. Eugenio del Hoyo. Monterrey: Publicaciones del Instituto Tecnologico y de Estudios Superiores de Monterrey.

Vetancurt, Agustin de. 1971. *Teatro Mexicano, Cronica de la Provincia del Santo Evangelio de Mexico, Menologio de Mexico*. Mexico City: Editorial Porrua, S.A.

Vizarraras, Luis. 1754. Letter to Joseph Antonio Rodriguez. Archivo del Convento de Santa Cruz, Convento de San Francisco, Celaya, Roll 9:1431–36, Old Spanish Missions Research Library, Our Lady of the Lake University, San Antonio, Texas.

Wade, Maria F. 1993. "Our Daily Bread: The Role of Grinding Technology in the Socio-Economics of South Texas during the 18th Century." M.A. thesis, Department of Anthropology, University of Texas at Austin.

———. 2003. *Native Americans of the Texas Edwards Plateau, 1582–1799*. Austin: University of Texas Press.

Wallis, Robert T. 2003. *Shamans/Neo-Shamans: Ecstasy, Alternative Archaeologies, and Contemporary Pagans.* London: Routledge.

Walter, Tamra L. 2007. *Espíritu Santo de Zúñiga: A Frontier Mission in South Texas.* Austin: University of Texas Press.

Webb, Edith B. 1952. *Indian Life at the Old Missions.* Lincoln: University of Nebraska Press.

Weber, David J. 1992. *The Spanish Frontier in North America.* New Haven, Conn.: Yale University Press.

———. 2004. *Spanish Bourbons and Wild Indians.* Waco, Tex.: Baylor University Press.

West, Delno C. 1989. "Medieval Ideas of Apocalyptic Mission and the Early Franciscans in Mexico." *The Americas* 45, no. 3:293–313.

Widmer, Randolph J. 1988. *The Evolution of the Calusa: A Nonagricultural Chiefdom on the Southwest Florida Coast.* Tuscaloosa: University of Alabama Press.

Wilbur, Marguerite E., trans. 1931/1972. *The Indian Uprising in Lower California 1734–1737 as Described by Father Sigismundo Taraval.* Los Angeles: The Quivira Society.

Williams, Jack S., and Anita G. Cohen-Williams. 2007. "Some Observations on the Archaeological Evidence in the Later Indian Village at Mission San Luis Rey, California." In *Proceedings of the 24th Annual Conference of the California Mission Studies Association,* ed. Rose Marie Beebe and Robert M. Senkewicz. Santa Clara, California: California Mission Studies Association.

Williams, Raymond. 1977. *Marxism and Literature.* Oxford: Oxford University Press.

Wood, Ian. 2001. *The Missionary Life Saints and the Evangelization of Europe, 400–1050.* Harlow, England: Pearson Education.

Xavier Ortiz, Francisco. 1745. Autos de Visita que quedan en cada una de las Missiones, Archivo del Convento de Santa Cruz, Convento de San Francisco, Celaya, Roll 9, Old Spanish Missions Research Library, Our Lady of the Lake University, San Antonio, Texas.

Index

Illustrations and maps are indicated by page numbers in *italics*.

www.ingramcontent.com/pod-product-compliance
Lightning Source LLC
Chambersburg PA
CBHW070556270326
41926CB00013B/2335